Ken Follett was born in Cardiff, Wales, in 1949. After taking a degree in Philosophy at University College, London, he became a newspaper reporter, first with the *South Wales Echo* and later with the London *Evening News*. While working on the *Evening News* he wrote his first novel, a mystery published under a pen name. It sold poorly, and he went to work for a publisher in an effort to find out where he had gone wrong. Ten assorted novels, mostly pseudonymous, were written before *Eye of the Needle* became an international bestseller. That book also won the Edgar award of the Mystery Writers of America and was filmed starring Donald Sutherland and Kate Nelligan. Subsequently Follett wrote *Triple*, *The Key to Rebecca*, and *The Man From St. Petersburg*, all No. 1 bestsellers.

He lives with his wife, Mary, to whom he has been married since 1968, and their two children, in an Edwardian country house in Surrey. They have a second home in New York City. As well as literature, Follett's interests include history and music.

Also by Ken Follett

THE KEY TO REBECCA
THE MAN FROM ST. PETERSBURG

and available from Corgi Books

Ken Follett

On Wings of Eagles

I bare you on eagles' wings,
and brought you unto myself.

EXODUS 19, 4.

CORGI BOOKS

ON WINGS OF EAGLES

A CORGI BOOK 0 552 12610 1

Originally published in Great Britain by
William Collins Sons & Co. Ltd.

PRINTING HISTORY
William Collins edition published 1983
Corgi edition published 1984
Corgi edition reprinted 1984
Corgi edition reprinted 1985

This book is set in 10/11pt Times

Corgi Books are published by Transworld Publishers Ltd.,
Century House, 61-63 Uxbridge Road,
Ealing, London W5 5SA.
Made and printed in Great Britain by
Hunt Barnard Printing Ltd., Aylesbury, Bucks.

Cast of characters

Dallas

Ross Perot, Chairman of the Board, Electronic Data
  Systems Corporation, Dallas, Texas.
Merv Stauffer, Perot's right-hand man.
T. J. Marquez, a vice-president of EDS.
Tom Walter, chief financial officer of EDS.
Mitch Hart, a former president of EDS who had good
  connections in the Democratic Party.
Tom Luce, founder of the Dallas law firm Hughes & Hill.
Bill Gayden, president of EDS World, a subsidiary of EDS.
Mort Meyerson, a vice-president of EDS.

Tehran

Paul Chiapparone, country manager, EDS Corporation
  Iran; Ruthie Chiapparone, his wife.
Bill Gaylord, Paul's deputy; Emily Gaylord, Bill's wife.
Lloyd Briggs, Paul's No. 3.
Rich Gallagher, Paul's administrative assistant; Cathy
  Gallagher, Rich's wife; Buffy, Cathy's poodle.
Paul Bucha, formerly country manager of EDS
  Corporation Iran, latterly based in Paris.
Bob Young, country manager for EDS in Kuwait.
John Howell, lawyer with Hughes & Hill.
Keane Taylor, manager of the Bank Omran project.

The team Col Arthur D. 'Bull' Simons, in command.
        Jay Coburn, second-in-command.
        Ron Davis, point.
        Ralph Boulware, shotgun.
        Joe Poché, driver.
        Glenn Jackson, driver.
        Pat Sculley, flank.
        Jim Schwebach, flank and explosives.

The Iranians Abolhasan, Lloyd Briggs's deputy and the most senior Iranian employee.

Majid, assistant to Jay Coburn; Fara, Majid's daughter.

Rashid, Seyyed, and 'the Cycle Man': trainee systems engineers.

Gholam, personnel/purchasing officer under Jay Coburn.

Hosain Dadgar, examining magistrate.

At the US Embassy William Sullivan, Ambassador.

Charles Naas, Minister Counselor, Sullivan's deputy.

Lou Goelz, Consul General.

Bob Sorenson, Embassy official.

Ali Jordan, Iranian employed by the Embassy.

Barry Rosen, press attaché.

Istanbul

'Mr Fish', resourceful travel agent.
Ilsman, employee of MIT, the Turkish intelligence agency.
'Charlie Brown', interpreter.

Washington

Zbigniew Brzezinski, National Security Adviser.
Cyrus Vance, Secretary of State.
David Newsom, Under Secretary at the State Department.
Henry Precht, Head of the Iran Desk at the State Department.
Mark Ginsberg, White House: State Deapartment liaison.
Admiral Tom Moorer, former Chairman of the Joint Chiefs of Staff.

Preface

This is a true story about a group of people who, accused of crimes they did not commit, decided to make their own justice.

When the adventure was over there was a court case, and they were cleared of all charges. The case is not part of my story, but because it established their innocence I have included details of the court's Findings and Judgment as an appendix to this book.

In telling the story I have taken two small liberties with the truth.

Several people are referred to by pseudonyms or nicknames, usually to protect them from the revenge of the Government of Iran. The false names are: Majid, Fara, Abolhasan, Mr Fish, Deep Throat, Rashid, the Cycle Man, Mehdi, Malek, Gholam, Seyyed and Charlie Brown. All other names are real.

Secondly, in recalling conversations which took place three or four years ago people rarely remember the exact words used; furthermore real-life conversation, with its gestures and interruptions and unfinished sentences, often makes no sense when it is written down. So the dialogue in this book is both reconstructed and edited. However, every reconstructed conversation has been shown to at least one of the participants for correction or approval.

With these two qualifications, I believe every word of what follows is true. This is not a 'fictionalization' or a 'non-fiction novel'. I have not invented anything. What you are about to read is what really happened.

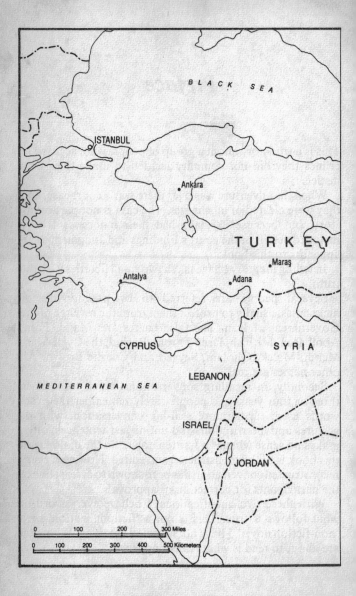

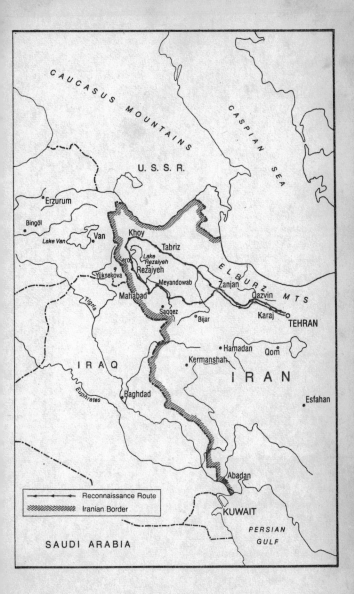

One

1

It all started on 5 December 1978.

Jay Coburn, Director of Personnel for EDS Corporation Iran, sat in his office in uptown Tehran with a lot on his mind.

The office was in a three-storey concrete building known as Bucharest (because it was in an alley off Bucharest Street). Coburn was on the first floor, in a room large by American standards. It had a parquet floor, a smart wood executive desk, and a picture of the Shah on the wall. He sat with his back to the window. Through the glass door he could see into the open-plan office where his staff sat at typewriters and telephones. The glass door had curtains, but Coburn never closed them.

It was cold. It was always cold: thousands of Iranians were on strike, the city's power was intermittent, and the heating was off for several hours most days.

Coburn was a tall, broad-shouldered man, five feet eleven inches and two hundred pounds. His red-brown hair was cut businessman-short and carefully combed, with a part. Although he was only thirty-two he looked nearer to forty. On closer examination, his youth showed in his attractive, open face and ready smile; but he had an air of early maturity, the look of a man who grew up too fast.

All his life he had shouldered responsibility: as a boy, working in his father's flower shop; at the age of twenty, as a helicopter pilot in Vietnam; as a young husband and father; and now, as Personnel Director, holding in his hands the safety of 131 American employees and their 220 dependents in a city where mob violence ruled the streets.

Today, like every day, he was making phone calls around Tehran trying to find out where the fighting was, where it would break out next, and what the prospects were for the next few days.

He called the US Embassy at least once a day. The Embassy had an information room which was manned twenty-four hours a day. Americans would call in from different areas of the city to report demonstrations and riots, and the Embassy would spread the news that this district or that was to be avoided. But for advance information and advice Coburn found the Embassy close to useless. At weekly briefings, which he attended faithfully, he would always be told that Americans should stay indoors as much as possible and keep away from crowds at all costs, but that the Shah was in control and evacuation was not recommended at this time. Coburn understood their problem – if the US Embassy said the Shah was tottering, the Shah would surely fall – but they were so cautious they hardly gave out any information at all.

Disenchanted with the Embassy, the American business community in Tehran had set up its own information network. The biggest US corporation in town was Bell Helicopter, whose Iran operation was run by a retired Major-General, Robert N. Mackinnon. Mackinnon had a first-class intelligence service and he shared everything. Coburn also knew a couple of intelligence officers in the US military and he called them.

Today the city was relatively quiet: there were no major demonstrations. The last outbreak of serious trouble had been three days earlier, on 2 December, the first day of the general strike, where seven hundred people had been reported killed in street fighting. According to Coburn's sources the lull could be expected to continue until 10 December, the Moslem holy day of Ashura.

Coburn was worried about Ashura. The Moslem winter holiday was not a bit like Christmas. A day of fasting and mourning for the death of the Prophet's grandson Husayn, its keynote was remorse. There would be massive street

14

processions, during which the more devout believers would flog themselves. In that atmosphere hysteria and violence could erupt fast.

This year, Coburn feared, the violence might be directed against Americans.

A series of nasty incidents had convinced him that anti-American feeling was growing rapidly. A card had been pushed through his door saying: 'If you value your life and possessions, get out of Iran.' Friends of his had received similar postcards. Spray-can artists had painted 'Americans live here' on the wall of his house. The bus which took his children to the Tehran American School had been rocked by a crowd of demonstrators. Other EDS employees had been yelled at in the streets and had their cars damaged. One scary afternoon, Iranians at the Ministry of Health and Social Welfare – EDS's biggest customer – had gone on the rampage, smashing windows and burning pictures of the Shah, while EDS executives in the building barricaded themselves inside an office until the mob went away.

In some ways the most sinister development was the change in the attitude of Coburn's landlord.

Like most Americans in Tehran, Coburn rented half of a two-family home: he and his wife lived upstairs, and the landlord's family lived on the ground floor. When the Coburns had arrived, in March of that year, the landlord had taken them under his wing. The two families had become friendly. Coburn and the landlord discussed religion: the landlord gave him an English translation of the Koran, and the landlord's daughter would read to her father out of Coburn's Bible. They all went on weekend trips to the countryside together. Scott, Coburn's seven-year-old son, played soccer in the street with the landlord's boys. One weekend the Coburns had the rare privilege of attending a Moslem wedding. It had been fascinating. Men and women had been segregated all day, so Coburn and Scott went with the men, his wife Liz and their three daughters went with the women, and Coburn never got to see the bride at all.

After the summer things had gradually changed. The

weekend trips stopped. The landlord's sons were forbidden to play with Scott in the street. Eventually all contact between the two families ceased even within the confines of the house and its courtyard, and the children would be reprimanded for just speaking to Coburn's family.

The landlord had not suddenly started hating Americans. One evening he had proved that he still cared for the Coburns. There had been a shooting incident in the street: one of his sons had been out after curfew, and soldiers had fired at the boy as he ran home and scrambled over the courtyard wall. Coburn and Liz had watched the whole thing from their upstairs verandah, and Liz had been scared. The landlord had come up to tell them what had happened and reassure them that all was well. But he clearly felt that for the safety of his family he could not be *seen* to be friendly with Americans: he knew which way the wind was blowing. For Coburn it was yet another bad sign.

Now, Coburn heard on the grapevine, there was wild talk in the mosques and bazaars of a holy war against Americans beginning on Ashura. It was five days away, yet the Americans in Tehran were surprisingly calm.

Coburn remembered when the curfew had been introduced: it had not even interfered with the monthly EDS poker game. He and his fellow-gamblers had simply brought their wives and children, turned it into a slumber party, and stayed until morning. They had got used to the sound of gunfire. Most of the heavy fighting was in the older, southern sector where the bazaar was, and in the area around the University; but everyone heard shots from time to time. After the first few occasions they had become curiously indifferent to it. Whoever was speaking would pause, then continue when the shooting stopped, just as he might in the States when a jet aircraft passed overhead. It was as if they could not imagine that shots might be aimed at *them*.

Coburn was *not* blasé about gunfire. He had been shot at rather a lot during his young life. In Vietnam he had piloted both helicopter gunships, in support of ground operations,

16

and troop/supply-carrying ships, landing and taking off in battlefields. He had killed people, and he had seen men die. In those days the Army gave an Air Medal for every twenty-five hours of combat flying: Coburn had come home with thirty-nine of them. He also got two Distinguished Flying Crosses, a Silver Star, and a bullet in his calf – the most vulnerable part of a helicopter pilot. He had learned, during that year, that he could handle himself pretty well in action, when there was so much to do and no time to be frightened. But every time he returned from a mission, when it was all over and he could think about what he had done, his knees would shake.

In a strange way he was grateful for the experience. He had grown up fast, and it had given him an edge over his contemporaries in business life. It had also given him a healthy respect for the sound of gunfire.

But most of his colleagues did not feel that way, nor did their wives. Whenever evacuation was discussed they resisted the idea. They had time, work and pride invested in EDS Corporation Iran, and they did not want to walk away from it. Their wives had turned the rented apartments into real homes, and they were making plans for Christmas. The children had their schools, their friends, their bicycles and their pets. Surely, they were telling themselves, if we just lie low and hang on, the trouble will blow over.

Coburn had tried to persuade Liz to take the kids back to the States, not just for their safety, but because the time might come when he had to evacuate some 350 people all at once, and he would need to give that job his complete undivided attention, without being distracted by private anxiety for his own family. Liz had refused to go.

He sighed when he thought of Liz. She was funny and feisty and everyone enjoyed her company, but she was not a good corporate wife. EDS demanded a lot from its executives: if you needed to work all night to get the job done, you worked all night. Liz resented that. Back in the States, working as a recruiter, Coburn had often been away from home Monday to Friday, travelling all over the country, and she had hated it. She was happy in Tehran because he was home every night. If he was going to stay here, she said, so was she. The children liked it here too. It was the first time they had lived outside the United States, and they were intrigued by the different language, and culture of Iran. Kim, the eldest at eleven, was too full of confidence to get worried. Kristi, the eight-year-old, was somewhat anxious, but then she was the emotional one, always the quickest to over-react. Both Scott, seven, and Kelly, the baby at four, were too young to comprehend the danger.

So they stayed, like everyone else, and waited for things to get better – or worse.

Coburn's thoughts were interrupted by a tap at the door, and Majid walked in. A short, stocky man of about fifty with a luxuriant moustache, he had once been wealthy: his tribe had owned a great deal of land and had lost it in the land reform of the sixties. Now he worked for Coburn as an administrative assistant, dealing with the Iranian bureaucracy. He spoke fluent English and was highly resourceful. Coburn liked him a lot: Majid had gone out of his way to be helpful when Coburn's family arrived in Iran.

'Come in,' Coburn said. 'Sit down. What's on your mind?'

'It's about Fara.'

Coburn nodded. Fara was Majid's daughter, and she worked with her father: her job was to make sure that all American employees always had up-to-date visas and work permits. 'Some problem?' Coburn said.

'The police asked her to take two American passports from our files *without telling anyone.*'

Coburn frowned. 'Any passports in particular?'

'Paul Chiapparone's and Bill Gaylord's.'

Paul was Coburn's boss, the head of EDS Corporation Iran. Bill was second-in-command and manager of their biggest project, the contract with the Ministry of Health. 'What the hell is going on?' Coburn said.

'Fara is in great danger,' Majid said. 'She was instructed not to tell anyone about this. She came to me for advice. Of course I had to tell you, but I'm afraid she will get into very serious trouble.'

'Wait a minute, let's back up,' Coburn said. 'How did this happen?'

'She got a telephone call this morning from the Police Department, Residence Permit Bureau, American Section. They asked her to come to the office. They said it was about James Nyfeler. She thought it was routine. She arrived at the office at eleven-thirty and reported to the Head of the American Section. First he asked for Mr Nyfeler's passport and residence permit. She told him that Mr Nyfeler is no longer in Iran. Then he asked about Paul Bucha. She said that Mr Bucha also was no longer in the country.'

'Did she?'

'Yes.'

Bucha *was* in Iran, but Fara might not have known that, Coburn thought. Bucha had been resident here, had left the country, and had come back in, briefly: he was due to fly back to Paris tomorrow.

Majid continued: 'The officer then said: "I suppose the other two are gone also?" Fara saw that he had four files on his desk, and she asked which other two. He told her Mr Chiapparone and Mr Gaylord. She said she had just picked up Mr Gaylord's residence permit earlier this morning. The officer told her to get the passports and residence permits of both Mr Gaylord and Mr Chiapparone and bring them to him. She was to do it quietly, not to cause alarm.'

'What did she say?' Coburn asked.

'She told him she could not bring them today. He instructed her to bring them tomorrow morning. He told her she was officially responsible for this, and he made sure there were witnesses to these instructions.'

'This doesn't make any sense,' Coburn said.

'If they learn that Fara has disobeyed them—'

'We'll think of a way to protect her,' Coburn said. He was wondering whether Americans were obliged to surrender their passports on demand. He had done so, recently, after a minor car accident, but had later been told he did not have to. 'They didn't say why they wanted the passports?'

'They did not.'

Bucha and Nyfeler were the predecessors of Chiapparone

19

and Gaylord. Was that a clue? Coburn did not know.

Coburn stood up. 'The first decision we have to make is what Fara is going to tell the police tomorrow morning,' he said. 'I'll talk to Paul Chiapparone and get back to you.'

On the ground floor of the building Paul Chiapparone sat in his office. He, too, had a parquet floor, an executive desk, a picture of the Shah on the wall and a lot on his mind.

Paul was thirty-nine years old, of middle height, and a little overweight, mainly because he was fond of good food. With his olive skin and thick black hair he looked very Italian. His job was to build a complete modern social security system in a primitive country. It was not easy.

In the early seventies Iran had had a rudimentary social security system which was inefficient at collecting contributions and so easy to defraud that one man could draw benefit several times over for the same illness. When the Shah decided to spend some of his twenty billion dollars a year oil revenues creating a welfare state, EDS got the contract. EDS ran Medicare and Medicaid programmes for several States in the US, but in Iran they had to start from scratch. They had to issue a social security card to each of Iran's thirty-two million people, organize payroll deductions so that wage-earners paid their contributions, and process claims for benefits. The whole system would be run by computers – EDS's speciality.

The difference between installing a data processing system in the States and doing the same job in Iran was, Paul found, like the difference between making a cake from a packet mix and making one the old-fashioned way with all the original ingredients. It was often frustrating. Iranians did not have the can-do attitude of American business executives, and seemed often to create problems instead of solving them. At EDS headquarters back in Dallas, Texas, not only were people expected to do the impossible, but it was usually due yesterday. Here in Iran everything was impossible and in any case not due until 'fardah' – usually translated 'tomorrow', in practice 'some time in the future'.

Paul had attacked the problems in the only way he knew: by hard work and determination. He was no intellectual genius. As a boy he had found school work difficult, but his Italian father, with the immigrant's typical faith in education, had pressured him to study, and he had got good grades. Sheer persistence had served him well ever since. He could remember the early days of EDS in the States, back in the sixties, when every new contract could make or break the company; and he had helped build it into one of the most dynamic and successful corporations in the world. The Iranian operation would go the same way, he had been sure, particularly when Jay Coburn's recruitment and training programme began to deliver more Iranians capable of top management.

He had been all wrong, and he was only just beginning to understand why.

When he and his family arrived in Iran, in August 1977, the petrodollar boom was already over. The government was running out of money. That year an anti-inflation programme increased unemployment just when a bad harvest was driving yet more starving peasants into the cities. The tyrannical rule of the Shah was weakened by the human-rights policies of American President Jimmy Carter. The time was ripe for political unrest.

For a while Paul did not take much notice of local politics. He knew there were rumblings of discontent, but that was true of just about every country in the world, and the Shah seemed to have as firm a grip on the reins of power as any ruler. Like the rest of the world, Paul missed the significance of the events of the first half of 1978.

On 7 January the newspaper *Etelaat* published a scurrilous attack on an exiled clergyman called Ayatollah Khomeini, alleging, among other things, that he was homosexual. The following day, eighty miles from Tehran in the town of Qom – the principal centre of religious education in the country – outraged theology students staged a protest sit-in which was bloodily broken up by the military and the police. The confrontation escalated, and seventy people were killed in two more days of disturbances. The clergy organized a memorial procession for the dead forty days later in accordance with Islamic tradition. There was more violence during the procession, and the dead were commemorated in another memorial forty days on . . . The processions continued, and grew larger and more violent, through the first six months of the year.

With hindsight, Paul could see that calling these marches 'funeral processions' had been a way to circumvent the Shah's ban on political demonstrations. But at the time he had had no idea that a massive political movement was building. Nor had anyone else.

In August this year Paul went home to the States on leave. (So did William Sullivan, the US Ambassador to Iran.) Paul loved all kinds of water sports, and he had gone to a sports fishing tournament in Ocean City, New Jersey, with his cousin Joe Porreca. His wife Ruthie and the children, Karen and Ann Marie, went to Chicago to visit Ruthie's parents. Paul was a little anxious because the Ministry of Health still had not paid EDS's bill for the month of June; but it was not the first time they had been late with a payment, and Paul had left the problem in the hands of his second-in-command, Bill Gaylord, and he was fairly confident Bill would get the money in.

While he was in the US the news from Iran was bad. Martial law was declared on 7 September, and the following day more than a hundred people were killed by soldiers during a demonstration in Jaleh Square in the heart of Tehran.

When the Chiapparone family came back to Iran the very air seemed different. For the first time Paul and Ruthie could hear shooting in the streets at night. They were alarmed: suddenly they realized that trouble for the Iranians meant trouble for *them*. There was a series of strikes. The electricity was continually being cut off, so they dined by candlelight and Paul wore his topcoat in the office to keep warm. It became more and more difficult to get money out of the banks, and Paul started a cheque-cashing service at the office for employees. When they got low on heating oil for their home Paul had to walk around the streets until he found a tanker, then bribe the driver to come to the house and deliver.

His business problems were worse. The Minister of Health and Social Welfare, Dr Sheikholeslamizadeh, had been arrested under Article 5 of martial law, which permitted a prosecutor to jail anyone without giving a reason. Also in jail was Deputy Minister Reza Neghabat, with whom Paul had worked closely. The Ministry still had not paid its June bill, nor any since, and now owed EDS more than four million dollars.

For two months Paul tried to get the money. The individuals he had dealt with previously had all gone. Their replacements usually did not return his calls. Sometimes someone would promise to look into the problem and call back. After waiting a week for the call that never came, Paul would telephone once again, to be told that the person he spoke to last week had now left the Ministry. Meetings would be arranged then cancelled. The debt mounted at the rate of $1.4 million a month.

On 14 November Paul wrote to Dr Heidargholi Emrani, the Deputy Minister in charge of the Social Security Organization, giving formal notice that if the Ministry did not pay up within a month EDS would stop work. The threat was repeated on 4 December by Paul's boss, the President of EDS World, at a personal meeting with Dr Emrani.

That was yesterday.

If EDS pulled out, the whole Iranian social security system would collapse. Yet it was becoming more and more apparent that the country was bankrupt and simply could not pay its bills. What, Paul wondered, would Dr Emrani do now?

He was still wondering when Jay Coburn walked in with the answer.

At first, however, it did not occur to Paul that the attempt to steal his passport might have been intended to keep him, and therefore EDS, in Iran.

When Coburn had given him the facts he said: 'What the hell did they do that for?'

'I don't know. Majid doesn't know, and Fara doesn't know.'

Paul looked at him. The two men had become close in the last month. For the rest of the employees Paul was putting on a brave face, but with Coburn he had been able to close the door and say Okay, what do you really think?

Coburn said: 'The first question is, What do we do about Fara? She could be in trouble.'

'She has to give them some kind of an answer.'

'A show of co-operation?'

'She could go back and tell them that Nyfeler and Bucha are no longer resident . . .'

'She already told them.'

'She could take their exit visas as proof.'

'Yeah,' Coburn said dubiously. 'But it's you and Bill they're really interested in now.'

'She could say that the passports aren't kept in the office.'

'They may know that's not true – Fara may even have taken passports down there in the past.'

'Say senior executives don't have to keep their passports in the office.'

'That might work.'

'Any convincing story to the effect that she was physically unable to do what they asked her.'

'Good. I'll discuss it with her and Majid.' Coburn thought for a moment. 'You know, Bucha has a reservation on a flight out tomorrow. He could just go.'

'He probably should – they think he's not here anyway.'

'You could do the same.'

Paul reflected. Maybe he should get out now. What would the Iranians do then? They might just try to detain someone else. 'No,' he said. 'If we're going, I should be the last to leave.'

'Are we going?' Coburn asked.

'I don't know.' Every day for weeks they had asked each

24

other that question. Coburn had developed an evacuation plan which could be put into effect instantly. Paul had been hesitating, with his finger on the button. He knew that his ultimate boss, back in Dallas, wanted him to evacuate – but it meant abandoning the project on which he had worked so hard for the last sixteen months. 'I don't know,' he repeated. 'I'll call Dallas.'

That night Coburn was at home, in bed with Liz, and fast asleep when the phone rang.

He picked it up in the dark. 'Yeah?'

'This is Paul.'

'Hello.' Coburn turned on the light and looked at his wristwatch. It was two a.m.

'We're going to evacuate,' Paul said.

'You got it.'

Coburn cradled the phone and sat on the edge of the bed. In a way it was a relief. There would be two or three days of frantic activity, but then he would know that the people whose safety had been worrying him for so long were back in the States, out of reach of these crazy Iranians.

He ran over in his mind the plans he had made for just this moment. First he had to inform a hundred and thirty families that they would be leaving the country within the next forty-eight hours. He had divided the city into sectors, with a team leader for each sector: he would call the leaders, and it would be their job to call the families. He had drafted leaflets for the evacuees telling them where to go and what to do. He just had to fill in the blanks with dates, times and flight numbers, then have the leaflets duplicated and distributed.

He had picked a lively and imaginative young Iranian systems engineer, Rashid, and given him the job of taking care of the homes, cars and pets which would be left behind by the fleeing Americans and – eventually – shipping their possessions to the US. He had appointed a small logistics group to organize plane tickets and transport to the airport.

Finally, he had conducted a small-scale rehearsal of the

evacuation with a few people. It had worked.

Coburn got dressed and made coffee. There was nothing he could do for the next couple of hours, but he was too anxious and impatient to sleep.

At four a.m. he called the half-dozen members of the logistics group, woke them, and told them to meet him at the 'Bucharest' office immediately after curfew.

Curfew began at nine each evening and ended at five in the morning. For an hour Coburn sat waiting, smoking and drinking a lot of coffee and going over his notes.

When the cuckoo clock in the hall chirped five he was at the front door, ready to go.

Outside there was a thick fog. He got into his car and headed for Bucharest, crawling along at fifteen miles per hour.

Three blocks from his house, half a dozen soldiers leaped out of the fog and stood in a semicircle in front of his car, pointing their rifles at his windscreen.

'Oh, shit,' Coburn said.

One of the soldiers was still loading his gun. He was trying to put the clip in backwards, and it would not fit. He dropped it, and went down on one knee, scrabbling around on the ground looking for it. Coburn would have laughed if he had not been scared.

An officer yelled at Coburn in Farsi. Coburn lowered the window. He showed the officer his wristwatch and said: 'It's after five.'

The soldiers had a conference. The officer came back and asked Coburn for his identification.

Coburn waited anxiously. This would be the worst possible day to get arrested. Would the officer believe that Coburn's watch was right and his was wrong?

At last the soldiers got out of the road and the officer waved Coburn on.

Coburn breathed a sigh of relief and drove slowly on.

Iran was like that.

26

Coburn's logistics group went to work making plane reservations, chartering buses to take people to the airport, and photocopying handout leaflets. At ten a.m. Coburn got the team leaders into Bucharest and started them calling the evacuees.

He got reservations for most of them on a Pan Am flight to Istanbul on Friday 8 December. The remainder – including Liz Coburn and the four children – would get a Lufthansa flight to Frankfurt that same day.

As soon as the reservations were confirmed, two top executives at EDS headquarters, Merv Stauffer and T. J. Marquez, left Dallas for Istanbul to meet the evacuees, shepherd them to hotels, and organize the next stage of their flight back home.

During the day there was a small change in plan. Paul was still reluctant to abandon his work in Iran. He proposed that a skeleton staff of about ten senior men stay behind, to keep the office ticking over, in the hope that Iran would quiet down and EDS would eventually be able to resume working normally. Dallas agreed. Among those who volunteered to stay were Paul himself, his deputy Bill Gaylord, Jay Coburn, and most of Coburn's evacuation logistics group. Two people who stayed behind reluctantly were Carl and Vickie Commons: Vickie was nine months pregnant and would leave after her baby was born.

On Friday morning Coburn's team, their pockets full of ten thousand rial (about $140) notes for bribes, virtually took over a section of Mehrabad Airport in western Tehran. Coburn had people writing tickets behind the Pan Am counter, people at passport control, people in the departure lounge, and people running baggage handling equipment. The plane was overbooked: bribes ensured that no one from EDS was bumped off the flight.

There were two especially tense moments. An EDS wife

with an Australian passport had been unable to get an exit visa because the Iranian government offices which issued exit visas were all on strike. (Her husband and children had American passports and therefore did not need exit visas.) When the husband reached the passport control desk, he handed over his passport and his children's in a stack with six or seven other passports. As the guard tried to sort them out, EDS people in the queue behind began to push forward and cause a commotion. Some of Coburn's team gathered around the desk asking loud questions and pretending to get angry about the delay. In the confusion the woman with the Australian passport walked through the departure lounge without being stopped.

Another EDS family had adopted an Iranian baby and had not yet been able to get a passport for the child. Only a few months old, the baby would fall asleep, lying face down, on its mother's forearm. Another EDS wife, Kathy Marketos – of whom it was said that she would try anything once – put the sleeping baby on her own forearm, draped her raincoat over it, and carried it out to the plane.

However, it was many hours before anyone got on to a plane. Both flights were delayed. There was no food to be bought at the airport and the evacuees were famished, so just before curfew some of Coburn's team drove around the city buying anything edible they could find. They purchased the entire contents of several *kuche* stalls – street-corner stands that sold candy, fruit and cigarettes – and they went into a Kentucky Fried Chicken and did a deal for its stock of bread rolls. Back at the airport, passing food out to EDS people in the departure lounge, they were almost mobbed by the other hungry passengers waiting for the same flights. On the way back downtown two of the team were caught and arrested for being out after curfew, but the soldier who stopped them got distracted by another car which tried to escape, and the EDS men drove off while he was shooting the other way.

The Istanbul flight left just after midnight. The Frankfurt flight took off the next day, thirty-one hours late.

Coburn and most of the team spent the night at Bucharest. They had no one to go home to.

While Coburn was running the evacuation, Paul had been trying to find out who wanted to confiscate his passport and why.

His administrative assistant, Rich Gallagher, was a young American who was good at dealing with Iranian bureaucracy. Gallagher was one of those who had volunteered to stay in Tehran. His wife Cathy had also stayed behind. She had a good job with the US military in Tehran. The Gallaghers did not want to leave. Furthermore, they had no children to worry about – just a poodle called Buffy.

The day Fara was asked to take the passports – 5 December – Gallagher visited the US Embassy with one of the people whose passports had been demanded: Paul Bucha, who no longer worked in Iran but happened to be in town on a visit.

They met with Consul General Lou Goelz. Goelz, an experienced consul in his fifties, was a portly balding man with a fringe of white hair: he would have made a good Santa Claus. With Goelz was an Iranian member of the consular staff, Ali Jordan.

Goelz advised Bucha to catch his plane. Fara had told the police – in all innocence – that Bucha was not in Iran, and they had appeared to believe her. There was every chance that Bucha could sneak out.

Goelz also offered to hold the passports and residence permits of Paul and Bill for safekeeping. That way, if the police made a formal demand for the documents, EDS would be able to refer them to the Embassy.

Meanwhile, Ali Jordan would contact the police and try to find out what the hell was going on.

Later that day the passports and papers were delivered to the Embassy.

Next morning Bucha caught his plane and got out. Gallagher called the Embassy. Ali Jordan had talked to General Biglari of the Tehran Police Department. Biglari had said that Paul and Bill were being detained in the country and would be arrested if they tried to leave.

Gallagher asked why.

They were being held as 'material witnesses in investigation', Jordan understood.

'*What* investigation?'

Jordan did not know.

Paul was puzzled, as well as anxious, when Gallagher reported all this. He had not been involved in a road accident, had not witnessed a crime, had no connections with the CIA . . . Who or what was being investigated? EDS? Or was the investigation just an excuse for keeping Paul and Bill in Iran so that they would continue to run the social security system's computers?

The police had made one concession. Ali Jordan had argued that the police were entitled to confiscate the residence permits, which were the property of the Iranian government, but not the passports, which were US Government property. General Biglari had conceded this.

Next day Gallagher and Ali Jordan went to the police station to hand the documents over to Biglari. On the way Gallagher asked Jordan whether he thought there was a chance Paul and Bill would be accused of wrongdoing.

'I doubt that very much,' said Jordan.

At the police station the General warned Jordan that the Embassy would be held responsible if Paul and Bill left the country by any means – such as a US military aircraft.

The following day – 8 December, the day of the evacuation – Lou Goelz called EDS. He had found out, through a 'source' at the Iranian Ministry of Justice, that the investigation in which Paul and Bill were supposed to be material witnesses was an investigation into corruption charges against the jailed Minister of Health, Dr Sheikholeslamizadeh.

It was something of a relief to Paul to know, at last, what the whole thing was about. He could happily tell the investigators the truth: EDS paid no bribes. He doubted whether anyone had bribed the Minister. Iranian bureaucrats were notoriously corrupt, but Dr Sheik – as Paul called him for short – seemed to come from a different mould. An orthopaedic surgeon by training, he had a perceptive mind and an impressive ability to master detail. In the Ministry of Health

30

he had surrounded himself with a group of progressive young technocrats who found ways to cut through red tape and get things done. The EDS project was only part of his ambitious plan to bring Iranian health and welfare services up to American standards. Paul did not think Dr Sheik was lining his own pockets at the same time.

Paul had nothing to fear – if Goelz's 'source' was telling the truth. But was he? Dr Sheik had been arrested three months ago. Was it a coincidence that the Iranians had suddenly realized that Paul and Bill were material witnesses when Paul told them that EDS would leave Iran unless the Ministry paid its bills?

After the evacuation, the remaining EDS men moved into two houses and stayed there, playing poker, during 10 and 11 December, the holy days of Ashura. There was a high-stakes house and a low-stakes house. Both Paul and Coburn were at the high-stakes house. For protection they invited Coburn's 'spooks' – his two contacts in military intelligence – who carried guns. No weapons were allowed at the poker table, so the spooks had to leave their firearms in the hall.

Contrary to expectations, Ashura passed relatively peacefully: millions of Iranians attended anti-Shah demonstrations all over the country, but there was little violence.

After Ashura, Paul and Bill again considered skipping the country, but they were in for a shock. As a preliminary they asked Lou Goelz at the Embassy to give them back their passports. Goelz said that if he did that he would be obliged to inform General Biglari. That would amount to a warning to the police that Paul and Bill were trying to sneak out.

Goelz insisted that he had told EDS, when he took the passports, that this was his deal with the police; but he must have said it rather quietly because no one could remember it.

Paul was furious. *Why* had Goelz had to make *any* kind of deal with the police? He was under no obligation to tell them what he did with an American passport. It was not his job to *help* the police detain Paul and Bill in Iran, for God's sake! The Embassy was there to help *Americans*, wasn't it?

Couldn't Goelz renege on his stupid agreement, and

return the passports quietly, perhaps informing the police a couple of days later, when Paul and Bill were safely home? Absolutely not, said Goelz. If he quarrelled with the police they would make trouble for everyone else, and Goelz had to worry about the other twelve thousand Americans still in Iran. Besides, the names of Paul and Bill were now on the 'stop list' held by the airport police: even with all their documents in order they would never get through passport control.

When the news that Paul and Bill were well and truly stuck in Iran reached Dallas, EDS and its lawyers went into high gear. Their Washington contacts were not as good as they would have been under a Republican administration, but they still had some friends. They talked to Bob Strauss, a high-powered White House troubleshooter who happened to be a Texan; Admiral Tom Moorer, a former Chairman of the Joint Chiefs of Staff, who knew many of the generals now running Iran's military government; and Richard Helms, past Director of the CIA and a former US Ambassador to Iran. As a result of the pressure they put on the State Department, the US Ambassador in Tehran, William Sullivan, raised the case of Paul and Bill in a meeting with the Iranian Prime Minister, General Azhari.

None of this brought any results.

The thirty days which Paul had given the Iranians to pay their bill ran out, and on 16 December he wrote to Dr Emrani formally terminating the contract. But he had not given up. He asked a handful of evacuated executives to come back to Tehran, as a sign of EDS's willingness to try to resolve its problems with the Ministry. Some of the returning executives, encouraged by the peaceful Ashura, even brought their families back.

Neither the Embassy nor EDS's lawyers in Tehran had been able to find out *who* had ordered Paul and Bill detained. It was Majid, Fara's father, who eventually got the information out of General Biglari. The investigator was examining magistrate Hosain Dadgar, a mid-level functionary within the office of the public prosecutor, in a department which dealt with crimes by civil servants and had very broad powers. Dadgar was conducting the inquiry into Dr Sheik, the jailed former Minister of Health.

Since the Embassy could not persuade the Iranians to let Paul and Bill leave the country, and would not give back their passports quietly, could they at least arrange for this Dadgar to question Paul and Bill as soon as possible so that they could go home for Christmas? Christmas did not mean much to the Iranians, said Goelz, but New Year did, so he would try to fix a meeting before then.

During the second half of December the rioting started again (and the first thing the returning executives did was plan for a second evacuation). The general strike continued, and petroleum exports – the government's most important source of income – ground to a halt, reducing to zero EDS's chances of getting paid. So few Iranians turned up for work at the Ministry that there was nothing for the EDS men to do, and Paul sent half of them home to the States for Christmas.

Paul packed his bags, closed up his house, and moved into the Hilton, ready to go home at the first opportunity.

The city was thick with rumours. Jay Coburn fished up most of them in his net and brought the interesting ones to Paul. One more disquieting than most came from Bunny Fleishhaker, an American woman with friends at the Ministry of Justice. Bunny had worked for EDS in the States, and she kept in touch here in Tehran although she was no longer with the company. She called Coburn to say that the Ministry of Justice planned to arrest Paul and Bill.

Paul discussed this with Coburn. It contradicted what they were hearing from the US Embassy. The Embassy's advice was surely better than Bunny Fleishhaker's, they agreed. They decided to take no action.

Paul spent Christmas Day quietly, with a few colleagues, at the home of Pat Sculley, a young EDS manager who had volunteered to return to Tehran. Sculley's wife Mary had also come back and she cooked Christmas dinner. Paul missed Ruthie and the children.

33

Two days after Christmas the Embassy called. They had succeeded in setting up a meeting for Paul and Bill with examining magistrate Hosain Dadgar. The meeting was to take place the following morning, 28 December, at the Ministry of Health building on Eisenhower Avenue.

Bill Gaylord came into Paul's office a little after nine, carrying a cup of coffee, dressed in the EDS uniform: business suit, white shirt, quiet tie, black brogue shoes.

Like Paul, Bill was thirty-nine, of middle height, and stocky; but there the resemblance ended. Paul had dark colouring, heavy eyebrows, deep-set eyes and a big nose: in casual clothes he was often mistaken for an Iranian until he opened his mouth and spoke English with a New York accent. Bill had a flat, round face and very white skin: nobody would take him for anything but an Anglo.

They had a lot in common. Both were Catholic, although Bill was more devout. They loved good food. Both had trained as systems engineers and joined EDS in the mid-sixties, Bill in 1965 and Paul in 1966. Both had had splendid careers with EDS, but although Paul had joined a year later he was now senior to Bill. Bill knew the health care business inside out, and he was a first-class 'people manager', but he was not as pushy and dynamic as Paul. Bill was a deep thinker and a careful organizer. Paul would never have to worry about Bill making an important presentation: Bill would have prepared every word.

They worked together well. When Paul was hasty, Bill would make him pause and reflect. When Bill wanted to plan his way around every bump in the road, Paul would tell him just to get in and drive.

They had been acquainted in the States but had got to know one another well in the last nine months. When Bill had arrived in Tehran, last March, he had lived at the Chiapparones' house until his wife Emily and the children came over. Paul felt almost protective toward him. It was a shame that Bill had had nothing but problems here in Iran.

Bill was much more worried by the rioting and the

shooting than most of the others – perhaps because he had not been here long, perhaps because he was more of a worrier by nature. He also took the passport problem more seriously than Paul. At one time he had even suggested that the two of them take a train to the north-east of Iran and cross the border into Russia, on the grounds that nobody would expect American businessmen to escape via the Soviet Union.

Bill also missed Emily and the children badly, and Paul felt somewhat responsible, because he had asked Bill to come to Iran.

Still, it was almost over. Today they would see Mr Dadgar and get their passports back. Bill had a reservation on a plane out tomorrow. Emily was planning a welcome-home party for him on New Year's Eve. Soon all this would seem like a bad dream.

Paul smiled at Bill. 'Ready to go?'

'Any time.'

'Let's get Abolhasan.' Paul picked up the phone. Abolhasan was the most senior Iranian employee, and advised Paul on Iranian business methods. The son of a distinguished lawyer, he was married to an American woman, and spoke very good English. One of his jobs was translating EDS's contracts into Farsi. Today he would translate for Paul and Bill at their meeting with Dadgar.

He came immediately to Paul's office and the three men left. They did not take a lawyer with them. According to the Embassy, this meeting would be routine, the questioning informal. To take lawyers along would not only be pointless, but might antagonize Mr Dadgar and lead him to suspect that Paul and Bill had something to hide. Paul would have liked to have a member of the Embassy staff present, but this idea also had been turned down by Lou Goelz: it was not normal procedure to send Embassy representatives to a meeting such as this. However, Goelz had advised Paul and Bill to take with them documents establishing when they had come to Iran, what their official positions were, and the scope of their responsibilities.

35

As the car negotiated its way through the usual insane Tehran traffic, Paul felt depressed. He was glad to be going home, but he hated to admit failure. He had come to Iran to build up EDS's business here, and he found himself dismantling it. Whatever way you looked at it the company's first overseas venture had been a failure. It was not Paul's fault that the government of Iran had run out of money, but that was small consolation: excuses did not make profits.

They drove down the tree-lined Eisenhower Avenue, as wide and straight as any American highway, and pulled into the courtyard of a square, ten-storey building set back from the street and guarded by soldiers with automatic rifles. This was the Social Security Organization of the Ministry of Health and Social Welfare. It was to have been the powerhouse of the new Iranian welfare state: here, side by side, the Iranian government and EDS had worked to build a social security system. EDS occupied the entire seventh floor. Bill's office was there.

Paul, Bill and Abolhasan showed their passes and went in. The corridors were dirty and poorly decorated, and the building was cold: the heat was off again. They were directed to the office Mr Dadgar was using.

They found him in a small room with dirty walls, sitting behind an old grey steel desk. In front of him on the desk were a notebook and a pen. Through the window Paul could see the data centre EDS was building next door.

Abolhasan introduced everyone. There was an Iranian woman sitting on a chair beside Dadgar's desk: her name was Mrs Nourbash, and she was Dadgar's interpreter.

They all sat down on dilapidated metal chairs. Tea was served. Dadgar began to speak in Farsi. His voice was soft but rather deep, and his expression was blank. Paul studied him as he waited for the translation. Dadgar was a short, stocky man in his fifties, and for some reason he made Paul think of Archie Bunker. His complexion was dark and his hair was combed forward, as if to hide the fact that it was receding. He had a moustache and glasses, and he wore a sober suit.

36

Dadgar finished speaking, and Abolhasan said: 'He warns you that he has the power to arrest you if he finds your answers to his questions unsatisfactory. In case you did not realize this, he says you may postpone the interview to give your lawyers time to arrange bail.'

Paul was surprised by this development, but he evaluated it fast, just like any other business decision. Okay, he thought, the worst thing that can happen is that he won't believe us and he will arrest us – but we're not murderers, we'll be out on bail in twenty-four hours. Then we might be confined to the country, and we would have to meet with our attorneys and try to work things out . . . which is no worse than the situation we're in now.

He looked at Bill. 'What do you think?'

Bill shrugged. 'Goelz says this meeting is routine. The stuff about bail sounds like a formality – like reading you your rights.'

Paul nodded. 'And the last thing we want is a postponement.'

'Then let's get it over with.'

Paul turned to Mrs Nourbash. 'Please tell Mr Dadgar that neither of us has committed a crime, and neither of us has any knowledge of anyone else committing a crime, so we are confident that no charges will be made against us, and we would like to get this finished up today so that we can go home.'

Mrs Nourbash translated.

Dadgar said he wanted first to interview Paul alone. Bill should come back in an hour.

Bill left.

Bill went up to his office on the seventh floor. He picked up the phone, called Bucharest, and reached Lloyd Briggs. Briggs was number three in the hierarchy after Paul and Bill.

'Dadgar says he has the power to arrest us,' Bill told Briggs. 'We might need to put up bail. Call the Iranian attorneys and find out what that means.'

'Sure,' Briggs said. 'Where are you?'

'In my office here at the Ministry.'

'I'll get back to you.'

Bill hung up and waited. The idea of his being arrested was kind of ridiculous – despite the widespread corruption of modern Iran, EDS had never paid bribes to get contracts. But even if bribes had been paid, Bill would not have paid them: his job was to deliver the product, not to win the order.

Briggs called back within a few minutes. 'You've got nothing to worry about,' he said. 'Just last week a man accused of murder had his bail set at a million and a half rials.'

Bill did a quick calculation: that was twenty thousand dollars. EDS could probably pay that in cash. For some weeks they had been keeping large amounts of cash, both because of the bank strikes and for use during the evacuation. 'How much do we have in the office safe?'

'Around seven million rials, plus fifty thousand dollars.'

So, Bill thought, even if we are arrested we'll be able to post bail immediately. 'Thanks,' he said. 'That makes me feel a lot better.'

Downstairs, Dadgar had written down Paul's full name, date and place of birth, schools attended, experience in computers, and qualifications: and he had carefully examined the document which officially named Paul as Country Manager for Electronic Data Systems Corporation Iran. Now he asked Paul to give an account of how EDS had secured its contract with the Ministry of Health.

Paul took a deep breath. 'First, I would like to point out that I was not working in Iran at the time the contract was negotiated and signed, so I do not have first-hand knowledge of this. However, I will tell you what I understand the procedure to have been.'

Mrs Nourbash translated and Dadgar nodded.

Paul continued, speaking slowly and rather formally to help the translator. 'In 1975 an EDS executive, Paul Bucha, learned that the Ministry was looking for a data processing company experienced in health insurance and social security work. He came to Tehran, had meetings with Ministry officials, and determined the nature and scale of the work the Ministry wanted done. He was told that the Ministry had already received proposals for the project from Louis Berger and Company, Marsh and McClennan, ISIRAN, and UNIVAC, and that a fifth proposal was on its way from Cap Gemini Sogeti. He said that EDS was the leading data processing company in the United States and that our company specialized in exactly this kind of health care work. He offered the Ministry a free preliminary study. The offer was accepted.'

When he paused for translation, Paul noticed, Mrs Nourbash seemed to say less than he had said; and what Dadgar wrote down was shorter still. He began to speak more slowly and pause more often. 'The Ministry obviously liked EDS's proposals, because they then asked us to perform a detailed study for two hundred thousand dollars. The results of our study were presented in October 1975. The Ministry accepted our proposal and began contract negotiations. By August 1976 the contract was agreed.'

'Was everything above board?' Dadgar asked through Mrs Nourbash.

'Absolutely,' Paul said. 'It took another three months to go through the lengthy process of getting all the necessary approvals from many government departments, including the Shah's court. None of these steps was omitted. The contract went into effect at the end of the year.'

'Was the contract price exorbitant?'

'It showed a maximum expected pre-tax profit of twenty per cent, which is in line with other contracts of this magnitude, both here and in other countries.'

'And has EDS fulfilled its obligations under the contract?'

This was something on which Paul *did* have first-hand knowledge. 'Yes, we have.'

'Could you produce evidence?'

'Certainly. The contract specifies that I should meet with Ministry officials at certain intervals to review progress:

39

those meetings have taken place and the Ministry has the minutes of the meetings on file. The contract lays down a complaints procedure for the Ministry to use if EDS fails to fulful its obligations: that procedure has never been used.'

Mrs Nourbash translated, but Dadgar did not write anything down. He must know all this anyway, Paul thought.

He added: 'Look out of the window. There is our data centre. Go and see it. There are computers in it. Touch them. They work. They produce information. Read the printouts. They are being *used.*'

Dadgar made a brief note. Paul wondered what he was really after.

The next question was: 'What is your relationship with the Mahvi group?'

'When we first came to Iran we were told that we had to have Iranian partners in order to do business here. The Mahvi group are our partners. However, their main role is to supply us with Iranian staff. We meet with them periodically, but they have little to do with the running of our business.'

Dadgar asked why Dr Towliati, a Ministry official, was on the EDS payroll. Was this not a conflict of interest?

Here at last was a question that made sense. Paul could see how Towliati's role could appear irregular. However, it was easily explained. 'In our contract we undertake to supply expert consultants to help the Ministry make the best use of the service we provide. Dr Towliati is such a consultant. He has a data processing background, and he is familiar with both Iranian and American business methods. He is paid by EDS, rather than by the Ministry, because Ministry salaries are too low to attract a man of his calibre. However, the Ministry is obliged to reimburse us for his salary, as laid down in the contract; so he is not *really* paid by us.'

Once again Dadgar wrote down very little. He could have got all this information from the files, Paul thought: perhaps he has.

Dadgar asked: 'But why does Dr Towliati sign invoices?'

'That's easy,' Paul replied. 'He does not, and never has. The closest he comes is this: he would inform the Minister

40

that a certain task has been completed, where the specification of that task is too technical for verification by a layman.' Paul smiled. 'He takes his responsibility to the Ministry very seriously – he is easily our harshest critic, and he will characteristically ask a lot of tough questions before verifying completion of a task. I sometimes wish I did have him in my pocket.'

Mrs Nourbash translated. Paul was thinking: What is Dadgar after? First he asks about the contract negotiations, which happened before my time; then about the Mahvi group and Dr Towliati, as if they were sensationally important. Maybe Dadgar himself doesn't know what he's looking for – maybe he's just fishing, hoping to come up with evidence of something illegal.

How long can this farce go on?

Bill was outside in the corridor, wearing his topcoat to keep out the cold. Someone had brought him a glass of tea, and he warmed his hands on it while he sipped. The building was dark as well as cold.

Dadgar had immediately struck Bill as being different from the average Iranian. He was cold, gruff and inhospitable. The Embassy had said Dadgar was 'favourably disposed' toward Bill and Paul, but that was not the impression Bill had.

Bill wondered what game Dadgar was playing. Was he trying to intimidate them, or was he seriously considering arresting them? Either way, the meeting was not turning out the way the Embassy had anticipated. Their advice, to come without lawyers or Embassy representatives, now looked mistaken: perhaps they just did not want to get involved. Anyway, Paul and Bill were on their own now. It was not going to be a pleasant day. But at the end of it they would be able to go home.

Looking out of the window, he saw that there was some excitement down on Eisenhower Avenue. Some distance along the street, dissidents were stopping cars and putting Khomeini posters on the windscreens. The soldiers guarding the Ministry building were stopping the cars and tearing the posters up. As he waited, the soldiers became more belligerent. They broke the headlight of a car, and the windscreen of another, as if to teach the drivers a lesson. Then they pulled a driver out of a car and punched him around.

The next car they picked on was a taxi, a Tehran orange cab. It went by without stopping, not surprisingly; but the soldiers seemed angered and chased it, firing their guns. Cab and pursuing soldiers disappeared from Bill's sight.

After that the soldiers ended their grim game and returned to their posts inside the walled courtyard in front of the Ministry building. The incident, with its queer mixture of childishness and brutality, seemed to sum up what was going on in Iran. The country was going down the drain. The Shah had lost control and the rebels were determined to drive him out or kill him. Bill felt sorry for the people in the cars, victims of circumstance who could do nothing but hope that things would get better. If Iranians are no longer safe, he thought, Americans must be in even more danger. We've got to get out of this country.

Two Iranians were hanging about in the same corridor, watching the fracas on Eisenhower. They seemed as appalled as Bill at what they saw.

Morning turned into afternoon. Bill got more tea and a sandwich for lunch. He wondered what was happening in the interrogation room. He was not surprised to be kept waiting: in Iran, 'an hour' meant nothing more precise than 'later,. maybe'. But as the day wore on he became more uneasy. Was Paul in trouble in there?

The Iranians stayed in the corridor all afternoon, doing nothing. Bill wondered vaguely who they were. He did not speak to them.

He wished the time would pass more quickly. He had a reservation on tomorrow's plane. Emily and the kids were in Washington, where both Emily's and Bill's parents lived. They had a big party planned for him on New Year's Eve. He could hardly wait to see them all again.

He should have left Iran weeks ago, when the firebombing started. One of the people whose homes had been bombed

42

was a girl with whom he had gone to high school in Washington. She was married to a diplomat at the US Embassy. Bill had talked to them about the incident. Nobody had been hurt, luckily, but it had been very scary. I should have taken heed, and got out then, he thought.

At last Abolhasan opened the door and called: 'Bill! Come in, please.'

Bill looked at his watch. It was five o'clock. He went in.

'It's cold,' he said as he sat down.

'It's warm enough in this seat,' Paul said with a strained smile. Bill looked at Paul's face. He seemed very uncomfortable.

Dadgar drank a glass of tea and ate a sandwich before he began to question Bill. Watching him, Bill thought: this guy is trying to trap us so he won't have to let us leave the country.

The interview started. Bill gave his full name, date and place of birth, schools attended, qualifications, and experience. Dadgar's face was blank as he asked the questions and wrote down the answers: he was like a machine.

Bill began to see why the interview with Paul had taken so long. Each question had to be translated from Farsi into English and each answer from English into Farsi. Mrs Nourbash did the translation, Abolhasan interrupting with clarifications and corrections.

Dadgar questioned him about EDS's performance of the Ministry contract. Bill answered at length and in detail, although the subject was both complicated and highly technical, and he was pretty sure that Mrs Nourbash could not really understand what he was saying. Anyway, no one could hope to grasp the complexities of the entire project by asking a handful of general questions. What kind of foolishness was this, he wondered? Why did Dadgar want to sit all day in a freezing cold room and ask stupid questions? It was some kind of Persian ritual, Bill decided. Dadgar needed to pad out his records, show that he had explored every avenue and protect himself in advance against possible criticism for letting them go. At the absolute worst, he might detain them

43

in Iran a while longer. Either way, it was just a matter of time.

Both Dadgar and Mrs Nourbash seemed hostile. The interview became more like a courtroom cross-examination. Dadgar said that EDS's progress reports to the Ministry had been false, and EDS had used them to make the Ministry pay for work that had not been done. Bill pointed out that Ministry officials, who were in a position to know, had never suggested that the reports were inaccurate. If EDS had fallen down on the job, where were the complaints? Dadgar could examine the Ministry's files.

Dadgar asked about Dr Towliati, and when Bill explained Towliati's role, Mrs Nourbash – speaking before Dadgar had given her anything to translate – replied that Bill's explanation was untrue.

There were several miscellaneous questions, including a completely mystifying one: did EDS have any Greek employees? Bill said they did not, wondering what that had to do with anything. Dadgar seemed impatient. Perhaps he had hoped that Bill's answers would contradict Paul's; and now, disappointed, he was just going through the motions. His questioning became perfunctory and hurried; he did not follow up Bill's answers with further questions or requests for clarifications; and he wound up the interview after an hour.

Mrs Nourbash said: 'You will now please sign your names against each of the questions and answers in Mr Dadgar's notebook.'

'But they're in Farsi – we can't read a word of it!' Bill protested. It's a trick, he thought; we'll be signing a confession to murder or espionage or some other crime Dadgar has invented.

Abolhasan said: 'I will look over his notes and check them.'

Paul and Bill waited while Abolhasan read through the notebook. It seemed a very cursory check. He put the book down on the desk.

'I advise you to sign.'

44

Bill was sure he should not – but he had no choice. If he wanted to go home, he had to sign.

He looked at Paul. Paul shrugged. 'I guess we'd better do it.'

They went through the notebook in turn, writing their names beside the incomprehensible squiggles of Farsi.

When they finished, the atmosphere in the room was tense. Now, Bill thought, he has to tell us we can go home.

Dadgar shuffled his papers into a neat stack while he talked to Abolhasan in Farsi for several minutes. Then he left the room. Abolhasan turned to Paul and Bill, his face grave.

'You are being arrested,' he said.

Bill's heart sank. No plane, no Washington, no Emily, no New Year's Eve party . . .

'Bail has been set at ninety million tomans, sixty for Paul and thirty for Bill.'

'Jesus!' Paul said. 'Ninety million tomans is . . .'

Abolhasan worked it out on a scrap of paper. 'A little under thirteen million dollars.'

'You're kidding!' Bill said. 'Thirteen *million*? A murderer's bail is twenty *thousand*.'

Abolhasan said: 'He asks whether you are ready to post the bail.'

Paul laughed. 'Tell him I'm a little short now, I'm going to have to go to the bank.'

Abolhasan said nothing.

'He can't be serious,' Paul said.

'He's serious,' said Abolhasan.

Suddenly Bill was mad as hell – mad at Dadgar, mad at Lou Goelz, mad at the whole damn world. It had been a sucker trap and they had fallen right into it. Why, they had walked in here of their own free will, to keep an appointment made by the US Embassy. They had done nothing wrong and nobody had a shred of evidence against them – yet they were going to jail, and worse, an Iranian jail!

Abolhasan said: 'You are allowed one phone call each.'

Just like the cop shows on TV – one phone call then into the slammer.

45

Paul picked up the phone and dialled. 'Lloyd Briggs, please. This is Paul Chiapparone . . . Lloyd? I can't make dinner tonight. I'm going to jail.'

Bill thought: Paul doesn't really believe it yet.

Paul listened for a moment, then said: 'How about calling Gayden, for a start?' Bill Gayden, whose name was so similar to Bill Gaylord's, was president of EDS World and Paul's immediate boss. As soon as this news reaches Dallas, Bill thought, these Iranian jokers will see what happens when EDS really gets into gear.

Paul hung up and Bill took his turn on the phone. He dialled the US Embassy and asked for the Consul General.

'Goelz? This is Bill Gaylord. We've just been arrested, and bail has been set at thirteen million dollars.'

'How did that happen?'

Bill was infuriated by Goelz's calm measured voice. 'You arranged this meeting and you told us we could leave afterwards!'

'I'm sure, if you've done nothing wrong—'

'What do you mean *if*?' Bill shouted.

'I'll have someone down at the jail as soon as possible,' Goelz said.

Bill hung up.

The two Iranians who had been hanging about in the corridor all day came in. Bill noticed they were big and burly, and realized they must be plain-clothes policemen.

Abolhasan said: 'Dadgar said it would not be necessary to handcuff you.'

Paul said, 'Gee, thanks.'

Bill suddenly recalled the stories he had heard about the torturing of prisoners in the Shah's jails. He tried not to think about it.

Abolhasan said: 'Do you want to give me your briefcases and wallets?'

They handed them over. Paul kept back a hundred dollars.

'Do you know where the jail is?' Paul asked Abolhasan.

'You're going to a Temporary Detention Facility at the Ministry of Justice on Khayyam Street.'

'Get back to Bucharest fast and give Lloyd Briggs all the details.'

'Sure.'

One of the plain-clothes policemen held the door open. Bill looked at Paul. Paul shrugged.

They went out.

The policemen escorted them downstairs and into a little car. 'I guess we'll have to stay in jail for a couple of hours,' Paul said. 'It'll take that long for the Embassy and EDS to get people down there to bail us out.'

'They might be there already,' Bill said optimistically.

The bigger of the two policemen got behind the wheel. His colleague sat beside him in the front. They pulled out of the courtyard and into Eisenhower Avenue, driving fast. Suddenly they turned into a narrow one-way street, heading the wrong way at top speed. Bill clutched the seat in front of him. They swerved in and out, dodging the cars and buses coming the other way, other drivers honking and shaking their fists.

They headed south and slightly east. Bill thought ahead to their arrival at the jail. Would people from EDS or the Embassy be there to negotiate a reduction in the bail so that they could go home instead of to a cell? Surely the Embassy staff would be outraged at what Dadgar had done. Ambassador Sullivan would intervene to get them released at once. After all, it was iniquitous to put two Americans in an Iranian jail when no crime had been committed and then set bail at thirteen million dollars. The whole situation was ridiculous.

Except that here he was, sitting in the back of this car, silently looking out of the windows and wondering what would happen next.

As they went farther south, what he saw through the window frightened him even more.

In the north of the city, where the Americans lived and worked, riots and fighting were still an occasional phenomenon, but here – Bill now realized – they must be continuous. The black hulks of burned buses smouldered in

47

the streets. Hundreds of demonstrators were running riot, yelling and chanting, setting fires and building barricades. Young teenagers threw Molotov cocktails – bottles of gasoline with blazing rag fuses – at cars. Their targets seemed random. We might be next, Bill thought. He heard shooting, but it was dark and he could not see who was firing at whom. The driver never went at less than top speed. Every other street was blocked by a mob, a barricade or a blazing car: the driver turned around, blind to all traffic signals, and raced through side streets and back alleys at breakneck speed to circumvent the obstacles. We're not going to get there alive, Bill thought. He touched the rosary in his pocket.

It seemed to go on forever – then, suddenly, the little car swung into a circular courtyard and pulled up. Without speaking, the burly driver got out of the car and went into the building.

The Ministry of Justice was a big place, occupying a whole city block. In darkness – the street lights were all off – Bill could make out what seemed to be a five-storey building. The driver was inside for ten or fifteen minutes. When he came out he climbed behind the wheel and drove around the block. Bill assumed he had registered his prisoners at the front desk.

At the rear of the building the car mounted the kerb and stopped on the sidewalk by a pair of steel gates set into a long, high brick wall. Somewhere over to the right, where the wall ended, there was a vague outline of a small park or garden. The driver got out. A peephole opened in one of the steel doors, and there was a short conversation in Farsi. Then the doors opened. The driver motioned Paul and Bill to get out of the car.

They walked through the doors.

Bill looked around. They were in a small courtyard. He saw ten or fifteen guards armed with automatic weapons scattered about. In front of him was a circular driveway with parked cars and trucks. To his left, up against the brick wall was a single-storey building. On his right was another steel door.

The driver went up to the second steel door and knocked. There was another exchange in Farsi through another peephole. Then the door was opened, and Paul and Bill were ushered inside.

They were in a small reception area with a desk and a few chairs. Bill looked around. There were no lawyers, no Embassy staff, no EDS executives here to spring him from jail. We're on our own, he thought, and this is going to be dangerous.

A guard stood behind the desk with a ballpoint pen and a pile of forms. He asked a question in Farsi. Guessing, Paul said: 'Paul Chiapparone', and spelled it.

Filling out the forms took close to an hour. An English-speaking prisoner was brought from the jail to help translate. Paul and Bill gave their Tehran addresses, phone numbers, and dates of birth, and listed their possessions. Their money was taken away and they were each given two thousand rials, about thirty dollars.

They were taken into an adjoining room and told to remove their clothes. They both stripped to their undershorts. Their clothing and their bodies were searched. Paul was told to get dressed again, but Bill was not. It was very cold: the heat was off here, too. Naked and shivering, Bill wondered what would happen now. Obviously they were the only Americans in the jail. Everything he had ever read or heard about being in prison was awful. What would the guards do to him and Paul? What would the other prisoners do? Surely, any minute now someone would come to get him released.

'Can I put on my coat?' he asked the guard.

The guard did not understand.

'Coat,' Bill said, and mimed putting on a coat.

The guard handed him his coat.

A little later another guard came in and told him to get dressed.

They were led back into the reception area. Once again Bill looked around expectantly for lawyers or friends; once again he was disappointed.

They were taken through the reception area. Another

49

door was opened. They went down a flight of stairs into the basement.

It was cold, dim and dirty. There were several cells, all crammed with prisoners, all of them Iranian. The stink of urine made Bill close his mouth and breathe shallowly through his nose. The guard opened the door to cell number nine. They walked in.

Sixteen unshaven faces stared at them, alive with curiosity. Paul and Bill stared back, horrified.

The cell door clanged shut behind them.

Two

1

Until this moment, life had been extremely good to Ross Perot.

On the morning of 28 December 1978 he sat at the breakfast table in his mountain cabin at Vail, Colorado, and was served breakfast by Holly, the cook.

Perched on the mountainside and half-hidden in the aspen forest, the 'log cabin' had six bedrooms, five bathrooms, a thirty-foot living room, and an après-ski recuperation room with a Jacuzzi pool in front of the fireplace. It was just a holiday home.

Ross Perot was rich.

He had started EDS with a thousand dollars, and now the shares in the company, more than half of which he still owned personally, were worth several hundred million dollars. He was the sole owner of the Petrus Oil and Gas Company which had reserves worth hundreds of millions. He also had an awful lot of Dallas real estate. It was difficult to figure out exactly how much money he had – a lot depended on just how you counted it – but it was certainly more than five hundred million dollars and probably less than a billion.

In novels, fantastically rich people were portrayed as greedy, power-mad, neurotic, hated and unhappy – always unhappy. Perot did not read many novels. He was happy.

He did not think it was the money that made him happy. He believed in money-making, in business and profits, because that was what made America tick; and he enjoyed a few of the toys money could buy – the cabin cruiser, the speedboats, the helicopter, but rolling around in hundred-dollar bills had never been one of his daydreams. He *had* dreamed of building a successful business that would employ thousands of people; but his greatest dream-come-true was right here in front of his eyes. Running around in thermal underwear, getting ready to go skiing, was his family. Here was Ross Junior, twenty years old, and if there was a finer young man in the state of Texas, Perot had yet to meet him. Here were four – count 'em, four – daughters: Nancy, Suzanne, Carolyn and Catherine. They were all healthy, smart and lovable. Perot had sometimes told interviewers that he would measure his success in life by how his children turned out. If they grew into good citizens with a deep concern for other people, he would consider his life worthwhile. (The interviewer would say: 'Hell, I believe you, but if I put stuff like that in the article the readers will think I've been bought off!' And Perot would just say: 'I don't care. I'll tell you the truth: you write whatever you like.') And the children had turned out just exactly how he had wished, so far. Being brought up in circumstances of great wealth and privilege had not spoiled them at all. It was almost miraculous.

Running around after the children with ski-lift tickets, wool socks and sunscreen lotion was the person responsible for this miracle, Margot Perot. She was beautiful, loving, intelligent, classy and a perfect mother. She could, if she had wanted to, have married a John Kennedy, a Paul Newman, a Prince Rainier, or a Rockefeller. Instead she had fallen in love with Ross Perot from Texarkana, Texas; five feet seven with a broken nose and nothing in his pocket but hopes. All his life Perot had believed he was lucky. Now, at the age of forty-eight, he could look back and see that the luckiest thing that ever happened to him was Margot.

He was a happy man with a happy family, but a shadow had fallen over them this Christmas. Perot's mother was dying. She had bone cancer. On Christmas Eve she had fallen at home. It was not a heavy fall, but because the cancer had weakened her bones, she had broken her hip and had to be rushed to Baylor Hospital in downtown Dallas.

Perot's sister, Bett, spent that night with their mother, then, on Christmas Day, Perot and Margot and the five children loaded the presents into the station wagon and drove to the hospital. Grandmother was in such good spirits that they all thoroughly enjoyed their day. However, she did not want to see them the following day: she knew they had planned to go skiing, and she insisted they go, despite her illness. Margot and the children left for Vail on 26 December, but Perot stayed behind.

There followed a battle of wills such as Perot had fought with his mother in childhood. Lulu May Perot was only an inch or two over five feet, and slight, but she was no more frail than a sergeant in the Marines. She told him he worked hard and he needed the holiday. He replied that he did not want to leave her. Eventually the doctors intervened, and told him he was doing her no good by staying against her will. The next day he joined his family in Vail. She had won, as she always did when he was a boy.

One of their battles had been fought over a Boy Scout trip. There had been flooding in Texarkana, and the Scouts were planning to camp near the disaster area for three days and help with relief work. Young Perot was determined to go, but his mother knew that he was too young – he would only be a burden to the scoutmaster. He kept on and on at her, and she just smiled sweetly and said no.

That time he won a concession from her: he was allowed to go and help pitch tents the first day, but he had to come home in the evening. It wasn't much of a compromise. But he was quite incapable of defying her. He just had to imagine the scene when he would come home, and think of the words he would use to tell her that he had disobeyed her – and he knew he could not do it.

He was never spanked. He could not remember even being yelled at. She did not rule him by fear. With her fair hair, blue eyes, and sweet nature, she bound him – and his sister Bette – in chains of love. She would just look you in the eye and tell you what to do, and you simply could not bring yourself to make her unhappy.

Even at the age of twenty-three, when he had been around the world and come home again, she would say: 'Who have you got a date with tonight? Where are you going? What time will you be back?' And when he came home he would always have to kiss her goodnight. But by this time their battles were few and far between, for her principles were so deeply embedded in him that they had become his own. She now ruled the family like a constitutional monarch, wearing the trappings of power and legitimizing the decision-makers.

He had inherited more than her principles. He also had her iron will. He, too, had a way of looking people in the eye. He had married a woman who resembled his mother. Blonde and blue-eyed, Margot also had the kind of sweet nature that Lulu May had. But Margot did not dominate Perot.

Everybody's mother has to die, and Lulu May was now eighty-two, but Perot could not be stoical about it. She was still a big part of his life. She no longer gave him orders, but she did give him encouragement. She had encouraged him to start EDS, and she had been the company's book-keeper during the early years as well as a founding director. He could talk over problems with her. He had consulted her in December 1969, at the height of his campaign to publicize the plight of American prisoners-of-war in North Vietnam. He had been planning to fly to Hanoi, and his colleagues at EDS had pointed out that if he put his life in danger the price of EDS stock might fall. He was faced with a moral dilemma: did he have the right to make shareholders suffer, even for the best of causes? He had put the question to his mother. Her answer had been unhesitating. 'Let them sell their shares.' The prisoners were dying, and that was far more important than the price of EDS stock.

It was the conclusion Perot would have come to on his own. He did not really need her to tell him what to do. Without her, he would be the same man and do the same things. He was going to miss her, that was all. He was going to miss her very badly indeed.

But he was not a man to brood. He could do nothing for

her today. Two years ago, when she had a stroke, he had turned Dallas upside down on a Sunday afternoon to find the best neurosurgeon in town and bring him to the hospital. He responded to a crisis with action. But if there was nothing to be done, he was able to shut the problem out of his mind, forgetting the bad news and going on with the next task. He would not now spoil his family's holiday by walking around with a mournful face. He would enter into the fun and games, and enjoy the company of his wife and children.

The phone rang, interrupting his thoughts, and he stepped into the kitchen to pick it up.

'Ross Perot,' he said.

'Ross, this is Bill Gayden.'

'Hi, Bill.' Gayden was an EDS old-timer, having joined the company in 1967. In some ways he was the typical salesman. He was a jovial man, everybody's buddy. He liked a joke, a drink, a smoke and a hand of poker. He was also a wizard financier, very good around acquisitions, mergers and deals, which was why Perot had made him president of EDS World. Gayden's sense of humour was irrepressible – he would find something funny to say in the most serious situations – but now he sounded sombre.

'Ross, we got a problem.'

It was an EDS catch-phrase: *We got a problem*. It meant bad news.

Gayden went on: 'It's Paul and Bill.'

Perot knew instantly what he was talking about. The way in which his two senior men in Iran had been prevented from leaving the country was highly sinister, and it had never been far from his mind, even while his mother lay dying. 'But they're supposed to be allowed out today.'

'They've been arrested.'

The anger began as a small, hard knot in the pit of Perot's stomach. 'Now, Bill, I was assured that they would be allowed to leave Iran as soon as this interview was over. Now I want to know how this has happened.'

'They just slung them in jail.'

'On what charges?'

55

'They didn't specify charges.'

'Under what law did they jail them?'

'They didn't say.'

'What are we doing to get them out?'

'Ross, they set bail at ninety million tomans. That's twelve million, seven hundred and fifty thousand dollars.'

'Twelve *million*?'

'That's right.'

'Now how the devil has this happened?'

'Ross, I've been on the phone with Lloyd Briggs for half an hour, trying to understand it, and the fact is that Lloyd doesn't understand it either.'

Perot paused. EDS executives were supposed to give him answers, not questions. Gayden knew better than to call without briefing himself as thoroughly as possible. Perot was not going to get any more out of him right now; Gayden just didn't have the information.

'Get Tom Luce into the office,' Perot said. 'Call the State Department in Washington. This takes priority over everything else. I don't want them to stay in that jail another damn minute!'

Margot pricked up her ears when she heard him say *damn*: it was most unusual for him to curse, especially in front of the children. He came in from the kitchen with his face set. His eyes were as blue as the Arctic Ocean, and as cold. She knew that look. It was not just anger: he was not the kind of man to dissipate his energy in a display of bad temper. It was a look of inflexible determination. It meant he had decided to do something and he would move heaven and earth to get it done. She had seen that determination, that strength in him when she had first met him, at the Naval Academy in Annapolis . . . could it really be twenty-five years ago? It was the quality that cut him out from the herd, made him different from the mass of men. Oh, he had other qualities – he was smart, he was funny, he could charm the birds out of the trees – but what made him *exceptional* was his strength of will. When he got that look in his eyes you could no more

56

stop him than you could stop a railway train on a downhill gradient.

'The Iranians put Paul and Bill in jail,' he said.

Margot's thoughts flew at once to their wives. She had known them both for years. Ruthie Chiapparone was a small, placid, smiling girl with a shock of fair hair. She had a vulnerable look: men wanted to protect her. She would take it hard. Emily Gaylord was tougher, at least on the surface. A thin blonde woman, Emily was vivacious and spirited: she would want to get on a plane and go spring Bill from jail herself. The difference in the two women showed in their clothes: Ruthie chose soft fabrics and gentle outlines; Emily went in for smart tailoring and bright colours. Emily would suffer on the inside.

'I'm going back to Dallas,' Ross said.

'There's a blizzard out there,' said Margot, looking out at the snowflakes swirling down the mountainside. She knew she was wasting her breath: snow and ice would not stop him now. She thought ahead: Ross would not be able to sit behind a desk in Dallas for very long while two of his men were in an Iranian jail. He's not going to Dallas, she thought; he's going to Iran.

'I'll take the four-wheel drive,' he said. 'I can catch a plane in Denver.'

Margot suppressed her fears and smiled brightly. 'Drive carefully, won't you,' she said.

Perot sat hunched over the wheel of the GM Suburban, driving carefully. The road was icy. Snow built up along the bottom edge of the windscreen, shortening the travel of the wipers. He peered at the road ahead. Denver was 106 miles from Vail. It gave him time to think.

He was still furious.

It was not just that Paul and Bill were in jail. They were in jail because they had gone to Iran, and they had gone to Iran because Perot had sent them there.

He had been worried about Iran for months. One day, after lying awake at night thinking about it, he had gone in to the office and said: 'Let's evacuate. If we're wrong, all we've lost is the price of three or four hundred plane tickets. Do it today.'

It had been one of the rare occasions on which his orders were not carried out. Everyone had dragged their feet, in Dallas and in Tehran. Not that he could blame them. He had lacked determination. If he had been firm they would have evacuated that day; but he had not, and the following day the passports had been called for.

He owed Paul and Bill a lot anyway. He felt a special debt of loyalty to the men who had gambled their careers by joining EDS when it was a struggling young company. Many times he had found the right man, interviewed him, got him interested, and offered him the job, only to find that, on talking it over with his family, the man had decided that EDS was just too small, too new, too risky.

Paul and Bill had not only taken the chance – they had worked their butts off to make sure their gamble paid. Bill had designed the basic computer system for the administration of Medicare and Medicaid programmes which, used now in many American States, formed the foundation of EDS's business. He had worked long hours, spent weeks away from home, and moved his family all over the country in those days. Paul had been no less dedicated: when the company had too few men and very little cash, Paul had done the work of three systems engineers. Perot could remember the company's first contract in New York, with Pepsico; and Paul walking from Manhattan across the Brooklyn Bridge in the snow, to sneak past a picket line – the plant was on strike – and go to work.

Perot owed it Paul and Bill to get them *out*.

He owed it to them to get the Government of the United States to bring the whole weight of its influence to bear on the Iranians.

America had asked for Perot's help, once; and he had given three years of his life – and a *bunch* of money – to the prisoners-of-war campaign. Now he was going to ask for America's help.

His mind went back to 1969, when the Vietnam war was at its height. Some of his friends from the Naval Academy had been killed or captured: Bill Leftwich, a wonderfully warm, strong, kind man, had been killed in battle at the age of thirty-nine; Bill Lawrence was a prisoner of the North Vietnamese. Perot found it hard to watch his country, the greatest country in the world, losing a war because of lack of will; and even harder to see millions of Americans protesting, not without justification, that the war was wrong and *should* not be won. Then, one day in 1969, he had met little Billy Singleton, a boy who did not know whether he had a father or not. Billy's father had gone missing in Vietnam before ever seeing his son: there was no way of knowing whether he was a prisoner, or dead. It was heartbreaking.

For Perot, sentiment was not a mournful emotion but a clarion call to action.

He learned that Billy's father was not unique. There were many, perhaps hundreds, of wives and children who did not know whether their husbands and fathers had been killed or just captured. The Vietnamese, arguing that they were not bound by the rules of the Geneva Convention because the United States had never declared war, refused to release the names of their prisoners.

Worse still, many of the prisoners were dying of brutality and neglect. President Nixon was planning to 'Vietnamize' the war and disengage in three years' time, but by then, according to CIA reports, half the prisoners would have died. Even if Billy Singleton's father were alive, he might not survive to come home.

Perot wanted to do something.

EDS had good connections with the Nixon White House. Perot went to Washington and talked to Chief Foreign Policy Advisor Henry Kissinger. And Kissinger had a plan.

The Vietnamese were maintaining, at least for the purposes of propaganda, that they had no quarrel with the American people – only with the US Government. Furthermore, they were presenting themselves to the world as the little guy in a David-and-Goliath conflict. It seemed that they valued their public image. It might be possible, Kissinger thought, to embarrass them into improving their treatment of prisoners, and releasing their names, by an international campaign to publicize the sufferings of the prisoners and their families.

The campaign must be privately financed, and must *seem* to be quite unconnected with the Government, even though in reality it would be closely monitored by a team of White House and State Department people.

Perot accepted the challenge. (Perot could resist anything but a challenge. His eleventh-grade teacher, one Mrs Duck, had realized this. 'It's a shame,' Mrs Duck had said, 'that you're not as smart as your friends.' Young Perot insisted he *was* as smart as his friends. 'Well, why do they make better grades than you?' It was just that they were interested in school and he was not, said Perot. 'Anybody can stand there and tell me that they *could* do something,' said Mrs Duck. 'But let's look at the record: your friends can do it and you can't.' Perot was cut to the quick. He told her that he would make straight As for the next six weeks. He made straight As, not just for six weeks, but for the rest of his high school career. The perceptive Mrs Duck had discovered the only way to manipulate Perot: challenge him.)

Accepting Kissinger's challenge, Perot went to J. Walter Thompson, the largest advertising agency in the world, and told them what he wanted to do. They offered to come up with a plan of campaign within thirty to sixty days and show some results in a year. Perot turned them down: he wanted to start today and see results tomorrow. He went back to Dallas and put together a small team of EDS executives who began calling newspaper executives and placing simple, unsophisticated advertisements which they wrote themselves.

And the mail came in truckloads.

For Americans who were pro-war, the treatment of the prisoners showed that the Vietnamese really were the bad guys; and for those who were anti-war the plight of the prisoners was one more reason for getting out of Vietnam. Only the most hard-line protesters resented the campaign. In 1970 the FBI told Perot that the Viet Cong had instructed the Black Panthers to murder him. (At the crazy end of the sixties this had not sounded particularly bizarre.) Perot hired body-guards. Sure enough, a few weeks later a squad of men climbed the fence around Perot's seventeen-acre Dallas property. They were chased off by savage dogs. Perot's family, including his indomitable mother, would not hear of him giving up the campaign for the sake of their safety.

His greatest publicity stunt took place in December 1969, when he chartered two planes and tried to fly into Hanoi with Christmas dinners for the prisoners-of-war. Of course, he was not allowed to land; but during a slow news period he created enormous international awareness of the problem. He spent two million dollars, but he reckoned the publicity would have cost sixty million to buy. And a Gallup poll he commissioned afterwards showed that the feelings of Americans toward the North Vietnamese were overwhelmingly negative.

During 1970 Perot used less spectacular methods. Small communities all over the United States were encouraged to set up their own POW campaigns. They raised funds to send people to Paris to badger the North Vietnamese delegation there. They organized telethons, and built replicas of the cages in which some of the POWs lived. They sent so many protest letters to Hanoi that the North Vietnamese postal system collapsed under the strain. Perot stumped the country, giving speeches anywhere he was invited. He met with North Vietnamese diplomats in Laos, taking with him lists of their people held in the south, mail from them, and film of their living conditions. He also took a Gallup associate with him, and together they went over the results of the poll with the North Vietnamese.

Some or all of it worked. The treatment of American POWs improved, mail and parcels began to get through to them, and the North Vietnamese started to release names. Most importantly, the prisoners heard of the campaign – from newly captured American soldiers – and the news boosted their morale enormously.

Eight years later, driving to Denver in the snow, Perot recalled another consequence of the campaign, a consequence which had then seemed no more than mildly irritating, but could now be important and valuable. Publicity for the POWs had meant, inevitably, publicity for Ross Perot. He had become nationally known. He would be remembered in the corridors of power – and especially in the Pentagon. That Washington monitoring committee had included Admiral Tom Moorer, then Chairman of the Joint Chiefs of Staff; Alexander Haig, then assistant to Kissinger and now Commander in Chief of NATO forces; William Sullivan, then a Deputy Assistant Secretary of State and now US Ambassador to Iran; and Kissinger himself.

These people would help Perot get inside the Government, find out what was happening, and promote help fast. He would call Richard Helms, who had in the past been both head of the CIA and US Ambassador to Tehran. He would call Kermit Roosevelt, son of Teddy, who had been involved in the CIA coup which put the Shah back on the throne in 1953 . . .

But what if none of this works? he thought.

It was his habit to think more than one step ahead.

What if the Carter administration could not or would not help?

Then, he thought, I'm going to break them out of jail.

How would we go about something like that? We've never done anything like it. Where would we start? Who could help us?

He thought of EDS executives Merv Stauffer and T. J. Marquez, and his secretary Sally Walther, who had been key organizers of the POW campaign: making complex arrangements half across the world by phone was meat and drink to them, but . . . a prison break? And who would staff the mission? Since 1968 EDS's recruiters had given priority to Vietnam veterans – a policy begun for patriotic reasons and continued when Perot found that the vets often made first-class businessmen – but the men who had once been lean, fit, highly-trained soldiers were now overweight, out-of-

62

condition computer executives, more comfortable with a telephone than with a rifle. And who would plan and lead the raid?

Finding the best man for the job was Perot's speciality. Although he was one of the most successful self-made men in the history of American capitalism, he was not the world's greatest computer expert, nor the world's greatest salesman, nor even the world's greatest business administrator. He did just one thing superbly well: pick the right man, give him the resources, motivate him, then leave him alone to do the job.

Now, as he approached Denver, he asked himself: who is the world's greatest rescuer?

Then he thought of Bull Simons.

A legend in the US Army, Colonel Arthur D. 'Bull' Simons had hit the headlines in November 1970 when he and a team of commandos raided the Son Tay prison camp, twenty-three miles outside Hanoi, in an attempt to rescue American prisoners of war. The raid had been a brave and well-organized operation, but the intelligence on which all the planning was based had been faulty: the prisoners had been moved, and were no longer at Son Tay. The raid was widely regarded as a fiasco which in Perot's opinion was grossly unfair. He had been invited to meet the Son Tay Raiders, to boost their morale by telling them that here was at least one American citizen who was grateful for their bravery. He had spent a day at Fort Bragg in North Carolina – and he had met Colonel Simons.

Peering through his windscreen, Perot could picture Simons against the cloud of falling snowflakes: a big man, just under six feet tall, with the shoulders of an ox. His white hair was cropped in a military crewcut, but his bushy eyebrows were still black. Either side of his big nose, two deep lines ran down to the corners of his mouth, giving him a permanently aggressive expression. He had a big head, big ears, a strong jaw, and the most powerful hands Perot had ever seen. The man looked as if he had been carved from a single block of granite.

After spending a day with him, Perot thought: in a world

of counterfeits, he is the genuine article.

That day and in years to come Perot learned a lot about Simons. What impressed him most was the attitude of Simons's men towards their leader. He reminded Perot of Vince Lombardi, the legendary coach of the Green Bay Packers: he inspired in his men emotions ranging from fear through respect and admiration to love. He was an imposing figure and an aggressive commander – he cursed a lot, and would tell a soldier: 'Do what I say or I'll cut your bloody head off!' – but that by itself could not account for his hold on the hearts of sceptical, battle-hardened commandos. Beneath the tough exterior there was a tough interior.

Those who had served under him liked nothing better than to sit around telling Simons stories. Although he had a bull-like physique, his nickname came not from that but, according to legend, from a game played by Rangers called The Bull Pen. A pit would be dug, six feet deep, and one man would get into it. The object of the game was to find out how many men it took to throw the first man out of the pit. Simons thought the game was foolish, but was once needled into playing it. It took fifteen men to get him out, and several of them spent the night in hospital with broken fingers and noses and severe bite wounds. After that he was called 'Bull'.

Perot learned later that almost everything in this story was exaggerated. Simons played the game more than once; it generally took four men to get him out; no one ever had any broken bones. Simons was simply the kind of man about whom legends are told. He earned the loyalty of his men not by displays of bravado but by his skill as a military commander. He was a meticulous, endlessly patient planner; he was cautious (one of his catch-phrases was: 'That's a risk we don't have to take') and he took a pride in bringing all his men back from a mission alive.

In the Vietnam war Simons had run Operation White Star. He went to Laos with 107 men and organized twelve battalions of Mao tribesmen to fight the Vietnamese. One of the battalions defected to the other side, taking as prisoners some of Simons's Green Berets. Simons took a helicopter and landed inside the stockade where the defecting battalion was. On seeing Simons, the Laotian colonel stepped forward, stood at attention, and saluted. Simons told him to produce the prisoners immediately, or he would call an airstrike and destroy the entire battalion. The colonel produced the prisoners. Simons took them away, then called the airstrike anyway. Simons had come back from Laos three years later with all his 107 men. Perot had never checked out this legend – he liked it the way it was.

The second time Perot met Simons was after the war. Perot virtually took over a hotel in San Francisco and threw a weekend party for the returning prisoners-of-war to meet the Son Tay Raiders. It cost Perot a quarter of a million dollars, but it was a hell of a party. Nancy Reagan, Clint Eastwood and John Wayne came. Perot would never forget the meeting between John Wayne and Bull Simons. Wayne shook Simons's hand with tears in his eyes and said: 'You *are* the man I play in the movies.'

Before the tickertape parade, Perot asked Simons to talk to his Raiders and warn them against reacting to demonstrators. 'San Francisco has had more than its share of anti-war demonstrations,' Perot said. 'You didn't pick your Raiders for their charm. If one of them gets irritated he might just snap some poor devil's neck and regret it later.'

Simons looked at Perot. It was Perot's first experience of The Simons Look. It made you feel as if you were the biggest fool in history. It made you wish you had not spoken. It made you wish the ground would swallow you up.

'I've already talked to them,' Simons said. 'There won't be a problem.'

That weekend and later, Perot got to know Simons better, and saw other sides of his personality. Simons could be very charming, when he chose to be. He enchanted Perot's wife Margot, and the children thought he was wonderful. With his men he spoke soldiers' language, using a great deal of profanity, but he was surprisingly articulate when talking at a banquet or press conference. His college major had been journalism. Some of his tastes were simple – he read

Westerns by the boxful, and enjoyed what his sons called 'supermarket music' – but he also read a lot of non-fiction, and had a lively curiosity about all sorts of things. He could talk about antiques or history as easily as battles and weaponry.

Perot and Simons, two wilful, dominating personalties, got along by giving one another plenty of room. They did not become close friends. Perot never called Simons by his first name, Art (although Margot did). Like most people, Perot never knew what Simons was thinking unless Simons chose to tell him. Perot recalled their first meeting in Fort Bragg. Before getting up to make his speech, Perot had asked Simons's wife Lucille: 'What is Colonel Simons really like?' She had replied: 'Oh, he's just a great big teddy bear.' Perot repeated this in his speech. The Son Tay Raiders fell apart. Simons never cracked a smile.

Perot did not know whether this impenetrable man would care to rescue two EDS executives from a Persian jail. Was Simons grateful for the San Francisco party? Perhaps. After that party, Perot had financed Simons on a trip to Laos to search for MIAs – American soldiers Missing In Action – who had not come back with the prisoners-of-war. On his return from Laos, Simons had remarked to a group of EDS executives: 'Perot is a hard man to say no to.'

As he pulled into Denver airport, Perot wondered whether, six years later, Simons would still find him a hard man to say no to.

But that contingency was a long way down the line. Perot was going to try everything else first.

He went into the terminal, bought a seat on the next flight to Dallas, and found a phone. He called EDS and spoke to T. J. Marquez, one of his most senior executives, who was known as T.J. rather than Tom because there were so many Toms around EDS. 'I want you to go find my passport, and get me a visa for Iran.'

T.J. said: 'Ross, I think that's the world's worst idea.'

T.J. would argue until nightfall if you let him. 'I'm not going to debate with you,' Perot said curtly. 'I talked Paul and Bill into going over there, and I'm going to get them out.'

He hung up the phone and headed for the departure gate. All in all, it had been a rotten Christmas.

T.J. was a little wounded. An old friend of Perot's as well as a vice-president of EDS, he was not used to being talked to like the office boy. This was a persistent failing of Perot's: when he was in high gear, he trod on people's toes and never knew he had hurt them. He was a remarkable man, but he was not a saint.

2

Ruthie Chiapparone also had a rotten Christmas.

She was staying at her parents' home, an eighty-five-year-old two-storey house on the southwest side of Chicago. In the rush of the evacuation from Iran she had left behind most of the Christmas presents she had bought for her daughters Karen, eleven, and Ann Marie, five; but soon after arriving in Chicago she had gone shopping with her brother Bill and bought some more. Her family did their best to make Christmas Day happy. Her sister and three brothers visited, and there were lots more toys for Karen and Anne Marie; but everyone asked about Paul.

Ruthie needed Paul. A soft, dependent woman, five years younger than her husband – she was thirty-four – she loved him partly because she could lean on his broad shoulders and feel safe. She had always been looked after. As a child, even when her mother was out at work – supplementing the wages of Ruthie's father, a truck driver – Ruthie had two older brothers and an older sister to take care of her.

When she first met Paul he had ignored her.

She was secretary to a Colonel; Paul was working on data processing for the Army in the same building. Ruthie used to go down to the cafeteria to get coffee for the Colonel, some of her friends knew some of the young officers, she sat down to talk with a group of them, and Paul was there and he ignored her. So she ignored him for a while, then all of a sudden he asked her for a date. They dated for a year and a half and then got married.

Ruthie had not wanted to go to Iran. Unlike most of the EDS wives, who had found the prospect of moving to a new country exciting, Ruthie had been highly anxious. She had never been outside the United States – Hawaii was the farthest she had ever travelled – and the Middle East seemed a weird and frightening place. Paul took her to Iran for a week in June of 1977, hoping she would like it, but she was not reassured. Finally she agreed to go, but only because the job was so important to him.

However, she ended up liking it. The Iranians were nice to her, the American community there was close-knit and sociable, and Ruthie's serene nature enabled her to deal calmly with the daily frustrations of living in a primitive country, like the lack of supermarkets and the difficulty of getting a washing machine repaired in less than about six weeks.

Leaving had been strange. The airport had been crammed, just an unbelievable number of people in there. She had recognized many of the Americans, but most of the people were fleeing Iranians. She had thought: 'I don't want to leave like this – why are you pushing us out? What are you doing?' She had travelled with Bill Gaylord's wife Emily. They went via Copenhagen, where they spent a freezing cold night in a hotel where the windows would not close: the children had to sleep in their clothes. When she got back to the States, Ross Perot had called her and talked about the passport problem, but Ruthie had not really understood what was happening.

During that depressing Christmas Day – so unnatural to have Christmas with the children and no Daddy – Paul had called from Tehran. 'I've got a present for you,' he had said.

'Your airline ticket?' she asked hopefully.

'No. I bought you a rug.'

'That's nice.'

He had spent the day with Pat and Mary Sculley, he told her. Someone else's wife had cooked his Christmas dinner, and he had watched someone else's children open their presents.

Two days later she heard that Paul and Bill had an appointment, the following day, to see the man who was making them stay in Iran. After the meeting they would be let go.

The meeting was today, 28 December. By midday Ruthie was wondering why nobody from Dallas had called her yet. Tehran was eight and a half hours ahead of Chicago; surely the meeting was over? By now Paul should be packing his suitcase to come home.

She called Dallas and spoke to Jim Nyfeler, an EDS man who had left Tehran last June. 'How did the meeting work out?' she asked him.

'It didn't go too well, Ruthie . . .'

'What do you mean, it didn't go too well?'

'They were arrested.'

'They were arrested? You're kidding!'

'Ruthie, Bill Gayden wants to talk to you.'

Ruthie held the line. Paul *arrested*? Why? For what? By whom?

Gayden, the president of EDS World and Paul's boss, came on the line. 'Hello, Ruthie.'

'Bill, what is all this?'

'We don't understand it,' Gayden said. 'The Embassy over there set up this meeting, and it was supposed to be routine, they weren't accused of any crime . . . Then, around six-thirty their time, Paul called Lloyd Briggs and told him they were going to jail.'

'Paul's in *jail*?'

'Ruthie, try not to worry too much. We got a bunch of lawyers working on it, we're getting the State Department on the case, and Ross is already on his way back from Colorado. We're sure we can straighten this out in a couple of days. It's just a matter of days, really.'

'All right,' said Ruthie. She was dazed. It didn't make

sense. How could her husband be in jail? She said goodbye to Gayden and hung up.

What was going on out there?

The last time Emily Gaylord had seen her husband Bill, she had thrown a plate at him.

Sitting in her sister Dorothy's home in Washington, talking to Dorothy and her husband Tim about how they might help to get Bill out of jail, she could not forget that flying plate.

It had happened in their house in Tehran. One evening in early December Bill came home and said that Emily and the children were to return to the States the very next day.

Bill and Emily had four children: Vickie, fifteen; Jackie, twelve; Jenny, nine; and Chris, six. Emily agreed that they should be sent back, but she wanted to stay. She might not be able to do anything to help Bill, but at least he would have someone to talk to.

It was out of the question, said Bill. She was leaving tomorrow. Ruthie Chiapparone would be on the same plane. All the other EDS wives and children would be evacuated a day or two later.

They argued. Emily got madder and madder until finally she could no longer express her frustration in words, so she picked up a plate and hurled it at him.

He would never forget it, she was sure: it was the only time in eighteen years of marriage that she had exploded like that. She was highly strung, spirited, excitable – but not violent. Mild, gentle Bill, it was the last thing he deserved . . .

When she first met him she was twelve, he was fourteen and she hated him. He was in love with her best friend Cookie, a strikingly attractive girl and all he ever talked about was who Cookie was dating and whether Cookie might like to go out and was Cookie allowed to do this or that . . . Emily's sisters and brother really liked Bill. She could not get away from him, for their families belonged to the same country club and her brother played golf with Bill. It was her brother who finally talked Bill into asking Emily for a date, long after he had forgotten Cookie; and, after years of mutual indifference, they fell madly in love.

By then Bill was in college, studying aeronautical engineering 240 miles away in Blacksburg, Virginia, and coming home for vacations and occasional weekends. They could not bear to be so far apart so, although Emily was only eighteen, they decided to get married.

It was a good match. They came from similar backgrounds, affluent Washington Catholic families, and Bill's personality – sensitive, calm, logical – complemented Emily's nervous vivacity. They went through a lot together over the next eighteen years. They lost a child with brain damage, and Emily had major surgery three times. Their troubles brought them closer together.

And here was a new crisis: Bill was in jail.

Emily had not yet told her mother. Mother's brother, Emily's Uncle Gus, had died that day, and Mother was already terribly upset. Emily could not talk to her about Bill yet. But she could talk to Dorothy and Tim.

Her brother-in-law Tim Reardon was a US Attorney in the Justice Department and had very good connections. Tim's father had been an administrative assistant to President John F. Kennedy, and Tim had worked for Ted Kennedy. Tim also knew personally the Speaker of the House of Representatives, Thomas P. 'Tip' O'Neill, and Maryland Senator Charles Mathias. He was familiar with the passport problem, for Emily had told him about it as soon as she got back to Washington from Tehran, and he had discussed it with Ross Perot.

'I could write a letter to President Carter, and ask Ted Kennedy to deliver it personally,' Tim was saying.

Emily nodded. It was hard for her to concentrate. She wondered what Bill was doing right now.

Paul and Bill stood just inside Cell No 9, cold, numb, and desperate to know what would happen next.

Paul felt very vulnerable: a white American in a business suit, unable to speak more than a few words of Farsi, faced

71

by a crowd of what looked like thugs and murderers. He suddenly remembered reading that men were frequently raped in jail, and he wondered grimly how he would cope with something like that.

Paul looked at Bill. His face was white with tension.

One of the inmates spoke to them in Farsi. Paul said: 'Does anyone here speak English?'

From another cell across the corridor a voice called: 'I speak English.'

There was a shouted conversation in rapid Farsi, then the interpreter called: 'What is your crime?'

'We haven't done anything,' Paul said.

'What are you accused of?'

'Nothing. We're just ordinary American businessmen with wives and children, and we don't know why we're in jail.'

This was translated. There was more rapid Farsi, then the interpreter said: 'The one who is talking to me, he is the boss of your cell, because he is there the longest.'

'We understand,' Paul said.

'He will tell you where to sleep.'

The tension eased as they talked. Paul took in his surroundings. The concrete walls were painted what might once have been orange but now just looked dirty. There was some kind of thin carpet or matting covering most of the concrete floor. Around the cell were six sets of bunks, stacked three high: the lowest bunk was no more than a thin mattress on the floor. The room was lit by a single dim bulb and ventilated by a grille in the wall which let in the bitterly cold night air. The cell was very crowded.

After a while a guard came down, opened the door of cell number nine, and motioned Paul and Bill to come out.

This is it, Paul thought; we'll be released now. Thank God I don't have to spend a night in that awful cell.

They followed the guard upstairs and into a little room. He pointed at their shoes.

They understood they were to take their shoes off.

The guard handed them each a pair of plastic slippers.

Paul realized with bitter disappointment that they were not about to be released; he *did* have to spend a night in the cell. He thought with anger of the Embassy staff: they had arranged the meeting with Dadgar, they had advised Paul against taking lawyers, they had said Dadgar was 'favourably disposed'. Ross Perot would say: 'Some people can't organize a two-car funeral.' That applied to the US Embassy. They were simply incompetent. Surely, Paul thought, after all the mistakes they have made, they ought to come here *tonight* and try to get us out?

They put on the plastic slippers and followed the guard back downstairs.

The other prisoners were getting ready for sleep, lying on the bunks and wrapping themselves in thin wool blankets. The cell boss, using sign language, showed Paul and Bill where to lie down. Bill was on the middle bunk of a stack, Paul below him with just a thin mattress between his body and the floor.

They lay down. The light stayed on, but it was so dim it hardly mattered. After a while Paul no longer noticed the smell, but he did not get used to the cold. With the concrete floor, the open vent, and no heating, it was almost like sleeping out of doors. What a terrible life criminals lead, Paul thought, having to endure conditions such as these; I'm glad I'm not a criminal. One night of this will be more than enough.

3

Ross Perot took a taxi from the Dallas/Fort Worth regional airport to EDS corporate headquarters at 7171 Forest Lane. At the EDS gate he rolled down the window to let the security guards see his face, then sat back again as the car wound along the quarter-mile driveway through the park. The site had once been a country club, and these grounds a golf course. EDS headquarters loomed ahead, a seven-storey office building, and next to it a tornado-proof blockhouse containing the vast computers with their thousands of miles of magnetic tape.

Perot paid the driver, walked into the office building, and took the elevator to the fifth floor, where he went to Gayden's corner office.

Gayden was at his desk. Gayden always managed to look untidy, despite the EDS dress code. He had taken his jacket off. His tie was loosened, the collar of his button-down shirt was open, his hair was mussed, and a cigarette dangled from the corner of his mouth. He stood up when Perot walked in.

'Ross, how's your mother?'

'She's in good spirits, thank you.'

'That's good.'

Perot sat down. 'Now, where are we on Paul and Bill?'

Gayden picked up the phone, saying: 'Lemme get T.J. in here.' He punched T.J. Marquez's number and said: 'Ross is here . . . Yeah. My office.' He hung up and said: 'He'll be right down. Uh . . . I called the State Department. The head of the Iran Desk is a man called Henry Precht. At first he wouldn't return my call. In the end I told his secretary, I said: "If he doesn't call me within twenty minutes, I'm going to call CBS and ABC and NBC and in one hour's time Ross Perot is going to give a press conference to say that we have two Americans in trouble in Iran and our country won't help them." He called back five minutes later.'

'What did he say?'

Gayden sighed. 'Ross, their basic attitude up there is that if Paul and Bill are in jail they must have done something wrong.'

'But what are they going to *do*?'

'Contact the Embassy, look into it, blah blah blah.'

'Well, we're going to have to put a firecracker under Precht's tail,' Perot said angrily. 'Now, Tom Luce is the man to do that.' Luce, an aggressive young lawyer, was the founder of the Dallas firm of Hughes & Hill, which handled most of EDS's legal business. Perot had retained him as EDS's counsel years ago, mainly because Perot could relate to a young man who, like himself, had left a big company to start his own business and was struggling to pay the bills. Hughes & Hill, like EDS, had grown rapidly. Perot had never regretted hiring Luce.

Gayden said: 'Luce is right here in the office somewhere.'

'How about Tom Walter?'

'He's here too.'

Walter, a tall Alabaman with a voice like molasses, was EDS's chief financial officer and probably the smartest man, in terms of sheer brains, in the company. Perot said: 'I want Walter to go to work on the bail. I don't want to pay it, but I will if we have to. Walter should figure out how we go about paying it. You can bet they won't take American Express.'

'Okay,' Gayden said.

A voice from behind said: 'Hi, Ross!'

Perot looked around and saw T. J. Marquez. 'Hi, Tom.' T.J. was a tall, slim man of forty with Spanish good looks: olive skin, short, curly black hair, and a big smile which showed lots of white teeth. The first employee Perot ever hired, he was living evidence that Perot had an uncanny knack of picking good men. T.J. was now a vice-president of EDS, and his personal shareholding in the company was worth millions of dollars. 'The Lord has been good to us,' T.J. would say. Perot knew that T.J.'s parents had really struggled to send him to college. Their sacrifices had been well rewarded. One of the best things about the meteoric success of EDS, for Perot, had been sharing the triumph with people like T.J.

T.J. sat down and talked fast. 'I called Claude.'

Perot nodded. Claude Chappelear was the company's in-house lawyer.

'Claude's friendly with Matthew Nimetz, counsellor to Secretary of State Vance. I thought Claude might get Nimetz to talk to Vance himself. Nimetz called personally a little later. He wants to help us. He's going to send a cable under Vance's name to the US Embassy in Tehran, telling them to get off their butts. And he's going to write a personal note to Vance about Paul and Bill.'

75

'Good.'

'We also called Admiral Moorer. He's up to speed on this whole thing because we consulted him about the passport problem. Moorer's going to talk to Ardeshir Zahedi. Now, Zahedi is not just the Iranian Ambassador in Washington but also the Shah's brother-in-law, and he's now back in Iran – running the country, some say. Moorer will ask Zahedi to vouch for Paul and Bill. Right now we're drafting a cable for Zahedi to send to the Ministry of Justice.'

'Who's drafting it?'

'Tom Luce.'

'Good.' Perot summed up. 'We've got the Secretary of State, the Head of the Iran Desk, the Embassy, and the Iranian Ambassador all working on the case. That's good. Now let's talk about what else we can do.'

T.J. said: 'Tom Luce and Tom Walter have an appointment with Admiral Moorer in Washington tomorrow. Moorer also suggested we call Richard Helms – he used to be Ambassador to Iran after he quit the CIA.'

'I'll call Helms,' Perot said. 'And I'll call Al Haig and Henry Kissinger. I want you two to concentrate on getting all our people out of Iran.'

Gayden said: 'Ross, I'm not sure that's necessary—'

'I don't want a discussion, Bill,' said Perot. 'Let's get it done. Now, Lloyd Briggs has to stay there and deal with the problem – he's the boss, with Paul and Bill in jail. Everyone else comes home.'

'You can't make them come home if they don't want to,' Gayden said.

'Who'll want to stay?'

'Rich Gallagher. His wife—'

'I know. Okay, Briggs and Gallagher stay. Nobody else.' Perot stood up. 'I'll get started on those calls.'

He took the elevator to the seventh floor and walked through his secretary's office. Sally Walther was at her desk. She had been with him for years, and had been involved in the prisoners-of-war campaign and the San Francisco party. (She had come back from that weekend with a Son Tay

Raider in tow, and Captain Udo Walther was now her husband.) Perot said to her: 'Call Henry Kissinger, Alexander Haig, and Richard Helms.'

He went through to his own office and sat at his desk. The office, with its panelled walls, costly carpet, and shelves of antiquarian books, looked more like a Victorian library in an English country house. He was surrounded by souvenirs and his favourite art. For the house Margot bought Impressionist paintings, but in his office Perot preferred American art: Norman Rockwell originals and the Wild West bronzes of Frederic Remington. Through the window he could see the slopes of the old golf course.

Perot did not know where Henry Kissinger might be spending the holidays: it could take Sally a while to find him. There was time to think about what to say. Kissinger was not a close friend. It would need all his salesmanship to grab Kissinger's attention and, in the space of a short phone call, win his sympathy.

The phone on his desk buzzed, and Sally called: 'Henry Kissinger for you.'

Perot picked it up. 'Ross Perot.'

'I have Henry Kissinger for you.'

Perot waited.

Kissinger had once been called the most powerful man in the world. He knew the Shah personally. But how well would he remember Ross Perot? The prisoners-of-war campaign had been big, but Kissinger's projects had been bigger: peace in the Middle East, rapprochement between the US and China, the ending of the Vietnam war . . .

'Kissinger here.' It was the familiar deep voice, its accent a curious mixture of American vowels and German consonants.

'Dr Kissinger, this is Ross Perot. I'm a businessman in Dallas, Texas, and—'

'Hell, Ross, I know who you are,' said Kissinger.

Perot's heart leaped. Kissinger's voice was warm, friendly and informal. This was great! Perot began to tell him about Paul and Bill: how they had gone voluntarily to see Dadgar, how the State Department had let them down. He assured Kissinger they were innocent, and pointed out that they had not been charged with any crime, nor had the Iranians produced an atom of evidence against them. 'These are my men, I sent them there, and I have to get them back,' he finished.

'I'll see what I can do,' Kissinger said.

Perot was exultant. 'I sure appreciate it!'

'Send me a short briefing paper with all the details.'

'We'll get it to you today.'

'I'll get back to you, Ross.'

'Thank you, sir.'

The line went dead.

Perot felt terrific. Kissinger had remembered him, had been friendly and willing to help. He wanted a briefing paper: EDS could send it today—

Perot was struck by a thought. He had no idea where Kissinger had been speaking from – it might have been London, Monte Carlo, Mexico . . .

'Sally?'

'Yes, sir?'

'Did you find out *where* Kissinger is?'

'Yes, sir.'

Kissinger was in New York, in his duplex at the exclusive River House apartment complex on East 52nd Street. From the window he could see the East River.

He remembered Ross Perot clearly. Perot was a rough diamond. He helped causes with which Kissinger was sympathetic, usually causes having to do with prisoners. In the Vietnam war Perot's campaign had been courageous, even though he had sometimes harassed Kissinger beyond the point of what was do-able. Now some of Perot's own people were prisoners.

Kissinger could readily believe that they were innocent. Iran was on the brink of civil war: justice and due process meant little over there now. He wondered whether he could help. He wanted to: it was a good cause. He was no longer in

78

office, but he still had friends. He would call Ardeshir Zahedi, he decided, as soon as the briefing paper arrived from Dallas.

Perot felt good about the conversation with Kissinger. *Hell, Ross, I know who you are.* That was worth more than money. The only advantage of being famous was that it sometimes helped get important things done.

T.J. came in. 'I have your passport,' he said. 'It already had a visa for Iran, but Ross, I don't think you should go. All of us here can work on the problem, but you're the key man. The last thing we need is for you to be out of contact – in Tehran or just up in a plane somewhere – at the moment when we have to make a crucial decision.'

Perot had forgotten all about going to Tehran. Everything he had heard in the last hour encouraged him to think it would not be necessary. 'You might be right,' he said to T.J. 'We have so many things going in the area of negotiation – only one of them has to work. I won't go to Tehran. Yet.'

4

Henry Precht was probably the most harassed man in Washington.

A long-serving State Department official with a bent for art and philosophy and a wacky sense of humour, he had been making American policy on Iran more or less by himself for much of 1978, while his superiors – right up to President Carter – focused on the Camp David agreement between Egypt and Israel.

Since early November, when things had really started to warm up in Iran, Precht had been working seven days a week from eight in the morning until nine at night. And those damn Texans seemed to think he had nothing else to do but talk to them on the phone.

The trouble was, the crisis in Iran was not the only power struggle Precht had to worry about. There was another fight going on, in Washington, between Secretary of State Cyrus Vance – Precht's boss – and Zbigniew Brzezinski, the President's National Security Advisor.

Vance believed, like President Carter, that American foreign policy should reflect American morality. The American people believed in freedom, justice and democracy, and they did not want to support tyrants. The Shah of Iran was a tyrant. Amnesty International had called Iran's human rights record the worst in the world, and the many reports of the Shah's systematic use of torture had been confirmed by the International Commission of Jurists. Since the CIA had put the Shah in power and the USA had kept him there, a President who talked a lot about human rights had to do something.

In January 1977 Carter had hinted that tyrants might be denied American aid. Carter was indecisive – later that year he visited Iran and lavished praise on the Shah – but Vance believed in the human-rights approach.

Zbigniew Brzezinski did not. The National Security Advisor believed in power. The Shah was an ally of the United States, and should be supported. Sure, he should be encouraged to stop torturing people – but not yet. His regime was under attack: this was no time to liberalize it.

'When would be the time?' asked the Vance faction. The Shah had been strong for most of his twenty-five years of rule, but had never shown much inclination toward moderate government. Brzezinski replied: 'Name one single moderate government in that region of the world.'

There were those in the Carter administration who thought that if America did not stand for freedom and democracy there was no point in having a foreign policy at all. But that was a somewhat extreme view, so they fell back on a pragmatic argument: the Iranian people had had enough of the Shah, and they were going to get rid of him regardless of what Washington thought.

'Rubbish,' said Brzezinski. 'Read history. Revolutions succeed when rulers make concessions, and fail when those in power crush the rebels with an iron fist. The Iranian army, four hundred thousand strong, can easily put down any revolt.'

The Vance faction – including Henry Precht – did not agree with the Brzezinski Theory of Revolutions: threatened tyrants make concessions because the rebels are strong, not the other way around, they said. More importantly, they did not believe that the Iranian army was four hundred thousand strong. Figures were hard to get, but soldiers were deserting at a rate which fluctuated around eight per cent per month, and there were whole units which would go over to the revolutionaries intact in the event of all-out civil war.

The two Washington factions were getting their information from different sources. Brzezinski was listening to Ardeshir Zahedi, the Shah's brother-in-law and the most powerful pro-Shah figure in Iran. Vance was listening to Ambassador Sullivan. Sullivan's cables were not as consistent as Washington could have wished, perhaps because the situation in Iran was sometimes confusing, but since September the general trend of his reports had been to say that the Shah was doomed.

Brzezinski said Sullivan was running around with his head cut off and could not be trusted. Vance's supporters said that Brzezinski dealt with bad news by shooting the messenger.

The upshot was that the United States did nothing. One time the State Department drafted a cable to Ambassador Sullivan, instructing him to urge the Shah to form a broad-based civilian coalition government: Brzezinski killed the cable. Another time Brzezinski phoned the Shah and assured him that he had the support of President Carter; the Shah asked for a confirming cable; the State Department did not send the cable. In their frustration both sides leaked stuff to the newspapers, so that the whole world knew that Washington's policy on Iran was paralyzed by in-fighting.

With all that going on, the last thing Precht needed was a gang of Texans on his tail thinking they were the only people in the world with a problem.

Besides, he knew, he thought, exactly why EDS was in trouble. On asking whether EDS was represented by an agent in Iran, he was told: 'Yes – Mr Abolfath Mahvi.' That explained everything. Mahvi was a well known Tehran middleman, nicknamed 'the king of the five percenters' for his dealings in military contracts. Despite his high-level contacts the Shah had put him on a blacklist of people banned from doing business in Iran. *This* was why EDS was suspected of corruption.

Precht would do what he could. He would get the Embassy in Tehran to look into the case, and perhaps Ambassador Sullivan might be able to put pressure on the Iranians to release Chiapparone and Gaylord. But there was no way the United States Government was going to put all other Iranian questions on the back burner. They were attempting to support the existing regime, and this was no time to unbalance that regime further by threatening a break in diplomatic relations over two jailed businessmen, especially when there were another twelve thousand US citizens in Iran, all of whom the State Department was supposed to look after. It was unfortunate, but Chiapparone and Gaylord would just have to sweat it out.

Henry Precht meant well. However, early in his involvement with Paul and Bill, he – like Lou Goelz – made a mistake which at first wrongly coloured his attitude to the problem and later made him defensive in all his dealings with EDS. Precht acted as if the investigation in which Paul and Bill were supposed to be witnesses was a legitimate judicial inquiry into allegations of corruption, rather than a barefaced act of blackmail. Goelz, on this assumption, decided to co-operate with General Biglari. Precht, making the same mistake, refused to treat Paul and Bill as criminally kidnapped Americans.

Whether Abolfath Mahvi was corrupt or not, the fact was that he had not made a penny out of EDS's contract with the Ministry. Indeed, EDS had got into trouble in its early days for *refusing* to give Mahvi a piece of the action.

It happened like this. Mahvi helped EDS get its first, small contract in Iran, creating a document control system for the Iranian Navy. EDS, advised that by law they had to have a local partner, promised Mahvi a third of the profit. When the contract was completed, two years later, EDS duly paid Mahvi four hundred thousand dollars.

But while the Ministry contract was being negotiated Mahvi was on the blacklist. Nevertheless, when the deal was about to be signed, Mahvi – who by this time was *off* the blacklist again – demanded that the contract be given to a joint company owned by him and EDS.

EDS refused. While Mahvi had earned his share of the Navy contract, he had done nothing for the Ministry deal.

Mahvi claimed that EDS's association with him had smoothed the way for the Ministry contract through the twenty-four different government bodies which had to approve it. Furthermore, he said, he had helped obtain a tax ruling favourable to EDS which was written into the contract: EDS only got the ruling because Mahvi had spent time with the Minister of Finance in Monte Carlo.

EDS had not asked for his help, and did not believe that he had given it. Furthermore, Ross Perot did not like the kind of 'help' that takes place in Monte Carlo.

EDS's Iranian attorney complained to the Prime Minister, and Mahvi was carpeted for demanding bribes. Nevertheless his influence was so great that the Ministry of Health would not sign the contract unless EDS made him happy.

EDS had a series of stormy negotiations with Mahvi. EDS still refused point blank to share profits with him. In the end there was a face-saving compromise: a joint company, acting as subcontractor to EDS, would recruit and employ all EDS's Iranian staff. In fact the joint company never made money, but that was later. At the time Mahvi accepted the compromise and the Ministry contract was signed.

So EDS had not paid bribes, and the Iranian government knew it; but Henry Precht did not, nor did Lou Goelz.

Consequently their attitude to Paul and Bill was equivocal. Both men spent many hours on the case but neither gave it top priority. When EDS's combative lawyer Tom Luce talked to them as if they were idle or stupid or both, they became indignant and said they might do better if he would get off their backs.

Precht in Washington and Goelz in Tehran were the crucial, ground-level operatives dealing with the case. Neither of them was idle. Neither was incompetent. But they both made mistakes, they both became somewhat hostile to EDS, and in those vital first few days they both failed to help Paul and Bill.

Three

1

A guard opened the cell door, looked around, pointed at Paul and Bill, and beckoned them.

Bill's hopes soared. Now they would be released.

They got up and followed the guard upstairs. It was good to see daylight through the windows. They went out of the door and across the courtyard to the little one-storey building beside the entrance gate. The fresh air tasted heavenly.

It had been a terrible night. Bill had lain on the thin mattress, dozing fitfully, startled by the slightest movement from the other prisoners, looking around anxiously in the dim light from the all-night bulb. He had known it was morning when a guard came with glasses of tea and rough hunks of bread for breakfast. He had not felt hungry. He had said a rosary.

Now it seemed his prayers were being answered.

Inside the one-storey building was a visiting room furnished with simple tables and chairs. Two people were waiting. Bill recognized one of them: it was Ali Jordan, the Iranian who worked with Lou Goelz at the Embassy. He shook hands and introduced his colleague, Bob Sorenson.

'We brought you some stuff,' Jordan said. 'A battery shaver – you'll have to share it – and some dungarees.'

Bill looked at Paul. Paul was staring at the two Embassy men, looking as if he were about to explode. 'Aren't you going to get us out of here?' Paul said.

'I'm afraid we can't do that.'

'God damn it, you got us in here!'

Bill sat down slowly, too depressed to be angry.

'We're very sorry this had happened,' said Jordan. 'It came as a complete surprise to us. We were told that Dadgar was favourably disposed towards you . . . The Embassy is filing a very serious protest.'

'But what are you doing to get us *out*?'

'You must work through the Iranian legal system. Your attorneys—'

'Jesus Christ,' Paul said disgustedly.

Jordan said: 'We have asked them to move you to a better part of the jail.'

'Gee, thanks.'

Sorenson asked: 'Uh, is there anything else you need?'

'There's nothing I need,' Paul said. 'I'm not planning to be here very long.'

Bill said: 'I'd like to get some eye drops.'

'I'll see that you do,' Sorenson promised.

Jordan said: 'I think that's all for now . . .' He looked at the guard.

Bill stood up.

Jordan spoke in Farsi to the guard, who motioned Paul and Bill to the door.

They followed the guard back across the courtyard. Jordan and Sorenson were low-ranking Embassy staff, Bill reflected. Why hadn't Goelz come? It seemed that the Embassy thought it was EDS's job to get them out: sending Jordan and Sorenson was a way of notifying the Iranians that the Embassy was concerned but at the same time letting Paul and Bill know that they could not expect much help from the US Government. We're a problem the Embassy wants to ignore, Bill thought angrily.

Inside the main building, the guard opened a door they had not been through before, and they went from the reception area into a corridor. On their right were three offices. On their left were windows looking out into the courtyard. They came to another door, this one made of thick steel. The guard unlocked it and ushered them through.

The first thing Bill saw was a TV set.

As he looked around he started to feel a little better. This part of the jail was more civilized than the basement. It was relatively clean and light, with grey walls and grey carpeting. The cell doors were open and the prisoners were walking around freely. Daylight came in through the windows.

They continued along a hall with two cells on the right and, on the left, what appeared to be a bathroom: Bill looked forward to a chance to get clean again after his night downstairs. Glancing through the last door on the right, he saw shelves of books. Then the guard turned left and led them down a long narrow corridor and into the last cell.

There they saw someone they knew.

It was Reza Neghabat, the Deputy Minister in charge of the Social Security Organization at the Ministry of Health. Both Paul and Bill knew him well and had worked closely with him before his arrest last September. They shook hands enthusiastically. Bill was relieved to see a familiar face, and someone who spoke English.

Neghabat was astonished. 'Why are you in here?'

Paul shrugged. 'I kind of hoped you might be able to tell us that.'

'But what are you accused of?'

'Nothing,' said Paul. 'We were interrogated yesterday by Mr Dadgar, the magistrate who's investigating your former Minister, Dr Sheik. He arrested us. No charges, no accusations. We're supposed to be "material witnesses", we understand.'

Bill looked around. On either side of the cell were paired stacks of bunks, three high, with another pair beside the window, making eighteen altogether. As in the cell downstairs, the bunks were furnished with thin foam rubber mattresses, the bottom bunk of the three being no more than a mattress on the floor, and grey wool blankets. However, here some of the prisoners seemed to have sheets as well. The window, opposite the door, looked out into a courtyard. Bill could see grass, flowers and trees, as well as parked cars belonging, presumably, to guards. He could also see the low building where they had just talked with Jordan and Sorenson.

Neghabat introduced Paul and Bill to their cellmates, who

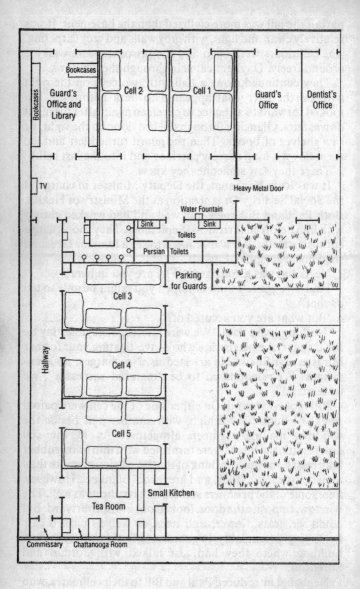

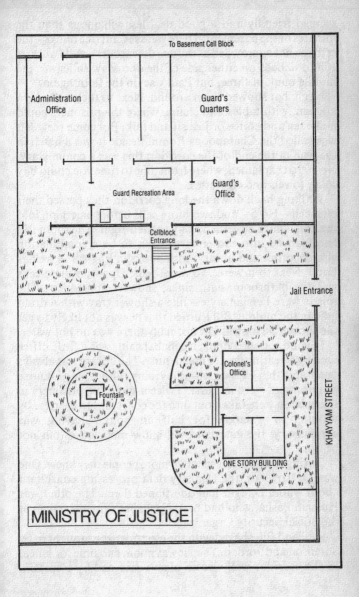

seemed friendly and a good deal less villainous than the inmates of the basement. There were several free bunks – the cell was not as crowded as the one downstairs – and Paul and Bill took beds on either side of the doorway. Bill's was the middle bunk of three, but Paul was on the floor again.

Neghabat showed them around. Next to their cell was a kitchen, with tables and chairs, where the prisoners could make tea and coffee or just sit and talk. For some reason it was called the Chatanooga Room. Beside it was a hatch in the wall at the end of the corridor: this was a commissary, Neghabat explained, where from time to time you could buy soap, towels and cigarettes.

Walking back down the long corridor, they passed their own cell – No 5 – and two more cells before emerging into the hall, which stretched away to their right. The room Bill had glanced into earlier turned out to be a combination guard's office and library, with books in English as well as Farsi. Next to it were two more cells. Opposite these cells was the bathroom, with sinks, showers and toilets. The toilets were Persian style – like a shower tray with a drain hole in the middle. Bill learned that he was not likely to get the shower he longed for: normally there was no hot water.

Beyond the steel door, Neghabat said, was a little office used by a visiting doctor and dentist. The library was always open and the TV was on all evening, although of course programmes were in Farsi. Twice a week the prisoners in this section were taken out into the courtyard to exercise by walking in a circle for half an hour. Shaving was compulsory: the guards would allow moustaches but not beards.

During the tour they met two more people they knew. One was Dr Towliati, the Ministry data processing consultant about whom Dadgar had questioned them. The other was Hussein Pasha, who had been Neghabat's financial man at the Social Security Organization.

Paul and Bill shaved with the electric razor brought in by Sorenson and Jordan. Then it was noon, and time for lunch. In the corridor wall was an alcove screened by a curtain.

From there the prisoners took a linoleum mat, which they spread on the cell floor, and some cheap tableware. The meal was steamed rice with a little lamb, plus bread and yoghurt, and tea or Pepsi-Cola to drink. They sat cross-legged on the floor to eat. For Paul and Bill, both gourmets, it was a poor lunch. However, Bill found he had an appetite: perhaps it was the cleaner surroundings.

After lunch they had more visitors: their Iranian attorneys. The lawyers did not know why they had been arrested, did not know what would happen next, and did not know what they could do to help. It was a desultory, depressing conversation. Paul and Bill had no faith in them anyway, for it was these lawyers who had advised Lloyd Briggs that the bail would not exceed twenty thousand dollars. They returned no wiser and no happier.

They spent the rest of the afternoon in the Chatanooga Room, talking to Neghabat, Towliati and Pasha. Paul described his interrogation by Dadgar in detail. Each of the Iranians was highly interested in any mention of his own name during the interrogation. Paul told Dr Towliati how his name had come up, in connection with a suggested conflict of interest. Towliati described how he, too, had been questioned by Dadgar in the same way before being thrown in jail. Paul recollected that Dadgar had asked about a memorandum written by Pasha. It had been a completely routine request for statistics, and nobody could figure out what was supposed to be special about it.

Neghabat had a theory as to why they were in jail. 'The Shah is making a scapegoat of us, to show the masses that he really is cracking down on corruption – but he picked a project where there was no corruption. There is nothing to crack down on – but if he releases us, he will look weak. If he had looked instead at the construction business he would have found an unbelievable amount of corruption . . .'

It was all very vague. Neghabat was just rationalizing. Paul and Bill wanted specifics: *who* ordered the crackdown, *why* pick on the Ministry of Health, *what* kind of corruption was supposed to have taken place, and *where* were the informants who had put the finger on the individuals who were now in jail? Neghabat was not being evasive – he simply had no answers. His vagueness was characteristically Persian: ask an Iranian what he had for breakfast and ten seconds later he would be explaining his philosophy of life.

At six o'clock they returned to their cell for supper. It was pretty grim – no more than the leftovers from lunch mashed into a dip to be spread on bread, with more tea.

After supper they watched TV. Neghabat translated the news. The Shah had asked an opposition leader, Shahpour Bakhtiar, to form a civilian government, replacing the generals who had ruled Iran since November. Neghabat explained that Shahpour was leader of the Bakhtiar tribe, and that he had always refused to have anything to do with the regime of the Shah. Nevertheless, whether Bakhtiar's government could end the turmoil would depend on the Ayatollah Khomeini.

The Shah had also denied rumours that he was leaving the country.

Bill thought this sounded encouraging. With Bakhtiar as Prime Minister the Shah would remain and ensure stability but the rebels would at last have a voice in governing their own country.

At ten o'clock the TV went off and the prisoners returned to their cells. The other inmates hung towels and pieces of cloth across their bunks to keep out the light: here, as downstairs, the bulb would shine all night. Neghabat said Paul and Bill could get their visitors to bring in sheets and towels for them.

Bill wrapped himself in the thin grey blanket and settled down to try to sleep. We're here for a while, he thought resignedly; we must make the best of it. Our fate is in the hands of others.

2

Their fate was in the hands of Ross Perot, and in the next two days all his high hopes came to nothing.

At first the news had been good. Kissinger had called back on Friday, 29 December, to say that Ardeshir Zahedi would get Paul and Bill released. First, though, US Embassy officials had to hold two meetings: one with people from the Ministry of Justice, the other with representatives of the Shah's court.

In Tehran the American Ambassador's deputy, Minister-Counsellor Charles Naas, was personally setting up those meetings.

In Washington, Henry Precht at the State Department was also talking to Ardeshir Zahedi. Emily Gaylord's brother-in-law, Tim Reardon, had spoken to Senator Kennedy. Admiral Moorer was working his contacts with the Iranian military government. The only disappointment in Washington had been Richard Helms, the former US Ambassador to Tehran: he had said candidly that his old friends no longer had any influence.

EDS consulted three separate Iranian lawyers. One was an American who specialized in representing US corporations in Tehran. The other two were Iranians: one had good contacts in pro-Shah circles, the other was close to the dissidents. All three had agreed that the way Paul and Bill had been jailed was highly irregular and that the bail was astronomical. The American, John Westberg, had said that the highest bail he had ever heard of in Iran was a hundred thousand dollars. The implication was that the magistrate who had jailed Paul and Bill was on weak ground.

Here in Dallas, EDS's chief financial officer Tom Walter, the slow-talking Alabaman, was working on how EDS might – if necessary – go about posting bail of $12,750,000. The lawyers had advised him that bail could be in one of three forms: cash; a letter of credit drawn on an Iranian bank; or a lien on property in Iran. EDS had no property worth that much in Tehran – the computers actually belonged to the Ministry – and, with the Iranian banks on strike and the country in turmoil, it was not possible to send in thirteen million dollars in cash; so Walter was organizing a letter of credit. T. J. Marquez, whose job it was to represent EDS to the investment community, had warned Perot that it might not be legal for a public company to pay that much money in what amounted to ransom. Perot deftly sidestepped that problem: he would pay the money personally.

Perot had been optimistic that he would get Paul and Bill out of jail in *one* of the three ways – legal pressure, political pressure, or by paying the bail.

Then the bad news started coming in.

The Iranian lawyers changed their tune. In turn they reported that the case was 'political', had 'high political content', and was 'a political hot potato'. John Westberg, the American, had been asked by his Iranian partners not to handle the case because it would bring the firm into disfavour with powerful people. Evidently, Examining Magistrate Hosain Dadgar was *not* on weak ground.

Lawyer Tom Luce and financial officer Tom Walter had gone to Washington and, accompanied by Admiral Moorer, had visited the State Department. They had expected to sit down around a table with Henry Precht and formulate an aggressive campaign for the release of Paul and Bill. But Henry Precht was cool. He had shaken hands with them – he could hardly do less, when they were accompanied by a former Chairman of the Joint Chiefs of Staff – but he had not sat down with them. He had handed them over to a subordinate. The subordinate reported that none of the State Department's efforts had achieved anything: neither Ardeshir Zahedi nor Charlie Naas had been able to get Paul and Bill released.

Tom Luce, who did not have the patience of Job, got mad as hell. It was the State Department's job to protect Americans abroad, he said, and so far all State had done was to get Paul and Bill thrown in jail! Not so, he was told; what State had done so far was above and beyond their normal duty. If Americans abroad committed crimes they were subject to foreign laws. The State Department's duties did not include springing people from jail. But, Luce argued, Paul and Bill had *not* committed a crime – they were being held hostage for thirteen million dollars! He was wasting his breath. He and Tom Walter returned to Dallas empty-handed.

Late last night Perot had called the US Embassy in Tehran and asked Charles Naas why he still had not met with the officials named by Kissinger and Zahedi. The answer was simple: those officials were making themselves unavailable to Naas.

Today Perot had called Kissinger again and reported this. Kissinger was sorry: he did not think there was anything more he could do. However, he would call Zahedi and try again.

One more piece of bad news completed the picture. Tom Walter had been trying to establish, with the Iranian lawyers, the conditions under which Paul and Bill might be released on bail. For example, would they have to promise to return to Iran for further questioning if required, or could they be interrogated outside the country? Neither, he was told: *if they were released from prison they still would not be able to leave Iran.*

Now it was New Year's Eve. For three days Perot had been living at the office, sleeping on the floor and eating cheese sandwiches. There was nobody to go home to – Margot and the children were still in Vail – and, because of the nine-and-a-half-hour time difference between Texas and Iran, important phone calls were often made in the middle of the night. He was leaving the office only to visit his mother, who was now out of hospital and recuperating at her Dallas home. Even with her he talked about Paul and Bill – she was keenly interested in the progress of events.

This evening he felt the need of hot food, and he decided to brave the weather – Dallas was suffering an ice storm – and drive a mile or so to a fish restaurant.

He left the building by the back door and got behind the wheel of his station wagon. Margot had a Jaguar, but Perot preferred nondescript cars.

He wondered just how much influence Kissinger had now, in Iran or anywhere. Zahedi and any other Iranian contacts Kissinger had might be like Richard Helms's friends – all out of the mainstream, powerless. The Shah seemed to be hanging on by the skin of his teeth.

On the other hand, that whole group might soon need

93

friends in America, and welcome the opportunity to do Kissinger a favour.

While he was eating, Perot felt a large hand on his shoulder, and a deep voice said: 'Ross, what are you doing here, eating all by yourself on New Year's Eve?'

He turned around to see Roger Staubach, quarterback for the Dallas Cowboys, a fellow Naval Academy graduate and an old friend. 'Hi, Roger! Sit down.'

'I'm here with the family,' Staubach said. 'The heat's off in our house on account of the ice storm.'

'Well, bring them over.'

Staubach beckoned to his family, then said: 'How's Margot?'

'Fine, thank you. She's skiing with the children in Vail. I had to come back – we've got a big problem.' He proceeded to tell the Staubach family all about Paul and Bill.

He drove back to the office in good spirits. There were still a *bunch* of good people in the world.

He thought again of Colonel Simons. Of all the schemes he had for getting Paul and Bill out, the jailbreak was the one with the longest lead time: Simons would need a team of men, a training period, equipment . . . And yet Perot still had not done anything about it. It had seemed such a distant possibility, a last resort: while negotiations had seemed promising he had blocked it out of his mind. He was still not ready to call Simons – he would wait for Kissinger to have one more try with Zahedi – but perhaps there was something he could do to prepare for Simons.

Back at EDS, he found Pat Sculley. Sculley, a West Point graduate, was a thin, boyish, restless man of thirty-one. He had been a project manager in Tehran and had come out with the 8 December evacuation. He had returned after Ashura, then come out again when Paul and Bill were arrested. His job at the moment was to make sure that the Americans remaining in Tehran – Lloyd Briggs, Rich Gallagher and his wife, Paul and Bill – had reservations on a flight out every day, just in case the prisoners should be released.

With Sculley was Jay Coburn, who had organized the evacuation and then, on 22 December, had come home to spend Christmas with his family. Coburn had been about to go back to Tehran when he got the news that Paul and Bill had been arrested, so he had stayed in Dallas and organized the second evacuation. A placid, stocky man, Coburn smiled a lot – a slow smile that began as a twinkle in his eye and often ended in a shoulder-shaking belly-laugh.

Perot liked and trusted both men. They were what he called eagles: high-flyers, who used their initiative, got the job done, gave him results not excuses. The motto of EDS's recruiters was: Eagles Don't Flock – You Have To Find Them One At A Time. One of the secrets of Perot's business success was his policy of going looking for men like this, rather than waiting and hoping they would apply for the job.

Perot said to Sculley: 'Do you think we're doing everything we need to do for Paul and Bill?'

Sculley responded without hesitation. 'No, I don't.'

Perot nodded. These young men were never afraid to speak out to the boss: that was one of the things that made them eagles. 'What do you think we ought to do?'

'We ought to break them out,' Sculley said. 'I know it sounds strange, but I really think that if we don't, they have a good chance of getting killed in there.'

Perot did not think it sounded strange: that fear had been at the back of his mind for three days. 'I'm thinking of the same thing.' He saw surprise on Sculley's face. 'I want you two to put together a list of EDS people who could help do it. We'll need men who know Tehran, have some military experience – preferably in Special Forces type action – and are one hundred per cent trustworthy and loyal.'

'We'll get on it right away,' Sculley said enthusiastically.

The phone rang and Coburn picked it up. 'Hi, Keane! Where are you . . . Hold on a minute.'

Coburn covered the mouthpiece with his hand and looked at Perot. 'Keane Taylor is in Frankfurt. If we're going to do something like this, he ought to be on the team.'

Perot nodded. Taylor, a former Marine sergeant, was

95

another of his eagles. Six feet two and elegantly dressed, Taylor was a somewhat irritable man, which made him the ideal butt for practical jokes. Perot said: 'Tell him to go back to Tehran. But don't explain why.'

A slow smile spread across Coburn's young-old face. 'He ain't gonna like it.'

Sculley reached across the desk and switched on the speaker so they could all hear Taylor blow his cool.

Coburn said: 'Keane, Ross wants you to go back to Iran.'

'What the hell for?' Taylor demanded.

Coburn looked at Perot. Perot shook his head. Coburn said: 'Uh, there's a lot we need to do, in terms of tidying up, administratively speaking—'

'You tell Perot I'm not going back in there for any administrative bullshit!'

Sculley started to laugh.

Coburn said: 'Keane, I have somebody else here who wants to talk to you.'

Perot said: 'Keane, this is Ross.'

'Oh. Uh, hello, Ross.'

'I'm sending you back to do *something very important*.'

'Oh.'

'Do you understand what I'm saying?'

There was a long pause, then Taylor said: 'Yes, sir.'

'Good.'

'I'm on my way.'

'What time is it there?' Perot asked.

'Seven o'clock in the morning.'

Perot looked at his own watch. It said midnight.

Nineteen seventy-nine had begun.

Taylor sat on the edge of the bed in his Frankfurt hotel room, thinking about his wife.

Mary was in Pittsburgh with the children, Mike and Dawn, staying at Taylor's brother's house. Taylor had called her from Tehran before leaving and told her he was coming home. She had been very happy to hear it. They had made plans for the future: they would return to Dallas, put the kids in school . . .

Now he had to call and tell her he would not be coming home after all.

She would be worried.

Hell, *he* was worried.

He thought about Tehran. He had not worked on the Ministry of Health project, but had been in charge of a smaller contract, to computerize the old-fashioned manual book-keeping systems of Bank Omran. One day about three weeks ago, a mob had formed outside the bank – Omran was the Shah's bank. Taylor had sent his people home. He and Glenn Jackson were the last to leave: they locked up the building and started walking north. As they turned the corner on to the main street, they walked into the mob. At that moment the army opened fire and charged down the street.

Taylor and Jackson ducked into a doorway. Someone opened the door and yelled at them to get inside. They did – but before their rescuer could lock it again four of the demonstrators forced their way in, chased by five soldiers.

Taylor and Jackson flattened themselves against the wall and watched the soldiers, with their truncheons and rifles, beat up the demonstrators. One of the rebels made a break for it. Two of his fingers were almost torn off his hand, and blood spurted all over the glass door. He got out but collapsed in the street. The soldiers dragged the other three demonstrators out. One was a bloody mess but conscious. The other two were out cold, or dead.

Taylor and Jackson stayed inside until the street was clear. The Iranian who had saved them kept saying: 'Get out while you can.'

And now, Taylor thought, I have to tell Mary that I've just agreed to go back into all that.

To do *something very important*.

Obviously it had to do with Paul and Bill; and if Perot could not talk about it on the phone, presumably it was something at least clandestine and quite possibly illegal.

In a way Taylor was glad, despite his fear of the mobs. While still in Tehran he had talked on the phone with Bill's wife, Emily Gaylord, and had promised not to leave without

Bill. The orders from Dallas, that everyone but Briggs and Gallagher had to get out, had forced him to break his word. Now the orders had changed, and perhaps he could keep his promise to Emily after all.

Well, he thought, I can't walk back, so I'd better find a plane. He picked up the phone again.

Jay Coburn remembered the first time he had seen Ross Perot in action. He would never forget it as long as he lived.

It happened in 1971. Coburn had been with EDS less than two years. He was a recruiter, working in New York City. Scott was born that year at a little Catholic hospital. It was a normal birth and, at first, Scott appeared to be a normal, healthy baby.

The day after he was born, when Coburn went to visit, Liz said Scott had not been brought in for his feed that morning. At the time Coburn took no notice. A few minutes later, a woman came in and said: 'Here are the pictures of your baby.'

'I don't remember any pictures being taken,' Liz said. The woman showed her the photographs. 'No, that's not my baby.'

The woman looked confused for a moment then said: 'Oh! That's right, yours is the one that's got the problem.'

It was the first Coburn and Liz had heard of any problem.

Coburn went to see the day-old Scott, and had a terrible shock. The baby was in an oxygen tent, gasping for air, and as blue as a pair of denim jeans. The doctors were in consultation about him.

Liz became almost hysterical, and Coburn called their family doctor and asked him to come to the hospital. Then he waited.

Something wasn't stacking up right. What kind of a hospital was it where they didn't tell you your new-born baby was dying? Coburn became distraught.

He called Dallas and asked for his boss, Gary Griggs. 'Gary, I don't know why I'm calling you, but I don't know what to do.' And he explained.

'Hold the phone,' said Griggs.

A moment later there was an unfamiliar voice on the line. 'Jay?'

'Yes.'

'This is Ross Perot.'

Coburn had met Perot, two or three times, but had never worked directly for him. Coburn wondered whether Perot even remembered what he looked like: EDS had more than a thousand employees at that time.

'Hello, Ross.'

'Now, Jay, I need some information.' Perot started asking questions: what was the address of the hospital? What were the doctors' names? What was their diagnosis? As he answered, Coburn was thinking bemusedly: does Perot even know who I am?

'Hold on a minute, Jay.' There was a short silence. 'I'm going to connect you with Doctor Urschel, a close friend of mine and a leading cardiac surgeon here in Dallas.' A moment later Coburn was answering more questions from the doctor.

'Don't you do a thing,' Urschel finished. 'I'm going to talk to the doctors on that staff. You just stay by the phone so we can get back in touch with you.'

'Yes, sir,' said Coburn dazedly.

Perot came back on the line. 'Did you get all that? How's Liz doing?'

Coburn thought: how the hell does he know my wife's name? 'Not too well,' Coburn answered. 'Her doctor's here and he's given her some sedation . . .'

While Perot was soothing Coburn, Dr Urschel was animating the hospital staff. He persuaded them to move Scott to New York University Medical Centre. Minutes later Scott and Coburn were in an ambulance on the way to the city.

They got stuck in a traffic jam in the Midtown Tunnel.

Coburn got out of the ambulance, ran more than a mile to the toll gate, and persuaded an official to hold up all lanes of traffic except the one the ambulance was in.

When they reached New York University Medical Centre there were ten or fifteen people waiting outside for them. Among them was the leading cardiovascular surgeon on the east coast, who had been flown in from Boston in the time it had taken the ambulance to reach Manhattan.

As baby Scott was rushed inside, Coburn handed over the envelope of X-rays he had brought from the other hospital. A woman doctor glanced at them. 'Where are the rest?'

'That's all,' Coburn replied.

'That's all they *took*?'

New X-rays revealed that, as well as a hole in the heart, Scott had pneumonia. When the pneumonia was treated the heart condition came under control.

And Scott survived. He turned into a soccer-playing, tree-climbing, creek-wading, thoroughly healthy little boy. And Coburn began to understand the way people felt about Ross Perot.

Perot's single-mindedness, his ability to focus narrowly on one thing and shut out distractions until he got the job done, had its disagreeable side. He could wound people. A day or two after Paul and Bill were arrested, he had walked into an office where Coburn was talking on the phone to Lloyd Briggs in Tehran. It had sounded to Perot like Coburn was giving instructions, and Perot believed strongly that people in head office should not give orders to those out there on the battlefield who knew the situation best. He had given Coburn a merciless telling-off in front of a room full of people.

Perot had other blind spots. When Coburn had worked in Recruiting, each year the company had named someone 'Recruiter of the Year'. The names of the winners were engraved on a plaque. The list went back years, and in time some of the winners left the company. When that happened Perot wanted to erase their names from the plaque. Coburn thought that was weird. So the guy left the company – so what? He had been Recruiter of the Year, one year, and why try to change history? It was almost as if Perot took it as a personal insult that someone should want to work elsewhere.

100

Perot's faults were of a piece with his virtues. His peculiar attitude toward people who left the company was the obverse of his intense loyalty to his employees. His occasional unfeeling harshness was just a part of the incredible energy and determination without which he would never have created EDS. Coburn found it easy to forgive Perot's shortcomings.

He had only to look at Scott.

'Mr Perot?' Sally called. 'It's Henry Kissinger.'

Perot's heart missed a beat. Could Kissinger and Zahedi have done it in the last twenty-four hours? Or was he calling to say he had failed?

'Ross Perot.'

'Hold the line for Henry Kissinger, please.'

A moment later Perot heard the familiar guttural accent. 'Hello, Ross?'

'Yes.' Perot held his breath.

'I have been assured that your men will be released tomorrow at ten a.m., Tehran time.'

Perot let out his breath in a long sigh of relief. 'Dr Kissinger, that's just about the best news I've heard since I don't know when. I can't thank you enough.'

'The details are to be finalized today by US Embassy officials and the Iranian Foreign Ministry, but this is a formality: I have been advised that your men will be released.'

'It's just great. We sure appreciate your help.'

'You're welcome.'

It was nine-thirty in the morning in Tehran, midnight in Dallas. Perot sat in his office, waiting. Most of his colleagues had gone home, to sleep in a bed for a change, happy in the knowledge that by the time they woke up Paul and Bill would be free. Perot was staying at the office to see it through to the end.

In Tehran, Lloyd Briggs was at the Bucharest office, and one of the Iranian employees was outside the jail. As soon as

Paul and Bill appeared, the Iranian would call Bucharest and Briggs would call Perot.

Now that the crisis was almost over, Perot had time to wonder where he had gone wrong. One mistake occurred to him immediately. When he had decided, on 4 December, to evacuate all his staff from Iran, he had not been determined enough and he had let others drag their feet and raise objections until it was too late.

But the big mistake had been doing business in Iran in the first place. With hindsight he could see that. At the time, he had agreed with his marketing people – and with many other American businessmen – that oil-rich, stable, Western-orientated Iran presented excellent opportunities. He had not perceived the strains beneath the surface, he knew nothing about the Ayatollah Khomeini, and he had not foreseen that one day there would be a President naïve enough to try to impose American beliefs and standards on a Middle Eastern country.

He looked at his watch. It was half past midnight. Paul and Bill should be walking out of that jail right now.

Kissinger's good news had been confirmed by a phone call from David Newsom, Cy Vance's deputy at the State Department. And Paul and Bill were getting out not a moment too soon. The news from Iran had been bad again today. Bakhtiar, the Shah's new Prime Minister, had been rejected by the National Front, the party which was now seen as the moderate opposition. The Shah had announced that he might take a vacation. William Sullivan, the American Ambassador, had advised the dependents of all Americans working in Iran to go home, and the embassies of Canada and Britain had followed suit. But the strike had closed the airports, and hundreds of women and children were stranded. However, Paul and Bill would not be stranded. Perot had had good friends at the Pentagon ever since the POW campaign: Paul and Bill would be flown out on a US Air Force jet.

At one o'clock Perot called Tehran. There was no news. Well, he thought, everyone says the Iranians have no sense of time.

The irony of this whole thing was that EDS had never paid bribes, in Iran or anywhere else. Perot hated the idea of bribery. EDS's Code of Conduct was set out in a 12-page booklet given to every new employee. Perot had written it himself. 'Be aware that federal law and the laws of most states prohibit giving anything of value to a government official with the intent to influence any official act . . . Since the absence of such intent might be difficult to prove, neither money nor anything of value should be given to a federal, state or foreign government official . . . A determination that a payment or practice is not forbidden by law does not conclude the analysis . . . It is always appropriate to make further inquiry into the ethics . . . Could you do business in complete trust with someone who acts the way you do? The answer must be *YES*.' The last page of the booklet was a form which the employee had to sign, acknowledging that he had received and read the Code.

When EDS first went to Iran, Perot's puritan principles had been reinforced by the Lockheed scandal. Daniel J. Haughton, chairman of the Lockheed Aircraft Corporation, had admitted to a Senate committee that Lockheed routinely paid millions of dollars in bribes to sell its planes abroad. His testimony had been an embarrassing performance which disgusted Perot: wriggling on his seat, Haughton had told the committee that the payments were not bribes but 'kickbacks'. Subsequently the Foreign Corrupt Practices Act made it an offence under US law to pay bribes in foreign countries.

Perot had called in lawyer Tom Luce and made him personally responsible for ensuring that EDS never paid bribes. During the negotiation of the Ministry of Health contract in Iran, Luce had offended not a few EDS executives by the thoroughness and persistence with which he had cross-examined them about the propriety of their dealings.

Perot was not hungry for business. He was already making millions. He did not *need* to expand abroad. If you have to pay bribes to do business there, he had said, why, we just won't do business there.

His business principles were deeply ingrained. His ancestors were Frenchmen who came to New Orleans and set up trading posts along the Red River. His father, Gabriel Ross Perot, had been a cotton broker. The trade was seasonal, and Ross Senior had spent a lot of time with his son, often talking about business. 'There's no point in buying cotton from a farmer *once*,' he would say. 'You have to treat him fairly, earn his trust, and develop a relationship with him, so that he'll be happy to sell you his cotton year after year. *Then* you're doing business.' Bribery just did not fit in there.

At one-thirty Perot called the EDS office in Tehran again. Still there was no news. 'Call the jail, or send somebody down there,' he said. 'Find out when they're getting out.'

He was beginning to feel uneasy.

What will I do if this doesn't work out? he thought. If I put up the bail, I'll have spent thirteen million dollars and still Paul and Bill will be forbidden to leave Iran. Other ways of getting them out using the legal system come up against the obstacle raised by the Iranian lawyers – that the case is political, which seems to mean that Paul's and Bill's innocence makes no difference. But political pressure had failed so far: neither the US Embassy in Tehran nor the State Department in Washington had been able to help; and if Kissinger should fail, that would surely be the end of all hope in that area. What then was left?

Force.

The phone rang. Perot snatched up the receiver. 'Ross Perot.'

'This is Lloyd Briggs.'

'Are they out?'

'No.'

Perot's heart sank. 'What's happening?'

'We spoke to the jail. They have no instructions to release Paul and Bill.'

Perot closed his eyes. The worst had happened. Kissinger had failed.

He sighed. 'Thank you, Lloyd.'

'What do we do next?'

'I don't know,' said Perot.

But he *did* know.

He said Goodbye to Briggs and hung up the phone.

He would not admit defeat. Another of his father's principles had been: take care of the people who work for you. Perot could remember the whole family driving twelve miles on Sundays to visit an old black man who had used to mow their lawn, just to make sure that he was well and had enough to eat. Perot's father would employ people he did not need, just because they had no job. Every year the Perot family car would go to the County Fair crammed with black employees, each of whom was given a little money to spend and a Perot business card to show if anyone tried to give him a hard time. Perot could remember one who had ridden a freight train to California and, on being arrested for vagrancy, had shown Perot's father's business card. The sheriff had said: 'We don't care whose nigger you are, we're throwing you in jail.' But he had called Perot Senior, who had wired the train fare for the man to come back. 'I been to California, and I'se back,' the man said when he reached Texarkana; and Perot Senior gave him back his job.

Perot's father did not know what civil rights were: this was how you treated other human beings. Perot had not known his parents were unusual until he grew up.

His father would not leave his employees in jail. Nor would Perot.

He picked up the phone: 'Get T. J. Marquez.'

It was two in the morning, but T. J. would not be surprised: this was not the first time Perot had woken him up in the middle of the night, and it would not be the last.

A sleepy voice said: 'Hello?'

'Tom, it doesn't look good.'

'Why?'

'They haven't been released and the jail says they aren't going to be.'

'Aw, *damn*.'

'Conditions are getting worse over there – did you see the news?'

'I sure did.'

'Do you think it's time for Simons?'

'Yeah, I think it is.'

'Do you have his number?'

'No, but I can get it.'

'Call him,' said Perot.

3

Bull Simons was going crazy.

He was thinking of burning down his house. It was an old wood-frame bungalow, and it would go up like a pile of matchwood, and that would be the end of it. The place was hell to him – but it was a hell he did not want to leave, for what made it hell was the bitter-sweet memory of the time when it had been heaven.

Lucille had picked the place. She saw it advertised in a magazine, and together they had flown down from Fort Bragg, North Carolina, to look it over. At Red Bay, in a dirt-poor part of the Florida Panhandle, the ramshackle house stood in forty acres of rough timber. But there was a two-acre lake with bass in it. Lucille had loved it.

That had been in 1971. It was time for Simons to retire. He had been a colonel for ten years, and if the Son Tay Raid could not get him promoted to general, nothing would. The truth was, he did not fit in the General's Club: he had always been a reserve officer, he had never been to a top military school such as West Point, his methods were unconventional, and he was no good at going to Washington cocktail parties and kissing ass. He knew he was a goddam fine soldier and if that was not good enough, why, Art Simons was not good enough. So he retired, and did not regret it.

He had passed the happiest years of his life here at Red Bay. All their married life he and Lucille had endured periods of separation, sometimes as much as a year without seeing one another, during his tours in Vietnam, Laos and Korea. From the moment he retired they were together all day and all night, every day of the year. Simons raised hogs. He knew nothing about farming, but he got the information he needed out of books, and built his own pens. Once the operation was under way he found there was not much to do but feed the pigs and look at them so he spent a lot of time fooling around with his collection of 150 guns, and eventually set up a little gunsmithing shop where he would repair his and his neighbours' weapons and load his own ammunition. Most days he and Lucille would wander, hand in hand, through the woods and down to the lake where they might catch a bass. In the evening, after supper, she would go to the bedroom as if she were preparing for a date, and come out later, wearing a housecoat over her nightgown and a red ribbon in her dark, dark hair, and sit on his lap . . .

Memories like these were breaking his heart.

Even the boys had seemed to grow up, at last, during those golden years. Harry, the younger, had come home one day and said: 'Dad, I've got a heroin habit and a cocaine habit and I need your help.' Simons knew little about drugs. He had smoked marijuana once, in a doctor's office in Panama, before giving his men a talk on drugs, just so that he could tell them that he knew what it was like; but all he knew about heroin was that it killed people. Still, he had been able to help Harry by keeping him busy, out in the open, building hog pens. It had taken a while. Many times Harry left the house and went into town to score dope, but he always came back, and eventually he did not go into town any more.

The episode had brought Simons and Harry together again. Simons would never be close to Bruce, his elder son; but at least he had been able to stop worrying about the boy. Boy? He was in his thirties, and just about as bull-headed as . . . well, as his father. Bruce had found Jesus and was determined to bring the rest of the world to the Lord – starting with Colonel Simons. Simons had practically thrown him out. However, unlike Bruce's other youthful enthusiasms – drugs, I Ching, back-to-nature communes –

Jesus had lasted, and at least Bruce had settled down to a stable way of life, as pastor of a tiny church in the frozen north-west of Canada.

Anyway, Simons was through agonizing about the boys. He had brought them up as well as he could, for better or worse, and now they were men, and had to take care of themselves. He was taking care of Lucille.

She was a tall, handsome, statuesque woman with a penchant for big hats. She looked pretty damn impressive behind the wheel of their black Cadillac. But in fact she was the reverse of formidable. She was soft, easygoing, and lovable. The daughter of two teachers, she had needed someone to make decisions for her, someone she could follow blindly and trust completely; and she had found what she needed in Art Simons. He in turn was devoted to her. By the time he retired, they had been married for thirty years, and in all that time he had never been in the least interested in another woman. Only his job, with its overseas postings, had come between them; and now that was over. He had told her: 'My retirement plans can be summed up in one word: you.'

They had seven wonderful years.

Lucille died of cancer on 16 March 1978.

And Bull Simons went to pieces.

Every man had a breaking-point, they said. Simons had thought the rule did not apply to him. Now he knew it did: Lucille's death broke him. He had killed many people, and seen more die, but he had not understood the meaning of death until now. For thirty-seven years they had been together, and now, suddenly, *she just wasn't there*.

Without her, he did not see what life was supposed to be about. There was no point in anything. He was sixty years old and he could not think of a single goddam reason for living another day. He stopped taking care of himself. He ate cold food from cans and let his hair – which had always been so short – grow long. He fed the hogs religiously at 3.45 p.m. every day, he knew perfectly well that it hardly mattered what time of day you fed a pig. He started taking in stray dogs, and soon had thirteen of them, scratching the furniture and messing on the floor.

He knew he was close to losing his mind, and only the iron self-discipline which had been part of his character for so long enabled him to retain his sanity. When he first thought of burning the place down, he knew his judgement was unbalanced, and he promised himself he would wait a year, and see how he felt then.

His brother Stanley was worried about him, he knew. Stan had tried to get him to pull himself together: had suggested he gave some lectures, had even tried to get him to join the Israeli army. Simons was Jewish by ancestry, but thought of himself as American: he did not want to go to Israel. He could not pull himself together. It was as much as he could do to live from day to day.

He did not need someone to take care of him – he had never needed that. On the contrary, he needed someone to take care of. That was what he had done all his life. He had taken care of Lucille, he had taken care of the men under his command. Nobody could rescue him from his depression, for his role in life was to rescue others. That was why he had been reconciled with Harry but not with Bruce: Harry had come to him asking to be rescued from his heroin habit, but Bruce had come offering to rescue Art Simons by bringing him to the Lord. In military operations, Simons's aim had always been to bring all his men back alive. The Son Tay Raid would have been the perfect climax to his career, if only there had been prisoners in the camp to rescue.

Paradoxically, the only way to rescue Simons was to ask him to rescue someone else.

It happened at two o'clock in the morning on 2 January 1979.

The phone woke him.

'Bull Simons?' The voice was vaguely familiar.

'Yeah.'

'This is T. J. Marquez from EDS in Dallas.'

Simons remembered: EDS, Ross Perot, the POW campaign, the San Francisco party . . . 'Hello, Tom.'

109

'Bull, I'm sorry to wake you.'

'It's okay. What can I do for you?'

'We have two people in jail in Iran, and it looks like we may not be able to get them out by any conventional means. Would you be willing to help us?'

Would he be *willing*? 'Hell, yes,' Simons said. 'When do we start?'

Four

1

Ross Perot drove out of EDS and turned left on Forest Lane then right on Central Expressway. He was heading for the Hilton Inn on Central and Mockingbird. He was about to ask seven men to risk their lives.

Sculley and Coburn had made their list. Their own names were at the top, followed by five more.

How many American corporate chiefs in the twentieth century had asked seven employees to perpetrate a jailbreak? Probably none.

During the night Coburn and Sculley had called the other five, who were scattered all over the United States, staying with friends and relations after their hasty departure from Tehran. Each had been told only that Perot wanted to see him in Dallas today. They were used to midnight phone calls and sudden summonses – that was Perot's style – and they had all agreed to come.

As they arrived in Dallas they had been steered away from EDS headquarters and sent to check in at the Hilton Inn. Most of them should be there by now, waiting for Perot.

He wondered what they would say when he told them he wanted them to go back to Tehran and bust Paul and Bill out of jail.

They were good men, and loyal to him, but loyalty to an employer did not normally extend to risking your life. Some of them might feel that the whole idea of a rescue by violence was foolhardy. Others would think of their wives and children, and for their sakes refuse – quite reasonably.

I have no right to ask these men to do this, he thought. I must take care not to put any pressure on them. No salesmanship today, Perot: just straight talk. They must understand that they're free to say: no, thanks, boss; count me out.

How many of them would volunteer?'

One in five, Perot guessed.

If that were the case it would take several days to get a team together, and he might end up with people who did not know Tehran.

What if *none* volunteered?

He pulled into the car park of the Hilton Inn and switched off the engine.

Jay Coburn looked around. There were four other men in the room: Pat Sculley, Glenn Jackson, Ralph Boulware and Joe Poché. Two more were on their way: Jim Schwebach was coming from Eau Claire, Wisconsin, and Ron Davis from Columbus, Ohio.

The Dirty Dozen they were not.

In their business suits, white shirts and sober ties, with their short haircuts and clean-shaven faces and well-fed bodies, they looked like what they were: ordinary American business executives. It was hard to see them as a squad of mercenaries.

Coburn and Sculley had made separate lists but these five men had been on both. Each had worked in Tehran – most had been on Coburn's evacuation team. Each had either military experience or some relevant skill. Each was a man Coburn trusted completely.

While Sculley was calling them in the early hours of this morning Coburn had gone to the personnel files and put together a folder on each man, detailing his age, height, weight, marital status and knowledge of Tehran. As they arrived in Dallas, each of them completed another sheet recounting his military experience, military schools attended, weapons training and other special skills. The folders were for Colonel Simons, who was on his way from Red Bay. But before Simons arrived, Perot had to ask these men whether they were willing to volunteer.

112

For Perot's meeting with them, Coburn had taken three adjoining rooms. Only the middle room would be used: the rooms on either side had been rented as a precaution against eavesdroppers. It was all rather melodramatic.

Coburn studied the others, wondering what they were thinking. They still had not been told what this was all about, but they had probably guessed.

He could not tell what Joe Poché was thinking: nobody ever could. A short, quiet man of thirty-two, Poché kept his emotions locked away. His voice was always low and even, his face generally blank. He had spent six years in the Army, and had seen action as commander of a howitzer battery in Vietnam. He had fired just about every weapon the army possessed up to some level of proficiency, and had killed time, in Vietnam, practising with a forty-five. He had spent two years with EDS in Tehran, first designing the enrolment system – the computer program which listed the names of people eligible for health care benefit – and later as the programmer responsible for loading the files which made up the data base for the whole system. Coburn knew him to be a deliberate, logical thinker, a man who would not give his assent to any idea or plan until he had questioned it from all angles and thought out all its consequences slowly and carefully. Humour and intuition were not among his strengths: brains and patience were.

Ralph Boulware was a full five inches taller than Poché. One of the two black men on the list, he had a chubby face and small, darting eyes, and he talked very fast. He had spent nine years in the Air Force as a technician, working on the complex inboard computer and radar systems of bombers. In Tehran for only nine months, he had started as data preparation manager and had swiftly been promoted to data centre manager. Coburn knew him well and liked him a lot. In Tehran they had got drunk together. Their children had played together and their wives had become friends. Boulware loved his family, loved his friends, loved his job, loved his life. He *enjoyed living* more than anyone else Coburn could think of, with the possible exception of Ross

113

Perot. Boulware was also a highly independent-minded son of a gun. He never had any trouble speaking out. Like many successful black men, he was a shade oversensitive, and liked to make it clear he was not to be pushed around. In Tehran over Ashura, when he had been in the high-stakes poker game with Coburn and Paul, everyone else had slept in the house for safety, as previously agreed; but Boulware had not. There had been no discussion, no announcement: Boulware just went home. A few days later he had decided that the work he was doing did not justify the risk to his safety, so he returned to the States. He was not a man to run with the pack just because it was a pack: if he thought the pack was running the wrong way he would leave it. He was the most sceptical of the group assembling at the Hilton Inn: if anyone was going to pour scorn on the idea of a jailbreak, Boulware would.

Glenn Jackson looked less like a mercenary than any of them. A mild man with spectacles, he had no military experience, but he was an enthusiastic hunter and an expert shot. He knew Tehran well, having worked there for Bell Helicopter as well as for EDS. He was such a straight, forthright, honest guy, Coburn thought, that it was hard to imagine him getting involved in the deception and violence that a jailbreak would entail. Jackson was also a Baptist – the others were Catholic, except for Poché who did not say what he was – and Baptists were famous for punching Bibles, not faces. Coburn wondered how Jackson would make out.

He had a similar concern about Pat Sculley. Sculley had a good military record – he had been five years in the Army, ending up as a Ranger instructor with the rank of captain – but he had no combat experience. Aggressive and outgoing in business, he was one of EDS's brightest up-and-coming young executives. Like Coburn, Sculley was an irrepressible optimist, but whereas Coburn's attitudes had been tempered by war, Sculley was youthfully naïve. If this thing gets violent, Coburn wondered, will Sculley be hard enough to handle it?

Of the two men who had not yet arrived, one was the most qualified to take part in a jailbreak, and the other perhaps the least.

Jim Schwebach knew more about combat than he did about computers. Eleven years in the army, he had served with the 5th Special Forces Group in Vietnam, doing the kind of commando work Bull Simons specialized in, clandestine operations behind enemy lines; and he had even more medals than Coburn. Because he had spent so many years in the military he was still a low-level executive, despite his age, which was thirty-five. He had been a trainee systems engineer when he went to Tehran, but he was mature and dependable, and Coburn had made him a team leader during the evacuation. Only five feet six inches, Schwebach had the erect, chin-up posture of many short men, and the indomitable fighting spirit which is the only defence of the smallest boy in the class. No matter what the score, it could be 12–0, ninth inning and two outs, Schwebach would be up on the edge of the dugout, clawing away and trying to figure out how to get an extra hit. Coburn admired him for volunteering – out of high-principled patriotism – for extra tours in Vietnam. In battle, Coburn thought, Schwebach would be the last guy you would want to take prisoner – if you had your druthers, you would make sure you killed the little son of a bitch before you captured him, he would make so much trouble.

However, Schwebach's feistiness was not immediately apparent. He was a very ordinary-looking fellow. In fact, you hardly noticed him. In Tehran he had lived farther south than anyone else, in a district where there were no other Americans, yet he had often walked around the streets, wearing a beat-up old field jacket, blue jeans and a knit cap, and had never been bothered. He could lose himself in a crowd of two – a talent which might be useful in a jailbreak.

The other missing man was Ron Davis. At thirty he was the youngest on the list. The son of a poor black insurance salesman, Davis had risen fast in the white world of corporate America. Few people who started, as he had, in operations ever made it to management on the customer side of the business. Perot was especially proud of Davis: 'Ron's career achievement is like a moonshot,' he would say. Davis had acquired a good knowledge of Farsi in a year and a half in Tehran, working under Keane Taylor, not on the Ministry contract but on a smaller, separate project to computerize Bank Omran, the Shah's bank. Davis was cheerful, flippant, full of jokes, a juvenile version of Richard Pryor, but without the profanity. Coburn thought he was the most *sincere* of the men on the list. Davis found it easy to open up and talk about his feelings and his personal life. For that reason Coburn thought of him as vulnerable. On the other hand, perhaps the ability to talk honestly about yourself to others was a sign of great inner confidence and strength.

Whatever the truth about Davis's emotional toughness, physically he was as hard as a nail. He had no military experience but he was a karate Black Belt. One time in Tehran, three men had attacked and attempted to rob him: he had beaten them all up in a few seconds. Like Schwebach's ability to be inconspicuous, Davis's karate was a talent which might become useful.

Like Coburn, all six men were in their thirties.

They were all married.

And they all had children.

The door opened and Perot walked in.

He shook hands, saying 'How are you?' and 'Good to see you!' as if he really meant it, remembering the names of their wives and children. He's *good* with people, Coburn thought.

'Schwebach and Davis didn't get here yet,' Coburn told him.

'All right,' Perot said, sitting down. 'I'll have to see them later. Send them to my office as soon as they arrive.' He paused. 'I'll tell them exactly what I'm going to tell y'all.'

He paused again, as if gathering his thoughts. Then he frowned and looked hard at them. 'I'm asking for volunteers for a project that might involve loss of life. At this stage I can't tell you what it's about, although you can probably guess. I want you to take five or ten minutes, or more, to

116

think about it, then come back and talk to me one at a time. Think *hard*. If you choose, *for any reason*, not to get involved, you can just say so, and no one outside this room will ever know about it. If you decide to volunteer, I'll tell you more. Now go away and think.'

They all stood up and, one by one, they left the room.

I could get killed on Central Expressway, thought Joe Poché.

He knew perfectly well what the dangerous project was: they were going to get Paul and Bill out of jail.

He had suspected as much since two-thirty a.m., when he had been woken up, at his mother-in-law's house in San Antonio, by a phone call from Pat Sculley. Sculley, the world's worst liar, had said: 'Ross asked me to call you. He wants you to come to Dallas in the morning to begin work on a study in Europe.'

Poché had said; 'Pat, why in hell are you calling me at two-thirty in the morning to tell me that Ross wants me to work on a study in Europe?'

'It is kind of important. We need to know when you can be here.'

Okay, Poché thought resignedly, it's something he can't talk about on the phone. 'My first flight is probably around six or seven o'clock in the morning.'

'Fine.'

Poché had made a plane reservation then gone back to bed. As he set his alarm clock for five a.m. he said to his wife: 'I don't know what this is all about, but I wish somebody would be straight, just for once.'

In fact he had a pretty good idea what it was all about, and his suspicions had been confirmed, later in the day, when Ralph Boulware had met him at the Coit Road bus station and, instead of taking him to EDS, had driven him to this hotel and refused to talk about what was going on.

Poché liked to think everything through, and he had had plenty of time to consider the idea of busting Paul and Bill out of jail. It made him glad, glad as hell. It reminded him of the old days, when there were only three thousand people in the whole of EDS, and they had talked about the Faith. It was their word for a whole bunch of attitudes and beliefs about how a company ought to deal with its employees. What it boiled down to was: EDS took care of its people. As long as you were giving your maximum effort to the company, it would stand by you through thick and thin: when you were sick, when you had personal or family problems, when you got yourself into any kind of trouble . . . It was a bit like a family. Poché felt good about that, although he did not talk about the feeling – he did not talk much about any of his feelings.

EDS had changed since those days. With ten thousand people instead of three thousand, the family atmosphere could not be so intense. Nobody talked about the Faith any more. But it was still there: this meeting proved it. And although his face was as expressionless as ever, Joe Poché was glad. Of *course* they would go in there and bust their friends out of jail. Poché was just happy to get a chance to be on the team.

Contrary to Coburn's expectation, Ralph Boulware did not pour scorn on the idea of a rescue. The sceptical, independent-minded Boulware was as hot for the idea as anyone.

He, too, had guessed what was going on, helped – like Poché – by Sculley's inability to lie convincingly.

Boulware and his family were staying with friends in Dallas. On New Year's Day Boulware had been doing nothing much, and his wife had asked him why he did not go to the office. He said there was nothing for him to do there. She did not buy that. Mary Boulware was the only person in the world who could bully Ralph, and in the end he went to the office. There he ran into Sculley.

'What's happening?' Boulware had asked.

'Oh, nothing,' Sculley said.

'What are you doing?'

'Making plane reservations, mostly.'

'Sculley's mood seemed strange. Boulware knew him well – in Tehran they had ridden to work together in the mornings – and his instinct told him Sculley was not telling the truth.

'Something's wrong,' Boulware said. 'What's going on?'

'There's nothing going on, Ralph!'

'What are they doing about Paul and Bill?'

'They're going through all the channels to try and get them out. The bail is thirteen million dollars, and we have to get the money into the country—'

'Bull *shit*. The whole government system, the whole judicial system has broken down over there. There ain't no channels *left*. What are y'all going to do?'

'Look, don't worry about it.'

'You guys ain't going to try to go in and get them out, are you?'

Sculley said nothing.

'Hey, count me in,' Boulware said.

'What do you mean, count you in?'

'It's obvious you're going to try to do something.'

'What do you mean?'

'Let's don't play games any more. *Count me in*.'

'Okay.'

For him it was a simple decision. Paul and Bill were his friends, and it could as easily have been Boulware in jail, in which case he would have wanted his friends to come and get him out.

There was another factor. Boulware was enormously fond of Pat Sculley. Hell, he *loved* Sculley. He also felt very protective toward him. In Boulware's opinion, Sculley really did not understand that the world was full of corruption and crime and sin: he saw what he wanted to see, a chicken in every pot, a Chevrolet on every driveway, a world of Mom and apple pie. If Sculley was going to be involved in a jailbreak, he would need Boulware to take care of him. It was an odd feeling to have about another man more or less your own age, but there it was.

That was what Boulware had thought on New Year's Day, and he felt the same today. So he went back into the

hotel room and said to Perot what he had said to Sculley:
'Count me in.'

Glenn Jackson was not afraid to die.

He knew what was going to happen after death, and he
had no fears. When the Lord wanted to call him home, why,
he was ready to go.

However, he was concerned about his family. They had
just been evacuated from Iran, and were now staying at his
mother's house in East Texas. He had not yet had time even
to start looking for a place for them all to live. If he got
involved in this, he was not going to have time to go off and
take care of family matters: it would be left to Carolyn. All
on her own, she would have to rebuild the life of the family
here in the States. She would have to find a house, get
Cheryl, Cindy and Glenn Junior into schools, buy or rent
some furniture . . .

Carolyn was kind of a dependent person. She would not
find it easy.

Plus, she was already mad at him. She had come to Dallas
with him that morning, but Sculley had told him to send her
home. She was not permitted to check in to the Hilton Inn
with her husband. That had made her angry.

But Paul and Bill had wives and families, too. 'Thou shalt
love thy neighbour as thyself.' It was in the Bible twice:
Leviticus, chapter 19, verse 18; and Matthew's Gospel,
chapter 19, verse 19. Jackson thought: If I were stuck in jail
in Tehran I'd sure love for somebody to do something for
me.

So he volunteered.

Sculley had made his choice days ago.

Before Perot started talking about a rescue Sculley had
been discussing the idea. It had first come up the day after
Paul and Bill were arrested, the day Sculley flew out of
Tehran with Joe Poché and Jim Schwebach. Sculley had
been upset at leaving Paul and Bill behind, all the more so
because Tehran had become dramatically more violent in

120

the last few days. At Christmas two Afghanis caught stealing in the bazaar had been summarily hung by a mob; and a taxi driver who tried to jump the queue at a gas station had been shot in the head by a soldier. What would they do to Americans, once they got started? It hardly bore thinking about.

On the plane Sculley had sat next to Jim Schwebach. They had agreed that Paul's and Bill's lives were in danger. Schwebach, who had experience in clandestine commando-type operations, had agreed with Sculley that it should be possible for a few determined Americans to rescue two men from an Iranian jail.

So Sculley had been surprised and delighted when, three days later, Perot had said: 'I've been thinking the same thing.'

Sculley had put his own name on the list.

He did not need time to think about it.

He volunteered.

Sculley had also put Coburn's name on the list – without telling Coburn.

Until this moment, happy-go-lucky Coburn, who lived from day to day, had not even thought about being on the team himself.

But Sculley had been right: Coburn wanted to go.

He thought: Liz won't like it.

He sighed. There were many things his wife did not like, these days.

She was clinging, he thought. She had not liked his being in the military, she did not like his having hobbies which took him away from her, and she did not like his working for a boss who felt free to call on him at all hours of the day or night for special tasks.

He had never lived the way she wanted, and it was probably too late to start now. If he went to Tehran to rescue Paul and Bill, Liz might hate him for it. But if he did not go, he would probably hate her for making him stay behind.

Sorry, Liz, he thought; here we go again.

Jim Schwebach arrived later in the afternoon but heard the same speech from Perot.

Schwebach had a highly developed sense of duty. (He had once wanted to be a priest, but two years in a Catholic seminary had soured him on organized religion.) He had spent eleven years in the Army, and had volunteered for repeated tours in Vietnam, out of that same sense of duty. In Asia he had seen a lot of people doing their jobs badly, and he knew he did his well. He had thought: if I walk away from this, someone else will do what I'm doing, but *he* will do it badly, and in consequence a man will lose his arm, his leg, or his life. I've been trained to do this, and I'm good at it, and I owe it to them to carry on doing it.

He felt much the same about the rescue of Paul and Bill. He was the only member of the proposed team who had actually done this sort of thing before. They needed him.

Anyway, he liked it. He was a fighter by disposition. Perhaps this was because he was five and a half feet tall. Fighting was his thing, it was where he lived. He did not hesitate to volunteer.

He couldn't wait to get started.

Ron Davis, the second black man on the list and the youngest of them all, did hesitate.

He arrived in Dallas early that evening and was taken straight to EDS Headquarters on Forest Lane. He had never met Perot, but had talked to him on the phone from Tehran during the evacuation. For a few days, during that period, they had kept a phone line open between Dallas and Tehran all day and all night. Someone had to sleep with the phone to his ear at the Tehran end, and frequently the job had fallen to Davis. One time Perot himself had come on the line.

'Ron, I know it's bad over there and we sure appreciate your staying. Now, is there anything I can do for you?'

Davis was surprised. He was only doing what his friends were doing, and he did not expect a special thank you. But he did have a special worry. 'My wife has conceived, and I haven't seen her for a while,' he told Perot. 'If you could have someone call her and tell her I'm okay and I'll be home as soon as possible, I'd appreciate it.'

Davis had been surprised to learn from Marva, later, that Perot had not had someone call her – he had called himself.

Now, meeting Perot for the first time, Davis was once again impressed. Perot shook his hand warmly and said: 'Hi, Ron, how are you?' just as if they had been friends for years.

However, listening to Perot's speech about 'loss of life', Davis had doubts. He wanted to know more about the rescue. He would be glad to help Paul and Bill, but he needed to be assured that the whole project would be well-organized and professional.

Perot told him about Bull Simons, and that settled it.

Perot was just so proud of them.

Every single one had volunteered.

He sat in his office. It was dark outside. He was waiting for Simons.

Smiling Jay Coburn; boyish Pat Sculley; Joe Poché, the man of iron; Ralph Boulware, tall, black and sceptical; mild-mannered Glenn Jackson; Jim Schwebach the scrapper; Ron Davis the comedian.

Every single one!

He was grateful as well as proud, for the burden they had shouldered was more his than theirs.

One way and another it had been quite a day. Simons had agreed instantly to come and help. Paul Walker, an EDS security man who had (coincidentally) served with Simons in Laos, had jumped on a plane in the middle of the night and flown to Red Bay to take care of Simons's pigs and dogs. And seven young executives had dropped everything at a moment's notice and agreed to take off for Iran to organize a jailbreak.

They were now down the hall, in the EDS boardroom, waiting for Simons, who had checked in to the Hilton Inn and gone to dinner with T. J. Marquez and Merv Stauffer.

Perot thought about Stauffer. Stocky, bespectacled, forty years old, an economics graduate, Stauffer was Perot's right-hand-man. He could remember vividly their first meeting, when he had interviewed Stauffer. A graduate of some college in Kansas, Merv had looked right off the farm, in his cheap coat and slacks. He had been wearing white socks.

During the interview, Perot had explained, as gently as he knew how, that white socks were not appropriate clothing for a business meeting.

But the socks were the only mistake Stauffer had made. He impressed Perot as being smart, tough, organized and used to hard work.

As the years went by Perot had learned that Stauffer had yet more useful talents. He had a wonderful mind for detail – something Perot lacked. He was completely unflappable. And he was a great diplomat. When EDS landed a contract, it often meant taking over an existing data processing department, with its staff. This could be difficult: the staff were naturally wary, touchy, and sometimes resentful. Merv Stauffer – calm, smiling, helpful, soft-spoken, gently determined – could smooth their feathers like no one else.

Since the late sixties he had been working directly with Perot. His speciality was taking a hazy, crazy idea from Perot's restless imagination, thinking it through, putting the pieces together and making it work. Occasionally he would conclude that the idea was impracticable – and when *Stauffer* said that, Perot began to think that maybe it *was* impracticable.

His appetite for work was enormous. Even among the workaholics on the seventh floor, Stauffer was exceptional. As well as doing whatever Perot had dreamed up in bed the previous night, he supervised Perot's real estate company and his oil company, managed Perot's investments and planned Perot's estate.

The best way to help Simons, Perot decided, would be to give him Merv Stauffer.

He wondered whether Simons had changed. It had been years since they last met. The occasion had been a banquet. Simons had told him a story.

124

During the Son Tay Raid, Simons's helicopter had landed in the wrong place. It was a compound very like the prison camp, but some four hundred yards distant, and it contained a barracks full of sleeping enemy soldiers. Awakened by the noise and the flares, the soldiers had begun to stumble out of the barracks, sleepy, half-dressed, carrying their weapons. Simons had stood outside the door, with a lighted cigar in his mouth. Beside him was a burly sergeant. As each man came through the door, he would see the glow of Simons's cigar, and hesitate. Simons would shoot him. The sergeant would heave the corpse aside, then they would wait for the next one.

Perot had been unable to resist the question: 'How many men did you kill?'

'Must have been seventy or eighty,' Simons had said in a matter-of-fact voice.

Simons had been a great soldier, but now he was a pig farmer. Was he still fit? He was sixty years old, and he had suffered a stroke even before Son Tay. Did he still have a sharp mind? Was he still a great leader of men?

He would want total control of the rescue, Perot was certain. The Colonel would do it his way or not at all. That suited Perot just fine: it was his way to hire the best man for the job then let him get on with it. But was Simons *still* the greatest rescuer in the world?

He heard voices in the outer office. They had arrived. He stood up, and Simons walked in with T. J. Marquez and Merv Stauffer.

'Colonel Simons, how are you?' said Perot. He never called Simons 'Bull' – he thought it was corny.

'Hello, Ross,' said Simons, shaking hands.

The handshake was firm. Simons was dressed casually, in khaki pants. His shirt collar was open, showing the muscles of his massive neck. He looked older: more lines in that aggressive face, more grey in the crewcut hair, which was also longer than Perot had ever seen it. But he seemed fit and hard. He still had the same deep, tobacco-roughened voice, with a faint but clear trace of a New York accent. He was carrying the folders Coburn had put together on the volunteers.

'Sit down,' said Perot. 'Did y'all have dinner?'

'We went to Dusty's,' said Stauffer.

Simons said: 'When was the last time this room was swept for bugs?'

Perot smiled. Simons was still sharp, as well as fit. Good. He replied: 'It's never been swept, Colonel.'

'From now on I want every room we use to be swept every day.'

Stauffer said: 'I'll see to that.'

Perot said: 'Whatever you need, Colonel, just tell Merv. Now, let's talk business for a minute. We ,sure appreciate you coming here to help us, and we'd like to offer you some compensation—'

'Don't even think about it,' Simons said gruffly.

'Well—'

'I don't want payment for rescuing Americans in trouble,' Simons said. 'I never got a bonus for it yet, and I don't want to start now.'

Simons was offended. The force of his displeasure filled the room. Perot backed off quickly: Simons was one of the very few people of whom he was wary.

The old warrior hasn't changed a bit, Perot thought.

Good.

'The team is waiting for you in the boardroom. I see you have the folders, but I know you'll want to make your own assessment of the men. They all know Tehran, and they all have either military experience or some skill which may be useful – but in the end the choice of the team is up to you. If for any reason you don't like these men, we'll get some more. You're in charge here.' Perot hoped Simons would not reject anyone, but he had to have the option.

Simons stood up. 'Let's go to work.'

T.J. hung back after Simons and Stauffer left. He said in a low voice: 'His wife died.'

'Lucille?' Perot had not heard. 'I'm sorry.'

'Cancer.'

126

'How did he take it, did you get an idea?'

T.J. nodded. 'Bad.'

As T.J. went out, Perot's twenty-year-old son, Ross Junior, walked in. It was common for Perot's children to drop by the office, but this time, when a secret meeting was in session in the boardroom, Perot wished his son had chosen another moment. Ross Junior must have seen Simons in the hall. The boy had met Simons before and knew who he was. By now, Perot thought, he's figured out that the only reason for Simons to be here is to organize a rescue.

Ross sat down and said: 'Hi, Dad. I've been by to see Grandmother.'

'Good,' Perot said. He looked fondly at his only son. Ross Junior was tall, broad-shouldered, slim, and a deal better-looking than his father. Girls clustered around him like flies: the fact that he was heir to a fortune was only one of the attractions. He handled it the way he handled everything: with immaculate good manners and a maturity beyond his years.

Perot said: 'You and I need to have a clear understanding about something. I expect to live to be a hundred, but if anything should happen to me, I want you to leave college and come home and take care of your mother and your sisters.'

'I would,' Ross said. 'Don't worry.'

'And if anything should happen to your mother, I want you to live at home and raise your sisters. I know it would be hard on you, but I wouldn't want you to hire people to do it. They would need *you*, a member of the family. I'm counting on you to live at home with them and see they're properly raised—'

'Dad, that's what I would have done if you'd never brought it up.'

'Good.'

The boy got up to go. Perot walked to the door with him.

Suddenly Ross put his arm around his father and said: 'Love you, Pop.'

Perot hugged him back.

He was surprised to see tears in his son's eyes.

Ross went out.

Perot sat down. He should not have been surprised by those tears: the Perots were a close family, and Ross was a warm-hearted boy.

Perot had no specific plans to go to Tehran, but he knew that if his men were going there to risk their lives, he would not be far behind. Ross Junior had known the same thing.

The whole family would support him, Perot knew. Margot might be entitled to say 'While you're risking your life for your employees, what about us?' but she would never say it. All through the prisoners-of-war campaign, when he had gone to Vietnam and Laos, when he had tried to fly into Hanoi, when the family had been forced to live with bodyguards, they had never complained, never said 'What about us?' On the contrary, they had encouraged him to do whatever he saw to be his duty.

While he sat thinking, Nancy, his eldest daughter walked in.

'Poops!' she said. It was her pet name for her father.

'Little Nan! Come in!'

She came around the desk and sat on his lap.

Perot adored Nancy. Eighteen years old, blonde, tiny but strong, she reminded him of his mother. She was determined and hard-headed, like Perot, and she probably had as much potential to be a business executive as her brother.

'I came to say goodbye – I'm going back to Vanderbilt.'

'Did you drop by Grandmother's house?'

'I sure did.'

'Good girl.'

She was in high spirits, excited about going back to school, oblivious of the tension and the talk of death here on the seventh floor.

'How about some extra funds?' she said.

Perot smile indulgently and took out his wallet. As usual, he was helpless to resist her.

She pocketed the money, hugged him, kissed his cheek,

jumped off his lap, and bounced out of the room without a care in the world.

This time there were tears in Perot's eyes.

It was like a reunion, Jay Coburn thought: the old Tehran hands in the boardroom waiting for Simons, chatting about Iran and the evacuation. There was Ralph Boulware talking at ninety miles an hour; Joe Poché sitting and thinking, looking about as animated as a robot in a sulk; Glenn Jackson saying something about rifles; Jim Schwebach smiling his lopsided smile, the smile that made you think he knew something you didn't; and Pat Sculley talking about the Son Tay Raid. They all knew, now, that they were about to meet the legendary Bull Simons. Sculley, when he had been a Ranger instructor, had taught Simons's famous raid, and he knew all about the meticulous planning, the endless rehearsals, and the fact that Simons had brought back all of his fifty-nine men alive.

The door opened and a voice said: 'All stand.'

They pushed back their chairs and stood up.

Coburn looked around.

Ron Davis walked in grinning all over his black face.

'Goddam you, Davis!' said Coburn, and they all laughed as they realized they had been fooled. Davis walked around the room slapping hands and saying hello.

That was Davis: always the clown.

Coburn looked at all of them and wondered how they would change when faced with physical danger. Combat was a funny thing, you could never predict how people would cope with it. The man you thought the bravest would crumble, and the one you expected to run scared would be solid as a rock.

Coburn would never forget what combat had done to him.

The crisis had come a couple of months after he arrived in Vietnam. He was flying support aircraft, called 'slicks' because they had no weapons systems. Six times a day he had come out of the battle zone with a full load of troops. It had been a good day: not a shot had been fired at his helicopter.

The seventh time was different.

A burst of 12.75 fire had hit the aircraft and severed the tail-rotor drive shaft.

When the main rotor of a helicopter turns, the body of the aircraft has a natural tendency to turn in the same direction. The function of the tail-rotor is to counteract this tendency. If the tail-rotor stops, the helicopter starts spinning.

Immediately after take-off, when the aircraft is only a few feet off the ground, the pilot can deal with tail-rotor loss by landing again before the spinning becomes too fast. Later, when the aircraft is at cruising height and normal flying speed, the flow of wind across the fuselage is strong enough to prevent the helicopter turning. But Coburn was at a height of 150 feet, the worst possible position, too high to land quickly but not yet travelling fast enough for the wind flow to stabilize the fuselage.

The standard procedure was a simulated engine stall. Coburn had learned and rehearsed the routine at flying school, and he went into it instinctively, but it did not work: the aircraft was already spinning too fast.

Within seconds he was so dizzy he had no idea where he was. He was unable to do anything to cushion the crash landing. The helicopter came down on its right skid (he learned afterwards) and one of the rotor blades flexed down under the impact, slicing through the fuselage and into the head of his co-pilot, who died instantly.

Coburn smelled fuel and unstrapped himself. That was when he realized he was upside down, for he fell on his head. But he got out of the aircraft, his only injury a few compressed neck vertebrae. His crew chief also survived.

The crew had been belted in, but the seven troops in the back had not. The helicopter had no doors, and the centrifugal force of the spin had thrown them out at a height of more than a hundred feet. They were all dead.

Coburn was twenty years old at the time.

A few weeks later he took a bullet in the calf, the most

vulnerable part of a helicopter pilot, who sits in an armoured seat but leaves his lower legs exposed.

He had been angry before, but now he just had the *ass*. Pissed off with being shot at, he went in to his commanding officer and demanded to be assigned to gunships so that he could kill some of those bastards down there who were trying to kill *him*.

His request was granted.

That was the point at which smiling Jay Coburn had turned into a cool-headed, cold-hearted professional soldier. He made no close friends in the Army. If someone in the unit was wounded Coburn would shrug and say: 'Well, that's what he gets combat pay for.' He suspected his comrades thought he was a little sick. He did not care. He was happy flying gunships. Every time he strapped himself in he knew he was going out there to kill or be killed. Clearing out areas in advance of ground troops, knowing that women and children and innocent civilians were getting hurt, Coburn just closed his mind and opened fire.

Eleven years later, looking back, he could think: I was an animal.

Schwebach and Poché, the two quietest men in the room, would understand: they had been there too, they knew how it had been. The others did not: Sculley, Boulware, Jackson and Davis. If this rescue turns nasty, Coburn wondered again, how will they make out?

The door opened, and Simons came in.

2

The room fell silent as Simons walked to the head of the conference table.

He's a *big* son of a bitch, Coburn thought.

T. J. Marquez and Merv Stauffer came in after Simons and sat near the door.

Simons threw a black plastic suitcase into a corner, dropped into a chair, and lit a small cigar.

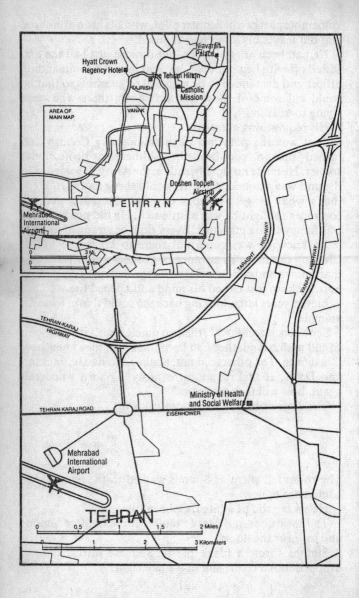

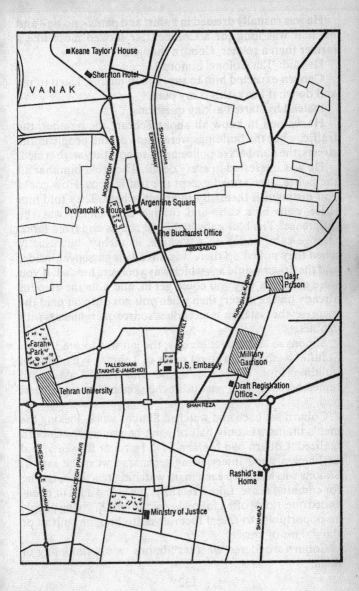

Keane Taylor's House

Sheraton Hotel

VANAK

Dvoranchik's House

Argentine Square

The Bucharest Office

ABBASABAD

Qasr Prison

Farah Park

ROOSEVELT

Military Garrison

TALLEGHANI (TAKHT-E-JAMSHID)

U.S. Embassy

Tehran University

Draft Registration Office

SHAH REZA

SHEMIRAN E-BAHMAN

MOSSADEGH (PAHLAVI)

Rashid's Home

Ministry of Justice

SHAHBAZ

MOSSADEGH (PAHLAVI)

SHAHANSHAHI EXPRESSWAY

KUROSH-E-KABIR

He was casually dressed in a shirt and pants – no tie – and his hair was long for a Colonel. He looked more like a farmer than a soldier, Coburn thought.

He said: 'I'm Colonel Simons.'

Coburn expected him to say, I'm in charge, listen to me and do what I say, this is my plan.

Instead he started asking questions.

He wanted to know all about Tehran: the weather, the traffic, what the buildings were made of, the people in the streets, the numbers of policemen and how they were armed.

He was interested in every detail. They told him that all the police were armed except the traffic cops. How could you distinguish them? By their white hats. They told him there were blue cabs and orange cabs. What was the difference? The blue cabs had fixed routes and fixed fares. Orange cabs would go anywhere, in theory, but usually when they pulled up there was already a passenger inside, and the driver would ask which way you were headed. If you were going his way you could get in, and note the amount already on the meter; then when you got out you paid the increase: the system was an endless source of arguments with cabbies.

Simons asked where, exactly, the jail was located. Merv Stauffer went to find street maps of Tehran. What did the building look like? Joe Poché and Ron Davis both remembered driving past it. Poché sketched it on an easel pad.

Coburn sat back and watched Simons work. Picking the men's brains was only half of what he was up to, Coburn realized. Coburn had been an EDS recruiter for years, and he knew a good interviewing technique when he saw it. Simons was sizing up each man, watching reactions, testing for common sense. Like a recruiter, he asked a lot of open-ended questions, often following with 'Why?', giving people an opportunity to reveal themselves, to brag or bullshit or show signs of anxiety.

Coburn wondered whether Simons would flunk any of them.

At one point he said: 'Who is prepared to die doing this?'

Nobody said a word.

'Good,' said Simons. 'I wouldn't take anyone who was planning on dying.'

The discussion went on for hours. Simons broke it up soon after midnight. It was clear by then that they did not know enough about the jail to begin planning the rescue. Coburn was deputized to find out more overnight: he would make some phone calls to Tehran.

Simons said: 'Can you ask people about the jail without letting them know why you want the information?'

'I'll be discreet,' Coburn said.

Simons turned to Merv Stauffer. 'We'll need a secure place for us all to meet. Somewhere that isn't connected with EDS.'

'What about the hotel?'

'The walls are thin.'

Stauffer considered for a moment. 'Ross has a little house at Lake Grapevine, out toward DFW airport. There won't be anyone out there swimming or fishing in this weather, that's for sure.'

Simons looked dubious.

Stauffer said: 'Why don't I drive you out there in the morning so you can look it over?'

'Okay.' Simons stood up. 'We've done all we can at this point in the game.'

They began to drift out.

As they were leaving, Simons asked Davis for a word in private.

'You ain't so goddam tough, Davis.'

Ron Davis stared at Simons in surprise.

'What makes you think you're a tough guy?' Simons said.

Davis was floored. All evening Simons had been polite, reasonable, quiet-spoken. Now he was making like he wanted to fight. What was happening?

Davis thought of his martial arts expertise, and of the three muggers he had disposed of in Tehran, but he said: 'I

133

don't consider myself a tough guy.'

Simons acted as if he had not heard. 'Against a pistol your karate is no bloody good whatsoever.'

'I guess not—'

'This team does not need any ba-ad black bastards spoiling for a fight.'

Davis began to see what this was all about. Keep cool, he told himself. 'I did not volunteer for this because I want to fight people, Colonel, I—'

'Then why *did* you volunteer?'

'Because I know Paul and Bill and their wives and children and I want to help.'

Simons nodded dismissively. 'I'll see you tomorrow.'

Davis wondered whether that meant he had passed the test.

In the afternoon on the next day, 3 January 1979, they all met at Perot's weekend house on the shore of Lake Grapevine.

The two or three other houses nearby appeared empty, as Merv Stauffer had predicted. Perot's house was screened by several acres of rough woodland, and had lawns running down to the water's edge. It was a compact wood-frame building, quite small – the garage for Perot's speedboats was bigger than the house.

The door was locked and nobody had thought to bring the keys. Schwebach picked a window lock and let them in.

There was a living-room, a couple of bedrooms, a kitchen and a bathroom. The place was cheerfully decorated in blue and white, with inexpensive furniture.

The men sat around the living-room with their maps and easel pads and magic markers and cigarettes. Coburn reported. Overnight he had spoken to Majid and two or three other people in Tehran. It had been difficult, trying to get detailed information about the jail while pretending to be only mildly curious, but he thought he had succeeded.

The jail was part of the Ministry of Justice complex which occupied a whole city block, he had learned. The jail entrance was at the rear of the block. Next to the entrance was a courtyard, separated from the street only by a twelve-foot-high fence of iron railings. This courtyard was the prisoners' exercise area. Clearly, it was also the prison's weak point.

Simons agreed.

All they had to do, then, was wait for an exercise period, get over the fence, grab Paul and Bill, bring them back over the fence, and get out of Iran.

They got down to details.

How would they get over the fence? Would they use ladders, or climb on each other's shoulders?

They would arrive in a van, they decided, and use its roof as a step. Travelling in a van rather than a car had another advantage: nobody would be able to see inside while they were driving to – and, more importantly, away from – the jail.

Joe Poché was nominated driver because he knew the streets of Tehran best.

How would they deal with the prison guards? They did not want to kill anyone. They had no quarrel with the Iranian man in the street, nor with the guards: it was not the fault of those people that Paul and Bill were unjustly imprisoned. Furthermore, if there was any killing, the subsequent hue-and-cry would be worse, making escape from Iran more hazardous.

But the prison guards would not hesitate to shoot *them*.

The best defence, Simons said, was a combination of surprise, shock and speed.

They would have the advantage of surprise. For a few seconds the prison guards would not understand what was happening.

Then the rescuers would have to do something to make the guards take cover. Shotgun fire would be best. A shotgun would make a big flash and a lot of noise, especially in a city street: the shock would cause the guards to react defensively instead of attacking the rescuers. That would given them a few more seconds.

135

With speed, those seconds might be enough.

And then they might not.

The room filled with tobacco smoke as the plan took shape. Simons sat there, chain-smoking his little cigars, listening, asking questions, guiding the discussion. This was a very democratic army, Coburn thought. As they got involved in the plan, his friends were forgetting about their wives and children, their mortgages, their lawn mowers and station wagons; forgetting, too, how outrageous was the very idea of their snatching prisoners out of a jail. Davis stopped clowning, Sculley no longer seemed boyish but became very cold and calculating. Poché wanted to talk everything to death, as usual; Boulware was sceptical, as usual.

Afternoon wore into evening. They decided the van would pull on to the pavement beside the iron railings. This sort of parking would not be in the least remarkable in Tehran, they told Simons. Simons would be sitting in the front seat, beside Poché, with a shotgun beneath his coat. He would jump out and stand in front of the van. The back door of the van would open and Ralph Boulware would get out, also with a shotgun under his coat.

So far, nothing out of the ordinary would appear to have happened.

With Simons and Boulware ready to give covering fire, Ron Davis would get out of the van, climb on the roof, step from the roof to the top of the fence, then jump down into the courtyard. Davis was chosen for this role because he was the youngest and fittest, and the jump – a twelve-foot drop – would be hard to take.

Coburn would follow Davis over the fence. He was *not* in good shape, but his face was more familiar than any other to Paul and Bill, so they would know as soon as they saw him that they were being rescued.

Next, Boulware would lower a ladder into the courtyard.

Surprise might take them this far, if they were quick; but at this point the guards were sure to react. Simons and

Boulware would now fire their shotguns into the air.

The prison guards would hit the dirt, the Iranian prisoners would run around in terrified confusion, and the rescuers would have gained a few more seconds.

What if there were interference from *outside* the jail, Simons asked – from police or soldiers in the street, revolutionary rioters or just public-spirited passers-by?

There would be two flanking guards, they decided; one at either end of the street. They would arrive in a car a few seconds before the van. They would be armed with handguns. Their job was simply to *stop* anyone who came to interfere with the rescue. Jim Schwebach and Pat Sculley were nominated. Coburn was sure Schwebach would not hesitate to shoot people if necessary; and Sculley, although he had never in his life shot anyone, had become so surprisingly ice-cool during the discussion that Coburn supposed he would be equally ruthless.

Glenn Jackson would drive the car: the question of Glenn the Baptist shooting people would not arise.

Meanwhile, in the confusion in the courtyard, Ron Davis would provide close cover, dealing with any nearby guards, while Coburn cut Paul and Bill out of the herd and urged them up the ladder. They would jump from the top of the fence to the roof of the van, then from there to the ground, and finally inside the van. Coburn would follow, then Davis.

'Hey, I'm taking the biggest risk of all,' said Davis. 'Hell, I'm first in and last out – maximum exposure.'

'No shit,' said Boulware. 'Next question.'

Simons would get into the front of the van, Boulware would jump in the back and close the door, and Poché would drive them away at top speed.

Jackson, in the car, would pick up the flanking guards, Schwebach and Sculley, and follow the van.

During the getaway, Boulware would be able to shoot through the back window of the van, and Simons would cover the road ahead. Any really serious pursuit would be taken care of by Sculley and Schwebach in the car.

At a prearranged spot they would dump the van and split up in several cars, then head for the air base at Doshen Toppeh, on the outskirts of the city. A US Air Force jet would fly them out of Iran: it would be Perot's job to arrange that somehow.

At the end of the evening they had the skeleton of a workable plan.

Before they left, Simons told them not to talk about the rescue – not to their wives, *not even to each other* – outside the lake house. They should each think up a cover story to explain why they would be going out of the US in a week or so. And, he added, looking at their full ashtrays and their ample waistlines, each man should devise his own exercise programme for getting in shape.

The rescue was no longer a zany idea in Ross Perot's mind: it was real.

Jay Coburn was the only one who made a serious effort to deceive his wife.

He went back to the Hilton Inn and called Liz. 'Hi, honey.'

'Hi, Jay! Where are you?'

'I'm in Paris . . .'.

Joe Poché also called his wife from the Hilton.

'Where are you?' she asked him.

'I'm in Dallas.'

'What are you doing?'

'Working at EDS, of course.'

'Joe, EDS in Dallas has been calling *me* to ask where you are!'

Poché realized that someone who was not in on the secret of the rescue team had been trying to locate him. 'I'm not working with those guys, I'm working directly with Ross. Somebody forgot to tell someone else, that's all.'

'What are you working on?'

'It has to do with some things that have to be done for Paul and Bill.'

138

'Oh . . .'

When Boulware got back to the home of the friends with whom his family was staying, his daughters, Stacy Elaine and Kecia Nicole, were asleep. His wife said: 'How was your day?'

I've been planning a jailbreak, Boulware thought. He said: 'Oh, okay.'

She looked at him strangely. 'Well, what did you do?'

'Nothing much.'

'For someone who was doing *nothing much*, you've been pretty busy. I called two or three times – they said they couldn't find you.'

'I was around. Hey, I think I'd like a beer.'

Mary Boulware was a warm, open woman to whom deceit was foreign. She was also intelligent. But she knew that Ralph had some firm ideas about the roles of husband and wife. The ideas might be old-fashioned but they worked in this marriage. If there was an area of his business life that he didn't want to tell her about, well, she wasn't about to fight him over it.

'One beer, coming up . . .'

Jim Schwebach did not try to fool his wife Rachel. She had already outguessed him. When Schwebach had got the original call from Pat Sculley, Rachel had asked: 'Who was that?'

'That was Pat Sculley in Dallas. They want me to go down there and work on a study in Europe.'

Rachel had known Jim for almost twenty years – they had started dating when he was sixteen, she eighteen – and she could read his mind. She said: 'They're going back over there to get those guys out of jail.'

Schwebach said feebly: 'Rachel, you don't understand, I'm out of that line of business, I don't do that any more.'

'That's what you're going to do . . .'

Pat Sculley could not lie successfully even to his colleagues, and with his wife he did not try. He told Mary everything.

Ross Perot told Margot everything.

And even Simons, who had no wife to pester him, broke security by telling his brother Stanley in New Jersey . . .

It proved equally impossible to keep the rescue plan from other senior executives at EDS. The first to figure it all out was Keane Taylor, the tall, irritable, well-dressed ex-Marine whom Perot had turned around in Frankfurt and sent back to Tehran.

Since that New Year's Day, when Perot had said: 'I'm sending you back to do *something very important*,' Taylor had been sure that a secret operation was being planned; and it did not take him long to figure out who was doing it.

One day, on the phone from Tehran to Dallas, he had asked for Ralph Boulware.

'Boulware's not here,' he was told.

'When will he be back?'

'We're not sure.'

Taylor, never a man to suffer fools gladly, had raised his voice. 'So, *where* has he gone?'

'We're not sure.'

'What do you *mean*, you're not sure?'

'He's on vacation.'

Taylor had known Boulware for years. It had been Taylor who gave Boulware his first management opportunity. They were drinking partners. Many times Taylor, drinking himself sober with Ralph in the early hours of the morning, had looked around and realized his was the only white face in an all-black bar. Those nights they would stagger back to whichever of their homes was nearest, and the unlucky wife who welcomed them would call the other and say: 'It's okay, they're here.'

Yes, Taylor knew Boulware; and he found it hard to believe that Ralph would go on vacation while Paul and Bill were still in jail.

Next day he asked for Pat Sculley, and got the same runaround.

Boulware *and* Sculley on vacation while Paul and Bill

140

were in jail?'

Bullshit.

Next day he asked for Coburn.

Same story.

It was beginning to make sense: Coburn had been with Perot when Perot sent Taylor back to Tehran. Coburn, Director of Personnel, evacuation mastermind, would be the right choice to organize a secret operation.

Taylor and Rich Gallagher, the other EDS man still in Tehran, started making a list.

Boulware, Sculley, Coburn, Ron Davis, Jim Schwebach and Joe Poché were all 'on vacation'.

That group had a few things in common.

When Paul Chiapparone had first come to Tehran he found that EDS's operation there was not organized to his liking: it had been too loose, too casual, too Persian. The Ministry contract had not been running to time. Paul had brought in a number of tough, down-to-earth EDS troubleshooters and together they had knocked the business back into shape. Taylor himself had been one of Paul's tough guys. So had Bill Gaylord. And Coburn, and Sculley, and Boulware, and all the guys who were now 'on vacation'.

The other thing they had in common was that they were all members of the EDS Tehran Roman Catholic Sunday Brunch Poker School. Like Paul and Bill, like Taylor himself, they were Catholics, with the exception of Joe Poché (and of Glenn Jackson, the only rescue team member Taylor failed to spot). Each Sunday they had met at the Catholic Mission in Tehran. After the service they would all go to the house of one of them for brunch. And while the wives were cooking and the children playing, the men would get into a poker game.

There was nothing like poker for revealing a man's true character.

If, as Taylor and Gallagher now suspected, Perot had asked Coburn to put together a team of completely trustworthy men, then Coburn was sure to have picked them

141

from the poker school.

'Vacation, my *ass*,' Taylor said to Gallagher. 'This is a rescue team.'

The rescue team returned to the lake house on the morning of 4 January and went over the whole plan again.

Simons had endless patience for detail, and he was determined to prepare for every possible snag that anyone could dream up. He was much helped by Joe Poché, whose tireless questioning – wearying though it was, to Coburn at least – was in fact highly creative, and led to numerous improvements of the rescue scenario.

First, Simons was dissatisfied with the arrangements for protecting the rescue team's flanks. The idea of Schwebach and Sculley, short but deadly, just plain *shooting* anyone who tried to interfere was crude. It would be better to have some kind of diversion, to distract any police or military types who might be nearby. Schwebach suggested setting fire to a car down the street from the jail. Simons was not sure that would be enough – he wanted to blow up a whole building. Anyway, Schwebach was given the job of designing a time bomb.

They thought of a small precaution which would shave a second or two off the time for which they would be exposed. Simons would get out of the van some distance from the jail and walk up to the fence. If all was clear he would give a hand signal for the van to approach.

Another weak element of the plan was the business of getting out of the van and climbing on its roof. All that jumping out and scrambling up would use precious seconds. And would Paul and Bill, after weeks in prison, be fit enough to climb a ladder and jump off the roof of a van?

All sorts of solutions were canvassed – an extra ladder, a mattress on the ground, grab handles on the roof – but in the end the team came up with a simple solution: they would cut a hole in the roof of the van and get in and out through that. Another little refinement, for those who had to jump back down through the hole, was a mattress on the floor of the van to soften their landing.

The getaway journey would give them time to alter their appearances. In Tehran they planned to wear jeans and casual jackets, and they were all beginning to grow beards and moustaches to look less conspicuous there; but in the van they would carry business suits and electric shavers, and before switching to the cars they would all shave and change their clothes.

Ralph Boulware, independent as ever, did not want to wear jeans and a casual jacket beforehand. In a business suit with a white shirt and a tie he felt comfortable and able to assert himself, especially in Tehran where good western clothing labelled a man as a member of the dominant class in society. Simons calmly gave his assent: the most important thing, he said, was for everyone to feel comfortable and confident during the operation.

At the Doshen Toppeh air base, from which they planned to leave in an Air Force jet, there were both American and Iranian planes and personnel. The Americans would of course be expecting them, but what if the Iranian sentries at the entrance gave them a hard time? They would all carry forged military identity cards, they decided. Some wives of EDS executives had worked for the military in Tehran and still had their ID cards: Merv Stauffer would get hold of one and use it as a model for the forgeries.

Throughout all this Simons was still very low-key, Coburn observed. Chain-smoking his cigars (Boulware told him: 'Don't worry about getting shot, you're going to die of cancer!') he did little more than ask questions. The plans were made in a round-table discussion, with everyone contributing, and decisions were arrived at by mutual agreement. Yet Coburn found himself coming to respect Simons more and more. The man was knowledgeable, intelligent, painstaking and imaginative. He also had a sense of humour.

Coburn could see that the others were also beginning to

get the measure of Simons. If anyone asked a dumb question, Simons would give a sharp answer. In consequence, they would hesitate before asking a question, and wonder what his reaction might be. In this way he was getting them to think like him.

Once on that second day at the lake house they felt the full force of his displeasure. It was, not surprisingly, young Ron Davis who angered him.

They were a humorous bunch, and Davis was the funniest. Coburn approved of that: laughter helped to ease the tension in an operation such at this. He suspected Simons felt the same. But one time Davis went too far.

Simons had a pack of cigars on the floor beside his chair, and five more packs out in the kitchen. Davis, getting to like Simons and characteristically making no secret of it, said with genuine concern: 'Colonel, you smoke too many cigars, it's bad for your health.'

By way of reply he got the Simons Look, but he ignored the warning.

A few minutes later he went into the kitchen and hid the five packs of cigars in the dishwasher.

When Simons finished the first pack he went looking for the rest and could not find them. He could not operate without tobacco. He was about to get in a car and go to a store when Davis opened the dishwasher and said: 'I have your cigars here.'

'You keep those, goddam it,' Simons growled, and he went out.

When he came back with another five packs he said to Davis: 'These are mine. Keep your goddam hands off them.'

Davis felt like a child who had been put in the corner. It was the first and last prank he played on Colonel Simons.

While the discussion went on, Jim Schwebach sat on the floor, trying to make a bomb.

To smuggle a bomb, or even just its component parts, through Iranian customs would have been dangerous – 'That's a risk we don't have to take,' Simons said – so

Schwebach had to design a device which could be assembled from ingredients readily available in Tehran.

The idea of blowing up a building was dropped: it was too ambitious and would probably kill innocent people. They would make do with a blazing car as a diversion. Schwebach knew how to make 'instant napalm' from gasoline, soap flakes and a little oil. The timer and the fuse were his two problems. In the States he would have used an electrical timer connected with a toy rocket motor; but in Tehran he would be restricted to more primitive mechanisms.

Schwebach enjoyed the challenge. He liked fooling around with anything mechanical: his hobby was an ugly-looking stripped-down '73 Oldsmobile Cutlass that went like a bullet out of a gun.

At first he experimented with an old-fashioned clockwork stove-top timer which used a striker to hit a bell. He attached a phosphorus match to the striker and substituted a piece of sandpaper for the bell, to ignite the match. The match in turn would light a mechanical fuse.

The system was unreliable, and caused great hilarity among the rest of team, who jeered and laughed every time the match failed to ignite.

In the end Schweback settled on the oldest timing device of all: a candle.

He test-burned a candle to see how long it took to burn down one inch, then he cut another candle off at the right length for fifteen minutes.

Next he scraped the heads off several old-fashioned phosphorus matches and ground up the inflammable material into a powder. This he packed tightly into a piece of aluminium kitchen foil. Then he stuck the foil into the base of the candle. When the candle burned all the way down, it heated the aluminium foil and the ground-up match-heads exploded. The foil was thinner at the bottom so that the explosion would travel downward.

The candle, with this primitive but reliable fuse in its base, was set into the neck of a plastic jar, about the size of a hip flask, full of jellied gasoline.

145

'You light the candle and walk away from it,' Schwebach told them when his design was complete. 'Fifteen minutes later you've got a nice little fire going.'

And any police, soldiers, revolutionaries or passers-by – plus, quite possibly, some of the prison guards – would have their attention fixed on a blazing automobile three hundred yards up the street while Ron Davis and Jay Coburn were jumping over the fence into the prison courtyard.

That day they moved out of the Hilton Inn. Coburn slept at the lake house, and the others checked in to the Airport Marina – which was closer to Lake Grapevine – all except Ralph Boulware, who insisted on going home to his family.

They spent the next four days training, buying equipment, practising their shooting, rehearsing the jailbreak, and further refining the plan.

Shotguns could be bought in Tehran, but the only kind of ammunition allowed by the Shah was birdshot. However, Simons was expert at reloading ammunition, so they decided to smuggle their own shot into Iran.

The trouble with putting buckshot into birdshot slugs would be that they would get relatively few shot into the smaller slugs: the ammunition would have great penetration but little spread. They decided to use No 2 shot, which would spread wide enough to knock down more than one man at a time, but had enough penetration to smash the windscreen of a pursuing car.

In case things turned really nasty, each member of the team would also carry a Walther PPK in a holster. Merv Stauffer got Bob Snyder, head of security at EDS and a man who knew when not to ask questions, to buy the PPKs at Ray's Sporting Goods in Dallas. Schwebach had the job of figuring out how to smuggle the guns into Iran.

Stauffer inquired which US airports did *not* fluoroscope outgoing baggage: one was Kennedy.

Schwebach bought two Vuitton trunks, deeper than ordinary suitcases, with reinforced corners and hard sides. With Coburn, Davis and Jackson he went to the woodwork

146

shop at Perot's Dallas home and experimented with ways of constructing false bottoms in the cases.

Schwebach was perfectly happy about carrying guns through Iranian customs in a false-bottom case. 'If you know how customs people work, you don't get stopped,' he said. His confidence was not shared by the rest of the team. In case he did get stopped and the guns were found, there was a fall-back plan. He would say the case was not his. He would return to the baggage claim area and there, sure enough, would be another Vuitton trunk just like the first, but full of personal belongings and containing no guns.

Once the team was in Tehran they would have to communicate with Dallas by phone. Coburn was quite sure that Iranians bugged the phone lines, so the team developed a simple code.

GR meant A, GS meant B, GT meant C, and so on through GZ which meant I; then HA meant J, HB meant K, through HR which meant Z. Numbers one through nine were IA through II; zero was IJ.

They would use the military alphabet, in which A is called Alpha, B is Bravo, C is Charlie and so on.

For speed, only key words would be coded. The sentence 'He is with EDS' would therefore become 'He is with Golf Victor Golf Uniform Hotel Kilo.'

Only three copies of the key to the code were made. Simons gave one to Merv Stauffer, who would be the team's contact here in Dallas. He gave the other two to Jay Coburn and Pat Sculley, who – though nothing was said formally – were emerging as his lieutenants.

The code would prevent an accidental leak through a casual phone tap, but – as computer men knew better than anyone – such a simple letter cipher could be broken by an expert in a few minutes. As a further precaution, therefore, certain common words had special code groups: Paul was AG, Bill was AH, the American Embassy was GC, and Tehran was AU. Perot was always referred to as The Chairman, guns were tapes, the prison was The Data Centre, Kuwait was Oil Town, Istanbul was Resort, and the attack on the prison was Plan A. Everyone had to memorize these special code words.

If anyone were questioned about the code he was to say that it was used to abbreviate teletype messages.

The code name for the whole rescue was Operation Hotfoot. It was an acronym, dreamed up by Ron Davis: Help Our Two Friends Out of Tehran. Simons was tickled by that. 'Hotfoot has been used so many times for operations,' he said, 'and this is the first time it's ever been appropriate.'

They rehearsed the attack on the prison at least a hundred times.

In the grounds of the lake house, Schwebach and Davis nailed up a plank between two trees at a height of twelve feet, to represent the courtyard fence. Merv Stauffer brought them a van borrowed from EDS security.

Time and time again Simons walked up to the 'fence' and gave a hand signal; Poché drove the van up and stopped it at the fence; Boulware jumped out of the back; Davis got on the roof and jumped over the fence; Coburn followed; Boulware climbed on the roof and lowered the ladder into the 'courtyard'; 'Paul' and 'Bill' – played by Schwebach and Sculley, who did not need to rehearse their roles as flanking guards – came up the ladder and over the fence, followed by Coburn and then Davis; everyone scrambled into the van; and Poché drove off at top speed.

Sometimes they switched roles so that each man learned how to do everyone else's job. They prioritized tasks so that, if one of them dropped out, wounded or for any other reason, they knew automatically who would take his place. Schweback and Sculley, playing the parts of Paul and Bill, sometimes acted sick and had to be carried up the ladder and over the fence.

The advantage of physical fitness became apparent during the rehearsals. Davis could come back over the fence in a second and a half, touching the ladder twice: nobody else could do it anywhere near that fast.

One time Davis went over too fast and landed awkwardly

on the frozen ground, straining his shoulder. The injury was not serious but it gave Simons an idea. Davis would travel to Tehran with his arm in a sling, carrying a bean bag for exercise. The bag would be weighted with No 2 shot.

Simons timed the rescue, from the moment the van stopped at the fence to the moment it pulled away with everyone inside. In the end, according to his stopwatch, they could do it in under thirty seconds.

They practised with the Walther PPKs at the Garland Public Shooting Range. They told the range operator that they were security men from all over the country on a course in Dallas, and they had to get their target practice in before they could go home. He did not believe them, especially after T. J. Marquez turned up looking just like a Mafia chieftain in a movie, with his black coat and black hat, and took ten Walther PPKs and five thousand rounds of ammunition out of the trunk of his black Lincoln.

After a little practice they could all shoot reasonably well except Davis. Simons suggested he try shooting lying down, since that was the position he would be in when he was in the courtyard; and he found he could do much better that way.

It was bitterly cold out in the open, and they all huddled in a little shack, trying to get warm, while they were not shooting – all except Simons, who stayed outside all day long, as if he were made of stone.

He was not made of stone: when he got into Merv Stauffer's car at the end of the day he said: 'Jesus *Christ* it's cold.'

He had begun to needle them about how soft they were. They were always talking about where they would go to eat and what they would order, he said. When *he* was hungry he would open a can. He would laugh at someone for nursing a drink: when *he* was thirsty he would fill a tumbler with water and drink it straight down, saying: 'I didn't pour it to look at it.' He showed them how he could shoot, one time: every bullet in the centre of the target. Once Coburn saw him with his shirt off: his physique would have been impressive on a man twenty years younger.

149

It was a tough-guy act, the whole performance. What was peculiar was that none of them ever laughed at it. With Simons, it was the real thing.

One evening at the lake house he showed them the best way to kill a man quickly and silently.

He had ordered – and Merv Stauffer had purchased – Gerber knives for each of them, short stabbing weapons with a narrow two-edge blade.

'It's kind of small,' said Davis, looking at his. 'Is it long enough?'

'It is unless you want to sharpen it when it comes out the other side,' Simons said.

He showed them the exact spot in the small of Glenn Jackson's back where the kidney was located. 'A single stab, right there, is lethal,' he said.

'Wouldn't he scream?' Davis asked.

'It hurts so bad he can't make a sound.'

While Simons was demonstrating Merv Stauffer had come in, and now he stood in the doorway, open-mouthed, with a McDonald's paper sack in either arm. Simons saw him and said: 'Look at this guy – he can't make a sound and nobody's stuck him yet.'

Merv laughed and started handing round the food. 'You know what the McDonald's girl said to me, in a completely empty restaurant, when I asked for thirty hamburgers and thirty orders of fries?'

'What?'

'What they always say – "Is this to eat here or to go?"'

Simons just loved working for private enterprise.

One of his biggest headaches in the Army had always been supplies. Even planning the Son Tay Raid, an operation in which the President himself was personally interested, it had seemed as if he had to fill in six requisition forms and get approval from twelve generals every time he needed a new pencil. Then, when all the paperwork was done, he would find that the items were out of stock, or there was a four-month wait for delivery, or – worst of all – when the stuff came it did not work. Twenty-two per cent of the blasting caps he ordered misfired. He had tried to get night-sights for his raiders. He learned that the Army had spent seventeen years trying to develop a night-sight, but by 1970 all they had were six hand-built prototypes. Then he discovered a perfectly good British-made night-sight available from Armalite Corporation for $49.50, and that was what the Son Tay Raiders took to Vietnam.

At EDS there were no forms to be filled and no permissions to be sought, at least not for Simons: he told Merv Stauffer what he needed and Stauffer got it, usually the same day. He asked for, and got, ten Walther PPKs and ten thousand rounds of ammunition; a selection of holsters, both left-handed and right-handed, in different styles so the men could pick the kind they felt most comfortable with; shotgun ammunition reloading kits in 12-gauge, 16-gauge and 20-gauge; and cold-weather clothes for the team including coats, mittens, shirts, socks and woollen stocking caps. One day he asked for a hundred thousand dollars in cash: two hours later T. J. Marquez arrived at the lake house with the money in an envelope.

It was different from the Army in other ways. His men were not soldiers who could be bullied into submission: they were some of the brightest young corporate executives in the United States. He had realized from the start that he could not *assume* command. He had to earn their loyalty.

These men would obey an order if they agreed with it. If not, they would discuss it. That was fine in the boardroom but useless on the battlefield.

They were squeamish, too. The first time they talked about setting fire to a car as a diversion, someone had objected on the grounds that innocent passers-by might get hurt. Simons needled them about their Boy Scout morality, saying they were afraid of losing their merit badges, and calling them 'you Jack Armstrongs' after the too-good-to-be-true radio character who went around solving crimes and helping old ladies cross the road.

151

They also had a tendency to forget the seriousness of what they were doing. There was a lot of joking and a certain amount of horseplay, particularly from young Ron Davis. A measure of humour was useful in a team on a dangerous mission, but sometimes Simons had to put a stop to it and bring them back to reality with a sharp remark.

He gave them all the opportunity to back out at any time. He got Ron Davis on his own again and said: 'You're going to be the first one over the fence – don't you have some reservations about that?'

'Yeah.'

'Good thing you do, otherwise I wouldn't take you. Suppose Paul and Bill don't come right away? Suppose they figure that if they head for the fence they'll get shot? You'll be stuck there and the guards will see you. You'll be in bad trouble.'

'Yeah.'

'Me, I'm sixty years old, I've lived my life. Hell, I don't have a thing to lose. But you're a young man – and Marva's pregnant, isn't she?'

'Yeah.'

'Are you really sure you want to do this?'

'Yeah.'

He worked on them all. There was no point in his *telling* them that his military judgement was better than theirs: they had to come to that conclusion themselves. Similarly, his tough-guy act was intended to let them know that from now on such things as keeping warm, eating, drinking, and worrying about innocent bystanders would not occupy much of their time or attention. The shooting practice and the knife lesson also had a hidden purpose: the last thing Simons wanted was any killing on this operation, but learning how to kill reminded the men that the rescue could be a life-and-death affair.

The biggest element in his psychological campaign was the endless practising of the assault on the jail. Simons was quite sure that the jail would *not* be exactly as Coburn had described it, and that the plan would have to be modified. A

152

raid *never* went precisely according to the scenario – as he knew better than most.

The rehearsals for the Son Tay Raid had gone on for weeks. A complete replica of the prison camp had been built, out of two-by-four timbers and target cloth, at Eglin Air Base in Florida. The bloody thing had to be dismantled every morning before dawn and put up again at night, because the Russian reconnaissance satellite Cosmos 355 passed over Florida twice every twenty-four hours. But it had been a beautiful thing: every goddam tree and ditch in the Son Tay prison camp had been reproduced in the mock-up. And then, after all those rehearsals, when they did it for real one of the helicopters – the one Simons was in – had landed in the wrong place.

Simons would never forget the moment he realized the mistake. His helicopter was taking off again, having discharged the raiders. A startled Vietnamese guard emerged from a foxhole and Simons shot him in the chest. Shooting broke out, a flare went up, and Simons saw that the buildings surrounding him were not the buildings of the Son Tay camp. 'Get that fucking chopper back in here!' he yelled to his radio operator. He told a sergeant to turn on a strobe light to mark the landing zone.

He knew where they were: four hundred yards from Son Tay, in a compound marked on intelligence maps as a school. This was no school. There were enemy troops everywhere. It was a barracks, and Simons realized that his helicopter pilot's mistake had been a lucky one, for now he was able to launch a pre-emptive attack and wipe out a concentration of enemy troops who might otherwise have jeopardized the whole operation.

That was the night he stood outside a barracks and shot eighty men in their underwear.

No, an operation never went exactly according to plan. But becoming proficient at executing the scenario was only half the purpose of rehearsals anyway. The other half – and, in the case of the EDS men, the important half – was learning to work together as a team. Oh, they were already

153

terrific as an *intellectual* team – give them each an office and a secretary and a telephone and they would computerize the world – but working together with their hands and their bodies was different. When they had started on 3 January, they would have had trouble launching a rowboat as a team. Five days later they were a machine.

And that was all that could be done here in Texas. Now they had to take a look at the real-life jail.

It was time to go to Tehran.

Simons told Stauffer he wanted to meet with Perot again.

3

While the rescue team was in training, President Carter got his last chance of preventing a bloody revolution in Iran.

And he blew it.

This is how it happened . . .

Ambassador William Sullivan went to bed content on the night of 4 January in his private apartment within the large, cool residence in the Embassy compound at the corner of Roosevelt and Takht-e-Jamshid avenues in Tehran.

Sullivan's boss, Secretary of State Cyrus Vance, had been busy with the Camp David negotiations all through November and December, but now he was back in Washington and concentrating on Iran – and boy, did it show. Vagueness and vacillation had ended. The cables containing Sullivan's instructions had become crisp and decisive. Most importantly, the United States at last had a strategy for dealing with the crisis: they were going to talk to the Ayatollah Khomeini.

It was Sullivan's own idea. He was now sure that the Shah would soon leave Iran and Khomeini would return in triumph. His job, he believed, was to preserve America's relationship with Iran through the change of government, so that when it was all over Iran would still be a stronghold of American influence in the Middle East. The way to do that was to help the Iranian armed forces to stay intact and to continue American military aid to any new regime.

Sullivan had called Vance on the secure telephone link and told him just that. The US should send an emissary to Paris to see the Ayatollah, Sullivan had urged. Khomeini should be told that the main concern of the US was to preserve the territorial integrity of Iran and deflect Soviet influence; that the Americans did not want to see a pitched battle in Iran between the Army and the Islamic revolutionaries; and that, once the Ayatollah was in power, the US would offer him the same military assistance and arms sales it had given the Shah.

It was a bold plan. There would be those who would accuse the US of abandoning a friend. But Sullivan was sure it was time for the Americans to cut their losses with the Shah and look to the future.

To his intense satisfaction, Vance had agreed.

So had the Shah. Weary, apathetic, and no longer willing to shed blood in order to stay in power, the Shah had not even put up a show of reluctance.

Vance had nominated, as his emissary to the Ayatollah, Theodore H. Eliot, a senior diplomat who had served as economic counsellor in Tehran and spoke Farsi fluently. Sullivan was delighted with the choice.

Ted Eliot was scheduled to arrive in Paris in two days' time, on 6 January.

In one of the guest bedrooms at the ambassadorial Residence, Air Force General Robert 'Dutch' Huyser was also going to bed. Sullivan was not as enthusiastic about the Huyser Mission as he was about the Eliot Mission. Dutch Huyser, the deputy commander (under Haig) of US forces in Europe, had arrived yesterday to persuade Iranian generals to support the new Bakhtiar government in Tehran. Sullivan knew Huyser. He was a fine soldier, but no diplomat. He spoke no Farsi and he did not know Iran. But even if he had been ideally qualified his task would have been hopeless. The Bakhtiar government had failed to gain the support even of the moderates, and Shahpour Bakhtiar himself had

155

been expelled from the centrist National Front party merely for accepting the Shah's invitation to form a government. Meanwhile the army which Huyser was trying futilely to swing to Bakhtiar continued to weaken as soldiers in their thousands deserted and joined the revolutionary mobs in the streets. The best Huyser could hope for was to hold the army together a little longer, while Eliot in Paris arranged for the peaceful return of the Ayatollah.

If it worked it would be a great achievement for Sullivan, something any diplomat could be proud of for the rest of his life: his plan would have strengthened the country *and* saved lives.

As he went to sleep, there was just one worry nagging at the back of his mind. The Eliot Mission, for which he had such high hopes, was a State Department scheme, identified in Washington with Secretary of State Vance. The Huyser Mission was the idea of Zbigniew Brzezinski, the National Security Advisor. The enmity between Vance and Brzezinski was notorious. And at this moment Brzezinski, after the summit meeting in Guadeloupe, was deep-sea fishing in the Caribbean with President Carter. As they sailed over the clear blue sea, what was Brzezinski whispering in the President's ear?

The phone woke Sullivan in the early hours of the morning.

It was the duty officer, calling from the communications vault in the Embassy building just a few yards away. An urgent cable had arrived from Washington. The Ambassador might want to read it immediately.

Sullivan got out of bed and walked across the lawns to the Embassy, full of foreboding.

The cable said that the Eliot Mission was cancelled.

The decision had been taken by the President. Sullivan's comments on the change of plan were *not* invited. He was instructed to tell the Shah that the United States Government no longer intended to hold talks with the Ayatollah Khomeini.

Sullivan was heartbroken.

156

This was the end of America's influence in Iran. It also meant that Sullivan personally had lost his chance of distinguishing himself as Ambassador by preventing a bloody civil war.

He sent an angry message back to Vance, saying the President had made a gross mistake and should reconsider.

He went back to bed, but he could not sleep.

In the morning another cable informed him that the President's decision would stand.

Wearily, Sullivan made his way up the hill to the palace to tell the Shah.

The Shah appeared drawn and tense that morning. He and Sullivan sat down and drank the inevitable cup of tea. Then Sullivan told him that President Carter had cancelled the Eliot Mission.

The Shah was upset. 'But *why* have they cancelled it?' he said agitatedly.

'I don't know,' Sullivan replied.

'But how do they expect to influence those people if they won't even talk to them?'

'I don't know.'

'Then what does Washington intend to do now?' asked the Shah, throwing up his hands in despair.

'I don't know,' said Sullivan.

4

'Ross, this is *idiotic*,' Tom Luce said loudly. 'You're going to destroy the company and you're going to destroy your*self*.'

Perot looked at his lawyer. They were sitting in Perot's office. The door was closed.

Luce was not the first to say this. During the week, as the news had spread through the seventh floor, several of Perot's top executives had come in to tell him that a rescue team was a foolhardy and dangerous notion, and he should drop the idea. 'Stop worrying,' Perot had told them. 'Just concentrate on what *you* have to do.'

Tom Luce was characteristically vociferous. Wearing an aggressive scowl and a courtroom manner, he argued his case as if a jury were listening.

'I can only advise you on the legal situation, but I'm here to tell you that this rescue can cause more problems, and *worse* problems, than you've got now. Hell, Ross, I can't make a *list* of the laws you're going to break!'

'Try,' said Perot.

'You'll have a mercenary army – which is illegal here, in Iran, and in every country the team would pass through. Anywhere they go they'd be liable to criminal penalties and you could have ten men in jail instead of two.

'But it's worse than that. Your men would be in a position much worse than soldiers in battle – international laws and the Geneva convention, which protect soldiers in uniform, would not protect the rescue team.

'If they get captured in Iran . . . Ross, they'll be *shot*. If they get captured in any country that has an extradition treaty with Iran, they'll be sent back and shot. Instead of two innocent employees in jail, you could have eight *guilty* employees *dead*.

'And if that happens the families of the dead men may turn on you – understandably, because this whole thing will look *stupid*. The widows will have *huge* claims against EDS in the American courts. They could bankrupt the company. Think of the ten thousand people who would be out of a job if that happened. Think of yourself – Ross, there might even be criminal charges against you which could put *you* in jail!'

Perot said calmly: 'I appreciate your advice, Tom.'

Luce stared at him. 'I'm not getting through to you, am I?'

Perot smiled. 'Sure you are. But if you go through life worrying about all the bad things that can happen, you soon convince yourself that it's best to do nothing at all.'

The truth was that Perot knew something Luce did not.

Ross Perot was lucky.

All his life he had been lucky.

As a twelve-year-old boy he had had a paper route in the

poor black district of Texarkana. The Texarkana Gazette cost twenty-five cents a week in those days, and on Sundays, when he collected the money, he would end up with forty or fifty dollars in quarters in his purse. And every Sunday, somewhere along the route, some poor man who had spent his week's wages in the bar the previous night would try to take the money from little Ross. This was why no other boy would deliver papers in that district. But Ross was never scared. He was on a horse; the attempts were never very determined; and he was lucky. He never lost his money.

He had been lucky again in getting admitted to the Naval Academy at Annapolis. Applicants had to be sponsored by a Senator or a Congressman, and of course the Perot family did not have the right contacts. Anyway, young Ross had never even *seen* the sea – the farthest he had ever travelled was to Dallas, 180 miles away. But there was a young man in Texarkana called Josh Morriss Junior who had been to Annapolis and told Ross all about it, and Ross had fallen in love with the Navy without ever seeing a ship. So he just kept writing to Senators begging for sponsorship. He succeeded – as he would many times during later life – because he was too dumb to know it was impossible.

It was not until many years later that he found out how it had happened. One day back in 1949 Senator W. Lee O'Daniel was clearing out his desk: it was the end of his term and he was not going to run again. An aide said: 'Senator, we have an unfilled appointment to the Naval Academy.'

'Does anyone want it?' the Senator said.

'Well, we've got this boy from Texarkana who's been trying for years . . .'

'Give it to him,' said the Senator.

The way Perot heard the story, his name was never actually mentioned during the conversation.

He had been lucky once again in setting up EDS when he did. As a computer salesman for IBM, he realized that his customers did not always make the best use of the machines he sold them. Data processing was a new and specialized skill. The banks were good at banking, the insurance

159

companies were good at insurance, the manufacturers were good at manufacturing – and the computer men were good at data processing. The customer did not want the *machine*, he wanted the fast, cheap information it could provide. Yet, too often, the customers spent so much time creating his new data processing department and learning how to use the machine that his computer caused him trouble and expense instead of saving them. Perot's idea was to sell a total package – a complete data processing department with machinery, software and staff. The customer had only to say, in simple language, what information he needed, and EDS would give it to him. Then he could get on with what he was good at – banking, insurance or manufacturing.

IBM turned down Perot's idea. It was a good concept but the pickings would be small. Out of every dollar spent on data processing, eighty cents went into hardware – the machinery – and only twenty cents into software, which was what Perot wanted to sell. IBM did not want to chase pennies under the table.

So Perot drew a thousand dollars out of his savings and started up on his own. Over the next decade the proportions changed until software was taking seventy cents of every data-processing dollar, and Perot became one of the richest self-made men in the world.

The chairman of IBM, Tom Watson, met Perot in a restaurant one day and said: 'I just want to know one thing, Ross. Did you foresee that the ratio would change?'

'No,' said Perot. 'The twenty cents looked good enough to me.'

Yes, he was lucky; but he had to give his luck room to operate. It was no good sitting in a corner being careful. You never got the chance to be lucky unless you took risks. All his life Perot had taken risks.

This one just happened to be the biggest.

Merv Stauffer walked into the office. 'Ready to go?' he said.

'Yes.'

Perot got up and the two men left the office. They went

down in the elevator and got into Stauffer's car, a brand-new four-door Lincoln Versailles. Perot read the nameplate on the dashboard: 'Merv and Helen Stauffer.' The interior of the car stank of Simons's cigars.

'He's waiting for you,' Stauffer said.

'Good.'

Perot's oil company, Petrus, had offices in the next building along Forest Lane. Merv had already taken Simons there, then come for Perot. Afterwards he would take Perot back to EDS then return for Simons. The object of the exercise was secrecy: as few people as possible were to see Simons and Perot together.

In the last six days, while Simons and the rescue team had been doing their thing out at Lake Grapevine, the prospects of a legal solution to the problem of Paul and Bill had receded. Kissinger, having failed with Ardeshir Zahedi, was unable to do anything else to help. Lawyer Tom Luce had been busy calling every single one of the twenty-four Texas Congressmen, both Texas Senators, and anyone else in Washington who would take his calls; but what they all did was to call the State Department to find out what was going on, and all the calls ended upon the desk of Henry Precht.

EDS's chief financial officer Tom Walter still had not found a bank willing to post a letter of credit for $12,750,000. The difficulty, Walter had explained to Perot, was this: under American law, an individual or a corporation could renege on a letter of credit if there was proof that the letter had been signed under illegal pressure, for example blackmail or kidnapping. The banks saw the imprisonment of Paul and Bill as a straightforward piece of extortion, and they knew EDS would be able to argue, in an American court, that the letter was invalid and the money should not be paid. In theory that would not matter, for by then Paul and Bill would be home, and the American bank would simply – and quite legally – refuse to honour the letter of credit when it was presented for payment by the Iranian government. However, most American banks had large loans outstanding with Iran, and their fear was that the

Iranians would retaliate by deducting $12,750,000 from what they owed. Walter was still searching for a large bank that did no business with Iran.

So, unfortunately, Operation Hotfoot was still Perot's best bet.

Perot left Stauffer in the car park and went into the oil company building.

He found Simons in the little office reserved for Perot. Simons was eating peanuts and listening to a portable radio. Perot guessed that the peanuts were his lunch and the radio was to swamp any eavesdropping devices that might be hidden in the room.

They shook hands. Perot noticed that Simons was growing a beard. 'How are things?' he said.

'They're good,' Simons answered. 'The men are beginning to pull together as a team.'

'Now,' said Perot, 'you realize you can reject any member of the team you find unsatisfactory.' A couple of days earlier Perot had proposed an addition to the team, a man who knew Tehran and had an outstanding military record, but Simons had turned him down after a short interview, saying: 'That guy believes his own bullshit.' Now Perot wondered whether Simons had found fault, during the training period, with any of the others. He went on: 'You're in charge of the rescue, and—'

'There's no need,' Simons said. 'I don't want to reject anyone.' He laughed softly. 'They're easily the most intelligent squad I've ever worked with, and that does create a problem, because they think orders are to be discussed, not obeyed. But they're learning to turn off their thinking switches when necessary. I've made it very clear to them that at some point in the game discussion ends and blind obedience is called for.'

Perot smiled. 'Then you've achieved more in six days than I have in sixteen years.'

'There's no more we can do here in Dallas,' Simons said. 'Our next step is to go to Tehran.'

Perot nodded. This might be his last chance to call off

162

Operation Hotfoot. Once the team left Dallas, they might be out of touch and they would be out of his control. The die would be cast.

Ross, this is idiotic. You're going to destroy the company and you're going to destroy yourself.

Hell, Ross, I can't make a list of the laws you're going to break!

Instead of two innocent employees in jail, you could have eight guilty employees dead.

Well, we've got this boy from Texarkana who's been trying for years . . .

'When do you want to leave?' Perot asked Simons.

'Tomorrow.'

'Good luck,' said Perot.

5

1

While Simons was talking to Perot in Dallas, Pat Sculley –
the world's worst liar – was in Istanbul, trying and failing to
pull the wool over the eyes of a wily Turk.

Mr Fish was a travel agent who had been 'discovered'
during the December evacuation by Merv Stauffer and T. J.
Marquez. They had hired him to make arrangements for the
evacuees' stopover in Istanbul, and he had worked miracles.
He had booked them all into the Sheraton and organized
buses to take them from the airport to the hotel. When they
arrived there had been a meal waiting for them. They had
left him to collect their baggage and clear it through
customs, and it appeared outside their hotel as if by magic.
Next day there had been video movies for the children and
sight-seeing tours for the adults to keep everyone occupied
while they waited for their flights to New York. Mr Fish
achieved all this while most of the hotel staff were on strike –
T. J. found out later that Mrs Fish had made the beds in the
hotel rooms. Once onward flights had been reserved, Merv
Stauffer had wanted to duplicate a handout sheet with
instructions for everyone, but the hotel's photocopier was
broken: Mr Fish got an electrician to mend it at five o'clock
on a Sunday morning. Mr Fish could *make it happen*.

Simons was still worried about smuggling the Walther
PPKs into Tehran, and when he heard how Mr Fish had
cleared the evacuees' baggage through Turkish customs he
proposed that the same man be asked to solve the problem
of the guns. Sculley had left for Istanbul on 8 January.

The following day he met Mr Fish at the coffee shop in the
Sheraton. Mr Fish was a big, fat man in his late forties,

164

dressed in drab clothes. But he was shrewd: Sculley was no match for him.

Sculley told him that EDS needed help with two problems. 'One, we need an aircraft that can fly into and out of Tehran. Two, we want to get some baggage through customs without it being inspected. Naturally, we'll pay you anything reasonable for help with these problems.'

Mr Fish looked dubious. 'Why do you want to do these things?'

'Well, we've got some magnetic tapes for computer systems in Tehran,' Sculley said. 'We've got to get them in there and we can't take any chances. We don't want anyone to X-ray those tapes or do anything that could damage them, and we can't risk having them confiscated by some petty customs official.'

'And for this, you need to hire a plane and get your bags through customs unopened?'

'Yes, that's right.' Sculley could see that Mr Fish did not believe a word of it.

Mr Fish shook his head. 'No, Mr Sculley. I have been happy to help your friends before, but I am a travel agent, not a smuggler. I will not do this.'

'What about the plane – can you get us a plane?'

Mr Fish shook his head again. 'You will have to go to Amman, Jordan. Arab Wings run charter flights from there to Tehran. That is the best suggestion I can make.'

Sculley shrugged. 'Okay.'

A few minutes later he left Mr Fish and went up to his room to call Dallas.

His first assignment as a member of the rescue team had not gone well.

When Simons got the news he decided to leave the Walther PPKs in Dallas.

He explained his thinking to Coburn. 'Let's not jeopardize the whole mission, right at the start, when we're not even sure we're going to need the handguns: that's a risk we don't have to take, not yet anyway. Let's get in the country and see what we're up against. If and when we need the guns, Schwebach will go back to Dallas and get 'em.'

The guns were put in the EDS vault, together with a tool Simons had ordered for filing off the serial numbers. (Since that was against the law it would not be done until the last possible moment.)

However, they would take the false-bottomed suitcase and do a dry run. They would also take the No 2 shot – Davis would carry it in his beanbag – and the equipment Simons needed for reloading the shot into birdshot cartridges – Simons would carry that himself.

There was now no point in going via Istanbul, so Simons sent Sculley to Paris to book hotel rooms there and try to get reservations for the team on a flight into Tehran.

The rest of the team took off from the Dallas/Fort Worth Regional Airport at 11.05 a.m. on 10 January aboard Braniff flight 341 to Miami, where they transferred to National 4 to Paris.

They met up with Sculley at Orly Airport, in the picture gallery between the restaurant and the coffee shop, the following morning.

Coburn noticed that Sculley was jumpy. Everyone was becoming infected with Simon's security-consciousness, he realized. Coming over from the States, although they had all been on the same plane, they had travelled separately, sitting apart and not acknowledging one another. In Paris Sculley had got nervous about the staff at the Orly Hilton and suspected that someone was listening to his phone calls, so Simons – who was always uneasy in hotels anyway – had decided they would talk in the picture gallery.

Sculley had failed in his second assignment, to get onward reservations from Paris to Tehran for the team. 'Half the airlines have just stopped flying to Iran, because of the political unrest and the strike at the airport,' he said. 'What flights there are, are overbooked with Iranians trying to get home. All I have is a rumour that Swissair are flying in from Zurich.'

They split into two groups. Simons, Coburn, Poché and Boulware would go to Zurich and try for the Swissair flight.

166

Sculley, Schweback, Davis and Jackson would stay in Paris.

Simon's group flew Swissair first class to Zurich. Coburn sat next to Simons. They spent the whole of the flight eating a splendid lunch of shrimp and steak. Simons raved about how good the food was. Coburn was amused, remembering how Simons had said: 'When you're hungry, you open a can.'

At Zurich airport the reservations desk for the Tehran flight was mobbed by Iranians. The team could get only one seat on the plane. Which of them should go? Coburn, they decided. He would be the logistics man. As Director of Personnel and as evacuation mastermind he had the most complete knowledge of EDS resources in Tehran: 150 empty houses and apartments, 60 abandoned cars and jeeps, 200 Iranian employees – those who could be trusted and those who couldn't – and the food, drink and tools left behind by the evacuees. Going in first, Coburn could arrange transport, supplies and a hideout for the rest of the team.

So Coburn said goodbye to his friends and got on the plane, heading for chaos, violence and revolution.

That same day, unknown to Simons and the rescue team, Ross Perot took British Airways flight 172 from New York to London. He, too, was on his way to Tehran.

The flight from Zurich to Tehran was all too short.

Coburn spent the time anxiously running over in his mind the things he had to do. He could not make a list: Simons would not allow anything to be written down.

His first job was to get through customs with the false-bottomed case. There were no guns in it: if the case was inspected and the secret compartment discovered, Coburn was to say that it was for carrying delicate photographic equipment.

Next he had to select some abandoned houses and apartments for Simons to consider as hideouts. Then he had to find cars and make sure there was a supply of gasoline for them.

His cover story, for the benefit of Keane Taylor, Rich Gallagher and EDS's Iranian employees, was that he was arranging shipment of evacuees' personal belongings back to the States. Coburn had told Simons that Taylor ought to be let in on the secret: he would be a valuable asset to the rescue team. Simons had said he would make that decision himself, after meeting Taylor.

Coburn wondered how to hoodwink Taylor.

He was still wondering when the plane landed.

Inside the terminal, all the airport staff were in Army uniforms. That was how the airport had been kept open despite the strike, Coburn realized: the military were running it.

He picked up the suitcase with the false bottom and walked through customs. No one stopped him.

The arrivals hall was a zoo. The waiting crowds were more unruly than ever. The army was not running the airport on military lines.

He fought his way through the crowd to the cab rank. He skirted two men who appeared to be fighting over a taxi, and took the next in line.

Riding into town, he noticed a good deal of military hardware on the road, especially near the airport. There were many more tanks about than there had been when he left. Was that a sign that the Shah was still in control? In the press the Shah was still talking as if he were in control, but then so was Bakhtiar. So, for that matter, was the Ayatollah, who had just announced the formation of a Council of the Islamic Revolution to take over the government, just as if he were already in power in Tehran instead of sitting in a villa outside Paris at the end of a telephone line. In truth, nobody was in charge; and while that hindered the negotiations for the release of Paul and Bill, it would probably help the rescue team.

The cab took him to the office they called Bucharest, where he found Keane Taylor. Taylor was in charge now, for Lloyd Briggs had gone to New York to brief EDS's lawyers in person. Taylor was sitting at Paul Chiapparone's desk, in an immaculate vested suit, just as if he were a million miles away from the nearest revolution instead of in the middle of it. He was astonished to see Coburn.

'Jay! When the hell did you get here?'

'Just arrived,' Coburn said.

'What's with the beard – you trying to get yourself fired?'

'I thought it might make me look less American here.'

'Did you ever see an Iranian with a ginger beard?'

'No,' Coburn laughed.

'So what are you here for?'

'Well, we're obviously not going to bring our people back in here in the foreseeable future, so I've come to police up everyone's personal belongings to get them shipped back to the States.'

Taylor shot him a funny look but did not comment. 'Where are you going to stay? We've all moved into the Hyatt Crown Regency, it's safer.'

'How about I use your old house?'

'Whatever you say.'

'Now, about these belongings. Do you have those envelopes everyone left, with their house keys and car keys and instructions for disposal of their household goods?'

'I sure do – I've been referring to them. Everything people don't want shipped, I've been selling – washers and dryers, refrigerators: I'm running a permanent garage sale here.'

'Can I have the envelopes?'

'Sure.'

'How's the car situation?'

'We've rounded up most of them. I've got them parked at a school, with some Iranians watching them, if they're not selling them.'

'What about gas?'

'Rich got four 55-gallon drums from the Air Force and we've got them full down in the basement.'

'I thought I smelled gas when I came in.'

'Don't strike a match down there in the dark, we'll all be blown to hell.'

'What do you do about topping up the drums?'

'We use a couple of cars as tankers – a Buick and a Chevy, with big US gas tanks. Two of our drivers spend all day waiting in gas lines. When they get filled up they come back here and we siphon the gas into the drums, then send the cars back to the filling station. Sometimes you can buy gas from the front of the line. Grab someone who's just filled up and offer him ten times the pump price for the gas in his car. There's a whole economy grown up around the gas lines.'

'What about fuel oil for the houses, for heating?'

'I've got a source, but he charges me ten times the old price. I'm spending money like a drunken sailor here.'

'I'm going to need twelve cars.'

'Twelve cars, huh, Jay?'

'That's what I said.'

'You'll have room to stash them, at my house – it's got a big walled courtyard. Would you . . . for any reason . . . like to be able to get the car refuelled without any of the Iranian employees seeing you?'

'I sure would.'

'Just bring an empty car to the Hyatt and I'll swap it for a full one.'

'How many Iranians do we still have?'

'Ten of the best, plus four drivers.'

'I'd like a list of their names.'

'Did you know Ross is on his way in?'

'Shit, no!' Coburn was astonished.

'I just got word. He's bringing Bob Young, from Kuwait, to take over this administrative stuff from me, and John Howell to work on the legal side. They want me to work with John on the negotiations and bail.'

'Is that a fact.' Coburn wondered what was on Perot's mind. 'Okay, I'm taking off for your place.'

'Jay, why don't you tell me what's up?'

'There's nothing I can tell you.'

'Screw you, Coburn. I want to know what's going down.'

'You got all I'm going to tell you.'

'Screw you again. Wait till you see what cars you get –

170

you'll be lucky if they have a steering wheel.'

'Sorry.'

'Jay . . .'

'Yeah?'

'That's the funniest looking suitcase I've ever seen.'

'So it is, so it is.'

'I *know* what you're up to, Coburn.'

Coburn sighed. 'Let's go for a walk.'

They went out into the street, and Coburn told Taylor about the rescue team.

Next day Coburn and Taylor went to work on hideouts.

Taylor's house, No 2 Aftab Street, was ideal. Conveniently close to the Hyatt for switching cars, it was also in the Armenian section of the city, which might be less hostile to Americans if the rioting got worse. It had a working phone and a supply of heating oil. The walled courtyard was big enough to park six cars, and there was a back entrance which could be used as an escape route if a squad of police came to the front door. And the landlord did not live on the premises.

Using the street map of Tehran on the wall of Coburn's office – which had, since the evacuation, been marked with the location of every EDS home in the city – they picked three more empty houses as alternative hideouts.

During the day, as Taylor got the cars gassed up, Coburn drove them one by one from Bucharest to the houses, parking three cars at each of the four locations.

Looking again at his wall map, he tried to recall which of the wives had worked for the American military, for the families with commissary privileges always had the best food. He listed eight likely prospects. Tomorrow he would visit them and pick up canned and dried food and bottled drinks for the hideouts.

He selected a fifth apartment, but did not visit it. It was to be a safe house, a hideout for a serious emergency: no one would go there until it had to be used.

That evening, alone in Taylor's apartment, he called

Dallas and asked for Merv Stauffer.

Stauffer was cheerful, as always. 'Hi Jay! How are you?'

'Fine.'

'I'm glad you called, because I have a message for you. Got a pencil?'

'Sure do.'

'Okay. Honky Keith Goofball Zero Honky Dummy—'

'Merv,' Coburn interrupted.

'Yeah?'

'What the hell are you talking about, Merv?'

'It's the code, Jay.'

'What is Honky Keith Goofball?'

'H for Honky, K for Keith—'

'Merv, H is Hotel, K is Kilo . . .'

'Oh!' said Stauffer. 'Oh, I didn't realize you were supposed to use certain particular words . . .'

Coburn started to laugh. 'Listen,' he said, 'get someone to give you the military alphabet before next time.'

Stauffer was laughing to himself. 'I sure will,' he said. 'I guess we'll have to make do with my own version this time, though.'

'Okay, off you go.'

Coburn took down the coded message, then – still using the code – he gave Stauffer his location and phone number. After hanging up, he decoded the message Stauffer had given him.

It was good news. Simons and Joe Poché were arriving in Tehran the next day.

2

By 11 January – the day Coburn arrived in Tehran and Perot flew to London – Paul and Bill had been in jail exactly two weeks.

In that time they had showered once. When the guards learned that there was hot water, they gave each cell five minutes in the showers. Modesty was forgotten as the men

172

crowded into the cubicles for the luxury of being warm and clean for a while. They washed not only themselves but all their clothes as well.

After a week the jail had run out of bottled gas for cooking, so the food, as well as being starchy and short on vegetables, was now cold. Fortunately they were allowed to supplement the diet with oranges, apples and nuts brought in by visitors.

Most evenings the electricity was off for an hour or two, and then the prisoners would light candles or flashlights. The jail was full of deputy Ministers, government contractors, and Tehran businessmen. Two members of the Empress's Court were in Cell No 5 with Paul and Bill. The latest arrival in their cell was Dr Siazi, who had worked at the Ministry of Health under Dr Sheik as manager of a department called Rehabilitation. Siazi was a psychiatrist, and he used his knowledge of the human mind to boost morale among his fellow prisoners. He was forever dreaming up games and diversions to enliven the dreary routine: he instituted a supper-time ritual whereby everyone in the cell had to tell a joke before they could eat. When he learned the amount of Paul's and Bill's bail he assured them they would have a visit from Farrah Fawcett Majors, whose husband was a mere Six Million Dollar Man.

Paul developed a curiously strong relationship with the 'father' of the cell, the longest resident who by tradition was cell boss. A small man in late middle age, he did what little he could to help the Americans, encouraging them to eat and bribing the guards for little extras for them. He knew only a dozen or so words of English, and Paul spoke little Farsi, but they managed halting conversations. Paul learned that he had been a prominent businessman, owning a construction company and a London hotel. Paul showed him the photographs which Taylor had brought in of Karen and Ann Marie, and the old man learned their names. For all Paul knew, he might have been as guilty as hell of whatever he was accused of; but the concern and warmth he displayed towards the foreigners was enormously heartening.

173

Paul was also touched by the bravery of his EDS colleagues in Tehran. Lloyd Briggs, who had now gone to New York; Rich Gallagher, who had never left; and Keane Taylor, who had come back; all risked their lives every time they drove through the riots to visit the jail. Each of them also faced the danger that Dadgar might take it into his head to seize them as additional hostages. Paul was particularly grateful when he heard that Bob Young was on his way in, for Bob's wife had a new baby, and this was an especially bad time for him to put himself in danger.

Paul had at first imagined he was going to be released any minute. Now he was telling himself he would get out any day.

One of their cellmates had been let out. He was Lucio Randone, an Italian builder employed by the construction company Condotti d'Acqua. Randone came back to visit, bringing two very large bars of Italian chocolate, and told Paul and Bill that he had talked to the Italian Ambassador in Tehran about them. The Ambassador had promised to see his American counterpart and reveal the secret of getting people out of jail.

But the biggest source of Paul's optimism was Dr Ahmad Houman, the attorney Briggs had retained to replace the Iranian lawyers who had given bad advice on the bail. Houman had visited them during their first week in jail. They had sat in the jail's reception area – not, for some reason, in the visiting room in the low building across the courtyard – and Paul had feared that this would inhibit a frank laywer-client discussion; but Houman was not intimidated by the presence of prison guards. 'Dadgar is trying to make a name for himself,' he had announced.

Could that be it? An over-enthusiastic prosecutor trying to impress his superiors – or perhaps the revolutionaries – with his anti-American diligence?'

'Dadgar's office is very powerful,' Houman went on. 'But in this case he is out on a limb. He did not have cause to arrest you, and the bail is exorbitant.'

Paul began to feel good about Houman. He seemed

174

knowledgeable and confident. 'So what are you going to do?'

'My strategy will be to get the bail reduced.'

'How?'

'First I will talk to Dadgar. I hope I will be able to make him see how outrageous the bail is. But if he remains intransigent, I will go to his superiors in the Ministry of Justice and persuade them to order him to reduce the bail.'

'And how long do you expect that to take?'

'Perhaps a week.'

It was taking more than a week, but Houman had made progress. He had come back to the jail to report that Dadgar's superiors at the Ministry of Justice had agreed to force Dadgar to back down and reduce the bail to a sum EDS could pay easily and swiftly out of funds currently in Iran. Exuding contempt for Dadgar and confidence in himself, he announced triumphantly that everything would be finalized at a second meeting between Paul and Bill and Dadgar on 11 January.

Sure enough, that day Dadgar came to the jail in the afternoon. He wanted to see Paul alone first, as he had before. Paul was in fine spirits as the guard walked him across the courtyard. Dadgar was just an over-enthusiastic prosecutor, he thought, and now he had been slapped down by his superiors and would have to eat humble pie.

Dadgar was waiting, with the same woman translator beside him. He nodded curtly, and Paul sat down, thinking: he doesn't look very humble.

Dadgar spoke in Farsi, and Mrs Nourbash translated: 'We are here to discuss the amount of your bail.'

'Good,' said Paul.

'Mr Dadgar has received a letter on this subject from officials at the Ministry of Health and Social Welfare.'

She began to translate the letter.

The Ministry officials were demanding that bail for the two Americans should be *increased* to twenty-three million dollars – almost double – to compensate for the Ministry's losses since EDS had switched off the computers.

175

It dawned on Paul that he was *not* going to be released today.

The letter was a put-up job. Dadgar had neatly out-manoeuvred Dr Houman. This meeting was nothing but a charade.

It made him *mad*.

To *hell* with being polite to this bastard, he thought.

When the letter had been read he said: 'Now I have something to say, and I want you to translate every word. Is that clear?'

'Of course,' said Mrs Nourbash.

Paul spoke loudly and clearly. 'You have now held me in jail for fourteen days. I have not been taken before a court. No charges have been brought against me. You have yet to produce a single piece of evidence implicating me in any crime whatsoever. You have not even specified what crime I might be accused of. Are you proud of Iranian justice?'

To Paul's surprise, the appeal seemed to melt Dadgar's icy gaze a little. 'I am sorry,' Dadgar said, 'that you have to be the one to pay for the things your company has done wrong.'

'No, no, no,' Paul said. 'I *am* the company. I am the person responsible. If the company had done wrong I should be the one to suffer. But we have done nothing wrong. In fact we have done far in excess of what we were committed to do. EDS got this contract because we are the only company in the world capable of doing this job – creating a fully automated welfare system in an underdeveloped country of thirty million subsistence farmers. *And we have succeeded.* Our data processing system issues social security cards. It keeps a register of deposits at the bank in the Ministry's account. Every morning it produces a summary of the welfare claims made the previous day. It prints the payroll for the entire Ministry of Health and Social Welfare. It produces weekly and monthly financial reports for the Ministry. Why don't you go to the Ministry and *look at the printouts*? No, wait a minute,' he said as Dadgar began to speak, 'I haven't finished.'

Dadgar shrugged.

176

Paul went on: 'There is readily available proof that EDS has fulfilled its contract. It is equally easy to establish that the Ministry has not kept its side of the deal, that is to say, it has not paid us for six months and currently owes us something in excess of ten million dollars. Now, think about the Ministry for a moment. Why hasn't it paid EDS? Because it hasn't got the money. Why not? You and I know it spent its entire budget during the first seven months of the current year and the government hasn't got the funds to top it up. There might well be a degree of incompetence in some departments. What about those people who overspent their budgets? Maybe they're looking for an excuse – someone to blame for what's gone wrong – a scapegoat. And isn't it convenient that they have EDS – a capitalist company, an American company – right in there working with them? In the current political atmosphere, people are eager to hear about the wickedness of the Americans, quick to believe that we are cheating Iran. *You* are not supposed to believe that the Americans are to blame unless there is evidence. Isn't it time you asked yourself *why* anyone should make false accusations against me and my company? *Isn't it time you started to investigate the goddam Ministry?*'

The woman translated the last sentence. Paul studied Dadgar: his expression had frozen again. He said something in Farsi.

Mrs Nourbash translated. 'He will see the other one now.'

Paul stared at her.

He had wasted his breath, he realized. He might just as well have recited nursery rhymes. Dadgar was immovable.

Paul was deeply depressed. He lay on his mattress, looking at the pictures of Karen and Ann Marie which he had stuck on the underside of the bunk above him. He missed the girls badly. Being unable to see them made him realize that in the past he had taken them for granted. Ruthie too. He looked at his watch: it was the middle of the night in the States now. Ruthie would be asleep, alone in a big bed. How good it would be to climb in beside her and hold her in his arms. He

177

put the thought out of his mind: he was just making himself miserable with self-pity. He had no need to worry about them. They were out of Iran, out of danger, and he knew that whatever might happen, Perot would take care of them. That was the good thing about Perot. He asked a lot of you – boy, he was just about the most demanding employer you could have – but when you needed to rely on him, he was like a rock.

Paul lit a cigarette. He had a cold. He could never get warm in the jail. He felt too down to do anything. He did not want to go to the Chattanooga Room and drink tea; he did not want to watch the news in gibberish on TV; he did not want to play chess with Bill. He did not want to go to the library for a new book. He had been reading *The Thorn Birds* by Colleen McCullough. He had found it a very emotional book. It was about several generations of families, and it made him think of his own family. The central character was a priest, and Paul as a Catholic had been able to associate with that. He had read the book three times. He had also read *Hawaii* by James Mitchener, *Airport* by Arthur Hailey, and *The Guinness Book of Records*. He never wanted to read another book for the rest of his life.

Sometimes he thought about what he would do when he got out, and let his mind wander on his favourite pastimes, boating and fishing. But that could be depressing.

He could not remember a time in his adult life when he had been at a loss for something to do. He was always busy. At the office he would typically have three days' work backed up. Never, *never*, did he lie down smoking and wondering how on earth he could keep himself amused.

But the worst thing of all was the helplessness. Although he had always been an employee, going where his boss sent him and doing what he was ordered to do, nevertheless he had always known that he could at any time get on a plane and go home, or quit his job, or say no to his boss. Ultimately the decisions had been his. Now he could not make any decisions about his own life. He could not even do anything about his plight. With every other problem he had

178

ever had, he had been able to work on it, try things, *attack* the problem. Now he just had to sit and suffer.

He realized that he had never known the meaning of freedom until he lost it.

The demonstration was relatively peaceful. There were several blazing cars, but otherwise no violence: the demonstrators were marching up and down carrying pictures of Khomeini and putting flowers in the turrets of tanks. The soldiers looked on passively.

The traffic was at a standstill.

It was 14 January, the day after Simons and Poché flew in. Boulware had gone back to Paris, and now he and the other four were waiting there for a flight to Tehran. Meanwhile Simons, Coburn and Poché were heading downtown to reconnoitre the jail.

After a few minutes Joe Poché turned off the car engine and sat there, silent and expressionless as usual.

By contrast Simons, sitting next to him, was animated. 'This is history being made in front of our eyes!' he said. 'Very few people get to observe first hand a revolution in progress.'

He was a history buff, Coburn had gathered, and revolutions were his speciality. Coming through the airport, on being asked what his occupation and the purpose of his visit, he said he was a retired farmer and this was his only chance he was ever likely to get of seeing a revolution. He had been telling the truth.

Coburn was *not* thrilled to be in the middle of it. He did not enjoy sitting in a little car – they had a Renault 4 – surrounded by excitable Muslim fanatics. Despite his new-grown beard he did not look Iranian. Nor did Poché. Simons did, however: his hair was longer now, he had olive skin and a big nose, and he had grown a white beard. Give him some worry beads and stand him on a corner and nobody would suspect for a minute that he was American.

But the crowd was not interested in Americans, and eventually Coburn became confident enough to get out of the car and go into a baker's shop. He bought barbari bread: long flat loaves with a delicate crust which were baked fresh every day and cost seven rials – ten cents. Like French bread, it was delicious when new but went stale very quickly. It was usually eaten with butter or cheese. Iran was run on barbari bread and tea.

They sat watching the demonstration and chewing on the bread until, at last, the traffic began to move again. Poché followed the route he had mapped out the previous evening. Coburn wondered what they would find when they reached the jail. On Simons's orders he had kept away from downtown until now. It was too much to hope that the jail would be exactly as he had described it eleven days ago at Lake Grapevine: the team had based a very precise attack plan on quite imprecise intelligence. Just how imprecise, they would soon find out.

They reached the Ministry of Justice and drove around to Khayyam Street, the side of the block on which the jail entrance was located.

Poché drove slowly, but not too slowly, past the jail.

Simons said, 'Oh, *shit*.'

Coburn's heart sank.

The jail was radically different from the mental picture he had built up.

The entrance consisted of two steel doors fourteen feet high. On one side was a single-storey building with barbed wire along its roof. On the other side was a taller building of grey stone, five storeys high.

There were no iron railings. There was no courtyard.

Simons said: 'So where's the fucking exercise yard?'

Poché drove on, made a few turns, and came back along Khayyam Street in the opposite direction.

This time Coburn did see a little courtyard with grass and trees, separated from the street by a fence of iron railings twelve feet high; but it plainly had nothing to do with the jail,

180

which was farther up the street. Somehow, in that telephone conversation with Majid, the exercise yard of the jail had got mixed up with this little garden.

Poché made one more pass around the block.

Simons was thinking ahead. 'We can get in there,' he said. 'But we have to know what we'll be up against once we're over the wall. Someone will have to go in and reconnoitre.'

'Who?' said Coburn.

'You,' said Simons.

Coburn walked up to the jail entrance with Rich Gallagher and Majid. Majid pressed the bell and they waited.

Coburn had become the 'outside man' of the rescue team. He had already been seen at Bucharest by Iranian employees, so his presence in Tehran could not be kept secret. Simons and Poché would stay indoors as much as possible and keep away from EDS premises: nobody need know they were here. It would be Coburn who would go to Hyatt to see Taylor and switch cars. And it was Coburn who went inside the jail.

As he waited he ran over in his mind all the points Simons had told him to watch out for – security, numbers of guards, weaponry, layout of the place, cover, high ground; it was a long list, and Simons had a way of making you anxious to remember every detail of his instructions.

A peephole in the door opened, Majid said something in Farsi.

The door was opened and the three of them went in.

Straight ahead of him Coburn saw a courtyard with a grassed traffic circle and cars parked on the far side. Beyond the cars a building rose five storeys high over the courtyard. To his left was the one-storey building he had seen from the street, with the barbed wire on its roof. To his right was another steel door.

Coburn was wearing a long, bulky down coat – Taylor had dubbed it the Michelin Man coat – under which he could easily have concealed a shotgun, but he was not searched by the guard at the gate. *I could have had eight weapons on me,* he thought. That was encouraging: security was slack.

He noted that the gate guard was armed with a small pistol.

The three visitors were led into the low building on the left. The Colonel in charge of the jail was in the visiting room, along with another Iranian. The second man, Gallagher had warned Coburn, was always present during visits, and spoke perfect English: presumably he was there to eavesdrop. Coburn had told Majid he did not want to be overheard while talking to Paul, and Majid agreed to engage the eavesdropper in conversation.

Coburn was introduced to the Colonel. In broken English, the man said he was sorry for Paul and Bill, and he hoped they would be released soon. He seemed sincere. Coburn noted that neither the Colonel nor the eavesdropper was armed.

The door opened, and Paul and Bill walked in.

They both stared at Coburn in surprise – neither of them had been forewarned that he was in town, and the beard was an additional shock.

'What the hell are you doing here?' Bill said, and smiled broadly.

Coburn shook hands warmly with both of them. Paul said: 'Boy, I can't believe you're here.'

'How's my wife?' Bill said.

'Emily's fine, so is Ruthie,' Coburn told them.

Majid started talking loudly in Farsi to the Colonel and the eavesdropper. He seemed to be telling them a complicated story with many gestures. Rich Gallagher began to speak to Bill, and Coburn sat Paul down.

Simons had decided that Coburn should question Paul about routines at the jail, and level with him about the rescue plan. Paul was picked rather than Bill because, in Coburn's opinion, Paul was likely to be the leader of the two.

'If you haven't guessed it already,' Coburn began, 'we're going to get y'all out of here by force if necessary.'

'I guessed it already,' Paul said. 'I'm not sure it's a good idea.'

'What?'

'People might get hurt.'

'Listen, Ross has retained just about the best man in the whole world for this kind of operation, and we have carte blanche—'

'I'm not sure I want it.'

'You ain't being asked for your permission, Paul.'

Paul smiled. 'Okay.'

'Now I need some information. Where do you exercise?'

'Right there in the courtyard.'

'When?'

'Thursdays.'

Today was Monday. The next exercise period would be 18 January. 'How long do you spend out there?'

'About an hour.'

'What time of day?'

'It varies.'

'Shit.' Coburn made an effort to look relaxed, to avoid lowering his voice conspicuously or glancing over his shoulder to see whether anyone might be listening: this had to look like a normal friendly visit. 'How many guards are there in this jail?'

'Around twenty.'

'All uniformed, all armed?'

'All uniformed, some armed with handguns.'

'No rifles?'

'Well . . . none of the regular guards have rifles, but . . . See, our cell is just across the courtyard and has a window. Well, in the morning there's a group of about twenty different guards, like an elite corps you might say. They have rifles and wear kind of shiny helmets. They have reveille right here, then I never see them for the rest of the day. I don't know where they go.'

'Try and find out.'

'I'll try.'

'Which is your cell?'

'When you go out of here, the window is more or less opposite you. If you start in the right-hand corner of the courtyard and count toward the left, it's the third window. But they close the shutters when there are visitors – so we can't see women coming in, they say.'

Coburn nodded, trying to memorize it all. 'You need to do two things,' he said. 'One: a survey of the inside of the jail, with measurements as accurate as possible. I'll come back and get the details from you so we can draw a plan. Two: get in shape. Exercise daily. You'll need to be fit.'

'Okay.'

'Now, tell me your daily routine.'

'They wake us up at six o'clock,' Paul began.

Coburn concentrated, knowing he would have to repeat all this to Simons. Nevertheless, at the back of his mind one thought nagged: if we don't know what time of day they exercise, how the hell do we know when to go over the wall?

'Visiting time is the answer,' Simons said.

'How so?' Coburn asked.

'It's the one situation when we can *predict* they will be out of the actual jail and vulnerable to a snatch, at a definite moment in time.'

Coburn nodded. The three of them were sitting in the living-room of Keane Taylor's house. It was a big room with a Persian carpet. They had drawn three chairs into the middle, around a coffee table. Beside Simons's chair, a small mountain of cigar ash was growing on the carpet. Taylor would be furious.

Coburn felt drained. Being debriefed by Simons was even more harrowing than he had anticipated. When he was sure he had told everything, Simons thought of more questions. When Coburn could not quite remember something, Simons made him think hard until he did remember. Simons drew from him information he had not consciously registered, just by asking the right questions.

'The van and the ladder – that scenario is out,' Simons said. 'Their weak point now is their loose routine. We can get two men in there as visitors, with shotguns or Walthers under their coats. Paul and Bill would be brought to that visiting area. Our two men should be able to overpower the Colonel and the eavesdropper without any trouble – and without making enough noise to alarm anyone else in the vicinity. Then . . .'

'Then what?'

'That's the problem. The four men would have to come out of the building, cross the courtyard, reach the gate, either open it or climb it, reach the street, and get in a car . . .'

'It sounds possible,' Coburn said. 'There's just one guard at the gate . . .'

'A number of things about this scenario bother me,' Simons said. 'One: the windows in the high building that overlooks the courtyard. While our men are in the courtyard, anyone looking out of any one of the windows will see them. Two: the elite guard with shiny helmets and rifles. Whatever happens, our people have to slow down at the gate. If there's just one guard with a rifle looking out of one of those high windows, he could pick off the four of them like shooting fish in a barrel.'

'We don't know the guards are in the high building.'

'We don't know they're *not*.'

'It seems like a small risk—'

'We're not going to take *any* risks we don't have to. Three: the traffic in this goddam city is a bastard. You just can't talk about jumping in a car and getting away. We could run into a demonstration fifty yards down the street. No. This snatch has got to be *quiet*. We must have *time*. What is that Colonel like, the one in charge of the place?'

'He was quite friendly,' Coburn said. 'He seemed genuinely sorry for Paul and Bill.'

'I wonder whether we can get to him. Do we know anything at all about him?'

'No.'

'Let's find out.'

185

'I'll put Majid on it.'

'The Colonel would have to make sure there were no guards around at visiting time. We could make it look good by tying him up, or even knocking him out . . . If he can be bribed, we can still bring this thing off.'

'I'll get on it right away,' said Coburn.

4

On 13 January Ross Perot took off from Amman, Jordan, in a Lear jet of Arab Wings, the charter operation of Royal Jordanian Airlines. The plane headed for Tehran. In the baggage hold was a net bag containing half a dozen professional-sized videotapes, the kind used by television crews: this was Perot's 'cover'.

As the little jet flew east, the British pilot pointed out the junction of the Tigris and Euphrates rivers. A few minutes later the plane developed hydraulic trouble and had to turn back.

It had been that kind of journey.

In London he had caught up with lawyer John Howell and EDS manager Bob Young, both of whom had been trying for days to get a flight into Tehran. Eventually Young discovered that Arab Wings was flying in, and the three men had gone to Amman. Arriving there in the middle of the night had been an experience all on its own: it looked to Perot as if all the bad guys of Jordan were sleeping at the airport. They found a taxicab to take them to a hotel. John Howell's room had no bathroom: the facilities were right there beside the bed. In Perot's room the toilet was so close to the bath that he had to put his feet in the tub when he sat on the john. And like that . . .

Bob Young had thought of the videotapes 'cover'. Arab Wings regularly flew tapes into and out of Tehran for NBC-

186

TV News. Sometimes NBC would have its own man to carry the tapes; other times the pilot would take them. Today, although NBC did not know it, Perot would be their bagman. He was wearing a sports jacket, a little plaid hat and no tie. Anyone watching for Ross Perot might not look twice at the regular NBC messenger with his regular net bag.

Arab Wings had agreed to this ruse. They had also confirmed that they could take Perot out again on this NBC tape run.

Back in Amman, Perot, Howell and Young and the pilot boarded a replacement jet and took off again. As they climbed high over the desert Perot wondered whether he was the craziest man in the world or the sanest.

There were powerful reasons why he should not go to Tehran. For one thing, the mobs might consider him the ultimate symbol of bloodsucking American capitalism and string him up on the spot. More likely, Dadgar might get to know that he was in town and try to arrest him. Perot was not sure he understood Dadgar's motives in jailing Paul and Bill, but the man's mysterious purposes would surely be even better served by having Perot behind bars. Why, Dadgar could set bail at a hundred million dollars and feel confident of getting it, if the money was what he was after.

But negotiations for the release of Paul and Bill were stalled, and Perot wanted to go to Tehran to kick ass in one last attempt at a legitimate solution before Simons and the team risked their lives in an assault on the prison.

There had been times, in business, when EDS had been ready to admit defeat but had gone on to victory because Perot himself had insisted on going one more mile. This was what leadership was all about.

That was what he told himself, and it was all true, but there was another reason for his trip. He simply could not sit in Dallas, comfortable and safe, while other people risked their lives on his instructions.

He knew only too well that if he were jailed in Iran he, and his colleagues, and his company, would be in much worse trouble than they were now. Should he do the prudent thing, and stay, he had wondered, or should he follow his deepest instincts, and go? It was a moral dilemma. He had discussed it with his mother.

She knew she was dying. And she knew that, even if Perot should come back alive and well after a few days, she might no longer be there. Cancer was rapidly destroying her body, but there was nothing wrong with her mind, and her sense of right and wrong was as clear as ever. 'You don't have a choice, Ross,' she had said. 'They're your men. You sent them over there. They didn't do anything wrong. Our government won't help them. *You* are responsible for them. It's up to you to get them out. You have to go.'

So here he was, feeling that he was doing the right thing, if not the smart thing.

The Lear jet left the desert behind and climbed over the mountains of western Iran. Unlike Simons and Coburn and Poché, Perot was a stranger to physical danger. He had been too young for World War Two and too old for Vietnam, and the Korean war had finished while Ensign Perot was on his way there aboard the destroyer USS *Sigourney*. He had been shot at just once, during the prisoners-of-war campaign, landing in a jungle in Laos aboard an ancient DC3: he had heard pinging noises but had not realized the aircraft had been hit until after it landed. His most frightening experience, since the days of the Texarkana paper-route thieves, had been in another plane over Laos, when a door right next to his seat fell off. He had been asleep. When he woke up he looked for a light for a second, before realizing he was leaning out of the aircraft. Fortunately he had been strapped in.

He was not sitting next to a door today.

He looked through the window and saw, in a bowl-shaped depression in the mountains, the city of Tehran, a mud-coloured sprawl dotted with white skyscrapers. The plane began to lose height.

Okay, he thought, now we're coming down. It's time to

start thinking and using your head, Perot.

As the plane landed he felt tense, wired, alert: he was pumping adrenalin.

The plane taxied to a halt. Several soldiers with machine-guns slung over their shoulders ambled casually across the tarmac.

Perot got out. The pilot opened the baggage hold and handed him the net bag of tapes.

Perot and the pilot walked across the tarmac. Howell and Young followed, carrying their suitcases.

Perot felt grateful for his inconspicuous appearance. He thought of a Norwegian friend, a tall, blond Adonis who complained of looking too impressive. 'You're lucky, Ross,' he would say. 'When you walk into a room no-one notices you. When people see me they expect too much – I can't live up to their expectations.' No one would ever take *him* for a messenger boy. But Perot, with his short stature and homely face and off-the-rack clothes, could be convincing in the part.

They entered the terminal. Perot told himself that the military, which was running the airport, and the Ministry of Justice, for which Dadgar worked, were two separate government bureaucracies; and if one of them knew what the other was doing, or whom it was seeking, why, this would have to be the most efficient operation in the history of government.

He walked up to the desk and showed his passport.

It was stamped and handed back to him.

He walked on.

He was not stopped by customs.

The pilot showed him where to leave the bag of television tapes. Perot put them down, then said goodbye to the pilot.

He turned around and saw another tall, distinguished-looking friend: Keane Taylor. Perot liked Taylor.

'Hi, Ross, how did it go?' Taylor said.

'Great,' Perot said with a smile. 'They weren't looking for the ugly American.'

They walked out of the airport. Perot said: 'Are you satisfied that I didn't send you back here for any administrative bullshit?'

'I sure am,' Taylor said.

They got into Taylor's car. Howell and Young got in the back.

As they pulled away, Taylor said: 'I'm going to take an indirect route, to avoid the worst of the riots.'

Perot did not find this reassuring.

The road was lined with tall, half-finished concrete buildings with cranes on top. Work seemed to have stopped. Looking closely, Perot saw that people were living in the shells. It seemed an apt symbol of the way the Shah had tried to modernize Iran too quickly.

Taylor was talking about cars. He had stashed all EDS's cars in a school playground and hired some Iranians to guard them, but he had discovered that the Iranians were busy running a used car lot, selling the damn things.

There were long lines at every gas station, Perot noticed. He found that ironic in a country rich in oil. As well as cars, there were people in the queues, holding cans. 'What are they doing?' Perot asked. 'If they don't have cars, why do they need gas?'

'They sell it to the highest bidder,' Taylor explained. 'Or you can rent an Iranian to stand in line for you.'

They were stopped briefly at a roadblock. Driving on, they passed several burning cars. A lot of civilians were standing around with machine-guns. The scene was peaceful for a mile or two, then Perot saw more burning cars, more machine-guns, another roadblock. Such sights ought to have been frightening, but somehow they were not. It seemed to Perot that the people were just enjoying letting loose for a change, now that the Shah's iron grip was at last being relaxed. Certainly the military was doing nothing to maintain order, as far as he could see.

There was always something weird about seeing violence as a tourist. He recalled flying over Laos in a light plane and watching people fighting on the ground: he had felt tranquil, detached. He supposed that battle was like that: it might be fierce if you were in the middle of it, but five minutes away nothing was happening.

They drove into a huge circle with a monument in its centre that looked like a spaceship of the far future, towering over the traffic on four gigantic splayed legs. 'What is *that*?' said Perot.

'The Shahyad Monument,' Taylor said. 'There's a museum in the top.'

A few minutes later they pulled into the forecourt of the Hyatt Crown Regency. 'This is a new hotel,' Taylor said. 'They've just opened it, poor bastards. It's good for us, though – wonderful food, wine, music in the restaurant in the evenings . . . We're living like kings in a city that's falling apart.'

They went into the lobby and took the elevator. 'You don't have to check in,' Taylor told Perot. 'Your suite is in my name. No sense in having your name written down anywhere.'

'Right.'

They got out at the eleventh floor. 'We've all got rooms along this hall,' Taylor said. He unlocked a door at the far end of the corridor.

Perot walked in, glanced around, and smiled. 'Would you look at this?' The sitting room was vast. Next to it was a large bedroom. He looked into the bathroom: it was big enough for a cocktail party.

'Is it all right?' Taylor said with a grin.

'If you'd seen the room I had last night in Amman you wouldn't bother to ask.'

Taylor left him to settle in.

Perot went to the window and looked out. His suite was at the front of the hotel, so he could look down and see the forecourt. I might hope to have a warning, he thought, if a squad of soldiers or a revolutionary mob comes for me.

But what would I do?

191

He decided to map an emergency escape route. He left his suite and walked up and down the corridor. There were several empty rooms with unlocked doors. At either end was an exit to a staircase. He went down the stairs to the floor below. There were more empty rooms, some without furniture or decoration: the hotel was unfinished, like so many buildings in this town.

I could take this staircase down, he thought, and if I heard them coming up I could duck back into one of the corridors and hide in an empty room. That way I could get to ground level.

He walked all the way down the stairs and explored the ground floor.

He wandered through several banqueting rooms which he supposed were unused most, if not all, of the time. There was a labyrinth of kitchens with a thousand hiding places: he particularly noticed some empty food containers big enough for a small man to climb into. From the banqueting area he could reach the health club at the back of the hotel. It was pretty fancy, with a sauna and a pool. He opened a door at the rear and found himself outside, in the hotel car park. Here he could take an EDS car and disappear into the city, or walk to the next hotel, the Evin; or just run into the forest of unfinished skyscrapers which began on the far side of the car park.

He re-entered the hotel and took the elevator. As he rode up, he resolved always to dress casually in Tehran. He had brought with him khaki pants and some chequered flannel shirts, and he also had a jogging outfit. He could not help looking American, with his pale, clean-shaven face and blue eyes and ultra-short crewcut; but, if he should find himself on the run, he could at least make sure he did not look like an *important* American, much less the multimillionaire owner of Electronic Data Systems Corporation.

He went to find Taylor's room and get a briefing. He wanted to go to the American Embassy and talk to Ambassador Sullivan; he wanted to go to the headquarters of MAAG, the US Military Assistance and Advisory Group, and see General Huyser and General Gast; he wanted to get Taylor and John Howell hyped up to put a bomb under Dadgar's tail; he wanted to *move*, to *go*, to get this problem *solved*, to get Paul and Bill *out*, and *fast*.

He banged on Taylor's door and walked in. 'Okay, Keane,' he said. 'Bring me up to speed.'

Six

1

John Howell was born in the ninth minute of the ninth hour
of the ninth day of the ninth month of 1946, his mother often
said.

He was a short, small man with a bouncy walk. His fine
light-brown hair was receding early, he had a slight squint,
and his voice was faintly hoarse, as if he had a permanent
cold. He spoke very slowly and blinked a lot.

Thirty-two years old, he was an associate in Tom Luce's
Dallas law firm. Like so many of the people around Ross
Perot, Howell had achieved a responsible position at a
young age. His greatest asset as a lawyer was stamina: 'John
wins by *outworking* the opposition,' Luce would say. Most
weekends Howell would spend either Saturday or Sunday at
the office, tidying up loose ends, finishing tasks that had
been interrupted by the phone, and preparing for the week
ahead. He would get frustrated when family activities
deprived him of that sixth working day. In addition, he often
worked late into the evening and missed dinner at home,
which sometimes made his wife Angela unhappy.

Like Perot, Howell was born in Texarkana. Like Perot, he
was short in stature and long on guts. Nevertheless, at
midday on 14 January he was scared. He was about to meet
Dadgar.

The previous afternoon, immediately after arriving in
Tehran, Howell had met with Ahmad Houman, EDS's new
local attorney. Dr Houman had advised him *not* to meet
Dadgar, at least not yet: it was perfectly possible that
Dadgar intended to arrest all the EDS Americans he could
find, and that might include lawyers.

194

Howell had found Houman impressive. A big, rotund man in his sixties, well dressed by Iranian standards, he was a former President of the Iran Bar Association. Although his English was not good – French was his second language – he seemed confident and knowledgeable.

Houman's advice gelled with Howell's instinct. He always liked to prepare very thoroughly for any kind of confrontation. He believed in the old maxim of trial lawyers: never ask a question unless you already know the answer.

Houman's advice was reinforced by Bunny Fleishhaker. An American woman with Iranian friends in the Ministry of Justice, Bunny had warned Jay Coburn, back in December, that Paul and Bill were going to be arrested, but at the time no-one had believed her. Events had given her retrospective credibility, and she was taken seriously when, early in January, she called Rich Gallagher's home at eleven o'clock one evening.

The conversation had reminded Gallagher of the phone calls in the movie *All The President's Men*, in which nervous informants talked to the newspaper reporters in improvised code. Bunny began by saying: 'D'you know who this is?'

'I think so,' Gallagher said.

'You've been told about me.'

'Yes.'

EDS's phones were bugged and the conversations were being taped, she explained. The reason she had called was to say that there was a strong chance Dadgar would arrest more EDS executives. She recommended they either leave the country or move into a hotel where there were lots of newspaper reporters. Lloyd Briggs, who as Paul's No 3 seemed the likeliest target for Dadgar, had left the country – he needed to return to the States to brief EDS's lawyers anyway. The others, Gallagher and Keane Taylor, had moved into the Hyatt.

Dadgar had not arrested any more EDS people – yet.

Howell needed no more convincing. He was going to stay out of Dadgar's way until he was sure of the ground rules.

Then, at eight-thirty this morning, Dadgar had raided Bucharest.

He had turned up with half a dozen investigators and demanded to see EDS's files. Howell, hiding in an office on another floor, had called Houman. After a quick discussion he had advised all EDS personnel to co-operate with Dadgar.

Dadgar had wanted to see Chiapparone's files. The filing cabinet in Paul's secretary's office was locked and nobody could find the key. Of course that made Dadgar all the more keen to see the files. Keane Taylor had solved the problem in characteristically direct fashion: he had got a crowbar and broken the cabinet open.

Meanwhile Howell snuck out of the building, met Dr Houman, and went to the Ministry of Justice.

That too had been scary, for he had been obliged to fight his way through an unruly crowd which was demonstrating, outside the Ministry, against the holding of political prisoners.

Howell and Houman had an appointment with Dr Kian, Dadgar's superior.

Howell told Kian that EDS was a reputable company which had done nothing wrong, and it was eager to co-operate in any investigation in order to clear its name, but it wanted to get its employees out of jail.

Kian said he had asked one of his assistants to ask Dadgar to review the case.

That sounded to Howell like nothing at all.

He told Kian he wanted to talk about a reduction in the bail.

The conversation took place in Farsi, with Houman translating. Houman said that Kian was not inflexibly opposed to a reduction in the bail. In Houman's opinion they might expect it to be halved.

Kian gave Howell a note authorizing him to visit Paul and Bill in jail.

The meeting had been just about fruitless, Howell thought afterwards, but at least Kian had not arrested him.

When he returned to Bucharest he found that Dadgar had not arrested anyone either.

His lawyer's instinct still told him not to see Dadgar; but now that instinct struggled with another side of his personality; impatience. There were times when Howell wearied of research, preparation, foresight, planning – times when he wanted to *move* on a problem instead of thinking about it. He liked to take the initiative, to have the opposition reacting to him, rather than the other way around. This inclination was reinforced by the presence in Tehran of Ross Perot, always up first in the morning, asking people what they had achieved yesterday and what tasks they intended to accomplish today, always on everyone's back. So impatience got the better of caution, and Howell decided to confront Dadgar.

This was why he was scared.

If he was unhappy, his wife was more so.

Angela Howell had not seen much of her husband in the last two months. He had spent most of November and December in Tehran, trying to persuade the Ministry to pay EDS's bill. Since getting back to the States he had been staying at EDS headquarters until all hours of the night, working on the Paul and Bill problem, when he was not dashing off to New York for meetings with Iranian lawyers there. On 31 December Howell had arrived home at breakfast-time, after working all night, at EDS, to find Angela and baby Michael, nine months old, huddled in front of a wood fire in a cold, dark house: the ice storm had caused a power failure. He had moved them into his sister's apartment and gone off to New York again.

Angela had had about as much as she could take, and when he announced he was going to Tehran again she had been upset. 'You *know* what's going on over there,' she had said. '*Why* do you have to go back?'

The trouble was that he did not have a simple answer to that question. It was not clear just what he was going to do in Tehran. He was going to work on the problem, but he did not know how. If he had been able to say, 'Look, this is what has to be done, and it's my responsibility, and I'm the only one who can do it,' she might have understood.

'John, we're a family. I need your help to take care of all this,' she had said, meaning the ice storm, the blackouts, and the baby.

'I'm sorry. Just do the best you can. I'll try to stay in touch,' Howell had said.

They were not the kind of married couple to express their feelings by yelling at each other. On the frequent occasions when he upset her by working late, leaving her to sit alone and eat the dinner she had fixed for him, a certain coolness was the closest they came to fighting. But this was worse than missing supper: he was abandoning her and the baby just when they needed him.

They had a long talk that evening. At the end of it she was no happier, but she was at least resigned.

He had called her several times since, from London and from Tehran. She was watching the riots on the TV news and worrying about him. She would have been even more worried if she had known what he was about to do now.

He pushed domestic concerns to the back of his mind and went to find Abolhasan.

Abolhasan was EDS's senior Iranian employee. When Lloyd Briggs had departed for New York, Abolhasan had been left in charge of EDS in Iran. (Rich Gallagher, the only American still there, was not a manager.) Then Keane Taylor had returned and assumed overall charge, and Abolhasan had been offended. Taylor was no diplomat. (Bill Gayden had coined the sarcastic phrase 'Keane's Marine Corps sensitivity training'.) There had been friction. But Howell got on fine with Abolhasan, who could translate not just the Farsi language but also Persian customs and methods for his American employers.

Dadgar knew Abolhasan's father, a distinguished lawyer, and had met Abolhasan himself at the interrogation of Paul and Bill, so this morning Abolhasan had been appointed liaison man with Dadgar's investigators, and had been instructed to make sure they had everything they asked for.

Howell said to Abolhasan: 'I've decided I should meet with Dadgar. What do you think?'

'Sure,' Abolhasan said. He had an American wife and spoke English with an American accent. 'I don't think that'll be a problem.'

'Okay. Let's go.'

Abolhasan led Howell to Paul Chiapparone's conference room. Dadgar and his assistants were sitting around the big table, going through EDS's financial records. Abolhasan asked Dadgar to step into the adjoining room, Paul's office; then he introduced Howell.

Dadgar gave a businesslike handshake.

They sat around the table in the corner of the office. Dadgar did not look to Howell like a monster, just a rather weary middle-aged man who was losing his hair.

Howell began by repeating to Dadgar what he had said to Dr Kian: 'EDS is a reputable company which has done nothing wrong, and we are willing to co-operate with your investigation. However, we cannot tolerate having two senior executives in jail.'

Dadgar's answer – translated by Abolhasan – surprised him. 'If you have done nothing wrong, why have you not paid the bail?'

'There's no connection between the two,' Howell said. 'Bail is a guarantee that someone will appear for trial, not a sum to be forfeited if he is guilty. Bail is repaid as soon as the accused man appears in court, regardless of the verdict.' While Abolhasan translated, Howell wondered whether 'bail' was the correct English translation of whatever Farsi word Dadgar was using to describe the $12,750,000 he was demanding. And now Howell recalled something else that might be significant. On the day Paul and Bill were arrested, he had talked on the phone with Abolhasan, who reported that the $12,750,000 was, according to Dadgar, the total amount EDS had been paid to date by the Ministry of Health, and Dadgar's argument had been that if the contract had been corruptly awarded then EDS was not entitled to that money. (Abolhasan had not translated this remark to Paul and Bill at the time.)

In fact EDS had been paid a good deal more than thirteen

million dollars, so the remark had not made much sense, and Howell had discounted it. Perhaps that had been a mistake: it might just be that Dadgar's arithmetic was wrong.

Abolhasan was translating Dadgar's reply. 'If the men are innocent, there is no reason why they should not appear for trial, so you would risk nothing by paying the bail.'

'An American corporation can't do that,' Howell said. He was not lying, but he was being deliberately deceitful. 'EDS is a publicly-traded company, and under American securities laws it can only use its money for the benefit of its shareholders. Paul and Bill are free individuals: the company cannot guarantee that they will show up for trial. Consequently we cannot spend the company's money this way.'

This was the initial negotiating position Howell had previously formulated; but as Abolhasan translated he could see it was making little impression on Dadgar.

'Their families have to put up the bail,' he went on. 'Right now they are raising money in the States, but thirteen million dollars is out of the question. Now, if the bail were lowered to a more reasonable figure, they might be able to pay it.' This was all lies, of course: Ross Perot was going to pay the bail, if he had to, and if Tom Walter could find a way to get the money into Iran.

It was Dadgar's turn to be surprised. 'Is it true that you could not force your men to appear for trial?'

'Sure it's true,' Howell said. 'What are we going to do, lock them in chains? We're not a police force. You see, you're holding *individuals* in jail for alleged crimes of a *corporation*.'

Dadgar's reply was: 'No, they are in jail for what they have done personally.'

'Which is?'

'They obtained money from the Ministry of Health by means of false progress reports.'

'This obviously cannot apply to Bill Gaylord, because the Ministry had paid none of the bills presented since he arrived in Tehran – so what is he accused of?'

'He falsified reports, and I will not be cross-examined by you, Mr Howell.'

Howell suddenly remembered that Dadgar could put him in jail.

Dadgar went on: 'I am conducting an investigation. When it is complete, I will either release your clients or prosecute them.'

Howell said, 'We're willing to co-operate with your investigation. In the meantime, what can we do to get Paul and Bill released?'

'Pay the bail.'

'And if they are released on bail, will they be permitted to leave Iran?'

'No.'

2

Jay Coburn walked through the double sliding glass doors into the lobby of the Sheraton. On his right was the long registration desk. To his left were the hotel shops. In the centre of the lobby was a couch.

In accordance with his instructions, he bought a copy of Newsweek magazine at the news-stand. He sat on the couch, facing the doors so that he could see everyone who came in, and pretended to read the magazine.

He felt like a character in a spy movie.

The rescue plan was in a holding pattern while Majid researched the Colonel in charge of the jail. Meanwhile Coburn was doing a job for Perot.

He had an assignation with a man nicknamed Deep Throat (after the secretive character who gave 'deep background' to reporter Bob Woodward in *All The President's Men*.) This Deep Throat was an American management consultant who gave seminars to foreign corporate executives on how to do business with the Iranians. Before Paul and Bill were arrested, Lloyd Briggs had engaged Deep Throat to help EDS get the Ministry to pay its bills. He had advised Briggs that EDS was in bad trouble, but for a payment of two and a half million dollars they could get the slate wiped clean. At the time EDS had scorned this advice: the government owed money to EDS, not vice versa; it was the Iranians who needed to get the slate wiped clean.

The arrest had given credibility to Deep Throat (as it had to Bunny Fleishhaker) and Briggs had contacted him again. 'Well, they're mad at you now,' he had said. 'It's going to be harder than ever, but I'll see what I can do.'

He called back yesterday. He could solve the problem, he said. He demanded a face-to-face meeting with Ross Perot.

Taylor, Howell, Young and Gallagher all agreed there was *no way* Perot was going to expose himself to such a meeting – they were horrified that Deep Throat even knew Perot was in town. So Perot asked Simons if he could send Coburn instead, and Simons consented.

Coburn had called Deep Throat and said he would be representing Perot.

'No, no,' said Deep Throat, 'it has to be Perot himself.'

'Then all deals are off,' Coburn had replied.

'Okay, okay.' Deep Throat had backed down and given Coburn instructions.

Coburn had to go to a certain phone box in the Vanak area, not far from Keane Taylor's house, at eight p.m.

At exactly eight o'clock the phone in the booth rang. Deep Throat told Coburn to go to the Sheraton, which was nearby, and sit in the lobby reading Newsweek. They would meet there and identify one another by a code. Deep Throat would say: 'Do you know where Pahlavi Avenue is?' It was a block away, but Coburn was to reply: 'No, I don't, I'm new in town.'

That was why he felt like a spy in a movie.

On Simons's advice he was wearing his long, bulky down coat, the one Taylor called his Michelin Man coat. The object was to find out whether Deep Throat would frisk him. If not, he would be able, at any future meetings, to wear a recording device under the coat and tape the conversation.

He flicked through the pages of Newsweek.

'Do you know where Pahlavi Avenue is?'

Coburn looked up to see a man of about his own height and weight, in his early forties, with dark slicked-down hair and glasses. 'No, I don't, I'm new in town.'

Deep Throat looked around nervously. 'Let's go,' he said. 'Over there.'

Coburn got up and followed him to the back of the hotel. They stopped in a dark passage. 'I'll have to frisk you,' said Deep Throat.

Coburn raised his arms. 'What are you afraid of?'

Deep Throat gave a scornful laugh. 'You can't trust anyone. There are no rules any more in this town.' He finished his search.

'Do we go back in the lobby now?'

'No. I could be under surveillance – I can't risk being seen with you.'

'Okay. What are you offering?'

Deep Throat gave the same scornful laugh. 'You guys are in *trouble*,' he said. 'You've already messed up once, by refusing to listen to people who *know* this country.'

'How did we mess up?'

'You think this is Texas. It's not.'

'But *how* did we mess up?'

'You could have got out of this for two and a half million dollars. Now it'll cost you six.'

'What's the deal?'

'Just a minute. You let me down last time. This is going to be your last chance. This time, there's no backing out at the last minute.'

Coburn was beginning to dislike Deep Throat. The man was a wise guy. His whole manner said *you're such fools, and I know so much more than you, it's hard for me to descend to your level.*

'Who do we pay the money to?' Coburn asked.

'A numbered account in Switzerland.'

'And how do we know we'll get what we're paying for?'

Deep Throat laughed. 'Listen, the way things work in this

203

country, you don't let go of your money until the goods are delivered. That's the way to get things done here.'

'Okay, so what's the arrangement?'

'Lloyd Briggs meets me in Switzerland and we open an escrow account and sign a letter of agreement which is lodged with the bank. The money is released from the account when Chiapparone and Gaylord get out – which will be immediately, if you'll just let me handle this.'

'Who gets the money?'

Deep Throat shook his head contemptuously.

Coburn said: 'Well, how do we know you really have a deal wired?'

'Look, I'm just passing on information from people close to the person who's causing you a problem.'

'You mean Dadgar?'

'You'll never learn, will you?'

As well as finding out what Deep Throat's proposal was, Coburn had to make a personal evaluation of the man. Well, he had made it now: Deep Throat was full of shit.

'Okay,' Coburn said. 'We'll be in touch.'

Keane Taylor poured a little rum into a big glass, added ice, and filled the glass with Coke. This was his regular drink.

Taylor was a big man, six feet two, 210 pounds, with a chest like a barrel. He had played football in the marines. He took care with his clothes, favouring suits with deep-plunging vests and shirts with button-down collars. He wore large gold-rimmed glasses. He was thirty-nine, and losing his hair.

The young Taylor had been a hell-raiser – a dropout from college, busted down from Sergeant in the Marines for disciplinary offences – and he still disliked close supervision. He preferred working in the World subsidiary of EDS because head office was so far away.

He was under close supervision now. After four days in Tehran Ross Perot was savage.

Taylor dreaded the evening debriefing sessions with his boss. After he and Howell had spent the day dashing around

204

the city, fighting the traffic, the demonstrations, and the intransigence of Iranian officialdom, they would then have to explain to Perot why they had achieved precisely nothing.

To make matters worse, Perot was confined to the hotel most of the time. He had gone out only twice: once to the US Embassy and once to US Military Headquarters. Taylor had made sure no-one offered him the keys to a car or any local currency, to discourage any impulse Perot might have had to take a walk. But the result was that Perot was like a caged bear, and being debriefed by him was like getting into the cage with the bear.

At least Taylor no longer had to pretend that he did not know about the rescue team. Coburn had taken him to meet Simons, and they had talked for three hours – or rather, Taylor had talked: Simons just asked questions. They had sat in the living room of Taylor's house, with Simons dropping cigar ash on Taylor's carpet, and Taylor had told him that Iran was like an animal with its head cut off: the head – the Ministers and officials – were still trying to give orders, but the body – the Iranian people – were off doing their own thing. Consequently, political pressure would not free Paul and Bill: they would have to be bailed out or rescued. For three hours Simons had never changed the tone of his voice, never offered an opinion, never even moved from this chair.

But the Simons ice was easier to deal with than the Perot fire. Each morning Perot would knock on the door while Taylor was shaving. Taylor got up a little earlier each day, in order to be ready when Perot came, but Perot got up earlier each day too, until Taylor began to fantasize that Perot listened outside the door all night, waiting to catch him shaving. Perot would be full of ideas which had come to him during the night: new arguments for Paul's and Bill's innocence, new schemes for persuading the Iranians to release them. Taylor and John Howell – the tall and the short, like Batman and Robin – would head off in the Batmobile to the Ministry of Justice or the Ministry of Health, where officials would demolish Perot's ideas in

205

seconds. Perot was still using a legalistic, rational, American approach, and, in Taylor's opinion, had yet to realize that the Iranians were not playing according to those rules.

This was not all Taylor had on his mind. His wife, Mary, and the children, Mike and Dawn, were staying with his parents in Pittsburgh. Taylor's mother and father were both over eighty, both in failing health. His mother had a heart condition. Mary was having to deal with that on her own. She had not complained, but he could tell, when he talked to her on the phone, that she was not happy.

Taylor sighed. He could not cope with all the world's problems at one time. He topped up his drink, then, carrying the glass, left his room and went to Perot's suite for the evening bloodbath.

Perot paced up and down the sitting-room of his suite, waiting for the negotiating team to gather. He was doing no good here in Tehran and he knew it.

He had suffered a chilly reception at the US Embassy. He had been shown into the office of Charles Naas, the Ambassador's deputy. Naas had been gracious, but had given Perot the same old story about how EDS should work through the legal system for the release of Paul and Bill. Perot had insisted on seeing the Ambassador. He had come halfway round the world to see Sullivan, and he was not going to leave before speaking to him. Eventually Sullivan came in, shook Perot's hand, and told him he was most unwise to come to Iran. It was clear that Perot was a *problem* and Sullivan did not want any more *problems*. He talked for a while, but did not sit down, and he left as soon as he could. Perot was not used to such treatment. He was, after all, an important American, and in normal circumstances a diplomat such as Sullivan would be at least courteous, if not deferential.

Perot also met Lou Goelz, who seemed sincerely concerned about Paul and Bill but offered no concrete help.

Outside Naas's office he ran into a group of military attachés who recognized him. Since the prisoners-of-war campaign Perot has always been able to count on a warm reception from the American military. He sat down with the attachés and told them his problem. They said candidly that they could not help. 'Look, forget what you read in the paper, forget what the State Department is saying publicly,' one of them told him. 'We don't have any power here, we don't have any control – you're wasting your time in the US Embassy.'

Perot had also wasted his time at US Military Headquarters. Cathy Gallagher's boss, Colonel Keith Barlow, chief of the US Support Activity Command in Iran, had sent a bulletproof car to the Hyatt. Perot had got in with Rich Gallagher. The driver had been Iranian: Perot wondered which side he was on.

They met with Air Force General Phillip Gast, chief of the US Military Assistance Advisory Group (MAAG) in Iran, and General 'Dutch' Huyser. Perot knew Huyser slightly, and remembered him as a strong, dynamic man; but now he looked drained. Perot knew from the newspapers that Huyser was President Carter's emissary, here to persuade the Iranian military to back the doomed Bakhtiar government; and Perot guessed that Huyser had no stomach for the job.

Huyser candidly said he would like to help Paul and Bill but at the moment he had no leverage with the Iranians: he had nothing to trade. Even if they got out of jail, Huyser said, they would be in danger here. Perot told them he had that taken care of: Bull Simons was here to look after Paul and Bill once they got out. Huyser burst out laughing, and a moment later Gast saw the joke: they knew who Simons was, and they knew he would be planning more than a babysitting job.

Gast offered to supply fuel to Simons, but that was all. Warm words from the military, cold words from the Embassy; little or no real help from either. And nothing but excuses from Howell and Taylor.

Sitting in a hotel room all day was driving Perot crazy. Today Cathy Gallagher had asked him to take care of her poodle, Buffy. She made it sound like an honour – a measure of her high esteem for Perot – and he had been so surprised that he had agreed. Sitting looking at the animal, he had realized that this was a funny occupation for the leader of a major international business, and he wondered how the hell he had let himself be talked into it. He got no sympathy from Keane Taylor, who thought it was funny as hell. After a few hours Cathy had come back from the hairdresser's or wherever she had been, and had taken the dog back; but Perot's mood remained black.

There was a knock at Perot's door, and Taylor came in, carrying his usual drink. He was followed by John Howell, Rich Gallagher and Bob Young. They all sat down.

'Now,' said Perot, 'did you tell them that we'd guarantee to produce Paul and Bill for questioning anywhere in the US or Europe, on thirty days' notice, at any time in the next two years?'

'They're not interested in that idea,' said Howell.

'What do you mean, they're not interested?'

'I'm just telling you what they said—'

'But if this is an investigation, rather than a blackmail attempt, all they need is to be sure that Paul and Bill will be available for questioning.'

'They're sure already. I guess they see no reason to make changes.'

It was maddening. There seemed no way to reason with the Iranians, no way to reach them. 'Did you suggest they release Paul and Bill into the custody of the US Embassy?'

'They turned that down, too.'

'Why?'

'They didn't say.'

'Did you ask them?'

'Ross, they don't have to give reasons. They're in charge here, and they know it.'

'But they're responsible for the safety of their prisoners.'

'It's a responsibility that doesn't seem to weigh too heavily on them.'

Taylor said: 'Ross, they're not playing to our rules.

Putting two men in jail is not a big deal to them. Paul and Bill's safety is not a big deal—'

'So what rules are they playing to? Can you tell me that?'

There was a knock on the door and Coburn walked in, wearing his Michelin Man coat and his black knit hat. Perot brightened: perhaps he would have good news. 'Did you meet with Deep Throat?'

'Sure did,' said Coburn, taking off his coat.

'All right, let's have it.'

'He says he can get Paul and Bill released for six million dollars. The money would be paid into an escrow account in Switzerland and released when Paul and Bill leave Iran.'

'Hell, that ain't bad,' said Perot. 'We get out with fifty cents on the dollar. Under US law it would even be legal – it's a ransom. What kind of guy is Deep Throat?'

'I don't trust the bastard,' said Coburn.

'Why?'

Coburn shrugged. 'I don't know, Ross . . . He's shifty, flaky . . . A bullshitter . . . I wouldn't give him sixty cents to go to the store and get me a pack of cigarettes. That's my gut feeling.'

'But, listen, what do you expect?' Perot said. 'This is bribery – pillars of the community don't get involved in this kind of thing.'

Howell said: 'You *said* it. This is bribery.' His deliberate, throaty voice was unusually passionate. 'I don't like this one bit.'

'I don't *like* it,' Perot said. 'But you've all been telling me that the Iranians aren't playing to our rules.'

'Yes, but *listen*,' Howell said fervently. 'The straw I've been clinging to all through this is that *we've done nothing wrong* – and someday, somehow, somewhere, some*body* is going to recognize that, and then all this will evaporate . . . I'd *hate* to give up that straw.'

'It hasn't got us far.'

'Ross, I believe that with time and patience we will succeed. But if we get involved in bribery we no longer have a case!'

209

Perot turned to Coburn. 'How do we *know* Deep Throat has a deal wired with Dadgar?'

'We don't know,' Coburn said. 'His argument is, we don't pay until we get results, so what do we have to lose?'

'Everything,' Howell said. 'Never mind what is legal in the United States, this could seal our fate in Iran.'

Taylor said: 'It stinks. The whole thing stinks.'

Perot was surprised by their reactions. He, too, hated the idea of bribery, but he was prepared to compromise his principles to get Paul and Bill out of jail. The good name of EDS was precious to him, and he was loath to let it be associated with corruption, just as John Howell was; but Perot knew something Howell did not know: that Colonel Simons and the rescue team faced risks more grave than this.

Perot said: 'Our good name hasn't done Paul and Bill any good so far.'

'It's not just our good name,' Howell persisted. 'Dadgar must be pretty sure by now that we aren't guilty of corruption – but if he could catch us in a bribe situation he could still save face.'

That was a point, Perot thought. 'Could this be a trap?'

'Yes!'

It made sense. Unable to get any evidence against Paul and Bill, Dadgar pretends to Deep Throat that he can be bribed, then – when Perot falls for it – announces to the world that EDS is, after all, corrupt. Then they would all be put in jail with Paul and Bill. And, being guilty, they would stay there.

'All right,' said Perot reluctantly. 'Call Deep Throat and tell him no, thanks.'

Coburn stood up. 'Okay.'

It had been another fruitless day, Perot thought. The Iranians had him all ways. Political pressure they ignored. Bribery could make matters worse. If EDS paid the bail, Paul and Bill would still be kept in Iran.

Simons's team still looked like the best bet.

But he was not going to tell the negotiating team that.

'All right,' he said. 'We'll just try again tomorrow.'

Tall Keane Taylor and short John Howell, like Batman and Robin, tried again on 17 January. They drove to the Ministry of Health building on Eisenhower Avenue, taking Abolhasan as interpreter, and met Dadgar at ten a.m. With Dadgar were officials of the Social Security Organization, the department of the Ministry which was run by EDS's computers.

Howell had decided to abandon his initial negotiating position, that EDS could not pay the bail because of American securities law. It was equally useless to demand to know the charges against Paul and Bill and what evidence there was: Dadgar could stonewall that approach by saying he was still investigating. But Howell did not have a new strategy to replace the old. He was playing poker with no cards in his hand. Perhaps Dadgar would deal him some today.

Dadgar began by explaining that the staff of the Social Security Organization wanted EDS to turn over to them what was known as the 125 Data Centre.

This small computer, Howell recalled, ran the payroll and pensions for the Social Security Organization staff. What these people wanted was to get their own wages, even while Iranians generally were not getting their social security benefits.

Keane Taylor said: 'It's not that simple. Such a turnover would be a very complex operation needing many skilled staff. Of course they are all back in the States.'

Dadgar replied: 'Then you should bring them back in.'

'I'm not that stupid,' Taylor said.

Taylor's Marine Corps sensitivity training was operating, Howell thought.

Dadgar said: 'If he speaks like that he will go to jail.'

'Just like my staff would if I brought them back to Iran,' said Taylor.

211

Howell broke in. 'Would you be able to give a legal guarantee that any returning staff would not be arrested or harassed in any way?'

'I could not give a formal guarantee,' Dadgar replied. 'However, I would give my personal word of honour.'

Howell darted an anxious glance at Taylor. Taylor did not speak, but his expression said he would not give two cents for Dadgar's word of honour. 'We could certainly investigate ways of arranging the turnover,' Howell said. Dadgar had at last given him something to bargain with, even though it was not much. 'There would have to be safeguards, of course. For example, you would have to certify that the machinery was handed over to you in a good condition . . .' Howell was shadow-boxing. If the data centre was handed over, there would be a price: the release of Paul and Bill.

Dadgar demolished that idea with his next sentence. 'Every day new complaints are being made about your company to my investigators, complaints which would justify increases in the bail. However, if you co-operate in the turnover of the 125 Data Centre, I can in return ignore the new complaints and refrain from increasing the bail.'

Taylor said: 'Goddam it, this is nothing but blackmail!'

Howell realized that the 125 Data Centre was a sideshow. Dadgar had raised the question, no doubt at the urging of these officials, but he did not care about it enough to offer serious concessions. So what *did* he care about?

Howell thought of Lucio Randone, the former cellmate of Paul and Bill. Randone's offer of help had been followed up by EDS manager Paul Bucha, who had gone to Italy to talk to Randone's company, Condotti d'Acqua. Bucha reported that the company had been building apartment blocks in Tehran when their Iranian financiers ran out of money. The company naturally stopped building; but many Iranians had already paid for apartments under construction. Given the present atmosphere it was not surprising that the foreigners got blamed, and Randone had been jailed as a scapegoat. The company had found a new source of finance and resumed building, and Randone had got out of jail at the same time, in a package deal arranged by an Iranian lawyer, Ali Azmayesh. Bucha also reported that the Italians kept saying: 'Remember, Iran will always be Iran, it never changes.' He took this to be a hint that a bribe was part of the package deal. Howell also knew that a traditional channel for paying a bribe was a lawyer's fee: the lawyer would do, say a thousand dollars' worth of work and pay a ten-thousand-dollar bribe, then charge his client eleven thousand dollars. This hint of corruption made Howell nervous, but despite that he had gone to see Azmayesh, who had advised him: 'EDS does not have a legal problem, it has a business problem.' If EDS could come to a business arrangement with the Ministry of Health, Dadgar would go away. Azmayesh had not mentioned bribery.

All this had started, Howell thought, as a business problem: the customer unable to pay, the supplier refusing to go on working. Might a compromise be possible, under which EDS would switch on the computers and the Ministry would pay at least some money? He decided to ask Dadgar directly.

'Would it help if EDS were to renegotiate its contract with the Ministry of Health?'

'This might be very helpful,' Dadgar answered. 'It would not be a legal solution to our problem, but it might be a practical solution. Otherwise, to waste all the work that has been done in computerizing the Ministry would be a pity.'

Interesting, thought Howell. They want a modern social security system – or their money back. Putting Paul and Bill in jail on thirteen million dollars bail was their way of giving EDS those two options – and no others. We're getting straight talk, at last.

He decided to be blunt. 'Of course, it would be out of the question to begin negotiations while Chiapparone and Gaylord are still in jail.'

Dadgar replied: 'Still, if you commit to good-faith negotiations, the Ministry will call me and the charges might be changed, the bail might be reduced, and Chiapparone

213

and Gaylord might even be released on their personal guarantees.'

Nothing could be plainer than that, Howell thought. EDS had better go see the Minister of Health.

Since the Ministry stopped paying its bills there had been two changes of government. Dr Sheikholeslamizadeh, who was now in jail, had been replaced by a general; and then, when Bakhtiar became Prime Minister, the general had in turn been replaced by a new Minister of Health. Who, Howell wondered, was the new guy; and what was he like?

'Mr Young, of the American company EDS, is calling you, Minister,' said the secretary.

Dr Razmara took a deep breath. 'Tell him that American businessmen may no longer pick up the phone and call Ministers of the Iranian government and expect to talk to us as if we were their employees,' he said. He raised his voice. 'Those days are over!'

Then he asked for the EDS file.

Manuchehr Razmara had been in Paris over Christmas. French-educated – he was a cardiologist – and married to a Frenchwoman, he considered France his second home, and spoke fluent French. He was also a member of the Iranian National Medical Council and a friend of Shahpour Bakhtiar, and when Bakhtiar had become Prime Minister he had called his friend Razmara in Paris and asked him to come home to be Minister of Health.

The EDS file was handed to him by Dr Emrani, the Deputy Minister in charge of social security. Emrani had survived the two changes of government: he had been here when the trouble had started.

Razmara read the file with mounting anger. The EDS project was insane. The basic contract price was forty-eight million dollars, with escalators taking it up to a possible ninety million. Razmara recalled that Iran had twelve thousand working doctors to serve a population of thirty-two million, and that there were sixty-four thousand villages without tap water; and he concluded that whoever had

214

signed the deal with EDS were fools or traitors, or both. How could they *possibly* justify spending millions on computers when the people lacked the fundamental necessities of public health like clean water? There could only be one explanation: they had been bribed.

Well they would suffer. Emrani had prepared this dossier, for the special court which prosecuted corrupt civil servants. Three people were in jail: former Minister Sheikholes-lamizadeh and two of his Deputy Ministers, Reza Neghabat and Nili Arame. That was as it should be. The blame for the mess they were in should fall primarily on Iranians. However, the Americans were also culpable. American businessmen and their government had encouraged the Shah in his mad schemes, and had taken their profits: now they must suffer. Furthermore, according to the file, EDS had been spectacularly incompetent: the computers were not yet working, after two and a half years, yet the automation project had so disrupted Emrani's department that the old-fashioned systems were not working either, with the result that Emrani could not monitor his department's expenditure. This was a principal cause of the Ministry's overspending its budget, the file said.

Razmara noted that the US Embassy was protesting about the jailing of the two Americans, Chiapparone and Gaylord, because there was no evidence against them. That was typical of the Americans. Of course there was no proof: bribes were not paid by cheque. The Embassy was also concerned for the safety of the two prisoners. Razmara found this ironic. *He* was concerned for *his* safety. Each day when he went to the office he wondered whether he would come home alive.

He closed the file. He had no sympathy for EDS or its jailed executives. Even if he had wanted to have them released, he would not have been able to, he reflected. The anti-American mood of the people was rising to fever pitch. The government of which Razmara was a part, the Bakhtiar regime, had been installed by the Shah and was therefore widely suspected of being pro-American. With the country

215

in such turmoil, any Minister who concerned himself with the welfare of a couple of greedy American capitalist lackeys would be sacked if not lynched – and quite rightly. Razmara turned his attention to more important matters.

The next day his secretary said: 'Mr Young, of the American company EDS, is here asking to see you, Minister.'

The arrogance of the Americans was infuriating. Razmara said: 'Repeat to him the message I gave you yesterday – then give him five minutes to get off the premises.'

4

For Bill, the big problem was time.

He was different from Paul. For Paul – restless, aggressive, strong-willed, ambitious – the worst of being in jail was the helplessness. Bill was more placid by nature: he accepted that there was nothing to do but pray, so he prayed. (He did not wear his religion on his sleeve: he did his praying late at night, before going to sleep, or early in the morning before the others woke up.) What got to Bill was the excruciating slowness with which time passed. A day in the real world – a day of solving problems, making decisions, taking phone calls, and attending meetings – was no time at all: a day in jail was endless. Bill devised a formula for conversion of real time to jail time.

Real Time		Jail Time
1 Second	=	1 Minute
1 Minute	=	1 Hour
1 Hour	=	1 Day
1 Week	=	1 Month
1 Month	=	1 Year

Time took on this new dimension for Bill after two or three weeks in jail, when he realized there was going to be no quick solution to the problem. Unlike a convicted criminal, he had not been sentenced to ninety days or five years, so he could gain no comfort from scratching a calendar on the wall as a countdown to freedom. It made no difference how many days had passed: his remaining time in jail was indefinite, therefore endless.

His Persian cellmates did not seem to feel this way. It was a revealing cultural contrast: the Americans, trained to get fast results, were tortured by suspense; the Iranians were content to wait for *'fardah'*, tomorrow, next week, sometime, eventually – just as they had been in business.

Nevertheless, as the Shah's grip weakened Bill thought he saw signs of desperation in some of them, and he came to mistrust them. He was careful not to tell them who was in town from Dallas or what progress was being made in the negotiations for his release: he was afraid that, clutching at straws, they would have tried to trade information to the guards.

He was becoming a well-adjusted jailbird. He learned to ignore dirt and bugs, and he got used to cold, starchy unappetizing food. He learned to live within a small, clearly defined personal boundary, the prisoner's 'turf'. He stayed active.

He found ways to fill the endless days. He read books, taught Paul chess, exercised in the hall, talked to the Iranians to get every word of the radio and TV news, and prayed. He made a minutely detailed survey of the jail, measuring the cells and the corridors and drawing plans and sketches. He kept a diary, recording every trivial event of jail life, plus everything his visitors told him and all the news. He used initials instead of names and sometimes put in invented incidents or altered versions of real incidents, so that if the diary were confiscated or read by the local authorities it would confuse them.

Like prisoners everywhere, he looked forward to visitors as eagerly as a child waiting for Christmas. The EDS people brought decent food, warm clothing, new books, and letters from home. One day Keane Taylor brought a picture of Bill's six-year-old son, Christopher, standing in front of the

Christmas tree. Seeing his little boy, even in a photograph, gave Bill strength: a powerful reminder of what he had to hope for, it renewed his resolve to hang on and not despair.

Bill wrote letters to Emily and gave them to Keane, who would read them to her over the phone. Bill had known Keane for ten years, and they were quite close – they had lived together after the evacuation. Bill knew that Keane was not as insensitive as his reputation would indicate – half of that was an act – but still it was embarrassing to write 'I love you' knowing that Keane would be reading it. Bill got over the embarrassment, because he wanted very badly to tell Emily and the children how much he loved them, just in case he never got another chance to say it in person. The letters were like those written by pilots on the eve of a dangerous mission.

The most important gift brought by the visitors was news. The all-too-brief meetings in the low building across the courtyard were spent discussing the various efforts being made to get Paul and Bill out. It seemed to Bill that time was the key factor. Sooner or later, one approach or another had to work. Unfortunately, as time passed, Iran went downhill. The forces of the revolution were gaining momentum. Would EDS get Paul and Bill out before the whole country exploded?

It was increasingly dangerous for the EDS people to come to the south of the city, where the jail was. Paul and Bill never knew when the next visit would come, or whether there would be a visit. As four days went by, then five, Bill would wonder whether all the others had gone back to the United States and left him and Paul behind. Considering that the bail was impossibly high, and the streets of Tehran impossibly dangerous, might they all give up Paul and Bill as a lost cause? They might be forced, against their wills, to leave in order to save their own lives. Bill recalled the American withdrawal from Vietnam, with the last Embassy officials being lifted off the roofs by helicopter; and he could imagine the scene repeated at the US Embassy in Tehran.

He was occasionally reassured by a visit from an Embassy official. They, too, were taking a risk in coming, but they never brought any hard news about Government efforts to help Paul and Bill, and Bill came to the conclusion that the State Department was inept.

Visits from Dr Houman, their Iranian attorney, were at first highly encouraging; but then Bill realized that in typically Iranian fashion Houman was promising much and producing little. The fiasco of the meeting with Dadgar was desperately depressing. It was frightening to see how easily Dadgar out-manoeuvred Houman, and how determined Dadgar was to keep Paul and Bill jailed. Bill had not slept that night.

When he thought about the bail he found it staggering. No one had ever paid that much ransom, anywhere in the world. He recalled news stories about American businessmen kidnapped in South America and held for a million or two million dollars. (They were usually killed.) Other kidnappings, of millionaires, politicians and celebrities had involved demands for three or four million – never thirteen. No one would pay that much for Paul and Bill.

Besides, even that much money would not buy them the right to leave the country. They would probably be kept under house arrest in Tehran, while the mobs took over. Bail sometimes seemed more like a trap than a way of escape. It was a catch-22.

The whole experience was a lesson in values. Bill learned that he could do without his fine house, his cars, fancy food, and clean clothes. It was no big deal to be living in a dirty room with bugs crawling across the walls. Everything he had in life had been stripped away, and he discovered that the only thing he cared about was his family. When you got right down to it, that was all that really counted: Emily, Vicki, Jackie, Jenny and Chris.

Coburn's visit had cheered him a little. Seeing Jay in that big down coat and woollen hat, with a growth of red beard on his chin, Bill had guessed that he was not in Tehran to work through legal channels. Coburn had spent most of the visit with Paul, and if Paul had learned more, he had not passed it on to Bill. Bill was content: he would find out as soon as he needed to know.

But the day after Coburn's visit there was bad news. On 16 January the Shah left Iran.

The television set in the hall of the jail was switched on, exceptionally, in the afternoon. Paul and Bill, with all the other prisoners, watched the little ceremony in the Imperial Pavilion at Mehrabad Airport. There was the Shah, with his wife, three of his four children, his mother-in-law, and a crowd of courtiers. There, to see them off, was Prime Minister Shahpour Bakhtiar, and a crowd of generals. Bakhtiar kissed the Shah's hand, and the royal party went out to the airplane.

The Ministry people in the jail were gloomy: most of them had been friends, of one kind or another, with the royal family or its immediate circle. Now their patrons were leaving: it meant, at the very least, that they had to resign themselves to a long stay in jail. Bill felt that the Shah had taken with him the last chance of a pro-American outcome in Iran. Now there would be more chaos and confusion, more danger to all Americans in Tehran – and less chance of a swift release for Paul and Bill.

Soon after the television showed the Shah's jet rising into the sky, Bill began to hear a background noise, like a distant crowd, from outside the jail. The noise quickly grew to a pandemonium of shouting and cheering and hooting of horns. The TV showed the source of the noise: a crowd of hundreds of thousands of Iranians was surging through the streets, yelling: *'Shah raft!'* The Shah has gone! Paul said it reminded him of the New Year's Day Parade in Philadelphia. All cars were driving with their headlights on and most were hooting continuously. Many drivers pulled their windscreen wipers forward, attached rags to them, and turned them on, so that they swayed from side to side, permanent mechanical flag-wavers. Truck-loads of jubilant youths careered around the streets celebrating, and all over the city crowds were pulling down and smashing statues of the Shah. Bill wondered what the mobs would do next. This led him to wonder what the guards and the other prisoners would do next. In the hysterical release of all this pent-up Iranian emotion, would Americans become targets?

He and Paul stayed in their cell for the rest of the day, trying to be inconspicuous. They lay on their bunks, talking desultorily. Paul smoked. Bill tried not to think about the terrifying scenes he had watched on TV, but the roar of that lawless multitude, the collective shout of revolutionary triumph, penetrated the prison walls and filled his ears, like the deafening crack and roll of nearby thunder a moment before the lightning strikes.

Two days later, on the morning of 18 January, a guard came to Cell No 5 and said something in Farsi to Reza Neghabat, the former Deputy Minister. Neghabat translated to Paul and Bill: 'You must get your things together. They are moving you.'

'Where to?' Paul asked.

'To another jail.'

Alarm bells rang in Bill's mind. What kind of jail were they going to? The kind where people were tortured and killed? Would EDS be told where they had gone, or would the two of them simply disappear? This place was not wonderful, but it was the devil they knew.

The guard spoke again, and Neghabat said: 'He tells you not to be concerned, this is for your own good.'

It was the work of minutes to put together their toothbrushes, their shared shaver, and their few spare clothes. Then they sat and waited – for three hours.

It was unnerving. Bill had got used to this jail, and – despite his occasional paranoia – basically he trusted his cellmates. He feared the change would be for the worse.

Paul asked Neghabat to try to get news of the move to EDS, maybe by bribing the Colonel in charge of the jail.

The cell father, the old man who had been so concerned for their welfare, was upset that they were leaving. He watched sadly as Paul took down the pictures of Karen and Anne Marie. Impulsively, Paul gave the photographs to the old man, who was visibly moved and thanked him profusely.

At last they were taken out into the courtyard and herded on to a minibus, along with half a dozen other prisoners from different parts of the jail. Bill looked around at the others, trying to figure out what they had in common. One was a Frenchman. Were all the foreigners being taken to a jail of their own, for their safety? But another was the burly Iranian who had been boss of the downstairs cell where they had spent their first night – a common criminal, Bill assumed.

As the bus pulled out of the courtyard, Bill spoke to the Frenchman. 'Do you know where we're going?'

'I am to be released,' the Frenchman said.

Bill's heart leaped. This was good news! Perhaps they were all to be released.

He turned his attention to the scene in the streets. It was the first time for three weeks he had seen the outside world. The government buildings all around the Ministry of Justice were damaged: the mobs really had run wild. Burned cars and broken windows were everywhere. The streets were full of soldiers and tanks but they were doing nothing, not maintaining order, not even controlling the traffic. It seemed to Bill only a matter of time before the weak Bakhtiar government would be overthrown.

What had happened to the EDS people – Taylor, Howell, Young, Gallagher and Coburn? They had not appeared at the jail since the Shah left. Had they been forced to flee, to save their own lives? Somehow Bill was sure they were still in town, still trying to get him and Paul out of jail. He began to hope that this transfer had been arranged by them. Perhaps, instead of taking the prisoners to a different jail, the bus would divert and take them to the US air base. The more he thought about it, the more he believed that everything had

222

been arranged for their release. No doubt the American Embassy had realized, since the departure of the Shah, that Paul and Bill were in serious danger, and had at last got on the case with some real diplomatic muscle. The bus ride was a ruse, a cover story to get them out of the Ministry of Justice jail without arousing the suspicion of hostile Iranian officials such as Dadgar.

The bus was heading north. It passed through districts with which Bill was familiar, and he began to feel safer as the turbulent south of the city receded behind him.

Also, the air base was to the north.

The bus entered a wide square dominated by a huge structure like a fortress. Bill looked interestedly at the building. Its walls were about twenty-five feet high and dotted with guard towers and machine-gun emplacements. The square was full of Iranian women in chadors, the traditional black robes, all making a heck of a noise. Was this some kind of palace, or mosque? Or perhaps a military base?

The bus approached the fortress and slowed down.

Oh, *no*.

A pair of huge steel doors were set centrally in the front. To Bill's horror, the bus drove up and stopped with its nose to the gateway.

This awesome place was the new prison, the new nightmare.

The gates opened and the bus entered.

They were not going to the air base, EDS had not arranged a deal, the Embassy had not got moving, they were not going to be released.

The bus stopped again. The steel doors closed behind it and a second pair of doors opened in front. The bus passed through and stopped in a massive compound dotted with buildings. A guard said something in Farsi, and all the prisoners stood up to get off the bus.

Bill felt like a disappointed child. Life is rotten, he thought. What did I do to deserve this?

What did I do?

'Don't drive so fast,' said Simons.

Joe Poché said: 'Do I drive unsafe?'

'No, I just don't want you violating the laws.'

'What laws?'

'Just be careful.'

Coburn interrupted: 'We're there.'

Poché stopped the car.

They all looked across the heads of the weird women in black and saw the vast fortress of Gasr Prison.

'Jesus Christ,' said Simons. His deep, rough voice was tinged with awe. 'Just look at that bastard.'

They all stared at the high walls, the enormous gates, the guard towers and the machine-gun nests.

Simons said: 'That place is worse than the Alamo.'

It dawned on Coburn that their little rescue team could not attack this place, not without the help of the entire US Army. The rescue they had planned so carefully and rehearsed so many times was now completely irrelevant. There would be no modifications or improvements to the plan, no new scenarios; the whole idea was dead.

They sat in the car for a while, each with his own thoughts.

'Who are those women?' Coburn wondered aloud.

'They have relatives in the jail,' Poché explained.

Coburn could hear a peculiar noise. 'Listen,' he said. 'What *is* that?'

'The women,' said Poché. 'Wailing.'

Colonel Simons had looked up at an impregnable fortress once before.

He had been Captain Simons then, and his friends had called him Art, not Bull.

It was October 1944. Art Simons, twenty-six years old, was commander of Company B, 6th Ranger Infantry Battalion. The Americans were winning the war in the Pacific, and were about to attack the Philippine Islands.

224

Ahead of the invading US forces, the 6th Rangers were already there, committing sabotage and mayhem behind enemy lines.

Company B landed on Homonhon Island in the Leyte Gulf and found there were no Japanese on the island. Simons raised the Stars and Stripes on a coconut palm in front of two hundred docile natives.

That day a report came in that the Japanese garrison on nearby Suluan Island was massacring civilians. Simons requested permission to take Suluan. Permission was refused. A few days later he asked again. He was told that no ships could be spared to transport Company B across the water. Simons asked permission to use native transportation. This time he got the okay.

Simons commandeered three native sailboats and eleven canoes and appointed himself Admiral of the Fleet. He sailed at two a.m. with eighty men. A storm blew up, seven of the canoes capsized, and Simons's fleet returned to shore with most of the navy swimming.

They set off again the next day. This time they sailed by daylight, and – since Japanese planes still controlled the air – the men stripped off and concealed their uniforms and equipment in the bottoms of the boats, so that they would look like native fishermen. The ruse worked, and Company B made landfall on Suluan Island. Simons immediately reconnoitred the Japanese garrison.

That was when he looked up at an impregnable fortress.

The Japanese were garrisoned at the south end of the island, in a lighthouse at the top of a three-hundred-foot coral cliff.

On the west side a trail led half way up the cliff to a steep flight of steps cut into the coral. The entire stairway and most of the trail were in full view of the sixty-foot lighthouse tower and three west-facing buildings on the lighthouse platform. It was a perfect defensive position: two men could have held off five hundred on that flight of coral steps.

But there was always a way.

Simons decided to attack from the east, by scaling the cliff.

The assault began at one a.m. on 2 November. Simons and fourteen men crouched at the foot of the cliff, directly below the garrison. Their faces and hands were blacked: there was a bright moon and the terrain was as open as an Iowa prairie. For silence they communicated by signals and wore their socks over their boots.

Simons gave the signal and they began to climb.

The sharp edges of the coral sliced into the flesh of their fingers and the palms of their hands. In places there were no footholds, and they had to go up climbing vines hand-over-hand. They were completely vulnerable: if one curious sentry should look over the platform, down the east side of the cliff, he would see them instantly, and could pick them off one by one: easy shooting.

They were half way up when the silence was rent by a deafening clang. Someone's rifle stock had banged against a coral cone. They all stopped and lay still against the face of the cliff. Simons held his breath and waited for the rifle shot from above which would begin the massacre. It never came.

After ten minutes they went on.

The climb took a full hour.

Simons was first over the top. He crouched on the platform, feeling naked in the bright moonlight. No Japanese were visible but he could hear voices from one of the low buildings. He trained his rifle on the lighthouse.

The rest of the men began to reach the platform. The attack was to start as soon as they got the machine-gun set up.

Just as the gun came over the edge of the cliff, a sleepy Japanese soldier wandered into view, heading for the latrine. Simons signalled to his point guard, who shot the Japanese; and the firefight began.

Simons turned immediately to the machine-gun. He held one leg and the ammunition box while the gunner held down the other leg and fired. The astonished Japanese ran out of the buildings straight into the deadly hail of bullets.

Twenty minutes later it was all over. Some fifteen of the enemy had been killed. Simons's squad suffered two casualties, neither fatal. And the 'impregnable' fortress had been taken.

There was always a way.

Seven

1

The American Embassy's Volkswagen minibus threaded its way through the streets of Tehran, heading for Gasr Square. Ross Perot sat inside. It was 19 January, the day after Paul and Bill were moved, and Perot was going to visit them in the new jail.

It was a little crazy.

Everyone had gone to great lengths to hide Perot in Tehran, for fear that Dadgar – seeing a far more valuable hostage than Paul or Bill – would arrest him and throw him in jail. Yet here he was, heading for the jail of his own free will, with his own passport in his pocket for identification.

His hopes were pinned on the notorious inability of government everywhere to let its right hand know what its left was doing. The Ministry of Justice might want to arrest him, but it was the military who ran the jails, and the military had no interest in him.

Nevertheless, he was taking precautions. He would go in with a group of people – Rich Gallagher and Jay Coburn were on the bus, as well as some Embassy people who were going in to visit an American woman in the jail – and he was wearing casual clothes and carrying a cardboard box containing groceries, books and warm clothing for Paul and Bill.

Nobody at the prison would know his face. He would have to give his name as he went in, but why would a minor clerk or prison guard recognize it? His name might be on a list at the airport, at police stations or at hotels; but the prison would surely be the *last* place Dadgar would expect him to turn up.

Anyway, he was determined to take the risk. He wanted to boost Paul's and Bill's morale, and to show them that he was willing to stick out his neck for them. It would be the only achievement of his trip: his efforts to get the negotiations moving had come to nothing.

The bus entered Gasr Square and he got his first sight of the new prison. It was formidable. He could not imagine how Simons and his little rescue team could possibly break in there.

In the square were scores of people, mostly women in chadors, making a lot of noise. The bus stopped near the huge steel doors. Perot wondered about the bus driver: he was Iranian, and he knew who Perot was . . .

They all got out. Perot saw a television camera near the prison entrance.

His heart missed a beat.

It was an *American* crew.

What the hell were they doing there?

He kept his head down as he pushed his way through the crowd, carrying his cardboard box. A guard looked out of a small window set into the brick wall beside the gates. The television crew seemed to be taking no notice of him. A minute later a little door in one of the gates swung open, and the visitors stepped inside.

The door clanged shut behind them.

Perot had passed the point of no return.

He walked on, through a second pair of steel doors, into the prison compound. It was a big place, with streets between the buildings, and chickens and turkeys running around loose. He followed the others through a doorway into a reception room.

He showed his passport. The clerk pointed to a register. Perot took out his pen and signed 'H. R. Perot' more or less legibly.

The clerk handed back the passport and waved him on.

He had been right. Nobody here had heard of Ross Perot.

He walked on into a waiting room – and stopped dead.

Standing there, talking to an Iranian in general's uniform,

was someone who knew perfectly well who Ross was.

It was Ramsey Clark, a Texan who had been US Attorney General under President Lyndon B. Johnson. Perot had met him several times and knew Clark's sister Mimi very well.

For a moment Perot froze. That explains the television cameras, he thought. He wondered whether he could keep out of Clark's sight. Any moment now, he thought, Ramsey will see me and say to the general: 'Lord, there's Ross Perot of EDS,' and if I look as if I'm trying to hide it will be even worse.

He made a snap decision.

He walked over to Clark, stuck out his hand, and said: 'Hello, Ramsey, what are you doing in jail?'

Clark looked down – he was six foot three – and laughed. They shook hands.

'How's Mimi?' Perot asked before Clark had a chance to perform introductions.

The general was saying something in Farsi to an underling.

Clark said: 'Mimi's fine.'

'Well, good to see you,' Perot said, and walked on.

His mouth was dry as he went out of the waiting-room and into the prison compound with Gallagher, Coburn and the Embassy people. That had been a close shave. An Iranian in colonel's uniform joined them: he had been assigned to take care of them, Gallagher said. Perot wondered what Clark was saying to the general now . . .

Paúl was sick. The cold he had caught in the first jail had recurred. He was coughing persistently and had pains in his chest. He could not get warm, in this jail or in the old one: for three whole weeks he had been cold. He had asked his EDS visitors to get him warm underwear, but for some reason they had not brought any.

He was also miserable. He really had expected that Coburn and the rescue team would ambush the bus that brought him and Bill here from the Ministry of Justice, and when the bus had entered the impregnable Gasr Prison he had been bitterly disappointed.

General Mohari, who ran the prison, had explained to Paul and Bill that he was in charge of all the jails in Tehran, and he had arranged for their transfer to this one for their own safety. It was small consolation: being less vulnerable to the mobs, this place was also more difficult, if not impossible, for the rescue team to attack.

The Gasr Prison was part of a large military complex. On its west side was the Old Gasr Ghazar Palace, which had been turned into a police academy by the Shah's father. The prison compound had once been the palace gardens. To the north was a military hospital; to the east an army camp where helicopters took off and landed all day.

The compound itself was bounded by an inner wall twenty-five or thirty feet high, and an outer wall twelve feet high. Inside were fifteen or twenty separate buildings, including a bakery, a mosque, and six cell blocks, one reserved for women.

Paul and Bill were in Building No 8. It was a two-storey block in a courtyard surrounded by a fence of tall iron bars covered with chicken wire. The environment was not bad, for a jail. There was a fountain in the middle of the courtyard, rose bushes around the sides, and ten or fifteen pine trees. The prisoners were allowed outside during the day, and could play volley-ball or ping-pong in the courtyard. However, they could not pass through the courtyard gate, which was manned by a guard.

The ground floor of the building was a small hospital with twenty or so patients, mostly mental cases. They screamed a lot. Paul and Bill and a handful of other prisoners were on the first floor. They had a large cell, about twenty feet by thirty, which they shared with only one other prisoner, an Iranian lawyer in his fifties who spoke English and French as well as Farsi. He had shown them pictures of his villa in France. There was a TV set in the cell.

Meals were prepared by some of the prisoners – who were paid for this by the others – and eaten in a separate dining room. The food here was better than at the first jail. Extra

231

privileges could be bought, and one of the other inmates, apparently a hugely wealthy man, had a private room and meals brought in from outside. The routine was relaxed: there were no set times for getting up and going to bed.

For all that Paul was thoroughly depressed. A measure of extra comfort meant little. What he wanted was freedom.

He was not much cheered when they were told, on the morning of 19 January, that they had visitors.

There was a visiting room on the ground floor of Building No 8, but today, without explanation, they were taken out of the building and along the street.

Paul realized they were headed for a building known as the Officers' Club, set in a small tropical garden with ducks and peacocks. As they approached the place he glanced around the compound and saw his visitors coming in the opposite direction.

He could not believe his eyes.

'My God!' he said delightedly. 'It's Ross!'

Forgetting where he was, he turned to run over to Perot: the guard jerked him back.

'Can you believe this?' he said to Bill. 'Perot's here!'

The guard hustled him through the garden. Paul kept looking back at Perot, wondering whether his eyes were deceiving him. He was led into a big circular room with banqueting tables around the outside and walls covered with small triangles of mirrored glass: it was like a small ballroom. A moment later Perot came in with Gallagher, Coburn and several other people.

Perot was grinning broadly. Paul shook his hand, then embraced him. It was an emotional moment. Paul felt the way he did when he listened to *The Star Spangled Banner*: a kind of shiver went up and down his spine. He was loved, he was cared for, he had friends, he belonged. Perot had come half across the world into the middle of a revolution just to visit him.

Perot and Bill embraced and shook hands. Bill said: 'Ross, what in the world are *you* doing here? Have you come to take us home?'

'Not quite,' Perot said. 'Not yet.'

The guards gathered at the far end of the room to drink tea. The Embassy staff who had come in with Perot sat around another table, talking to a woman prisoner.

Perot put his box on a table. 'There's some long underwear in here for you,' he said to Paul. 'We couldn't buy any, so this is mine, and I want it back, you hear?'

'Sure,' Paul grinned.

'We brought you some books as well, and groceries – peanut butter and tuna fish and juice and I don't know what.' He took a stack of envelopes from his pocket. 'And your mail.'

Paul glanced at his. There was a letter from Ruthie. Another envelope was addressed to 'Chapanoodle'. Paul smiled: that would be from his friend David Behne, whose son Tommy, unable to pronounce 'Chiapparone' had dubbed Paul 'Chapanoodle'. He pocketed the letter to read later, and said: 'How's Ruthie?'

'She's just fine. I talked to her on the phone,' Perot said. 'Now, we have assigned one man to each of your wives, to make sure everything necessary is done to take care of them. Ruthie's in Dallas now, staying with Jim and Cathy Nyfeler. She's buying a house, and Tom Walter is handling all the legal details for her.'

He turned to Bill. 'Emily has gone to visit her sister Vickie in North Carolina. She needed a break. She's been working with Tim Reardon in Washington, putting pressure on the State Department. She wrote to Rosalynn Carter – you know, as one wife to another – she's trying everything. Matter of fact, we're all trying everything . . .'

As Perot ran down the long list of people who had been asked to help – from Texas Congressmen all the way up to Henry Kissinger – Bill realized that the main purpose of Perot's visit was to boost his and Paul's morale. It was something of an anticlimax. For a moment back there, when he had seen Perot walking across the compound with the other guys, grinning all over his face, Bill had thought: here

233

comes the rescue party – at last they've got this damn thing solved, and Perot is coming to tell us personally. He was disappointed. But he cheered up as Perot talked. With his letters from home and his box of goodies Perot was like Santa Claus; and his presence here, and the big grin on his face, symbolized a tremendous defiance of Dadgar, the mobs and everything that threatened them.

Bill was worried, now, about Emily's morale. He knew instinctively what was going on in his wife's mind. The fact that she had gone to North Carolina told him she had given up hope. It had become too much for her to keep up a façade of normality with the children at her parents' house. He knew, somehow, that she had started smoking again. That would puzzle little Chris. Emily had given up smoking when she went into hospital to have her gall bladder removed, and she had told Chris then that she had had her smoker taken out. Now he would wonder how it had got back in.

'If all this fails,' Perot was saying, 'we have another team in town who will get you out of here by other methods. You'll recognize all the members of the team except one, the leader, an older man.'

Paul said: 'I have a problem with that, Ross. Why should a bunch of guys get cut up for the sake of two?'

Bill wondered just what was being planned. Would a helicopter fly over the compound and pick them up? Would the US Army storm the walls? It was hard to imagine – but with Perot, anything could happen.

Coburn said to Paul: 'I want you to observe and memorize all the details you can about the compound and the prison routine, just like before.'

Bill was feeling embarrassed about his moustache. He had grown it to make him look more Iranian. EDS executives were not allowed to have moustaches or beards, but he had not expected to see Perot. It was silly, he knew, but he felt uncomfortable about it. 'I apologize for this,' he said, touching his upper lip. 'I'm trying to be inconspicuous. I'll shave it off as soon as I get out of here.'

'Keep it,' Perot said with a smile. 'Let Emily and the

children see it. Anyway, we're going to change the dress code. We've had the results of the employee attitude survey, and we'll probably permit moustaches, and coloured shirts too.'

Bill looked at Coburn. 'And beards?'

'No beards. Coburn has a very special excuse.'

The guards came to break up the party. Visiting time was over.

Perot said: 'We don't know whether we'll get you out quickly or slowly. Tell yourselves it will be slowly. If you get up each morning thinking "Today could be the day", you may have a lot of disappointments and become demoralized. Prepare yourselves for a long stay, and you may be pleasantly surprised. But always remember this: we *will* get you out.'

They all shook hands. Paul said: 'I really don't know how to thank you for coming, Ross.'

Perot smiled. 'Just don't leave without my underwear.'

They all walked out of the building. The EDS men headed across the compound towards the prison gate, leaving Paul and Bill and their guards watching. As his friends disappeared, Bill was seized by a longing just to go with them.

Not today, he told himself; not today.

Perot wondered whether he would be allowed to leave.

Ramsey Clark had had a full hour to let the cat out of the bag. What had he said to the general? Would there be a reception committee waiting in the administration block at the prison entrance?

His heart beat faster as he entered the waiting room. There was no sign of the general or of Clark. He walked through and into the reception area. Nobody looked at him.

With Coburn and Gallagher close behind, he walked through the first set of doors.

Nobody stopped him.

He was going to get away with it.

He crossed the little courtyard and waited by the big gates.

235

The small door set in one of the gates was opened.

Perot walked out of the prison.

The TV cameras were still there.

All I need, he thought, having gotten this far, is to have the US networks show my picture . . .

He pushed his way through the crowd to the Embassy minibus and climbed aboard.

Coburn and Gallagher got on with him, but the Embassy people had lagged behind.

Perot sat on the bus, looking out of the window. The crowd in the square seemed malevolent. They were shouting in Farsi. Perot had no idea what they were saying.

He wished the Embassy people would hurry up.

'Where *are* those guys?' he said tetchily.

'They're coming,' Coburn said.

'I thought we'd all just come on out, get in the bus and *leave.*'

A minute later the prison door opened again and the Embassy people came out. They got on the bus. The driver started the engine and pulled away across the Gasr Square.

Perot relaxed.

He need not have worried quite so much. Ramsey Clark, who was there at the invitation of Iranian human-rights groups, did not have such a good memory. He had known that Perot's face was vaguely familiar, but thought he was Colonel Frank Borman, the president of Eastern Airlines.

2

Emily Gaylord sat down with her needlepoint. She was making a nude for Bill.

She was back at her parents' house in Washington, and it was another normal day of quiet desperation. She had driven Vicki to high school then returned and taken Jackie, Jenny and Chris to elementary school. She had dropped by her sister Dorothy's place and talked for a while with her and her husband, Tim Reardon. Tim was still working through Senator Kennedy and Congressman Tip O'Neill to put pressure on the State Department.

Emily was becoming obsessed with Dadgar, the mystery man who had the power to put her husband in jail and keep him there. She wanted to confront Dadgar herself, and ask him personally why he was doing this to her. She had even asked Tim to try to get her a diplomatic passport, so she could go to Iran and just knock on Dadgar's door. Tim had said it was a pretty crazy idea, and she realized he was right; but she was desperate to do something, anything, to get Bill back.

Now she was waiting for the daily call from Dallas. It was usually Ross, T. J. Marquez or Jim Nyfeler who called. After that she would pick up the children then help them with their homework for a while. Then there was nothing ahead but the lonely night.

She had only recently told Bill's parents that he was in jail. Bill had asked her, in a letter read over the phone by Keane Taylor, not to tell them until it was absolutely necessary, because Bill's father had a history of strokes and the shock might be dangerous. But after three weeks the pretence had become impossible, so she had broken the news; and Bill's father had been angry at having been kept in the dark so long. Sometimes it was hard to know the right thing to do.

The phone rang, and she snatched it up. 'Hello?'

'Emily? This is Jim Nyfeler.'

'Hi, Jim, what's the news?'

'Just that they've been moved to another jail.'

Why was there *never* any good news?

'It's nothing to worry about,' Jim said. 'In fact, it's good. The old jail was in the south of the city, where the fighting is. This one is further north, and more secure – they'll be safer there.'

Emily lost her cool. 'But Jim,' she yelled, 'You've been telling me for three weeks that they're perfectly safe in jail, now you say they've been moved to a new jail and *now* they'll be safe!'

'Emily—'

'Come on, please don't lie to me!'

'Emily—'

'Just tell it like it is and be upfront, okay?'

'Emily, I don't think they have been in danger up till now, but the Iranians are taking a sensible precaution, okay?'

Emily felt ashamed of herself for getting mad at him. 'I'm sorry, Jim.'

'That's all right.'

They talked a little longer, then Emily hung up and went back to her needlepoint. I'm losing my grip, she thought. I'm going around in a trance, taking the kids to school, talking to Dallas, going to bed at night and getting up in the morning . . .

Visiting her sister Vickie for a few days had been a good idea, but she didn't really need a change of scene – what she needed was Bill.

It was hard to keep on hoping. She began to think about how life might be without Bill. She had an aunt who worked in Woody's department store in Washington: maybe she could get a job there. Or she could talk to her father about getting secretarial work. She wondered whether she would ever fall in love with anyone else, if Bill should die in Tehran. She thought not.

She remembered when they were first married. Bill had been at college, and they were short of money, but they had gone ahead and done it because they could not bear to be apart any longer. Later, as Bill's career began to take off, they prospered, and gradually bought better cars, bigger houses, more expensive clothes . . . more *things*. How worthless those *things* were, she thought now; how little it mattered whether she was rich or poor. Bill was what she wanted, and he was all she needed. He would always be enough for her, enough to make her happy.

If he ever came back.

Karen Chiapparone said: 'Mommy, why doesn't Daddy call? He always calls when he's away.'

Jay Coburn: holding in his hands the safety of
131 employees in a city where mob violence ruled the streets.

Paul and Bill:
their bail was $13 million.

Ross Perot: until this moment, life had been good to him.

Perot's parents:
he had his father's love of jo[
his mother's iron will.

Bull Simons.
ABOVE, with Lucille.
BELOW, the San Francisco party.

ABOVE,
the Seventh Floor Squad.
FROM LEFT: gentle Merv Stauffer, aggressive Tom Luce,
slow-talking Tom Walter, and argumentative T. J. Marquez.

BELOW,
Tehran negotiators.
FROM LEFT:
jovial Bill Gayden,
persistent John Howell,
and quick-tempered
Keane Taylor.

Sculley:
world's worst liar

Schwebach:
explosives

Boulware:
independent

The Dirty Dozen
they were not.

Davis:
karate

Jackson:
rocket man

Poché:
iron man

ABOVE, the code.
BELOW, Ross Perot and his son.

Fire and smoke seen from the roof of the EDS Bucharest office.

Iran exploded into revolution on Friday, February 9, 1979.

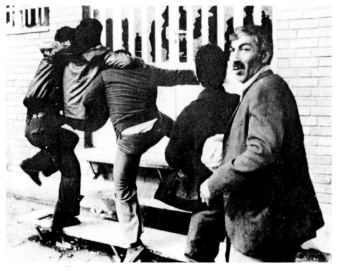

ON THE RUN

Keane Taylor in cold-weather gear.

Lunch break. FROM LEFT: Rashid, Simons, Gayden, and Bill.

The mountains of
northwest Iran.

Davis and Gayden.

A beautiful sight:
the bus at the border.

ABOARD THE "PERSIAN WHOREHOUSE"

Pilot John Carlen.

Simons and Boulware.

Davis, Perot, and Gayden.

Taylor and Coburn.

Simons and Coburn

Paul.

Perot.

Sculley.

TOGETHER AGAIN

Bill and Emily.

Paul and Ruthie.

John Howell with
Angela and baby Michael.

Bob, Molly, and Christine Young.

Perot and Simons
tell the story.

Bill with Emily and
daughters Vicki
and Jacqueline.

'He called today,' Ruthie lied. 'He's fine.'

'Why did he call when I was at school? I'd like to talk to him.'

'Honey, it's difficult to get through from Tehran, the lines are so busy, he just has to call when he can.'

'Oh.'

Karen wandered off to watch TV, and Ruthie sat down. It was getting dark outside. She was finding it increasingly difficult to lie to everyone about Paul.

That was why she had left Chicago and come to Dallas. Living with her parents and keeping the secret from them had become impossible. Mom would say: 'Why do Ross and the fellows from EDS keep calling you?'

'They just want to make sure we're okay, you know,' Ruthie would say with a forced smile.

'That is so nice of Ross to call.'

Here in Dallas she could at least talk openly to other EDS people. Moreover, now that the Iran business was certain to be closed down, Paul would be based at EDS headquarters, at least for a while, so Dallas would be their home; and Karen and Anne Marie had to go to school.

They were all living with Jim and Cathy Nyfeler. Cathy was especially sympathetic, for her husband had been on the original list of four men whose passports Dadgar had asked for: if Jim had happened to be in Iran at the time, he would now be in jail with Paul and Bill. Stay with us, Cathy had said; it will only be for maybe a week, then Paul will be back. That had been at the beginning of January. Since then Ruthie had proposed getting an apartment of her own, but Cathy would not hear of it.

Right now Cathy was at the hairdresser's, the children were watching TV in another room, and Jim was not yet home from work, so Ruthie was alone with her thoughts.

With Cathy's help she was keeping busy and putting on a brave face. She had enrolled Karen in school and found a kindergarten for Ann Marie. She went out to lunch with Cathy and some of the other EDS wives – Mary Boulware, Liz Coburn, Mary Sculley, Marva Davis, and Toni

239

Dvoranchik. She wrote bright optimistic letters to Paul, and listened to his bright, optimistic replies read over the phone from Tehran. She shopped and went to dinner parties.

She had killed a lot of time house-hunting. She did not know Dallas well, but she remembered Paul saying that Central Expressway was a nightmare, so she looked for houses well away from it. She had found one she liked and decided to buy it, so there would be a real home for Paul to come back to, but there were legal problems because he was not here to sign the papers: Tom Walter was trying to sort that out.

Ruthie was making it look good, but inside she was dying.

She rarely slept more than an hour at night. She kept waking up wondering whether she would ever see Paul again. She tried to think about what she would do if he did not come back. She supposed she would return to Chicago and stay with Mom and Dad for a while, but she would not want to live with them permanently. No doubt she could get some kind of a job . . . But it was not the practical business of living without a man and taking care of herself that bothered her: it was the idea of being without Paul, forever. She could not imagine what life would be like if he were not there. What would she do, what would she care about, what would she want, what could possibly make her happy? She was completely dependent on him, she realized. She could not live without him.

She heard a car outside. That would be Jim, home from work: perhaps he would have some news.

A moment later he came in. 'Hi, Ruthie. Cathy not home?'

'She's at the hairdresser's. What happened today?'

'Well . . .'

She knew from his expression that he had nothing good to tell her and he was trying to find an encouraging way of saying so.

'Well, they had a meeting scheduled to talk about the bail, but the Iranians didn't turn up. Tomorrow—'

'But *why*?' Ruthie fought to keep calm. 'Why don't they turn up when they arrange these meetings?'

'You know, sometimes they're called out on strike, and sometimes people just can't move around the city because of . . . because of the demonstrations, and so on . . .'

She seemed to have been hearing reports like this for weeks. There were always delays, postponements, frustrations. 'But, Jim,' she began; then the tears started and she could not stop them. 'Jim . . .' Her throat tightened up until she could not speak. She thought: all I want is my husband! Jim stood there looking helpless and embarrassed. All the misery she had kept locked up for so long suddenly flooded out, and she could not control herself any longer. She burst into tears and ran from the room. She rushed to her bedroom, threw herself on the bed and lay there sobbing her heart out.

Liz Coburn sipped her drink. Across the table were Pat Sculley's wife, Mary, and another EDS wife who had been evacuated from Tehran, Toni Dvoranchik. The three women were at Recipes, a restaurant on Greenville Avenue, Dallas. They were drinking strawberry Daiquiris.

Toni Dvoranchik's husband was here in Dallas. Liz knew that Pat Sculley had disappeared, like Jay, in the direction of Europe. Now Mary Sculley was talking as if Pat had gone not just to Europe but to Iran.

'Is Pat in Tehran?' Liz asked.

'They're all in Tehran, I guess,' Mary said.

Liz was horrified. 'Jay in Tehran . . .' She wanted to cry. Jay had told her he was in Paris. Why couldn't he tell the truth? Pat Sculley had told Mary the truth. But Jay was different. Some men would play poker for a few hours, but Jay had to play all night and all the next day. Other men would play nine or eighteen holes of golf: Jay would play thirty-six. Lots of men had demanding jobs, but Jay had to work for EDS. Even in the Army, when the two of them had been not much more than kids, Jay had to volunteer for one of the most dangerous assignments, helicopter pilot. Now he had gone to Tehran in the middle of a revolution. Same old thing, she thought: he's gone away, he's lying to me, and he's

241

in danger. She suddenly felt cold all over, as if she were in shock. He's not coming back, she thought numbly. He's not going to get out of there alive.

3

Perot's good spirits soon passed. He had got into the prison, defying Dadgar, and had cheered up Paul and Bill; but Dadgar still held all the cards. After six days in Tehran he understood why the political pressure he had been putting on in Washington had been ineffectual: the old regime in Iran was struggling for survival and had no control. Even if he posted the bail – and a lot of problems had to be solved before that could happen – Paul and Bill would still be held in Iran. And Simons's rescue plan was now in tatters, ruined by the move to the new prison. There seemed to be no hope.

That night Perot went to see Simons.

He waited until dark, for safety. He wore his jogging suit with tennis shoes and a dark businessman's overcoat. Keane Taylor drove him.

The rescue team had moved out of Taylor's house. Taylor had now met Dadgar face-to-face, and Dadgar had started examining EDS's records: it was possible, Simons had reasoned, that Dadgar would raid Taylor's house, looking for incriminating documents. So Simons, Coburn and Poché were living in the home of Bill and Toni Dvoranchik, who were now back in Dallas. Two more of the team had made it to Tehran from Paris: Pat Sculley and Jim Schwebach, the short but deadly duo who had been flank guards in the original, now useless, rescue scenario.

In a typical Tehran arrangement, Dvoranchik's home was the ground floor of a two-storey house, with the landlord living upstairs. Taylor and the rescue team left Perot alone with Simons. Perot looked around the living-room distastefully. No doubt the place had been spotless when Toni Dvoranchik lived here, but now, inhabited by five men none of whom was very interested in housekeeping, it was dirty

242

and run-down, and it stank of Simons's cigars.

Simons's huge frame was slumped in an armchair. His white whiskers were bushy and his hair long. He was chain-smoking, as usual; drawing heavily on his little cigar and inhaling with relish.

'You've seen the new prison,' Perot said.

'Yeah,' Simons rasped.

'What do you think?'

'The idea of taking that place with the kind of frontal attack we had in mind just isn't worth talking about.'

'That's what I figured.'

'Which leaves a number of possibilities.'

It does? thought Perot.

Simons went on: 'One. I understand there are cars parked in the prison compound. We may find a way to get Paul and Bill driven out of there in the trunk of a car. As part of that plan, or as an alternative, we may be able to bribe or blackmail this general who is in charge of the place.'

'General Mohari.'

'Right. One of your Iranian employees is getting us a rundown on the man.'

'Good.'

'Two. The negotiating team. If they can get Paul and Bill released under house arrest, or something of that kind, we can snatch the two of them. Get Taylor and those guys to concentrate on this house arrest idea. Agree to any conditions the Iranians care to name, but get 'em out of that jail. Working on the assumption that they would be confined to their homes and kept under surveillance, we're developing a new rescue scenario.'

Perot was beginning to feel better. There was an aura of confidence about this massive man. A few minutes ago Perot had felt almost helpless: now Simons was calmly listing fresh approaches to the problem, as if the move to the new jail, the bail problems, and the collapse of the legitimate government were minor snags rather than total catastrophe.

'Three,' Simons went on. 'There's a revolution going on here. Revolutions are predictable. The same things happen every damn time. You can't say *when* they'll occur, only that they *will*, sooner or later. And one of the things that always happens is, the mob storms the prisons and lets everyone out.'

Perot was intrigued. 'Is that so?'

Simons nodded. 'Those are the three possibilities. Of course, at this point in the game we can't pick one: we have to prepare for each of them. Whichever of the three happens first, we'll need a plan for getting everyone out of this goddam country just as soon as Paul and Bill are in our hands.'

'Yes.' Perot was worried about his own departure: that of Paul and Bill would be a good deal more hazardous. 'I've had promises of help from the American military—'

'Sure,' Simons said. 'I'm not saying they're insincere, but I will say they have higher priorities, and I'm not prepared to place a great deal of reliance on their promises.'

'All right.' That was a matter for Simons's judgement, and Perot was content to leave it to him. In fact, he was content to leave everything to Simons. Simons was probably the best qualified man in the world to do this job, and Perot had complete faith in him. 'What can I do?'

'Get back to the States. For one thing, you're in danger here. For another, I need you over there. Chances are, when we eventually come out, it won't be on a scheduled flight. We may not fly at all. You'll have to pick us up somewhere – it could be Iraq, Kuwait, Turkey or Afghanistan – and that will take organizing. Go home and stay ready.'

'Okay.' Perot stood up. Simons had done to him what Perot sometimes did to his staff: inspired them with the strength to go one more mile when the game seemed lost. 'I'll leave tomorrow.'

He got a reservation on British Airways flight 200, Tehran to London via Kuwait, leaving at 10.20 a.m. on 20 January, the next day.

He called Margot and asked her to meet him in London. He wanted a few days alone with her: they might not get another chance, once the rescue started to unfold.

They had had good times in London in the past. They would stay at the Savoy Hotel. (Margot liked Claridge's, but Perot did not: they turned the heat too high, and if he opened the windows he was kept awake by the roar of the all-night traffic along Brook Street.) He and Margot would see plays and concerts, and go to Margot's favourite London nightclub, Annabel's. For a few days they would enjoy life.

If he got out of Iran.

In order to minimize the amount of time he would have to spend at the airport, he stayed at the hotel until the last minute. He called the airport to find out whether the flight would leave on time, and was told that it would.

He checked in a few minutes before ten o'clock.

Rich Gallagher, who accompanied him to the airport, went off to enquire whether the authorities were planning to give Perot a hard time. Gallagher had done this before. Together with an Iranian friend who worked for Pan Am, he walked through to passport control carrying Perot's passport. The Iranian explained that a VIP was coming through, and asked to clear the passport in advance. The official at the desk obligingly looked through the loose-leaf folder which contained the stop list and said there would be no problems for Mr Perot. Gallagher returned with the good news.

Perot remained apprehensive. If they wanted to pick him up, they might be smart enough to lie to Gallagher.

Affable Bill Gayden, the president of EDS World, was flying in to take over direction of the negotiating team. Gayden had left Dallas for Tehran once before, but had turned back in Paris on hearing about Bunny Fleishhaker's warning of more arrests to come. Now he, like Perot, had decided to risk it. By chance his flight came in while Perot was waiting to leave, and they had an opportunity to talk.

In his suitcase Gayden had eight American passports belonging to EDS executives who looked vaguely like Paul or Bill.

Perot said: 'I thought you were getting forged passports

for them. Couldn't you find a way?'

'Yeah, we found a way,' Gayden said. 'If you need a passport in a hurry, you can take all the documentation down to the courthouse in Dallas, then they put everything in an envelope and you carry it to New Orleans, where they issue the passport. It's just a plain government envelope sealed with scotch tape, so you could open it on the way to New Orleans, take out the photographs, replace them with photographs of Paul and Bill – which we have – re-seal the envelope, and, bingo, you've got passports for Paul and Bill in false names. But it's against the law.'

'So what did you do instead?'

'I told all the evacuees that I had to have their passports in order to get their belongings shipped over from Tehran. I got a hundred or two passports, and I picked the best eight. I bogused up a letter from someone in the States to someone here in Tehran saying: "Here are the passports you asked for us to return so you could deal with the immigration authorities," just so that I've got a piece of paper to show if I'm asked why the hell I'm carrying eight passports.'

'If Paul and Bill use those passports to cross a frontier, they'll be breaking the law anyway.'

'If we get that far, we'll break the law.'

Perot nodded. 'It makes sense.'

His flight was called. He said goodbye to Gayden and to Taylor, who had driven him to the airport and would take Gayden to the Hyatt. Then he went off to discover the truth about the stop list.

He went first through a 'Passengers Only' gate where his boarding pass was checked. He walked along a corridor to a booth where he paid a small sum as airport tax. Then, on his right, he saw a series of passport control desks.

Here the stop list was kept.

One of the desks was manned by a girl who was absorbed in a paperback book. Perot approached her. He handed over his passport and a yellow exit form. The form had his name at the top.

The girl took the yellow sheet, opened his passport,

stamped it, and handed it back without looking at him. She returned to her book immediately.

Perot walked into the departure lounge.

The flight was delayed.

He sat down. He was on tenterhooks. At any moment the girl could finish her book, or just get bored with it, and start checking the stop list against the names on the yellow forms. Then, he imagined, they would come for him, the police or the military or Dadgar's investigators, and he would go to jail, and Margot would be like Ruthie and Emily, not knowing whether she would ever see her husband again.

He checked the departures board every few seconds: it just said DELAYED.

He sat on the edge of his chair for the first hour.

Then he began to feel resigned. If they were going to catch him they would, and there was nothing he could do about it. He started to read a magazine. Over the next hour he read everything in his briefcase. Then he started talking to the man sitting next to him. Perot learned that the man was an English engineer working in Iran on a project for a large British company. They chatted for a while, then swapped magazines.

In a few hours, Perot thought, I'll be in a beautiful hotel suite with Margot – or in an Iranian jail. He pushed the thought from his mind.

Lunchtime went by, and the afternoon wore on. He began to believe they were not going to come for him.

The flight was finally called at six o'clock.

Perot stood up. If they come for me now . . .

He joined the crowd and approached the departure gate. There was a security check. He was frisked and waved through.

I've almost made it, he thought as he boarded the plane. He sat between two fat people in an economy seat – it was an all-economy flight. I think I've made it.

The doors were closed and the plane began to move.

It taxied on to the runway and gathered speed.

The plane took off.

247

He had made it.

He had always been lucky.

His thoughts turned to Margot. She was handling this crisis the way she had handled the prisoners-of-war adventures: she understood her husband's concept of duty and she never complained. That was why he could stay focused on what he had to do, and block out negative thoughts that would excuse inaction. He was lucky to have her. He thought of all the lucky things that had happened to him: good parents, getting into the Naval Academy, meeting Margot, having such fine children, starting EDS, getting good people to work for him, brave people like the volunteers he had left behind in Iran . . .

He wondered superstitiously whether an individual had a certain limited quantity of luck in his life. He saw his luck as sand in an hour-glass, slowly but steadily running out. What happens, he thought, when it's all gone?

The plane descended towards Kuwait. He was out of Iranian airspace. He had escaped.

While the plane was refuelling he walked to the open door and stood there, breathing the fresh air and ignoring the stewardess who kept asking him to return to his seat. There was a nice breeze blowing across the tarmac, and it was a relief to get away from the fat people sitting either side of him. The stewardess eventually gave up and went to do something else. He watched the sun go down. Luck, he thought; I wonder how much I've got left?

Eight

1

The rescue team in Tehran now consisted of Simons, Coburn, Poché, Sculley and Schwebach. Simons decided that Boulware, Davis and Jackson would not come to Tehran. The idea of rescuing Paul and Bill by frontal assault was now dead, so he did not need such a big team. He sent Glenn Jackson to Kuwait, to investigate that end of the southerly route out of Iran. Boulware and Davis went back to the States to await further orders.

Majid reported to Coburn that General Mohari, the man in charge of Gasr Prison, was not easily corruptible, but had two daughters at school in the United States. The team briefly discussed kidnapping the girls and forcing Mohari to help Paul and Bill escape; but they rejected the idea. (Perot hit the roof when he learned they had even *discussed* it.) The idea of sneaking Paul and Bill out in the trunk of a car was put on the back burner for a while.

For two or three days they concentrated on what they would do if Paul and Bill were released under house arrest. They went to look at the houses the two men had occupied before the arrest. The snatch would be easy unless Dadgar put Paul and Bill under surveillance. The team would use two cars, they decided. The first car would pick up Paul and Bill. The second, following at a distance, would contain Sculley and Schwebach, who would be responsible for eliminating anyone who tried to tail the first car. Once again, the deadly duo would do the killing.

The two cars would keep in touch by short-wave radio, they decided. Coburn called Merv Stauffer in Dallas and ordered the equipment. Boulware would take the radios to

London: Schwebach and Sculley would go to London to meet him and pick them up. While in London, the deadly duo would try to get hold of some good maps of Iran, for use during the escape from the country, should the team have to leave by road. (No good maps of the country were to be found in Tehran, as the Jeep Club had learned in happier days: Gayden said Persian maps were at the 'Turn left by the dead horse' level.)

Simons wanted also to prepare for the third possibility – that Paul and Bill would be released by a mob storming the prison. What should the team do in that eventuality? Coburn was continuously monitoring the situation in the city, calling his contacts in US military intelligence and several trustworthy Iranian employees: if the prison were overrun he would know very quickly. What then? Someone would have to look for Paul and Bill and bring them to safety. But a bunch of Americans driving into the middle of a riot would be asking for trouble: Paul and Bill would be safer mingling inconspicuously with the crowd of escaping prisoners. Simons told Coburn to speak to Paul about this possibility, next time he visted the jail, and instruct Paul to head for the Hyatt Hotel.

However, an Iranian could go looking for Paul and Bill in the riots. Simons asked Coburn to recommend an Iranian employee of EDS who was really street-smart.

Coburn thought immediately of Rashid.

He was a dark-skinned, rather good-looking twenty-three-year-old from an affluent Tehran family. He had completed EDS's training programme for systems engineers. He was intelligent and resourceful, and he had bags of charm. Coburn recalled the last time Rashid had demonstrated his talent for improvisation. Ministry of Health employees who were on partial strike had refused to key the data for the payroll system, but Rashid had got all the input together, taken it down to Bank Omran, talked someone there into keying the data, then run the program on the Ministry computer. The trouble with Rashid was that you had to keep an eye on him, because he never consulted anyone before implementing his unconventional ideas. Getting the data keyed the way he had constituted strike-breaking, and might have got EDS in big trouble – indeed, when Bill had heard about it he had been more anxious than pleased. Rashid was excitable and impulsive, and his English was not so good, so he tended to dash off and do his own crazy thing without telling anyone, a tendency which made his managers nervous. But he always got away with it. He could talk his way into and out of anything. At the airport, meeting people or seeing them off, he always managed to pass through all the 'Passengers Only' barriers even though he never had a boarding card, ticket or passport to show. Coburn knew him well, and liked him enough to have brought him home for supper several times. Coburn also trusted him completely, especially since the strike, when Rashid had been one of Coburn's informants among the hostile Iranian employees.

However, Simons would not trust Rashid on Coburn's say-so. Just as he had insisted on meeting Keane Taylor before letting him in on the secret, so he would want to talk to Rashid.

So Coburn arranged a meeting.

When Rashid was eight years old he had wanted to be President of the United States.

At twenty-three he knew he could never be President, but he still wanted to go to America, and EDS was going to be his ticket. He knew he had it in him to be a great businessman. He was a student of the psychology of the human being, and it had not taken him long to understand the mentality of EDS people. They wanted results, not excuses. If you were given a task, it was always better to do a little more than was expected. If for some reason the task was difficult, or even impossible, it was best not to say so: they hated to hear people whining about problems. You never said: 'I can't do that because . . .' You always said: 'This is the progress I have made so far, and this is the problem I am working on right now . . .' It so happened that these attitudes suited Rashid perfectly. He had made himself useful to EDS, and he knew the company appreciated it.

His greatest achievement had been installing computer terminals in offices where the Iranian staff were suspicious and hostile. So great was the resistance that Pat Sculley had been able to install no more than two per month: Rashid had installed the remaining eighteen in two months. He had planned to capitalize on this. He had composed a letter to Ross Perot, who – he understood – was the head of EDS, asking to be allowed to complete his training in Dallas. He had intended to ask all the EDS managers in Tehran to sign the letter, but events had overtaken him, most of the managers had been evacuated and EDS in Iran was falling to pieces. He never mailed the letter. So he would think of something else.

He could always find a way. Everything was possible for Rashid. He could do anything. He had even got out of the army. At a time when thousands of young middle-class Iranians were spending fortunes in bribes to avoid military service, Rashid, after a few weeks in uniform, had convinced the doctors that he was incurably ill with a twitching disease. His comrades and the officers over him knew that he was in perfect health, but every time he saw the doctor he twitched uncontrollably. He went before medical boards and twitched for hours – an absolutely exhausting business, he discovered. Finally, so many doctors had certified him ill that he got his discharge papers. It was crazy, ridiculous, impossible – but doing the impossible was Rashid's normal practice.

So he *knew* that he would go to America. He did not know *how*, but careful and elaborate planning was not his style anyway. He was a spur-of-the-moment man, an improviser, an opportunist. His chance would come and he would seize it.

Mr Simons interested him. He was not like the other EDS managers. They were all in their thirties and forties, but Simons was nearer to sixty. His long hair and white whiskers and big nose seemed more Iranian than American. Finally, he did not come right out with whatever was on his mind. People like Sculley and Coburn would say: 'This is the situation and this is what I want you to do and you need to have it done by tomorrow morning . . .' Simons just said: 'Let's go for a walk.'

They strolled around the streets of Tehran. Rashid found himself talking about his family, his work at EDS, and his views on the psychology of the human being. They could hear continual shooting, and the streets were alive with people marching and chanting. Everywhere they saw the wreckage of past battles, overturned cars and burned-out buildings. 'The Marxists smash up expensive cars and the Moslems trash the liquor stores,' Rashid told Simons.

'Why is this happening?' Simons asked him.

'This is the time for Iranians to prove themselves, to accomplish their ideas, and to gain their freedom.'

They found themselves in Gasr Square, facing the prison. Rashid said: 'There are many Iranians in these jails simply because they ask for freedom.'

Simons pointed at the crowd of women in chadors. 'What are they doing?'

'Their husbands and sons are unjustly imprisoned, so they gather here, wailing and crying to the guards to let the prisoners go.'

Simons said: 'Well, I guess I feel the same about Paul and Bill as those women do about their men.'

'Yes. I, too, am very concerned about Paul and Bill.'

'But what are you doing about it?' Simons asked.

Rashid was taken aback. 'I am doing everything I can to help my American friends,' he said. He thought of the dogs and cats. One of his tasks at the moment was to care for all the pets left behind by EDS evacuees – including four dogs and twelve cats. Rashid had never had pets and did not know how to deal with large aggressive dogs. Every time he went to the apartment where the dogs were stashed to feed them, he had to hire two or three men off the streets to help him restrain the animals. Twice now he had taken them all to the airport in cages, having heard that there was a flight out which would accept them; and both times the flight had been cancelled. He thought of telling Simons about this, but somehow he knew that Simons would not be impressed.

Simons was up to something, Rashid thought, and it was not a business matter. Simons struck him as an experienced man – you could see that just by looking at his face. Rashid did not believe in experience. He believed in fast education. Revolution, not evolution. He liked the inside track, short cuts, accelerated development, superchargers. Simons was different. He was a patient man, and Rashid, analysing Simons's psychology, guessed that the patience came from a strong will. When he is ready, Rashid thought, he will let me know what he wants from me.

'Do you know anything about the French Revolution?' Simons asked.

'A little.'

'This place reminds me of the Bastille – a symbol of oppression.'

It was a good comparison, Rashid thought.

Simons went on: 'The French revolutionaries stormed the Bastille and let all the prisoners out.'

'I think the same will happen here. It's a possibility, at least.'

Simons nodded. 'If it happens, someone ought to be here to take care of Paul and Bill.'

'Yes.' That will be me, Rashid thought.

They stood together in Gasr Square, looking at the high walls and huge gates, and the wailing women in their black robes. Rashid recalled his principle: always do a little more than EDS asks of you. What if the mobs ignored Gasr Prison? Maybe he should make sure they did not. The mob was nothing but people like Rashid – young, discontented Iranian men who wanted to change their lives. He might not only join the mob – he might lead it. He might lead an attack on the prison. He, Rashid, might rescue Paul and Bill.

Nothing was impossible.

Coburn did not know all that was going on in Simons's mind at this point. He had not been in on Simons's conversations with Perot and Rashid, and Simons did not volunteer much information. From what Coburn did know, the three possibilities – the trunk-of-a-car-trick, the house-arrest-and-snatch routine, and the storming of the Bastille – seemed pretty vague. Furthermore, Simons was doing nothing to *make it happen*, but appeared content to sit around the Dvoranchik place discussing ever-more-detailed scenarios. Yet none of this made Coburn uneasy. He was an optimist anyway; and he – like Ross Perot – figured there was no point in second-guessing the world's greatest rescue expert.

While the three possibilities were simmering, Simons concentrated on routes out of Iran, the problem Coburn thought of as 'Getting Out of Dodge'.

Coburn looked for ways of flying Paul and Bill out. He poked around warehouses at the airport, toying with the idea of shipping Paul and Bill as freight. He talked to people at each of the airlines, trying to develop contacts. He eventually had several meetings with the chief of security at Pan Am, telling him everything except the names of Paul and Bill. They talked about getting the two fugitives on a scheduled flight wearing Pan Am cabin crew uniforms. The security chief wanted to help, but the airline's liability proved in the end to be an insuperable problem. Coburn then considered stealing a helicopter. He scouted a chopper base in the south of the city, and decided the theft was feasible. But, given the chaos of the Iranian military, he suspected the aircraft were not being properly maintained, and he knew they were short of spare parts. Then again, some of them might have contaminated fuel.

He reported all this to Simons. Simons was already uneasy about airports, and the snags uncovered by Coburn reinforced his prejudice. There were always police and military around airports; if something went wrong there was no escape – airports were designed to prevent people wandering where they should not go; at an airport you always had to put yourself in the hands of others. Furthermore, in that situation your worst enemy could be the people escaping: they needed to be *very* cool. Coburn thought Paul and Bill had the nerves to go through something like that, but there was no point telling Simons so: Simons always had to make his own assessment of a man's character, and he had never met Paul or Bill.

So, in the end, the team focused on getting out by road.

There were six ways.

To the north was the USSR, not a hospitable country. To the east were Afghanistan, equally inhospitable, and Pakistan, whose border was too far away – almost a thousand miles, mostly across desert. To the south was the Persian Gulf, with friendly Kuwait just fifty or a hundred miles across the water. That was promising. To the west was unfriendly Iraq; to the north-west, friendly Turkey.

Kuwait and Turkey were the destinations they favoured.

Simons asked Coburn to have a trustworthy Iranian employee drive south all the way to the Persian Gulf, to find out whether the road was passable and the countryside peaceful. Coburn asked the Cycle Man, so called because he zipped around Tehran on a motorcycle. A trainee systems engineer like Rashid, the Cycle Man was about twenty-five, short, and street-smart. He had learned English at school in California, and could talk with any regional American accent – Southern, Puerto Rican, anything. EDS had hired him despite his lack of a college degree because he scored remarkably high marks in aptitude tests. When EDS's Iranian employees had joined the general strike, and Paul and Coburn had called a mass meeting to discuss it with them, the Cycle Man had astonished everyone by speaking out vehemently against his colleagues and in favour of the management. He made no secret of his pro-American feelings, yet Coburn was quite sure the Cycle Man was involved with the revolutionaries. One day he had asked Keane Taylor for a car. Taylor had given him one. Next day he asked for another. Taylor obliged. The Cycle Man always used his motorcycle anyway: Taylor and Coburn were pretty sure the cars were for the revolutionaries. They did not care: it was more important that the Cycle Man became obligated to them.

So, in return for past favours, the Cycle Man drove to the Persian Gulf.

He came back a few days later and reported that anything was possible if you had enough money. You could get to the Gulf and you could buy or rent a boat.

He had no idea what would happen when you disembarked in Kuwait.

That question was answered by Glenn Jackson.

As well as being a hunter and a Baptist, Glenn Jackson was a Rocket Man. His combination of first-class mathematical brain and ability to stay calm under stress had got him into Mission Control at NASA's Manned Spacecraft Centre in Houston as a flight controller. His job had been to design and operate the computer programs which calculated trajectories for in-flight manoeuvring.

Jackson's unflappability had been severely tested on Christmas Day, 1968, during the last mission he worked on, the lunar flyby. When the spacecraft came out from behind the moon, astronaut Jim Lovell had read down the list of numbers, called residuals, which told Jackson how close the craft was to its planned course. Jackson had got a fright: the numbers were way outside the acceptable limits of error. Jackson asked CAPCOM to have the astronaut read them down again, to double-check. Then he told the flight director that if those numbers were correct, the three astronauts were as good as dead: there was not enough fuel to correct such a huge divergence.

Jackson asked for Lovell to read the numbers a third time, extra carefully. They were the same. Then Lovell said: 'Oh, wait a minute, I'm reading these wrong . . .'

When the real numbers came through it turned out that the manoeuvre had been almost perfect.

All that was a long way from busting into a prison.

Still, it was beginning to look like Jackson would never get the chance to perpetrate a jailbreak. He had been cooling his heels for a week when he got instructions from Simons, via Dallas, to go to Kuwait.

He flew to Kuwait and moved into Bob Young's house. Young had gone to Tehran to help the negotiating team, and his wife Kris and her new baby were in the States on vacation. Jackson told Malloy Jones, who was Acting Country Manager in Young's absence, that he had come to help with the preliminary study EDS was doing for Kuwait's central bank. He did a little work for the benefit of his cover story, then started looking around.

He spent some time at the airport, watching the immigration officers. They were being very tough, he soon learned. Hundreds of Iranians without passports were flying in to Kuwait: they were being handcuffed and put on the next flight back. Jackson concluded that Paul and Bill could not possibly fly in to Kuwait.

Assuming they could get in by boat, would they later be allowed to *leave* without passports? Jackson went to see the American consul, saying that one of his children seemed to have lost a passport, and asking what was the procedure for replacing it. In the course of a long and rambling discussion the consul revealed that the Kuwaitis had a way of checking, when they issued an exit visa, whether the person had entered the country legally.

That was a problem, but perhaps not an insoluble one: once inside Kuwait Paul and Bill would be safe from Dadgar, and surely the US Embassy would then give them back their passports. The main question was: assuming the fugitives could reach the south of Iran and embark on a small boat, would they be able to land unnoticed in Kuwait? Jackson travelled the sixty-mile length of the Kuwait coast, from the Iraqui border in the north to the Saudi-Arabian border in the south. He spent many hours on the beaches,

258

collecting seashells in winter. Normally, he had been told, coastal patrols were very light. But the exodus from Iran had changed everything. There were thousands of Iranians who wanted to leave the country almost as badly as Paul and Bill did, and those Iranians, like Simons, could look at a map and see the Persian Gulf to the south with friendly Kuwait just across the water. The Kuwait coastguard was wise to all this. Everywhere Jackson looked he saw, out at sea, at least one patrol boat. And they appeared to be stopping *all* small craft.

The prognosis was gloomy. Jackson called Merv Stauffer in Dallas and reported that the Kuwait exit was a no-no.

That left Turkey.

Simons had favoured Turkey all along. It involved a shorter drive than Kuwait. Furthermore Simons knew Turkey. He had served there in the fifties as part of the American military aid programme, training the Turkish Army. He even spoke a little of the language.

So he sent Ralph Boulware to Istanbul.

Ralph Boulware grew up in bars. His father, Benjamin Russell Boulware, was a tough and independent black man who had a series of small businesses: a grocery store, house property, bootlegging, but mostly bars. Ben Boulware's theory of child-raising was that if he knew where they were he knew what they were doing, so he kept his boys mostly within his sight, which meant mostly in the bar. It was not much of a childhood, and it left Ralph feeling that he had been an adult all his life.

He had realized he was different from other boys his age when he went to college and found his contemporaries getting all excited about gambling, drinking and going with women. He knew all about gamblers, drunks and whores already. He dropped out of college and joined the Air Force.

In nine years in the Air Force he had never seen action, and while he was on the whole glad about that, it had left him wondering whether he had what it took to fight in a shooting war. The rescue of Paul and Bill might give him the chance to find out, he had thought; but Simons had sent him from Paris back to Dallas. It looked like he was going to be ground crew again. Then new orders came.

They came via Merv Stauffer, Perot's right-hand man who was now Simons's link with the scattered rescue team. Stauffer went to Radio Shack and bought six five-channel two-way radios, ten rechargers, a supply of batteries, and a device for running the radios off a dashboard cigar lighter. He gave the equipment to Boulware and told him to meet Sculley and Schwebach in London before going on to Istanbul.

Stauffer also gave him forty thousand dollars in cash, for expenses, bribes, and general purposes.

The night before Boulware left, his wife started giving him a hard time about money. He had taken a thousand dollars out of the bank, without telling her, before he went to Paris – he believed in carrying cash money – and she had subsequently discovered how little was left in their account. Boulware did not want to explain to her why he had taken the money and how he had spent it. Mary insisted that she needed money. Boulware was not too concerned about that: she was staying with good friends and he knew she would be looked after. But she didn't buy his brush-off, and – as often happened when she was really determined – he decided to make her happy. He went into the bedroom, where he had left the box containing the radios and the forty thousand dollars, and counted out five hundred. Mary came in while he was doing it, and saw what was in the box.

Boulware gave her the five hundred and said: 'Will that hold you?'

'Yes,' she said.

She looked at the box, then at her husband. 'I'm not even going to ask,' she said; and she went out.

Boulware left the next day. He met Schwebach and Sculley in London, gave them five of the six radio sets, kept one for himself, and flew on to Istanbul.

He went from the airport straight to the office of Mr Fish, the travel agent.

Mr Fish met him in an open-plan office with three or four other people sitting around.

'My name is Ralph Boulware, and I work for EDS,' Boulware began. 'I think you know my daughters, Stacy Elaine and Kecia Nicole.' The girls had played with Mr Fish's daughters during the evacuees' stopover in Istanbul.

Mr Fish was not very warm.

'I need to talk to you,' Boulware said.

'Fine, talk to me.'

Boulware looked around the room. 'I want to talk to you in private.'

'Why?'

'You'll understand when I talk to you.'

'These are my partners. There are no secrets here.'

Mr Fish was giving Boulware a hard time. Boulware could guess why. There were two reasons. First, after all that Mr Fish had done during the evacuation, Don Norsworthy had tipped him $150, which was derisory, in Boulware's opinion. ('I didn't know what to do!' Norsworthy had said. 'The man's bill was twenty-six thousand dollars. What should I have tipped him – ten per cent?')

Secondly, Pat Sculley had approached Mr Fish with a transparent tale about smuggling computer tapes into Iran. Mr Fish was neither a fool nor a criminal, Boulware guessed; and of course he had refused to have anything to do with Sculley's scheme.

Now Mr Fish thought EDS people were (a) cheapskates and (b) dangerously amateurish law-breakers.

But Mr Fish was a small businessman. Boulware understood small businessmen – his father had been one. They spoke two languages: straight talk, and cash money. Cash money would solve problem (a) and straight talk problem (b).

'Okay, let's start again,' Boulware said. 'When EDS was here you really helped those people, treated the children nice, and did a great deal for us. When they left there was a mix-up about showing you our appreciation. We're embarrassed that this was not handled properly and I need

261

to settle that score.'

'It's no big deal—'

'We're sorry,' Boulware said, and he gave Mr Fish a thousand dollars in hundred-dollar bills.

The room went very quiet.

'Well, I'm going to check in to the Sheraton,' Boulware said. 'Maybe we can talk later.'

'I'll come with you,' said Mr Fish.

He personally checked Boulware into the hotel and ensured that he got a good room, then agreed to meet him for dinner that night in the hotel coffee shop.

Mr Fish was a high-class hustler, Boulware thought as he unpacked. The man had to be smart, to have what appeared to be a very prosperous business in this dirt-poor country. The evacuees' experience showed that he had the enterprise to do more than issue plane tickets and make hotel bookings. He had the right contacts to oil the wheels of bureaucracy, judging by the way he had got everyone's baggage through customs. He had also helped solve the problem of the adopted Iranian baby with no passport. EDS's mistake had been to see that he was a hustler and overlook the fact that he was high-class – deceived perhaps, by his unimpressive appearance: he was rather fat and dressed in drab clothes. Boulware, learning from past mistakes, thought he could handle Mr Fish.

That night over dinner Boulware told him he wanted to go to the Iran—Turkey border to meet some people coming out.

Mr Fish was horrified. 'You don't understand,' he said. 'That is a *terrible* place. The people are Kurds and Azerbaijanis – wild mountain men, they don't obey any government. You know how they live up there? By smuggling, robbery and murder. I personally would not dare to go there. If you, an American, go there, you will never come back. Never.'

Boulware thought he was probably exaggerating. 'I have to go there, even if it's dangerous,' he said. 'Now, can I buy a light plane?'

Mr Fish shook his head. 'It is illegal in Turkey for individuals to own airplanes.'

'A helicopter?'

'Same thing.'

'All right, can I charter a plane?'

'It is possible. Where there is no scheduled flight, you can charter.'

'Are there scheduled flights to the border area?'

'No.'

'All right.'

'However, chartering is so unusual that you will surely attract the attention of the authorities . . .'

'We have no plans to do anything illegal. All the same, we don't need the hassle of being investigated. So let's set up the option of chartering. Find out about price and availability, but hold off from making any kind of booking. Meanwhile, I want to know more about getting there by land. If you don't want to escort me, fine, but maybe you can find somebody who will.'

'I'll see what I can do.'

They met several times over the next few days. Mr Fish's initial coolness totally disappeared, and Boulware felt they were becoming friends. Mr Fish was alert and articulate. Although he was no criminal, he would break the law if the risks and rewards were proportionate, Boulware guessed. Boulware had some sympathy with that attitude – he, too, would break the law under the right circumstances. Mr Fish was also a shrewd interrogator, and bit by bit Boulware told him the full story. Paul and Bill would probably have no passports, he admitted; but once in Turkey they would get new ones at the nearest American Consulate. Paul and Bill might have some trouble getting out of Iran, he said, and he wanted to be prepared to cross the border himself, perhaps in a light aircraft, to bring them out. None of this fazed Mr Fish as much as the idea of travelling in bandit country.

However, a few days later he introduced Boulware to a man who had relatives among the mountain bandits. Mr Fish whispered that the man was a criminal, and he certainly looked the part: he had a scar on his face and little beady eyes. He said he could guarantee Boulware safe passage to the border and back, and his relatives could even take Boulware across the border into Iran, if necessary.

Boulware called Dallas and told Merv Stauffer about the plan. Stauffer relayed the news to Coburn, in code; and Coburn told Simons. Simons vetoed it. If the man is a criminal, Simons pointed out, we can't trust him.

Boulware was annoyed. He had gone to some trouble to set it up. Did Simons imagine it was easy to get these people? And if you wanted to travel in bandit country, who else but a bandit would escort you? But Simons was the boss, and Boulware had no option but to ask Mr Fish to start all over again.

Meanwhile, Sculley and Schwebach flew in to Istanbul.

The deadly duo had been on a flight from London to Tehran via Copenhagen when the Iranians had closed their airport again, so Sculley and Schwebach joined Boulware in Istanbul. Cooped up in the hotel, waiting for something to happen, the three of them got cabin fever. Schwebach reverted to his Green Beret role and tried to make them all keep fit by running up and down the hotel stairs. Boulware did it once and then gave up. They became impatient with Simons, Coburn and Poché, who seemed to be sitting in Tehran doing nothing: why didn't those guys *make it happen*? Then Simons sent Sculley and Schwebach back to the States. They left the radios with Boulware.

When Mr Fish saw the radios he had a fit. It was highly illegal to own a radio transmitter in Turkey, he told Boulware. Even ordinary transistor radios had to be registered with the government, for fear their parts would be used to make transmitters for terrorists. 'Don't you understand how *conspicuous* you are?' he said to Boulware. 'You're running up a phone bill of a couple of thousand dollars a week, and you're paying *cash*. You don't appear to be doing business here. The maids are sure to have seen the radios and talked about it. By now you must be under surveillance. Forget your friends in Iran – *you* are going to end up in jail.'

Boulware agreed to get rid of the radios. The snag about Simons's apparently endless patience was that further delay caused new problems. Now Sculley and Schwebach could not get back into Iran, yet still nobody had any radios. Meanwhile Simons kept saying no to things. Mr Fish pointed out that there were two border crossings from Iran to Turkey, one at Sero and the other at Barzagan. Simons had picked Sero. Barzagan was a bigger and more civilized place, Mr Fish pointed out; everyone would be a little safer there. Simons said no.

A new escort was found to take Boulware to the border. Mr Fish had a business colleague whose brother-in-law was in the Milli Istihbarat Teskilati, or MIT, the Turkish equivalent of the CIA. The name of this secret policeman was Ilsman. His credentials would secure for Boulware army protection in bandit country. Without such credentials, Mr Fish said, the ordinary citizen was in danger not only from bandits but from the Turkish army.

Mr Fish was very jumpy. On the way to meet Ilsman, he took Boulware through a whole cloak-and-dagger routine, changing cars and switching to a bus for part of the journey, as if he were trying to shake off a tail. Boulware could not see the need for all that if they were really going to visit a perfectly upright citizen who just happened to work in the intelligence community. But Boulware was a foreigner in a strange country, and he just had to go along with Mr Fish and trust the man.

They ended up at a big, run-down apartment building in an unfamiliar section of the city. The power was off – just like Tehran – so it took Mr Fish a while to find the right apartment in the dark. At first he could get no answer. His attempt to be secretive fell apart at this point, for he had to hammer on the door for what seemed like half an hour, and every other inhabitant of the building got a good look at the visitors in the meantime. Boulware just stood there feeling like a white man in Harlem. At last a woman opened up, and they went in.

It was a small, drab apartment crowded with ancient furniture and dimly lit by a couple of candles. Ilsman was a short man of about Boulware's age, thirty-five. He had not seen his feet for many years – he was *gross*. He made Boulware think of the stereotyped fat police sergeant in the movies, with a suit too small and a sweaty shirt and a wrinkled tie wrapped around the place where his neck would have been if he had had a neck.

They sat down, and the woman – Mrs Ilsman, Boulware presumed – served tea – just like Tehran! Boulware explained his problem, with Mr Fish translating. Ilsman was suspicious. He cross-questioned Boulware about the two fugitive Americans. How could Boulware be sure they were innocent? Why did they have no passpoorts? What would they bring into Turkey? In the end he seemed convinced that Boulware was levelling with him, and he offered to get Paul and Bill from the border to Istanbul for eight thousand dollars, all in.

Boulware wondered if Ilsman was for real. Smuggling Americans into the country was a funny pastime for an intelligence agent. And if Ilsman really was MIT, who was it that Mr Fish thought might have been following him and Boulware across town?

Perhaps Ilsman was freelancing. Eight thousand dollars was a lot of money in Turkey. It was even possible that Ilsman would tell his superiors what he was doing. After all – Ilsman might figure – if Boulware's story were true no harm would be done by helping; and if Boulware were lying, the best way to find out what he was really up to might be to accompany him to the border.

Anyway, at this point Ilsman seemed to be the best Boulware could get. Boulware agreed the price, and Ilsman broke out a bottle of scotch.

While other members of the rescue team were fretting in various parts of the world, Simons and Coburn were driving the road from Tehran to the Turkish border.

Reconnaissance was a watchword with Simons, and he wanted to be familiar with every inch of his escape route before he embarked on it with Paul and Bill. How much fighting was there in that part of the country? What was the police presence? Were the roads passable in winter? Were the filling stations open?

In fact there were two routes to Sero, the border crossing he had chosen. (He preferred Sero because it was a little-used frontier post at a tiny village, so there would be few people and the border would be lightly guarded, whereas Barzagan – the alternative Mr Fish kept recommending – would be busier.) The nearest large town to Sero was Rezaiyeh. Directly across the path from Tehran to Rezaiyeh lay Lake Rezaiyeh, a hundred miles long: you had to drive around it, either to the north or to the south. The northerly route went through large towns and would have better roads. Simons therefore preferred the southerly route, provided the roads were passable. On this reconnaissance trip, he decided, they would check out both routes, the northerly going and the southerly on the return.

He decided that the best kind of car for the trip was a Range Rover. There were no dealerships or used car lots open in Tehran now, so Coburn gave the Cycle Man the job of getting hold of two Range Rovers. The Cycle Man's solution to the problem was characteristically ingenious. He had a notice printed with his telephone number and the message: 'If you would like to sell your Range Rover, call this number.' Then he went around on his motorcycle and put a copy under the windscreen wipers of every Range Rover he saw parked on the streets.

He got two vehicles for $20,000 each, and he also brought tools and spare parts for all but the most major repairs.

Simons and Coburn took two Iranians with them: Majid, and a cousin of Majid's who was a professor at an agricultural college in Rezaiyeh. The professor had come to Tehran to put his American wife and their children on a plane to the States: taking him back to Rezaiyeh was Simons's cover story for the trip.

They left Tehran early in the morning, with one of Keane Taylor's 55-gallon drums of gasoline in the back. For the first hundred miles, as far as Qazvin, there was a modern

267

freeway. After Qazvin the road was a two-lane blacktop. The hillsides were covered with snow, but the road itself was clear. If it's like this all the way to the border, Coburn thought, we could get there in a day.

They stopped at Zanjan, two hundred miles from Tehran and the same distance from Rezaiyeh, and spoke to the local chief of police, who was related to the professor. (Coburn could never quite work out the family relationships of Iranians: they seemed to use the word 'cousin' rather loosely.) This part of the country was peaceful, the police chief said, if they were to encounter any problems it would happen in the area of Tabriz.

They drove on through the afternoon, on narrow but good country roads. After another hundred miles they entered Tabriz. There was a demonstration going on, but it was nothing like the kind of battle they had got used to in Tehran, and they even felt secure enough to take a stroll around the bazaar.

Along the way Simons had been talking to Majid and the professor. It seemed like a casual conversation, but by now Coburn was familiar with Simons's technique, and he knew that the Colonel was feeling these two out, deciding whether he could trust them. So far the prognosis seemed good, for Simons began to drop hints about the real purpose of the trip.

The professor said that the countryside around Tabriz was pro-Shah, so before they moved on Simons stuck a photograph of the Shah on the windscreen.

The first sign of trouble came a few miles north of Tabriz, where they were stopped by a roadblock. It was an amateur affair, just two tree-trunks laid across the road in such a way that cars could manoeuvre around them but could not pass through at speed. It was manned by villagers armed with axes and sticks.

Majid and the professor talked to the villagers. The professor showed his university identity card, and said that the Americans were scientists come to help him with a research project. It was clear, Coburn thought, that the rescue team would need to bring Iranians when and if they did the trip with Paul and Bill, to handle situations like this.

The villagers let them pass.

A little later, Majid stopped and waved down a car coming in the opposite direction. The professor talked to the driver of the other car for a few minutes, then reported that the next town, Khoy, was anti-Shah. Simons took down the picture of the Shah from the windscreen and replaced it with one of the Ayatollah Khomeini. From then on they would stop oncoming cars regularly and change the picture according to local politics.

On the outskirts of Khoy there was another roadblock.

Like the first one, it looked unofficial, and was manned by civilians; but this time the ragged men and boys standing behind the tree-trunks were holding guns.

Majid stopped the car and they all got out.

To Coburn's horror a teenage boy pointed a gun at him.

Coburn froze.

The gun was a 9mm Llama pistol. The boy looked about sixteen. He had probably never handled a firearm before today, Coburn thought. Amateurs with guns were *dangerous*. The boy was holding the gun so tightly that his knuckles showed white.

Coburn was scared. He had been shot at many times, in Vietnam, but what frightened him now was the possibility that he would be killed by goddam *accident*.

'Rooskie,' the boy said. 'Rooskie.'

He thinks I'm a Russian, Coburn realized.

Perhaps it was because of the bushy red beard and the little black wool cap.

'No, American,' Coburn said.

The boy kept his pistol levelled.

Coburn stared at those white knuckles and thought: I just hope the punk doesn't *sneeze*.

The villagers searched Simons, Majid and the professor. Coburn, who could not take his eyes off the kid, heard Majid say: 'They're looking for weapons.' The only weapon they had was a little knife which Coburn was wearing in a

269

scabbard behind his back, under his shirt.

A villager began to search Coburn, and at last the kid lowered his pistol.

Coburn breathed again.

Then he wondered what would happen when they found his knife.

The search was not thorough, and the knife was not found.

The vigilantes believed the story about the scientific project. 'They apologize for searching the old man,' Majid said. The 'old man' was Simons, who was now looking just like an elderly Iranian peasant. 'We can go on,' Majid added.

They climbed back into the car.

Outside Khoy they turned south, looping over the top end of the lake, and drove down the western shore to the outskirts of Rezaiyeh.

The professor guided them into the town by remote roads, and they saw no roadblocks. The journey from Tehran had taken them twelve hours, and they were now an hour away from the border crossing at Sero.

That evening they all had dinner – chella kebab, the Iranian dish of rice and lamb – with the professor's landlord, who happened to be a customs official. Majid gently pumped the landlord for information, and learned that there was very little activity at the Sero frontier station.

They spent the night at the professor's house, a two-storey villa on the outskirts of the town.

In the morning Majid and the professor drove to the border and back. They reported that there were no roadblocks and the route was safe. Then Majid went into town to seek out a contact from whom he could buy firearms, and Simons and Coburn went to the border.

They found a small frontier post with only two guards. It had a customs warehouse, a weighbridge for lorries, and a guard house. The road was barred by a low chain stretched betwen a post on one side and the wall of the guard house on the other. Beyond the chain was about two hundred yards of no-man's land, then another, smaller frontier post on the Turkish side.

They got out of the car to look around. The air was pure and bitingly cold. Simons pointed across the hillside. 'See the tracks?'

Coburn followed Simons's finger. In the snow, close behind the border station, was a trail where a small caravan had crossed the border, impudently close to the guards.

Simons pointed again, this time above their heads. 'Easy to cut the guards off.' Coburn looked up and saw a single telephone wire leading down the hill from the station. A quick snip and the guards would be isolated.

The two of them walked down the hill and took a side road, no more than a dirt track, into the hills. After a mile or so they came to a small village, just a dozen or so houses made of wood or mud brick. Speaking halting Turkish, Simons asked for the chief. A middle-aged man in baggy trousers, waistcoat and headdress appeared. Coburn listened without understanding as Simons talked. Finally Simons shook the chief's hand, and they left.

'What was all that about?' Coburn asked as they walked away.

'I told him I wanted to cross the border on horseback at night with some friends.'

'What did he say?'

'He said he could arrange it.'

'How did you know the people in that particular village were smugglers?'

'Look around you,' Simons said.

Coburn looked around at the bare snow-covered slopes.

'What do you see?' Simons asked.

'Nothing.'

'Right. There is no agriculture here, no industry. How do you think these people make a living? They're *all* smugglers.'

They returned to the Range Rover and drove back into Rezaiyeh. That evening Simons explained his plan to Coburn.

Simons, Coburn, Poché, Paul and Bill would drive from

271

Tehran to Rezaiyeh in the two Range Rovers. They would bring Majid and the professor with them as interpreters. In Rezaiyeh they would stay at the professor's house. The villa was ideal: no one else lived there, it was detached from other houses, and from there quiet roads led out of the city. Between Tehran and Rezaiyeh they would be unarmed: judging by what had happened at the roadblocks, guns would get them into trouble. However, at Rezaiyeh they would buy guns. Majid had made a contact in the city who would sell them Browning 12-gauge shotguns for six thousand dollars apiece. The same man could also get Llama pistols.

Coburn would cross the border legitimately in one of the Range Rovers and link up with Boulware, who would also have a car, on the Turkish side. Simons, Poché, Paul and Bill would cross on horseback with the smugglers. (That was why they needed the guns: in case the smugglers should decide to 'lose' them in the mountains.) On the other side they would meet Coburn and Boulware. They would all drive to the nearest American consulate and get new passports for Paul and Bill. Then they would fly to Dallas.

It was a good plan, Coburn thought; and he now saw that Simons was right to insist on Sero rather than Barzagan, for it would be difficult to sneak across the border in a more civilized, heavily populated area.

They returned to Tehran the next day. They left late and did most of the journey by night, so as to be sure to arrive in the morning, after curfew was lifted. They took the southerly route, passing through the small town of Mahabad. The road was a single-lane dirt track through the mountains, and they had the worst possible weather: snow, ice, and high winds. Nevertheless the roads were passable, and Simons determined to use this route, rather than the northerly one, for the escape itself.

If it ever happened.

One evening Coburn went to the Hyatt and told Keane Taylor he needed twenty-five thousand dollars in Iranian rials by the following morning.

He didn't say why.

Taylor got twenty-five thousand dollars in hundreds from Gayden, then called a carpet dealer he knew in the south of the city and agreed an exchange rate.

Taylor's driver, Ali, was highly reluctant to take him downtown, especially after dark, but after some argument he agreed.

They went to the shop. Taylor sat down and drank tea with the carpet dealer. Two more Iranians came in: one was introduced as the man who would exchange Taylor's money; the other was his bodyguard, and looked like a hoodlum.

Since Taylor's phone call, the carpet dealer said, the exchange rate had changed rather dramatically – in the carpet dealer's favour.

'I'm insulted!' Taylor said angrily. 'I'm not going to do business with you people!'

'This is the best exchange rate you can get,' said the carpet man.

'The hell it is!'

'It's very dangerous for you to be in this part of the city, carrying all that money.'

'I'm not alone,' Taylor said. 'I've got six people waiting for me.'

He finished his tea and stood up. He walked slowly out of the shop and jumped in the car. 'Ali, let's get out of here, fast.'

They drove north. Taylor directed Ali to another carpet dealer, an Iranian Jew with a shop near the palace. The man was just closing up when Taylor walked in.

'I need to change some dollars for rials,' Taylor said.

'Come back tomorrow,' said the man.

'No, I need them tonight.'

'How much?'

'Twenty-five thousand dollars.'

'I don't have anything like that much.'

'I've really got to have them tonight.'

'What's it for?'

'It's to do with Paul and Bill.'

The carpet dealer nodded. He had done business with several EDS people and he knew that Paul and Bill were in jail. 'I'll see what I can do.'

He called his brother from the back of the shop and sent him out. Then he opened his safe and took out all his rials. He and Taylor stood there counting money: the dealer counted the dollars and Taylor the rials. A few minutes later a kid came in with his hands full of rials and dumped them on the counter. He left without speaking. Taylor realized the carpet dealer was rounding up all the cash he could lay his hands on.

A young man came up on a motor scooter, parked outside, and walked in with a bag full of rials. While he was in the shop someone stole his motor scooter. The young man dropped the bag of money and ran after the thief, yelling at the top of his voice.

Taylor went on counting.

Just another business day in revolutionary Tehran.

John Howell was changing. With each day that went by he became a little less the upright American lawyer and a little more the devious Persian negotiator. In particular, he began to see bribery in a different light.

Mehdi, an Iranian accountant who had done occasional work for EDS, had explained things to him like this: 'In Iran many things are achieved by friendship. There are several ways to become Dadgar's friend. Me, I would sit outside his house every day until he talked to me. Another way for me to become his friend would be to give him two hundred thousand dollars. If you like I could arrange something like this for you.'

Howell discussed this proposal with the other members of the negotiating team. They assumed that Mehdi was offering himself as a bribe intermediary, as Deep Throat had. But this time Howell was not so quick to reject the idea of a corrupt deal for Paul's and Bill's freedom.

They decided to play along with Mehdi. They might be able to expose the deal and discredit Dadgar. Alternatively, they might decide the arrangement was solid and pay up. Either way, they wanted a clear sign from Dadgar that he was bribeable.

Howell and Keane Taylor had a series of meetings with Mehdi. The accountant was as jumpy as Deep Throat had been, and would not let the EDS people come to his office during normal working hours: he always met them early in the morning or late at night, or at his house or down back alleys. Howell kept pressing him for an unmistakable signal: Dadgar was to come to a meeting wearing odd socks, or with his tie on backwards. Mehdi would propose ambiguous signals, such as Dadgar giving the Americans a hard time. On one occasion Dadgar did give them a hard time, as Mehdi had forecast, but that might have happened anyway.

Dadgar was not the only one giving Howell a hard time. Howell was talking to Angela on the phone every four or five days, and she wanted to know when he was coming home. He did not know. Paul and Bill were naturally pressing him for hard news, but his progress was so slow and indefinite that he could not possibly give them deadlines. He found this frustrating, and when Angela started questioning him on the same point he had to suppress his irritation.

The Mehdi initiative came to nothing. Mehdi introduced Howell to a lawyer who claimed to be close to Dadgar. The lawyer did not want a bribe – just normal legal fees. EDS retained him, but at the next meeting Dadgar said: 'Nobody has any special relationship with me. If anybody tries to tell you differently, don't believe them.'

Howell was not sure what to make of all this. Had there been nothing in it right from the start? Or had EDS's caution frightened Dadgar into dropping a demand for a bribe? He would never know.

On 30 January Dadgar told Howell he was interested in Abolfath Mahvi, EDS's Iranian partner. Howell began to prepare a dossier on EDS's dealings with Mahvi.

Howell now believed that Paul and Bill were straightforward commercial hostages. Dadgar's investigation into corruption might be genuine, but he knew by now that Paul and Bill were innocent, therefore he must be holding them on orders from above. The Iranians had originally wanted either their promised computerized welfare system or their money back. Giving them their welfare system meant renegotiating the contract – but the new government was not interested in renegotiating and in any case was unlikely to stay in power long enough to consummate a deal.

If Dadgar could not be bribed, convinced of Paul's and Bill's innocence, or ordered by his superior to release them on the basis of a new contract between EDS and the Ministry, there remained to Howell only one option: pay the bail. Dr Houman's efforts to get the amount reduced had come to nothing. Howell now concentrated on ways of getting thirteen million dollars from Dallas to Tehran.

He had learned, bit by bit, that there was an EDS rescue team in Tehran. He was astonished that the head of an American corporation would set in motion something like that. He was also reassured, for if he could only get Paul and Bill out of jail, somebody else was standing by to get them out of Iran.

Liz Coburn was frantic with worry.

She sat in the car with Toni Dvoranchik and Toni's husband Bill. They were heading for the Royal Tokyo restaurant. It was on Greenville Avenue, not far from Recipes, the place where Liz and Toni had drunk Daiquiris with Mary Sculley and Mary had shattered Liz's world by saying: 'They're all in Tehran, I guess.'

Since that moment Liz had been living in constant, stark terror.

Jay was everything to her. He was Captain America, he was Superman, he was her whole life. She did not see how

276

she could live without him. The thought of losing him scared her to death.

She called Tehran constantly but never reached him. She called Merv Stauffer every day, saying: 'When is Jay coming home? Is he all right? Will he get out alive?' Merv tried to soothe her, but he would not give her any information and so she would demand to speak to Ross Perot. Merv would tell her that was not possible. Then she would call her mother and burst into tears and pour out all her anxiety and fear and frustration over the phone.

The Dvoranchiks were kind. They were trying to take her mind off her worries.

'What did you do today?' Toni asked.

'I went shopping,' Liz said.

'Did you buy anything?'

'Yes.' Liz started to cry. 'I bought a black dress. Because Jay isn't coming home.'

During those days of waiting, Jay Coburn learned a good deal about Simons.

One day Merv Stauffer called from Dallas to say that Simons's son Harry had been on the phone, worried. Harry had called his father's house and spoken to Paul Walker, who was minding the farm. Walker had said he did not know where Simons was, and had advised Harry to call Merv Stauffer at EDS. Harry was naturally worried, Stauffer said. Simons called Harry from Tehran and reassured him.

Simons told Coburn that Harry had had some problems, but he was a good boy at heart. He spoke of his son with a kind of resigned affection. (He never mentioned Bruce, and it was not until much later that Coburn realized Simons had two sons.)

Simons talked a lot about his late wife, Lucille, and how happy the two of them had been after Simons retired. They had been very close during the last few years, Coburn gathered, and Simons seemed to regret that it had taken him so long to realize how much he loved her. 'Hold on to your

277

mate,' he advised Coburn. 'She's the most important person in your life.'

Paradoxically, Simons's advice had the opposite effect on Coburn. He envied the companionship Simons and Lucille had had, and he wanted that for himself; but he was so sure he could never achieve it with Liz that he wondered if someone else would be his true soul-mate.

One evening Simons laughed and said: 'You know, I wouldn't do this for anyone else.'

It was a characteristically cryptic Simons remark. Sometimes, Coburn had learned, you got an explanation, sometimes you did not. This time Coburn got an explanation: Simons told him why he felt indebted to Ross Perot.

The aftermath of the Son Tay Raid had been a bitter experience for Simons. Although the raiders had not brought back any American POWs, it had been a brave try, and Simons expected the American public to see it that way. Indeed, he had argued, at a breakfast meeting with Defence Secretary Melvin Laird, in favour of releasing the news of the raid to the press. 'This is a perfectly legitimate operation,' he had told Laird. 'These are American prisoners. This is something Americans traditionally do for Americans. For Christ's sake, what is it we're afraid of here?'

He soon found out. The press and the public saw the raid as a failure and yet another intelligence foul-up. The banner headline on the front page of the next day's Washington Post read: US RAID TO RESCUE POWS FAILS. When Senator Robert Dole introduced a resolution praising the raid and said 'Some of these men have been languishing in prison for five years,' Senator Kennedy replied: 'And they're still there!'

Simons went to the White House to receive the Distinguished Service Cross for 'extraordinary heroism' from President Nixon. The rest of the raiders were to be decorated by Defence Secretary Laird. Simons was enraged to learn that over half of his men were to get nothing more than the Army Commendation Ribbon, only slightly better than a Good Conduct Ribbon, and known to soldiers as a Green Weenie. Mad as hell, he picked up the phone and asked for the Army Chief of Staff, General Westmoreland. He got the Acting Chief, General Palmer. Simons told Palmer about the Green Weenies and said: 'General, I don't want to embarrass the Army, but one of my men is just likely to shove an Army Commendation Ribbon up Mr Laird's ass.' He got his way. Laird awarded four Distinguished Service Crosses, fifty Silver Stars, and no Green Weenies.

The PoWs got a huge morale boost from the Son Tay Raid (which they heard about from incoming prisoners). An important side-effect of the raid was that the PoW camps – where many prisoners had been kept permanently in solitary confinement – were closed, and all the Americans were brought in to two large prisons where there was not enough room to keep them apart. Nevertheless, the world branded the raid a failure, and Simons felt a grave injustice had been done to his men.

The disappointment rankled with him for years – until, one weekend, Ross Perot threw a mammoth party in San Francisco, persuaded the Army to round up the Son Tay Raiders from all over the world, and introduced them to the prisoners they had tried to rescue. That weekend, Simons felt, his raiders had at last got the thanks they deserved. And Ross Perot had been responsible.

'That's why I'm here,' Simons told Coburn. 'Sure as hell, I wouldn't do this for anyone else.'

Coburn, thinking of his son Scott, knew exactly what Simons meant.

4

On 22 January hundreds of homafars – young Air Force officers – mutinied at bases in Dezful, Hamadan, Isfahan and Mashad, and declared themselves loyal to the Ayatollah Khomeini.

The significance of the event was not apparent to National Security Adviser Zbigniew Brzezinski, who still expected the Iranian military to crush the Islamic revolution; nor to Premier Shahpour Bakhtiar, who was talking about meeting the revolutionary challenge with a minimum of force; nor to the Shah, who instead of going to the United States was hanging on in Egypt, waiting to be summoned back to save his country in its hour of need.

Among the people who did see its significance were Ambassador William Sullivan and General Abbas Gharabaghi, the Iranian Chief of Staff.

Sullivan told Washington that the idea of a pro-Shah counter-coup was moonshine, the revolution was going to succeed and the US had better start thinking about how it would live with the new order. He received a harsh reply from the White House suggesting that he was disloyal to the President. He decided to resign, but his wife talked him out of it: he had a responsibility to the thousands of Americans still in Iran, she pointed out, and he could hardly walk out on them now.

General Gharabaghi also contemplated resigning. He was in an impossible situation. He had sworn his oath of loyalty, not to the parliament or the government of Iran, but to the Shah personally; and the Shah was gone. For the time being Gharabaghi took the view that the military owed loyalty to the Constitution of 1906, but that meant little in practice. Theoretically the military ought to support the Bakhtiar government. Gharabaghi had been wondering for some weeks whether he could rely on his soldiers to follow orders and fight for Bakhtiar against the revolutionary forces. The revolt of the homafars showed that he could not. He realized – as Brzezinski did not – that the army was not a machine to be switched on and off at will, but a collection of people, sharing the aspirations, the anger and the revivalist religion of the rest of the country. The soldiers wanted a revolution as much as the civilians. Gharabaghi concluded that he could no longer control his troops, and he decided to resign. On the day that he announced his intention to his fellow-generals, Ambassador William Sullivan was summoned to Prime Minister Bakhtiar's office at six o'clock in the evening. Sullivan had heard, from US General 'Dutch' Huyser, of Gharabaghi's intended resignation, and he assumed that this was what Bakhtiar wanted to talk about.

Bakhtiar waved Sullivan to a seat, saying with an enigmatic smile: *'Nous serons trois.'* There will be three of us. Bakhtiar always spoke French with Sullivan.

A few minutes later General Gharabaghi walked in. Bakhtiar spoke of the difficulties that would be created if the general were to resign. Gharabaghi began to reply in Farsi, but Bakhtiar made him speak French. As the general talked, he toyed with what seemed to be an envelope in his pocket. Sullivan guessed it was his letter of resignation.

As the two Iranians argued in French, Bakhtiar kept turning to the American Ambassador for support. Sullivan secretly thought Gharabaghi was absolutely right to resign, but his orders from the White House were to encourage the military to support Bakhtiar, so he doggedly argued, against his own convictions, that Gharabaghi should not resign. After a discussion of half an hour, the general left without delivering his letter of resignation. Bakhtiar thanked Sullivan profusely for his help. Sullivan knew it would do no good.

On 24 January Bakhtiar closed Tehran's airport to stop Khomeini entering Iran. It was like opening an umbrella against a tidal wave. On 26 January soldiers killed fifteen pro-Khomeini protestors in street fighting in Tehran. Two days later Bakhtiar offered to go to Paris for talks with the Ayatollah. For a ruling Prime Minister to offer to visit an exiled rebel was a fantastic admission of weakness, and Khomeini saw it that way: he refused to talk unless Bakhtiar first resigned. On 29 January thirty-five people died in the fighting in Tehran and another fifty in the rest of the country. Gharabaghi, bypassing his Prime Minister, began talks with the rebels in Tehran, and gave his consent for the return of the Ayatollah. On 30 January Sullivan ordered the evacuation of all nonessential Embassy personnel and all dependents. On 1 February Khomeini came home.

His Air France jumbo jet landed at 9.15 a.m. Two million Iranians turned out to greet him. At the airport the Ayatollah made his first public statement. 'I beg God to cut off the hands of all evil foreigners and all their helpers.'

Simons saw it all on TV, then he said to Coburn: 'That's it. The people are going to do it for us. The mob will take that jail.'

Nine

1

At midday on 5 February John Howell was on the point of getting Paul and Bill out of jail.

Dadgar had said that he would accept bail in one of three forms: cash, a bank guarantee, or a lien on property. Cash was out of the question. Firstly, anyone who flew into the lawless city of Tehran with $12,750,000 in a suitcase might never reach Dadgar's office alive. Secondly, Dadgar might take the money and still keep Paul and Bill, either by raising the bail or by rearresting them on some new pretext. (Tom Walter suggested using counterfeit money but nobody knew where to get it.) There had to be a *document* which gave Dadgar the money and at the same time gave Paul and Bill their freedom. In Dallas, Tom Walter had at last found a bank willing to issue a letter of credit for the bail, but Howell and Taylor were having trouble finding an Iranian bank to accept it and issue the guarantee Dadgar required. Meanwhile, Howell's boss Tom Luce thought about the third option, a lien on property, and came up with a wild and whacky idea that just might work: pledging the US Embassy in Tehran as bail for Paul and Bill.

The State Department was by now loosening up but was not quite ready to pledge its Tehran embassy as bail. However, it was ready to give the guarantee of the United States Government. That in itself was unique: the USA standing bail for two jailed men!

First, Tom Walter in Dallas got a bank to issue a letter of credit in favour of the State Department for $12,750,000. Because this transaction took place entirely within the US it was accomplished in hours rather than days. Once the State Department in Washington had the letter, Minister

283

Counsellor Charles Naas – Ambassador Sullivan's deputy – would deliver a diplomatic note saying that Paul and Bill, once released, would make themselves available to Dadgar for questioning, otherwise the bail would be paid by the Embassy.

Right now Dadgar was in a meeting with Lou Goelz, Consul General at the Embassy. Howell had not been invited to attend, but Abolhasan was there for EDS.

Howell had had a preliminary meeting with Goelz yesterday. Together they had gone over the terms of the guarantee, with Goelz reading the phrases in his quiet, precise voice. Goelz was changing. Two months ago Howell had found him maddeningly correct: it was Goelz who had refused to give back Paul's and Bill's passports without telling the Iranians. Now Goelz seemed ready to try the unconventional. Perhaps living in the middle of a revolution had made the old boy unbend a little.

Goelz had told Howell that the decision to release Paul and Bill would be made by Prime Minister Bakhtiar, but it must first be cleared with Dadgar. Howell was hoping Dadgar would not make trouble, for Goelz was not the type of man to bang the table and force Dadgar to back down.

There was a tap at the door and Abolhasan walked in.

Howell could tell from his face that he brought bad news.

'What happened?'

'He turned us down,' Abolhasan said.

'Why?'

'He won't accept the guarantee of the United States Government.'

'Did he give a reason?'

'There's nothing in the law that says he can accept that as bail. He has to have cash, a bank guarantee—'

'Or a lien on property, I know.' Howell felt numb. There had been so many disappointments, so many dead ends, he was no longer capable of resentment or anger. 'Did you say anything about the Prime Minister?'

'Yes. Goelz told him we would take this proposal to Bakhtiar.'

284

'What did Dadgar say to that?'

'He said it was typical of the Americans. They try to resolve things by bringing influence t⌣ bear at high levels, with no concern for what is happening at lower levels. He also said that if his superiors did not like the way he was handling the case, they could take him off it, and he would be very happy, because he was weary of it.'

Howell frowned. What did all this mean? He had recently concluded that what the Iranians really wanted was the money. Now they had flatly turned it down. Was this genuinely because of the technical problem that the law did not specify a government guarantee as an acceptable form of bail – or was that an excuse? Perhaps it was genuine. The EDS case had always been politically sensitive, and now that the Ayatollah had returned, Dadgar might well be terrified of doing anything that could be construed as pro-American. Bending the rules to accept an unconventional form of bail might get him into trouble. What would happen if Howell succeeded in putting up bail in the legally required form? Would Dadgar then feel he had covered his rear, and release Paul and Bill? Or would he invent another excuse?

There was only one way to find out.

The week the Ayatollah returned to Iran, Paul and Bill asked for a priest.

Paul's cold seemed to have turned to bronchitis. He had asked for the prison doctor. The doctor did not speak English, but Paul had no trouble explaining his problem: he coughed, and the doctor nodded.

Paul was given some pills which he assumed were penicillin, and a bottle of cough medicine. The taste of the medicine was strikingly familiar, and he had a sudden, vivid flashback: he saw himself as a little boy, and his mother pouring the glutinous syrup from an old-fashioned bottle on to a spoon and dosing him with it. This was exactly the same stuff. It eased his cough, but he had already done some damage to the muscles in his chest, and he suffered a sharp pain every time he breathed deeply.

He had a letter from Ruthie which he read and re-read. It was an ordinary, newsy kind of letter. Karen was in a new school, and having some trouble adjusting. This was normal: every time she changed schools, Karen would be sick to her stomach for the first couple of days. Ann Marie, Paul's younger daughter, was much more happy-go-lucky. Ruthie was still telling her mother that Paul would be home in a couple of weeks, but the story was becoming implausible for that two-week deadline had now been stretched for two months. She was buying a house, and Tom Walter was helping her with the legal processes. Whatever emotions Ruthie was going through, she did not put them in the letter.

Keane Taylor was the most frequent visitor to the jail. Each time he came, he would hand Paul a pack of cigarettes with fifty or a hundred dollars folded inside. Paul and Bill could use the money in jail to buy special privileges, such as a bath. During one visit the guard left the room for a moment, and Taylor handed over four thousand dollars.

On another visit Taylor brought Father Williams.

Williams was pastor of the Catholic Mission where, in happier times, Paul and Bill had met with the EDS Tehran Roman Catholic Sunday Brunch Poker School. Williams was eighty years old, and his superiors had given him permission to leave Tehran, because of the danger. He had preferred to stay at his post. This kind of thing was not new to him, he told Paul and Bill: he had been a missionary in China during World War Two, when the Japanese had invaded, and later, during the revolution which brought Mao-Tse Tung to power. He himself had been imprisoned, so he understood what Paul and Bill were going through.

Father Williams boosted their morale almost as much as Ross Perot had. Bill, who was more devout than Paul, felt deeply strengthened by the visit. It gave him the courage to face the unknown future. Father Williams granted them absolution for their sins before he left. Bill still did not know whether he would get out of the jail alive, but now he felt prepared to face death.

Iran exploded into revolution on Friday 9 February 1979.

In just over a week Khomeini had destroyed what was left of legitimate government. He had called on the military to mutiny and the members of parliament to resign. He had appointed a 'provisional government' despite the fact that Bakhtiar was still officially Prime Minister. His supporters, organized into revolutionary committees, had taken over responsibility for law and order and garbage collection, and had opened more than a hundred Islamic co-operative stores in Tehran. On 8 February a million people or more marched through the city in support of the Ayatollah. Street fighting went on continually between stray units of loyalist soldiers and gangs of Khomeini men.

On 9 February, at two Tehran air bases – Doshen Toppeh and Farahabad – formations of homafars and cadets gave a salute to Khomeini. This infuriated the Javadan Brigade, which had been the Shah's personal bodyguard, and they attacked both air bases. The homafars barricaded themselves in and repelled the loyalist troops, helped by crowds of armed revolutionaries milling around inside and outside the bases.

Units of both the Marxist Fedayeen and the Muslim Mujahedeen guerrillas rushed to Doshen Toppeh. The armoury was broken open and weapons were distributed indiscriminately to soldiers, guerrillas, revolutionaries, demonstrators, and passers-by.

That night at eleven o'clock the Javadan Brigade returned in force. Khomeini supporters within the military warned the Doshen Toppeh rebels that the Brigade was on its way, and the rebels counter-attacked before the Brigade reached the base. Several senior officers among the loyalists were killed early in the battle. The fighting continued all night, and spread to a large area around the base.

By noon on the following day, the battlefield had widened to include most of the city.

That day John Howell and Keane Taylor went downtown for a meeting.

Howell was convinced they would get Paul and Bill released within hours. They were all set to pay the bail.

Tom Walter had a Texas bank ready to issue a letter of credit for $12,750,000 to the New York branch of Bank Melli. The plan was that the Tehran branch of Bank Melli would then issue a bank guarantee to the Ministry of Justice, and Paul and Bill would be bailed out. It had not worked quite that way. The deputy managing director of Bank Melli, Sadr-Hashemi, had recognized – as had all the bankers – that Paul and Bill were commercial hostages, and that once they were out of jail EDS could argue in an American court that the money had been extorted and should not be paid. If that happened, Bank Melli in New York would not be able to collect on the letter of credit – but Bank Melli in Tehran would still have to pay the money to the Iranian Ministry of Justice. Sadr-Hashemi said he would change his mind only if his New York lawyers told him there was no way EDS could block payment on the letter of credit. Howell knew perfectly well that no decent American attorney would issue such an option.

Then Keane Taylor thought of Bank Omran. EDS had a contract to install an on-line computerized accounting system for Bank Omran, and Taylor's job in Tehran had been to supervise this contract, so he knew the bank's officials. He met with Farhad Bakhtiar, who was one of the top men there as well as being a relative of Prime Minister Shahpour Bakhtiar. It was clear that the Prime Minister was going to fall from power any day, and Farhad was planning to leave the country. Perhaps that was why he was less concerned than Sadr-Hashemi about the possibility that the $12,750,000 would never be paid. Anyway, for whatever reason, he had agreed to help.

Bank Omran did not have a US branch. How, then, could EDS pay the money? It was agreed that the Dallas bank would lodge its letter of credit with the Dubai branch of Bank Omran by a system called Tested Telex. Dubai would then call Tehran on the phone to confirm that the letter of credit had been received, and the Tehran branch of Bank

Omran would issue the guarantee to the Ministry of Justice.

There were delays. Everything has to be approved by the board of directors of Bank Omran, and by the bank's lawyers. Everyone who looked at the deal suggested small changes in the language. The changes, in English and Farsi, had to be communicated to Dubai and to Dallas, then a new telex had to be sent from Dallas to Dubai, tested, and approved by phone with Tehran. Because the Iranian weekend was Thursday and Friday, there were only three days in the week when both banks were open; and because Tehran was nine and a half hours ahead of Dallas there was never a time of day when both banks were open. Furthermore, the Iranian banks were on strike a good deal of the time. Consequently a two-word change could take a week to arrange.

The last people who had to approve the deal were the Iranian central bank. Getting that approval was the task Howell and Taylor had set themselves for Saturday 10 February.

The city was relatively quiet at 8.30 in the morning when they drove to Bank Omran. They met with Farhad Bakhtiar. To their surprise he said that the request for approval was already with the central bank. Howell was delighted – for once something was happening ahead of time in Iran! He left some documents with Farhad, including a signed letter of agreement, and he and Taylor drove farther downtown to the central bank.

The city was waking up now, the traffic was even more nightmarish than usual, but dangerous driving was Taylor's speciality, and he tore through the streets, cutting across lanes of traffic, U-turning in the middle of freeways, and generally beating the Iranian drivers at their own game.

At the central bank they had a long wait to see Mr Farhang, who would give approval. Eventually he stuck his head out of his office door and said the deal had already been approved and the approval notified to Bank Omran.

This was good news!

They got back into the car and headed for Bank Omran.

Now they could tell that there was serious fighting in parts of the city. The noise of gunfire was continuous, and plumes of smoke rose from burning buildings. Bank Omran was opposite a hospital, and the dead and wounded were being brought in from the battle zones in cars, pick-up trucks and buses, all the vehicles having white cloths tied to their radio antennae to signify emergency, all hooting constantly. The street was jammed with people, some coming to give blood, others to visit the sick, still others to identify corpses.

They had resolved the bail problem not a moment too soon. Not only Paul and Bill, but now Howell and Taylor and all of them were in grave danger. They had to get out of Iran fast.

Howell and Taylor went into the bank and found Farhad.

'The central bank has approved the deal,' Howell told him.

'I know.'

'Is the letter of agreement all right?'

'No problems.'

'Then, if you give us the bank guarantee, we can go to the Ministry of Justice with it right away.'

'Not today.'

'*Why not*?'

'Our lawyer, Dr Emami has reviewed the credit document and wishes to make some small changes.'

Taylor muttered: 'Jesus *Christ*.'

Farhad said: 'I have to go to Geneva for five days.'

Forever was more likely.

'My colleagues will look after you, and if you have any problems just call me in Switzerland.'

Howell suppressed his anger. Farhad knew perfectly well that things were not that simple: with him away everything would be more difficult. But nothing would be accomplished by an emotional outburst, so Howell just said: 'What are the changes?'

Farhad called in Dr Emami.

'I also need the signatures of two more directors of the bank,' Farhad said. 'I can get those at the board meeting tomorrow. And I need to check the references of the National Bank of Commerce in Dallas.'

'And how long will that take?'

'Not long. My assistants will deal with it while I am away.'

Dr Emami showed Howell the changes he proposed in the language of the credit letter. Howell was happy to agree to them, but the rewritten letter would have to go through the time-consuming process of being transmitted from Dallas to Dubai by Tested Telex and from Dubai to Tehran by telephone.

'Look,' said Howell. 'Let's try to get all this done *today*. You could check the references of the Dallas bank *now*. We could find those other two bank directors, wherever in the city they are, and get their signatures *this afternoon*. We could call Dallas, give them the language changes, and get them to send the telex *now*. Dubai could confirm to you *this afternoon*. You could issue the bank guarantee—'

'There is a holiday in Dubai today,' said Farhad.

'All right, Dubai can confirm tomorrow morning—'

'There is a strike tomorrow. Nobody will be here at the bank.'

'Monday, then—'

The conversation was interrupted by the sound of a siren. A secretary put her head around the door and said something in Farsi. 'There is an early curfew,' Farhad translated. 'We must all leave now.'

Howell and Taylor sat there looking at each other. Two minutes later they were alone in the office. They had failed yet again.

That evening, Simons said to Coburn: 'Tomorrow is the day.'

Coburn thought he was full of shit.

291

In the morning on Sunday 11 February the negotiating team
went as usual to the EDS office they called 'Bucharest'. John
Howell left, taking Abolhasan with him, for an eleven
o'clock meeting with Dadgar at the Ministry of Health. The
others – Keane Taylor, Bill Gayden, Bob Young and Rich
Gallagher – went up on the roof to watch the city burn.

Bucharest was not a high building but it was located on a
slope of the hills which rose to the north of Tehran, so from
the roof they could see the city laid out like a tableau. To the
south and east, where modern skyscrapers rose out of the
low-rise villas and slums, great palls of smoke billowed up
into the murky air, while helicopter gunships buzzed around
the fires like wasps at a barbecue. One of EDS's Iranian
drivers brought a transistor radio up to the roof and tuned it
to a station which had been taken over by the revolutionaries.
With the help of the radio and the driver's translation they
tried to identify the burning buildings.

Keane Taylor, who had abandoned his elegant vested
suits for jeans and cowboy boots, went downstairs to take a
phone call. It was the Cycle Man.

'You need to get out of there,' the Cycle Man told Taylor.
'Get out of the country as quickly as you can.'

'You know we can't do that,' Taylor said. 'We can't leave
without Paul and Bill.'

'It's going to be very dangerous for you.'

Taylor could hear, at the other end of the line, the noise of
a terrific battle. 'Where the hell are you, anyway?'

'Near the bazaar,' said the Cycle Man. 'I'm making
Molotov cocktails. They brought in helicopters this
morning and we just figured out how to shoot them down.
We burned four tanks—'

The line went dead.

Incredible, Taylor thought as he cradled the phone. In the
middle of a battle, he suddenly thinks of his American

friends, and calls to warn us. Iranians will never cease to surprise me.

He went back up on the roof.

'Look at this,' Bill Gayden said to him. Gayden, the jovial president of EDS World, had also switched to off-duty clothes: nobody was even pretending to do business any more. He pointed to a column of smoke in the east. 'If that isn't the Gasr Prison burning, it's damn close.'

Taylor peered into the distance. It was hard to tell.

'Call Dadgar's office at the Ministry of Health,' Gayden told Taylor. 'Howell should be there now. Get him to ask Dadgar to release Paul and Bill to the custody of the Embassy, for their own safety. If we don't get them out they're going to burn to death.'

John Howell had hardly expected Dadgar to turn up. The city was a battlefield, and an investigation into corruption under the Shah now seemed an academic exercise. But Dadgar was there in his office, waiting for Howell. Howell wondered what the hell was driving the man. Dedication? Hatred of Americans? Fear of the incoming revolutionary government? He would probably never know.

Dadgar had asked Howell about EDS's relationship with Abolfath Mahvi, and Howell had promised a complete dossier. It seemed the information was important to Dadgar's mysterious purposes, for a few days later he had pressed Howell for the dossier, saying: 'I can interrogate the people here and get the information I need,' which Howell took as a threat to arrest more EDS executives.

Howell had prepared a twelve-page dossier in English, with a covering letter in Farsi. Dadgar read the covering letter, then spoke. Abolhasan translated: 'Your company's helpfulness is laying the ground for a change in my attitude towards Chiapparone and Gaylord. Our legal code provides for such leniency towards those who supply information.'

It was farcical. They could all be killed in the next few hours, and here was Dadgar still talking about applicable provisions of the legal code.

293

Abolhasan began to translate the dossier aloud into Farsi. Howell knew that choosing Mahvi as an Iranian partner had not been the smartest move EDS ever made: Mahvi had got the company its first, small contract in Iran, but subsequently he had been blacklisted by the Shah and had caused trouble over the Ministry of Health contract. However, EDS had nothing to hide. Indeed, Howell's boss Tom Luce, in his eagerness to place EDS above suspicion, had filed details of the EDS–Mahvi relationship with the American Securities Exchange Commission, so that much of what was in the dossier was already public knowledge.

The phone interrupted Abolhasan's translation. Dadgar picked it up then handed it to Abolhasan, who listened for a moment then said: 'It's Keane Taylor.'

A minute later he hung up and said to Howell: 'Keane has been up on the roof at Bucharest. He says there are fires down by Gasr Prison. If the mob attacks the prison Paul and Bill could get hurt. He suggested we ask Dadgar to turn them over to the American Embassy.'

'Okay,' Howell said. 'Ask him.'

He waited while Abolhasan and Dadgar conversed in Farsi.

Finally, Abolhasan said: 'According to our laws, they have to be kept in an Iranian prison. He can't consider the US Embassy to be an Iranian prison.'

Crazier and crazier. The whole country was falling apart and Dadgar was still consulting his book of rules. Howell said: 'Ask him how he proposes to guarantee the safety of two American citizens who have not been charged with any crime.'

Dadgar's reply was: 'Don't be concerned. The worst that could happen is that the prison might be overrun.'

'And what if the mob decides to attack Americans?'

'Chiapparone will probably be safe – he could pass for Iranian.'

'Terrific,' said Howell. 'And what about Gaylord?'

Dadgar just shrugged.

Rashid left his house early that morning.

His parents, his brother and his sister planned to stay indoors all day, and they had urged him to do the same, but he would not listen. He knew it would be dangerous on the streets, but he could not hide at home while his countrymen were making history. Besides, he had not forgotten his conversation with Simons.

He was living by impulse. On Friday he had found himself at Farahabad air base during the clash between the homafars and the loyalist Javadan Brigade. For no particular reason, he had gone into the armoury and started passing out rifles. After half an hour of that he got bored and left.

The same day he had seen a dead man for the first time. He had been at the mosque when a bus driver who had been shot by soldiers had been brought in. On impulse Rashid had uncovered the face of the corpse. A whole section of the head was destroyed, a mixture of blood and brains: it had been sickening. The incident seemed like a warning, but Rashid was in no mood to heed warnings. The streets were where things were happening, and he had to be there.

This morning the atmosphere was electric. Crowds were everywhere. Hundreds of men and boys were toting automatic rifles. Rashid, wearing a flat English cap and an open-neck shirt, mingled with them, feeling the excitement. Anything could happen today.

He was vaguely heading for Bucharest. He still had duties: he was negotiating with two shipping companies to transport the belongings of the EDS evacuees back to the States; and he had to feed the abandoned dogs and cats. The scenes on the streets changed his mind. Rumour said that the Evin Prison had been stormed last night; today it might be the turn of the Gasr Prison, where Paul and Bill were.

Rashid wished he had an automatic rifle like the others.

He passed an army building which appeared to have been invaded by the mob. It was a six-storey block containing an armoury and a draft registration office. Rashid had a friend who worked there, Malek. It occurred to him that Malek

295

might be in trouble. If he had come to work this morning, he would be wearing his Army uniform – and that alone might be enough to get him killed today. I could lend Malek my shirt, Rashid thought; and impulsively he went into the building.

He pushed his way through the crowd on the ground floor and found the staircase. The rest of the building seemed empty. As he climbed, he wondered whether soldiers were hiding out on the upper floors: if so, they might shoot anyone who came along. He went on regardless. He climbed to the top floor. Malek was not there; nobody was there. The Army had abandoned the place to the mob.

Rashid returned to the ground floor. The crowd had gathered around the entrance to the basement armoury, but no one was going in. Rashid pushed his way to the front and said: 'Is this door locked?'

'It might be booby-trapped,' someone said.

Rashid looked at the door. All thoughts of going to Bucharest had now left him. He wanted to go to the Gasr Prison, and he wanted to carry a gun.

'I don't think this armoury is booby-trapped,' he said, and he opened the door.

He went down the staircase.

The basement consisted of two rooms divided by an archway. The place was dimly lit by narrow strip windows high in the walls, just above street level. The floor was of black mosaic tiles. In the first room were open boxes of loaded magazines. In the second were G3 machine guns.

After a minute some of the crowd upstairs followed him down.

He grabbed three machine guns and a sack of magazines and left. As soon as he got outside the building, people jumped all over him, asking for weapons: he gave away two of the guns and some of the ammunition.

Then he walked away, heading for Gasr Square.

Some of the mob went with him.

On the way they had to pass a military garrison. A skirmish was going on there. A steel door in the high brick wall around the garrison had been smashed down, as if a tank had rolled through it, and the brickwork on either side of the entrance had crumbled. A burning car stood across the way in.

Rashid went around the car and through the entrance.

He found himself in a large compound. From where he stood, a bunch of people were shooting haphazardly at a building a couple of hundreds yards away. Rashid took cover behind a wall. The people who had followed him joined in the shooting, but he held his fire. Nobody was really aiming. They were just trying to scare the soldiers in the building. It was a funny kind of battle. Rashid had never imagined the revolution would be like this: just a disorganized crowd with guns they hardly knew how to use, wandering around on a Sunday morning, firing at walls, encountering half-hearted resistance from invisible troops.

Suddenly a man near him fell dead.

It happened so quickly: Rashid did not even see him fall. At one moment the man was standing four feet away from Rashid, firing his rifle; next moment he lay on the ground with his forehead blown away.

They carried the corpse out of the compound. Someone found a jeep. They put the body in the jeep and drove off. Rashid returned to the skirmish.

Ten minutes later, for no apparent reason, a piece of wood with a white undershirt tied to its end was waved out of one of the windows in the building they had been shooting at. The soldiers had surrendered.

Just like that.

There was a sense of anticlimax.

This is my chance, Rashid thought.

It was easy to manipulate people if you understood the psychology of the human being. You just had to study the people, comprehend their situation, and figure out their needs. These people, Rashid decided, want excitement and adventure. For the first time in their lives they have guns in their hands: they need a target, and anything that symbolizes the regime of the Shah will do.

297

Right now they were standing around wondering where to go next.

'Listen!' Rashid shouted.

They all listened – they had nothing better to do.

'I'm going to the Gasr Prison!'

Someone cheered.

'The people in there are prisoners of the regime – if we are against the regime we should let them out!'

Several people shouted their agreement.

He started walking.

They followed him.

It's the mood they're in, he thought; they'll follow anyone who seems to know where to go.

He started with a band of twelve or fifteen men and boys, but as he walked the group grew: everyone with nowhere to go automatically joined in.

Rashid had become a revolutionary leader.

Nothing was impossible.

He stopped just before Gasr Square and addressed his army. 'The jails must be taken over by the people, just like the police stations and the garrisons; this is our responsibility. There are people in Gasr Prison who are guilty of nothing. They are just like us – our brothers, our cousins. Like us, they only want their freedom. But they were braver than us, for *they* demanded their freedom while the Shah was here, and they were thrown in jail for it. Now we shall let them out!'

They all cheered.

He remembered something Simons had said. 'The Gasr Prison is our Bastille!'

They cheered louder.

Rashid turned and ran into the square.

He took cover on the street corner opposite the huge steel entrance gates of the prison. There was a fair-sized mob in the square already, he realized; probably the prison would be stormed today with or without his help. But the important thing was to help Paul and Bill.

He raised his gun and fired in the air.

The mob in the square scattered, and the shooting began in earnest.

Once again the resistance was half-hearted. A few guards fired back from the gun towers on the walls and from the windows close to the gates. As far as Rashid could see, no one on either side was hit. Once again, the battle ended not with a bang but with a whimper: the guards simply disappeared from the walls and the shooting stopped.

Rashid waited a couple of minutes, to make sure they had gone, then he ran across the square to the prison entrance.

The gates were locked.

The mob crowded around. Someone fired a burst at the gates, trying to shoot them open. Rashid thought: he's seen too many cowboy movies. Another man produced a crowbar from somewhere, but it was impossible to force the gates open. We would need dynamite, Rashid thought.

In the brick wall beside the gates was a little barred window, through which a guard could see who was outside. Rashid smashed the glass with his gun, then started to attack the brickwork in which the bars were embedded. The man with the crowbar helped him, then three or four others crowded around, trying to loosen the bars with their hands, their gun barrels, and anything else that came to hand. Soon the bars came out and fell to the ground.

Rashid wriggled through the window.

He was inside.

Anything was possible.

He found himself in a little guardroom. There were no guards. He put his head out of the door. Nobody.

He wondered where the keys to the cell blocks were kept.

He went out of the office and past the big gates to another guardroom on the far side of the entrance. There he found a big bunch of keys.

He returned to the gates. Inset into one of them was a small door secured by a simple bar.

Rashid lifted the bar and opened the door.

The mob poured in.

Rashid stood back. He handed keys to anyone who would

299

take them, saying, 'Open every cell – let the people go!'

They swarmed past him. His career as a revolutionary leader was over. He had achieved his objective. He, Rashid, had led the storming of the Gasr Prison!

Once again, Rashid had done the impossible.

Now he had to find Paul and Bill among the eleven thousand eight hundred inmates of the jail.

Bill woke up at six o'clock. All was quiet.

He had slept well, he realized with some surprise. He had not expected to sleep at all. The last thing he remembered was lying on his bunk listening to what sounded like a pitched battle outside. If you're tired enough, he thought, I suppose you can sleep anywhere. Soldiers sleep in foxholes. You become acclimatized. No matter how frightened you may be, in the end your body takes control and you nod off.

He said a rosary.

He washed, brushed his teeth, shaved, and dressed, then he sat looking out of the window, waiting for breakfast, wondering what EDS was planning for today.

Paul woke up around seven. He looked at Bill and said: 'Couldn't sleep?'

'Sure I slept,' Bill said. 'I've been up an hour or so.'

'I didn't sleep well. The shooting was heavy most of the night.' Paul got out of his bunk and went to the bathroom.

A few minutes later breakfast came: bread and tea. Bill opened a can of orange juice that had been brought in by Keane Taylor.

The shooting started again around eight o'clock.

The prisoners speculated about what might be going on outside, but no one had any hard information. All they could see was the helicopters darting across the skyline, apparently shooting down at rebel positions on the ground. Every time a helicopter flew over the prison Bill watched for a ladder to come dropping out of the sky into the courtyard of Building No 8. This was his regular daydream. He also fantasized about a small group of EDS people, led by Coburn and an older man, swarming over the prison wall

300

with rope ladders; or a large force of American military arriving at the last minute, like the cavalry in the western movies, blasting a huge gap in the wall with dynamite.

He had done more than daydream. In his quiet, apparently casual way, he had inspected every inch of the building and courtyard, estimating the fastest way out under various imagined circumstances. He knew how many guards there were and how many rifles they possessed. Whatever might happen, he was ready.

It began to look as if today would be the day.

The guards were not following their normal routines. In jail everything was done by routine: a prisoner, with little else to do, observed the patterns and quickly became familiar with them. Today everything was different. The guards appeared nervous, whispering in corners, hurrying everywhere. The sounds of battle outside grew louder. With all this going on, was it *possible* that today would end like any other day? We might escape, Bill thought, or we might get killed; but surely we won't be turning off the TV and lying down on our bunks as usual tonight.

At about ten-thirty he saw most of the officers crossing the prison compound, heading north, as if they were going to a meeting. They hurried back half an hour later. The major in charge of building No 8 went into his office. He emerged a couple of minutes later – in civilian clothes! He carried a shapeless parcel – his uniform? – out of the building. Looking through the window, Bill saw him put the parcel in the trunk of his BMW, which was parked outside the courtyard fence, then get in the car and drive away.

What did that mean? Would all the officers leave? Was that how it would happen – would Paul and Bill be able just to walk out?

Lunch came a little before noon. Paul ate but Bill was not hungry. The firing seemed very close now, and they could hear shouting and chanting from the streets.

Three of the guards in Building No 8 suddenly appeared in civilian clothes.

This *had* to be the end.

301

Paul and Bill went downstairs and into the courtyard. The mental patients on the ground floor all seemed to be screaming. Now the guards in the gun towers were firing into the streets outside: the prison must be under attack.

Was that good news or bad, wondered Bill. Did EDS know this was happening? Could it be part of Coburn's rescue? There had been no visitors for two days. Had they all gone home? Were they still alive?

The sentry who normally guarded the courtyard gate had gone, and the gate was open.

The gate was open!

Did the guards *want* the prisoners to leave?

Other cell blocks must have been open too, for there were now prisoners as well as guards running around the compound. Bullets whistled through the trees and ricocheted off buildings.

A slug landed at Paul's feet.

They both stared at it.

The guards in the gun towers were now firing *into* the compound.

Paul and Bill turned and ran back into Building No 8.

They stood at a window, watching the mounting chaos in the compound. It was ironic: for weeks they had thought of little else but their freedom, yet now that they could walk out, they hesitated.

'What do you think we should do?' said Paul.

'I don't know. Is it more dangerous in here or out there?'

Paul shrugged.

'Hey, there's the billionaire.' They could see the rich prisoner from Building No 8 – the one who had a private room and meals brought in from outside – crossing the compound with two of his henchmen. He had shaved off his luxuriant handlebar moustache. Instead of his mink-lined camel coat, he wore a shirt and pants: he was stripped for action, travelling light, ready to move fast. He was heading north, away from the prison gates: did that mean there was a back way out?

The guards from Building No 8, all now in civilian clothes,

crossed the little courtyard and went out through the gate.

Everyone, was leaving, yet still Paul and Bill hesitated.

'See that motorcycle?' said Paul.

'I see it.'

'We could leave on that. I used to ride a motorcycle.'

'How would we get it over the wall?'

'Oh, yeah.' Paul laughed at his own foolishness.

Their cellmate had found a couple of big bags and he began to pack his clothes. Bill felt the urge to take off, just to get out of here, whether or not that was part of the EDS plan. Freedom was so close. But bullets were flying around out there, and the mob attacking the jail might well be anti-American. On the other hand, if the authorities were somehow to regain control of the prison, Paul and Bill would have lost their last chance of escape . . .

'I wonder where Gayden is now, the son of a bitch,' said Paul. 'The only reason I'm here is because he sent me to Iran.'

Bill looked at Paul and realized he was only joking.

The patients from the ground-floor hospital swarmed out into the courtyard: someone must have unlocked their doors. Bill could hear a tremendous commotion, like crying, from the women's cell block on the other side of the street. There were more and more people out in the compound, flocking towards the prison entrance. Looking that way, Bill saw smoke. Paul saw it at the same moment.

Bill said: 'If they're going to burn the place . . .'

'We'd better get out.'

The fire tipped the balance: their decision was made.

Bill looked around the cell. The two of them had few possessions. Bill thought of the diary he had kept faithfully for the last forty-three days. Paul had written lists of things he would do when he got back to the States, and had figured out, on a sheet of paper, the finance on the new house Ruthie was buying. They both had precious letters from home which they had read over and over again.

Paul said: 'We're probably better off not carrying anything that shows we're Americans.'

303

Bill had picked up his diary. Now he dropped it again. 'You're right,' he said reluctantly.

. They put on their coats: Paul had a blue London Fog raincoat and Bill an overcoat with a fur collar.

They had about two thousand dollars each, money which Keane Taylor had brought in. Paul had some cigarettes. They took nothing else.

They went out of the building and crossed the little courtyard, then hesitated at the gate. The street was now a sea of people, like the crowd leaving a sports stadium, walking and running in one mass towards the prison gates.

Paul stuck out his hand. 'Hey, good luck, Bill.'

Bill shook his hand. 'Good luck to you.'

Probably we'll both die in the next few minutes, Bill thought, most likely from a stray bullet. I'll never see the kids grow up, he realized sadly. The thought that Emily would have to manage on her own made him angry.

Amazingly enough, he felt no fear.

They stepped through the little gate, and then there was no more time for reflection.

They were swept into the throng, like twigs dropped into a fast-flowing stream. Bill concentrated on sticking close to Paul and staying upright, not to get trampled. There was still a lot of shooting. One lone guard had stayed at his post and seemed to be firing into the crowd from his gun tower. Two or three people fell – one of them was the American woman they had seen before – but it was not clear whether they had been shot or had merely stumbled. I don't want to die yet, Bill thought; I've got plans, things I want to do with my family, in my career; this is not the time, not the place for me to die; what a rotten hand of cards I've been dealt . . .

They passed the officers' club where they had met with Perot just three weeks ago – it seemed like years. Vengeful prisoners were smashing up the club and wrecking the officers' cars outside. Where was the sense in that? For a moment the whole scene seemed unreal, like a dream, or a nightmare.

The chaos around the main prison entrance was worse.

Paul and Bill held back, and managed to detach themselves from the crowd, for fear of being crushed. Bill recalled that some of the prisoners had been here for twenty-five years: it was no wonder, after that length of time, that when they smelled freedom they went berserk.

It seemed that the prison gates must still be shut, for scores of people were trying to climb the immense exterior wall. Some were standing on cars and trucks which had been pushed up against the wall. Others were climbing trees and crawling precariously along overhanging branches. Still more had leaned planks against the brickwork and were trying to scramble up those. A few people had reached the top of the wall by one means or another and were letting down ropes and sheets to those below, but the ropes were not long enough.

Paul and Bill stood watching, wondering what to do. They were joined by some of the other foreign prisoners from Building No 8. One of them, a New Zealander charged with drug smuggling, had a big grin all over his face as if he were enjoying the whole thing hugely. There was a kind of hysterical elation in the air, and Bill began to catch it. Somehow, he thought, we're going to get out of this mess alive.

He looked around. To the right of the gates the buildings were burning. To the left, some distance away, he saw an Iranian prisoner waving as if to say: This way! There had been some construction work on that section of the wall – a building seemed to be going up on the far side – and there was a steel door in the wall to allow access to the site. Looking more closely, Bill could see that the waving Iranian had got the steel door open.

'Hey – look over there!' said Bill.

'Let's go,' said Paul.

They ran over. Several other prisoners followed. They went through the door – and found themselves trapped in a kind of cell without doors or windows. There was a smell of new cement. Builders' tools lay around. Someone grabbed a pickaxe and swung it at the wall. The fresh concrete

305

crumbled quickly. Two or three others joined in, hacking away with anything that came to hand. Soon the hole was big enough: they dropped their tools and crawled through.

They were now between the two prison walls. The inner wall, behind them, was the high one – twenty-five or thirty feet. The outer wall, which stood between them and freedom, was only ten or twelve feet high.

An athletic prisoner managed to get up on to the top of the wall. Another man stood at its foot and beckoned. A third prisoner went forward. The man on the ground pushed him up, the one on top pulled, and the prisoner went over the wall.

It happened very quickly then.

Paul took a run at the wall.

Bill was right behind him.

Bill's mind was a blank. He ran. He felt a push, helping him up; then a pull; then he was at the top, and he jumped.

He landed on the pavement.

He got to his feet.

Paul was right beside him.

We're free! thought Bill. We're free!

He felt like dancing.

Coburn put down the phone and said: 'That was Majid. The mob has overrun the prison.'

'Good,' said Simons. He had told Coburn, earlier that morning, to send Majid down to Gasr Square.

Simons was very cool, Coburn thought. This was it – this was the big day! Now they could get out of the apartment, get on the move, activate their plans for 'Getting Out of Dodge'. Yet Simons showed no signs of excitement.

'What do we do now?' said Coburn.

'Nothing. Majid is there, Rashid is there. If those two can't take care of Paul and Bill we sure as hell won't be able to. If Paul and Bill don't turn up by nightfall, we'll do what we discussed: you and Majid will go out on a motorcycle and search.'

'And meanwhile?'

306

'We stick to the plan. We sit tight. We wait.'

There was a crisis at the US Embassy.

Ambassador William Sullivan had got an emergency call for help from General Gast, head of the Military Assistance Advisory Group. MAAG headquarters was surrounded by a mob. Tanks were drawn up outside the building and shots were being exchanged. Gast and his officers, together with most of the Iranian general staff, were in a bunker underneath the building.

Sullivan had every able-bodied man in the Embassy making phone calls, trying to find revolutionary leaders who might have the authority to call off the mob. The phone on Sullivan's desk was ringing constantly. In the middle of the crisis he got a call from Under Secretary Newsom in Washington.

Newsom was calling from the Situation Room in the White House, where Zbigniew Brzezinski was chairing a meeting on Iran. He asked for Sullivan's assessment of the current position in Tehran. Sullivan gave it to him in a few short phrases, and told him that right at that moment he was preoccupied with saving the life of the senior American military officer in Iran.

A few minutes later Sullivan got a call from an Embassy official who had succeeded in reaching Ibrahim Yazdi, a Khomeini sidekick. The official was telling Sullivan that Yazdi might help when the call was overridden and Newsom came on the line again.

Newsom said: 'The National Security Advisor has asked for your view of the possibility of a coup d'etat by the Iranian military to take over from the Bakhtiar government, which is clearly faltering.'

The question was so ridiculous that Sullivan blew his cool. 'Tell Brzezinski to fuck off,' he said.

'That's not a very helpful comment,' said Newsom.

'You want it translated into Polish?' Sullivan said, and he hung up the phone.

On the roof of Bucharest, the negotiating team could see the fires spreading uptown. The noise of shooting was also coming closer to where they stood.

John Howell and Abolhasan returned from their meeting with Dadgar. 'Well?' Gayden said to Howell. 'What did that bastard say?'

'He won't let them go.'

'Bastard.'

A few minutes later they all heard a noise which sounded distinctly like a bullet whizzing by. A moment later the noise came again. They decided to get off the roof.

They went down to the offices and watched from the windows. They began to see, in the street below, boys and young men with rifles. It seemed the mob had broken into a nearby armoury. This was too close for comfort: it was time to abandon Bucharest and go to the Hyatt, which was farther uptown.

They went out and jumped into two cars, then headed up the Shahanshahi Expressway at top speed. The streets were packed, and there was a carnival atmosphere. People were leaning out of their windows yelling '*Allahar Akbar!*' God is great! Most of the traffic was headed downtown, towards the fighting. Taylor drove straight through three road-blocks, but nobody minded: they were all dancing.

They reached the Hyatt and assembled in the sitting-room of the eleventh-floor corner suite which Gayden had taken over from Perot. They were joined by Rich Gallagher's wife Cathy and her white poodle Buffy.

Gayden had stocked the suite with booze from the abandoned homes of EDS evacuees, and he now had the best bar in Tehran; but no one felt much like drinking.

'What do we do next?' Gayden asked.

Nobody had any ideas.

Gayden got on the phone to Dallas, where it was now six a.m. He reached Tom Walter and told him about the fires, the fighting, and the kids on the streets with their automatic rifles.

'That's all I got to report,' he finished.

308

In his slow Alabama drawl, Walter said: 'Other than that a quiet day, huh?'

They discussed what they would do if the phone lines went down. Gayden said he would try to get messages through via the US military: Cathy Gallagher worked for the army and she thought she could swing it.

Keane Taylor went into the bedroom and lay down. He thought about his wife, Mary. She was in Pittsburgh, staying with his parents. Taylor's mother and father were both past eighty and in failing health. Mary had called to tell him his mother had been rushed to hospital: it was her heart. Mary wanted Taylor to come home. He had spoken to his father, who had said ambiguously: 'You know what you have to do.' It was true: Taylor knew he had to stay here. But it was not easy, not for him nor for Mary.

He was dozing on Gayden's bed when the phone rang. He reached out on the bedside table and picked it up. 'Hello?' he said sleepily.

A breathless Iranian voice said: 'Are Paul and Bill there?'

'What?' said Taylor. 'Rashid – is that you?'

'Are Paul and Bill there?' Rashid repeated.

'No. What do you mean?'

'Okay, I'm coming, I'm coming.'

Rashid hung up.

Taylor got off the bed and went into the sitting-room. 'Rashid just called,' he told the others. 'He asked me if Paul and Bill were here.'

'What did he mean?' said Gayden. 'Where was he calling from?'

'I couldn't get anything else out of him. He was all excited, and you know how bad his English is when he gets wound up.'

'Didn't he say any more?'

'He said: "I'm coming", then he hung up.'

'Shit.' Gayden turned to Howell. 'Give me the phone.' Howell was sitting with the phone to his ear, saying nothing: they were keeping the line to Dallas open. At the other end an EDS switchboard operator was listening, waiting for

309

someone to speak. Gayden said: 'Let me talk to Tom Walter again, please.'

As Gayden told Walter about Rashid's call, Taylor wondered what it meant. Why would Rashid imagine Paul and Bill might be at the Hyatt? They were in jail – weren't they?

A few minutes later Rashid burst into the room, dirty, smelling of gunsmoke, with clips of G3 ammunition falling out of his pockets, talking a mile a minute so that nobody could understand a word. Taylor calmed him down. Eventually he said: 'We hit the prison. Paul and Bill were gone.'

Paul and Bill stood at the foot of the prison wall and looked around.

The scene in the street reminded Paul of a New York parade. In the apartment buildings across from the jail everyone was at the windows, cheering and applauding as they watched the prisoners escape. At the street corner a vendor was selling fruit from a stall. There was gunfire not far away, but in the immediate vicinity nobody was shooting. Then, as if to remind Paul and Bill that they were not yet out of danger, a car full of revolutionaries raced by with guns sticking out of every window.

'Let's get out of here,' said Paul.

'Where do we go? The US Embassy? The French Embassy?'

'The Hyatt.'

Paul started walking, heading north. Bill walked a little behind him, with his coat collar turned up and head bent to hide his pale American face. They came to an intersection. It was deserted: no cars, no people. They started across. A shot rang out.

Both of them ducked and ran back the way they had come.

It was not going to be easy.

'How are you doing?' said Paul.

'Still alive.'

They walked back past the prison. The scene was the same: at least the authorities had not yet got organized enough to start rounding up the escapers.

Paul headed south and east through the streets, hoping to circle around until he could go north again. Everywhere there were boys, some only thirteen or fourteen, with automatic rifles. On every corner was a sandbagged bunker, as if the streets were divided up into tribal territories. Farther on they had to push their way through a crowd of yelling, chanting, almost hysterical people: Paul carefully avoided meeting people's eyes, for he did not want them to notice him, let alone speak to him – if they were to learn there were two Americans in their midst they might turn ugly.

The rioting was patchy. It was like New York, where you had only to walk a few steps and turn a corner to find the character of the district completely changed. Paul and Bill went through a quiet area for half a mile, then ran into a battle. There was a barricade of overturned cars across the road and a bunch of youngsters with rifles shooting across the barricade towards what looked like a military installation. Paul turned away quickly, fearful of being hit by a stray bullet.

Each time he tried to turn north he ran into some obstruction. They were now farther from the Hyatt than they had been when they started. They were moving south, and the fighting was always worse in the south.

They stopped outside an unfinished building. 'We could duck in there and hide until nightfall,' Paul said. 'After dark nobody will notice that you're American.'

'We might get shot for being out after curfew.'

'You think there's still a curfew?'

Bill shrugged.

'We're doing all right so far,' Paul said. 'Let's go on a little longer.'

They went on.

It was two hours – two hours of crowds and street battles and stray sniper fire – before at last they could turn north.

Then the scene changed. The gunfire receded, and they found themselves in a relatively affluent area of pleasant villas. They saw a child on a bicycle, wearing a T-shirt that said something about Southern California.

Paul was tired. He had been in jail for forty-five days, and during most of that time he had been sick: he was no longer strong enough to walk for hours. 'What do you say we hitchhike?' he asked Bill.

'Let's give it a try.'

Paul stood at the roadside and waved at the next car that came along. (He remembered not to stick out his thumb the American way – this was an obscene gesture in Iran.) The car stopped. There were two Iranian men in it. Paul and Bill got in the back.

Paul decided not to mention the name of the hotel. 'We're going to Tajrish,' he said. That was a bazaar area to the north of the city.

'We can take you part of the way,' said the driver.

'Thanks.' Paul offered them cigarettes, then sat back gratefully and lit one for himself.

The Iranians dropped them of at Kurosh-e-Kabir, several miles south of Tajrish, not far from where Paul had lived. They were in a main street, with plenty of traffic and a lot more people around. Paul decided not to make himself conspicuous by hitch-hiking here.

'We could take refuge in the Catholic Mission,' Bill suggested.

Paul considered. The authorities presumably knew that Father Williams had visited them in Gasr Prison just two days ago. 'The Mission might be the first place Dadgar looks for us.'

'Maybe.'

'We should go to the Hyatt.'

'The guys may not be there any longer.'

'But there'll be phones, some way to get plane tickets . . .'

'And hot showers.'

'Right.'

They walked on.

Suddenly a voice called: 'Mr Paul! Mr Bill!'

Paul's heart stopped. He looked around. He saw a car full of people moving slowly along the road beside him. He recognized one of the passengers: it was a guard from the Gasr Prison.

The guard had changed into civilian clothes, and looked as if he had joined the revolution. His big smile seemed to say: 'Don't tell who I am, and I won't tell who you are.'

He waved, then the car gathered speed and passed on.

Paul and Bill laughed with a mixture of amusement and relief.

They turned into a quiet street, and Paul started to hitch-hike again. He stood in the road waving while Bill stayed on the sidewalk, so that motorists might think there was only one man, an Iranian.

A young couple stopped. Paul got into the car and Bill jumped in after him.

'We're headed north,' Paul said.

The woman looked at her man.

The man said: 'We could take you to Niavron Palace.'

'Thank you.'

The car pulled away.

The scene in the streets changed again. They could hear much more gunfire, and the traffic became heavier and more frantic, with all the cars honking continually. They saw press cameramen and television crews standing on car roofs taking pictures. The mob was burning the police stations near where Bill had lived. The Iranian couple looked nervous as the car inched through the crowd: having two Americans in their car could get them into trouble in this atmosphere.

It began to get dark.

Bill leaned forward. 'Boy, it's getting a bit late,' he said. 'It sure would be nice if y'all could take us to the Hyatt Hotel. We'd be happy to, you know, thank you and give you something for taking us there.'

'Okay,' said the driver.

He did not ask how much.

They passed the Niavron Palace, the Shah's winter residence. There were tanks outside, as always, but now they had white flags attached to their antennae: they had surrendered to the revolution.

The car went on, past wrecked and burning buildings, turned back every now and again by street barricades.

At last they saw the Hyatt.

'Oh, boy,' Paul said feelingly. 'An American hotel.'

They drove into the forecourt.

Paul was so grateful that he gave the Iranian couple two hundred dollars.

The car drove off. Paul and Bill waved, then walked into the hotel.

Suddenly Paul wished he were wearing his EDS uniform of business suit and white shirt, instead of prison dungarees and a dirty raincoat.

The magnificent lobby was deserted.

They walked to the reception desk. After a moment someone came out from an office.

Paul asked for Bill Gayden's room number.

The clerk checked, then told him there was no one of that name registered.

'How about Bob Young?'

'No.'

'Rich Gallagher?'

'No.'

'Jay Coburn?'

'No.'

I've got the wrong hotel, Paul thought. How could I have made a mistake like that?

'What about John Howell?' he said, remembering the lawyer.

'Yes,' the clerk said at last, and he gave them a room number on the eleventh floor.

They went up in the elevator.

They found Howell's room and knocked. There was no answer.

314

'What do you think we ought to do?' Bill said.

'I'm going to check in,' said Paul. 'I'm tired. Why don't we check in, have a meal. We'll call the States, tell them we're out of jail, everything will be fine.'

'Okay.'

They walked back to the elevator.

Bit by bit, Keane Taylor got the story out of Rashid.

He had stood just inside the prison gates for about an hour. The scene was a shambles; eleven thousand people were trying to get out through a small doorway, and in the panic women and old men were getting trampled. Rashid had waited, thinking of what he would say to Paul and Bill when he saw them. After an hour the flood of people slowed to a trickle, and he concluded that most people were out. He started asking: 'Have you seen any Americans?' Someone told him that all the foreigners had been kept in Building No 8. He went there and found it empty. He searched every building in the compound. He then returned to the Hyatt by the route Paul and Bill were most likely to take. Walking and hitching rides, he had looked for them all the way. At the Hyatt he had been refused admission because he was still carrying his rifle. He gave the gun away to the nearest youngster and came in.

While he was telling his story Coburn arrived, all set to go looking for Paul and Bill on Majid's motorcycle. He had a crash helmet with a vizor that would hide his white face.

Rashid offered to take an EDS car and drive the route between the hotel and the prison, making one more sweep there and back before Coburn risked his neck in the mobs. Taylor gave him the keys to a car. Gayden got on the phone to tell Dallas the latest news. Rashid and Taylor left the suite and walked down the corridor.

Suddenly Rashid yelled: 'I thought you were dead!' and broke into a run.

Then Taylor saw Paul and Bill.

Rashid was hugging them both, screaming: 'I couldn't find you! I couldn't find you!'

Taylor ran up and embraced Paul and Bill. 'Thank God!' he said.

Rashid ran back into Gayden's suite, yelling: 'Paul and Bill are here! Paul and Bill are here!'

An instant later Paul and Bill walked in, and all hell broke loose.

Ten

It was an unforgettable moment.

Everyone was yelling, no one was listening, and they all wanted to hug Paul and Bill at the same time.

Gayden was bellowing into the phone: 'We got the guys! We got the guys! Fantastic! They just walked in the door! Fantastic!'

Somebody yelled: 'We beat them! We beat those sonsabitches!'

'We did it!'

'In your ear, Dadgar!'

Buffy barked like a mad thing.

Paul looked around at his friends, and realized that they had stayed here in the middle of a revolution to help him, and he found he had difficulty speaking.

Gayden dropped the phone and came over to shake hands. Paul, with tears in his eyes, said: 'Gayden, I just saved you twelve and a half million dollars – I think you ought to buy me a drink.'

Gayden fixed him a stiff scotch.

Paul tasted his first alcoholic drink for six weeks.

Gayden said into the phone: 'I have somebody would like to speak to you.' He handed the phone to Paul.

Paul said: 'Hello.'

He heard the syrupy voice of Tom Walter. 'Hi, there, buddy!'

'God almighty,' said Paul, out of general exhaustion and relief.

'We were wondering where you guys were!'

'So was I, for the last three hours.'

'How d'you get to the hotel, Paul?'

Paul did not have the energy to tell Walter the whole story. 'Fortunately, Keane left me a lot of money one day.'

'Fantastic. Golly, Paul! Is Bill okay?'

'Yeah, he's a little shook up but he's all right.'

'We're *all* a little shook up. Oh, boy. Boy, it's good to hear you.'

Another voice came on the line. 'Paul? This is Mitch.' Mitch Hart was a former president of EDS. 'I figured that Italian street fighter would get out of there.'

'How's Ruthie?' said Paul.

Tom Walter answered. They must be using the telephone conference circuit, Paul guessed. 'Paul, she's great. I just talked to her a little while ago. Jean's calling her right now, she's on the other phone.'

'Kids doing all right?'

'Yeah, fine. Boy, she'll be glad to hear!'

'Okay, I'll let you talk to my other half.' Paul handed the phone to Bill.

While he had been speaking, an Iranian employee, Gholam, had arrived. He had heard about the jailbreak and had gone looking for Paul and Bill in the streets around the prison.

Jay Coburn was worried by the arrival of Gholam. For a few minutes there, Coburn had been too full of tearful joy to think of anything else, but now he reverted to his role as Simons's lieutenant. He quietly left the suite, found another open door, went into the room, and called the Dvoranchik apartment.

Simons answered the phone.

'It's Jay. They got here.'

'Good.'

'The security is all shot to hell here. They're using the names over the phone, everybody's wandering around, we have Iranian employees walking in . . .'

'Get a couple of rooms away from the others. We'll be right there.'

'Okay.' Coburn hung up.

He went down to the reception desk and asked for a two-bedroom suite on the twelfth floor. There was no problem: the hotel had hundreds of empty rooms. He gave a false name. He was not asked for his passport.

He returned to Gayden's suite.

A few minutes later Simons walked in and said: 'Hang up the goddam phone.'

Bob Young, who was holding the line open to Dallas, put down the phone.

Joe Poché walked in behind Simons and started closing the curtains.

It was incredible. Suddenly Simons was in charge. Gayden, the president of EDS World, was the senior man there; and an hour ago he had told Tom Walter that 'The Sunshine Boys' – Simons, Coburn and Poché – seemed useless and ineffectual; yet now he deferred to Simons without even thinking about it.

'Take a look around, Joe,' Simons said to Poché. Coburn knew what this meant. The team had scouted the hotel and its grounds during their weeks of waiting, and Poché would now see whether there had been any changes.

The phone rang. John Howell answered it. 'It's Abolhasan,' he said to the others. He listened for a couple of minutes, then said: 'Hold on.' He covered the mouthpiece with his hand and spoke to Simons. 'This is an Iranian employee who translates for me at meetings with Dadgar. His father is a friend of Dadgar's. He's at his father's house, and just got a call from Dadgar.'

The room went very quiet.

'Dadgar said: "Did you know the Americans are out of jail?" Abolhasan said: "It's news to me." Dadgar said: "Get hold of EDS and tell them that if they find Chiapparone and Gaylord they are to turn them in, that I'm now willing to renegotiate the bail and it ought to be much more reasonable."'

Gayden said: 'Fuck *him*.'

'All right,' Simons said. 'Tell Abolhasan to give Dadgar a message. Say we are searching for Paul and Bill, but

319

meanwhile we hold Dadgar personally responsible for their safety.'

Howell smiled and nodded, and began speaking to Abolhasan.

Simons turned to Gayden. 'Call the American Embassy. Yell at them a little. They got Paul and Bill thrown in jail, now the jail has been stormed and we don't know where Paul and Bill are, but we hold the Embassy responsible for their safety. Make it convincing. There *must* be Iranian spies at the Embassy – you can bet your ass Dadgar will have the text of the message in minutes.'

Gayden went to find a phone.

Simons, Coburn and Poché, with Paul and Bill, moved to the new suite Coburn had taken on the floor above.

Coburn ordered two steak dinners for Paul and Bill. He told room service to send them to Gayden's suite: there was to be no unnecessary traffic in and out of the new rooms.

Paul took a hot bath. He had been longing for it. He had not had a bath for six weeks. He revelled in the clean white bathroom, the piping hot water, the fresh cake of soap . . . He would never take such things for granted again. He washed the Gasr Prison out of his hair. There were clean clothes waiting for him: someone had retrieved his suitcase from the Hilton, where he had been staying until he was arrested.

Bill took a shower. His euphoria had gone. He had imagined that the nightmare was over when he walked into Gayden's suite, but gradually it had dawned on him that he was still in danger, there was no US Air Force jet to fly him home at twice the speed of sound. Dadgar's message via Abolhasan, the appearance of Simons, and the new security precautions – this suite, Poché closing the curtains, the shuttling of the food – all made him realize that the escape had only just begun.

All the same, he enjoyed his steak dinner.

Simons was still uneasy. The Hyatt was near the Evin Hotel where the US military stayed, the Evin Prison, and an armoury: all these were natural targets for the revolutionaries. Dadgar's phone call was also worrying. Plenty of Iranians knew that the EDS people were staying at the Hyatt: Dadgar could easily find out, and send men to search for Paul and Bill.

While Simons, Coburn and Bill were discussing this in the sitting room of the suite, the phone rang.

Simons stared at it.

It rang again.

'Who the fuck knows we're here?' Simons said.

Coburn shrugged.

Simons picked up the phone and said: 'Hello?'

There was a pause.

'Hello?'

He hung up. 'Nobody there.'

At that moment Paul walked in in his pyjamas. Simons said: 'Change your clothes, we're going to leave.'

'Why?' Paul protested.

Simons repeated: 'Change your clothes, we're going to leave.'

Paul shrugged and went back to the bathroom.

Bill found it hard to believe. On the run again already! Somehow Dadgar was staying in authority through all the violence and chaos of the revolution. But who was working for him? The guards had fled the jails, the police stations had been burned, the army had surrendered – who was left to carry out Dadgar's orders?

The Devil and all his hordes, Bill thought.

Simons went down to Gayden's suite while Paul was dressing. He got Gayden and Taylor in a corner. 'Get all these turkeys out of here,' he said in a low voice. 'The story is, Paul and Bill are in bed for the night. You'll all come to our place tomorrow morning. Leave at seven o'clock, just as if you were going to the office. Don't pack any bags, don't check out, don't pay your hotel bill. Joe Poché will be waiting for you outside and he'll have figured out a safe route to the house. I'm taking Paul and Bill there *now* – but don't tell the others that until the morning.'

'Okay,' said Gayden.

Simons went back upstairs. Paul and Bill were ready. Coburn and Poché were waiting. The five of them walked to the elevator.

As they were going down, Simons said: 'Now, let's just walk out of here like it was the normal thing to do.'

They reached the ground floor. They walked across the vast lobby and out into the forecourt. The two Range Rovers were parked there.

As they crossed the forecourt a big dark car drew up, and four or five ragged men with machine-guns jumped out.

Coburn muttered: 'Oh, shit.'

The five Americans kept walking.

The revolutionaries ran over to the doorman.

Poché threw open the doors of the first Range Rover. Paul and Bill jumped in. Poché started the engine and pulled away fast. Simons and Coburn got into the second car and followed.

The revolutionaries went into the hotel.

Poché headed down the Vanak Highway, which passed both the Hyatt and the Hilton. They could hear constant machine-gun fire over the sound of the car engines. A mile up the road, at the intersection with Pahlavi Avenue near to the Hilton, they ran into a roadblock.

Poché pulled up. Bill looked around. He and Paul had come through this intersection a few hours earlier, with the Iranian couple who had brought them to the Hyatt; but then there had been no roadblock, just one burned-out car. Now there were several burning cars, a barricade, and a crowd of revolutionaries armed with an assortment of military firearms.

One of them approached the Range Rover, and Joe Poché rolled down the window.

'Where are you going?' the revolutionary said in perfect English.

'I'm going to my mother-in-law's house in Abbas Abad,' Poché said.

Bill thought: my god, what an idiotic story to tell.

Paul was looking away, hiding his face.

322

Another revolutionary came up and spoke in Farsi. The first man said: 'Do you have any cigarettes?'

'No, I don't smoke,' said Poché.

'Okay, go ahead.'

Poché drove on down the Shahanshahi Expressway.

Coburn pulled the second car forward to where the revolutionaries stood.

'Are you with them?' he was asked.

'Yes.'

'Do you have any cigarettes?'

'Yes.' Coburn took a pack out of his pocket and tried to shake out a cigarette. His hands were unsteady and he could not get one out.

Simons said: 'Jay.'

'Yes.'

'*Give him the fucking pack.*'

Coburn gave the revolutionary the whole pack, and he waved them on.

2

Ruthie Chipparone was in bed, but awake, at the Nyfeler's house in Dallas when the phone rang.

She heard footsteps in the hall. The ringing stopped, and Jim Nyfeler's voice said: 'Hello? . . . Well, she's sleeping.'

'I'm awake,' Ruthie called. She got out of bed, slipped on a robe, and went into the hall.

'It's Tom Walter's wife, Jean,' said Jim, handing her the phone.

Ruthie said: 'Hi, Jean.'

'Ruth, I have good news for you. The guys are free. They got out of jail.'

'Oh, thank God!' said Ruthie.

She had not yet begun to wonder how Paul would get out of Iran.

When Emily Gaylord got back from church her mother said:

'Tom Walter called from Dallas. I said you'd call back.'

Emily snatched up the phone, dialled EDS's number, and asked for Walter.

'Hi, Em'ly,' Walter drawled. 'Paul and Bill got out of jail.'

'Tom, that's wonderful!'

'There was a jailbreak. They're safe, and they're in good hands.'

'When are they coming home?'

'We're not sure yet, but we'll keep you posted.'

'Thank you, Tom,' said Emily. 'Thank you!'

Ross Perot was in bed with Margot. The phone woke them both. Perot reached out and picked it up. 'Yes?'

'Ross, this is Tom Walter. Paul and Bill got out of jail.'

Suddenly Perot was wide awake. He sat up. 'That's great!'

Margot said sleepily: 'They're out?'

'Yes.'

She smiled. 'Oh, good!'

Tom Walter was saying: 'The jail was overrun by the revolutionaries, and Paul and Bill walked out.'

Perot's mind was clicking into gear. 'Where are they now?'

'At the hotel.'

'That's dangerous, Tom. Is Simons there?'

'Uh, when I was talking to them he was not there.'

'Tell them to call him. Taylor knows the number. And get them out of that hotel!'

'Yes, sir.'

'Call everyone into the office right away. I'll be there in a few minutes.'

'Yes, sir.'

Perot hung up. He got out of bed, threw on some clothes, kissed Margot, and ran down the stairs. He went through the kitchen and out of the back door. A security man, surprised to see him up so early, said: 'Good morning, Mr Perot.'

'Morning.' Perot decided to take Margot's Jaguar. He jumped in and raced down the driveway to the gate.

For six weeks he had felt as if he were living inside a

popcorn popper. He had been trying everything, and nothing had worked; bad news had hit him from every direction, he had made no progress. Now at last things were *moving*.

He tore along Forest Lane, running red lights and breaking the speed limit. Getting them out of jail was the easy part, he reflected; now we have to get them out of Iran. The hard part hasn't even started.

In the next few minutes the whole team gathered at EDS headquarters on Forest Lane: Tom Walter, T. J. Marquez, Merv Stauffer, Perot's secretary Sally Walther, lawyer Tom Luce, and Mitch Hart, who – though he no longer worked at EDS – had been trying to use his connections in the Democratic Party to help Paul and Bill.

Until now, communications with the negotiating team in Tehran had been organized from Bill Gayden's office on the fifth floor, while on the seventh floor Merv Stauffer was quietly handling support and communications with the illegal rescue team, talking on the phone in code. Now they all realized that Simons was the key figure in Tehran, and that whatever happened next would probably be illegal; so they moved up to Stauffer's office, which was also more private.

'I'm going to go to Washington right away,' Perot told them. 'Our best hope is still an Air Force jet out of Tehran.'

Stauffer said: 'I don't know about flights to Washington from DFW on Sundays—'

'Charter a jet,' Perot said.

Stauffer picked up the phone.

'We're going to need secretaries here twenty-four hours a day for the next few days,' Perot went on.

'I'll see to that,' said T.J.

'Now, the military has promised to help us but we can't rely on them – they may have bigger fish to fry. The likeliest alternative is for the team to drive out via Turkey. In that event, the plan is for us to meet them at the border or if necessary fly into the north-west of Iran to pull them out. We need to assemble the Turkish Rescue Team. Boulware is already in Istanbul, Schwebach, Sculley and Davis are in the States – somebody call them and have the three of them meet me in Washington. We may also need a helicopter pilot and another pilot for small fixed-wing aircraft, in case we want to sneak into Iran. Sally, call Margot and ask her to pack me a case – I'll need casual clothes, a flashlight, all-weather boots, thermal underwear, a sleeping bag and a tent.'

'Yes, sir.' Sally left the room.

'Ross, I don't think that's a good idea,' T.J. said. 'Margot might get scared.'

Perot suppressed a sigh: it was just like T.J. to argue. But he was right. 'Okay, I'll go home and do it myself. Come with me so we can talk while I'm packing.'

'Sure.'

Stauffer put down the phone and said: 'There's a Lear jet waiting for you at Love Field.'

'Good.'

Perot and T.J. went downstairs and got in their cars. They left EDS and turned right on Forest Lane. A few seconds later, T.J. looked at his speedo and saw that he was doing eighty – and Perot, in Margot's Jaguar, was losing him.

At Page Terminal in Washington Perot ran into two old friends: Bill Clements, Governor of Texas and former Deputy Secretary of Defence; and Clements's wife Rita.

Clements said: 'Hi, Ross! What the hell are you doing in Washington on a Sunday afternoon?'

'I'm up here on business,' said Perot.

'No, what are you doing *really*,' said Clements with a grin.

'Have you got a minute?'

Clements had a minute. The three of them sat down, and Perot told the story of Paul and Bill.

When he had finished Clements said: 'There's a guy you need to talk to. I'll write down his name.'

'How am I going to get him on a Sunday afternoon?'

'Hell, I'll get him.'

The two men walked over to a pay phone. Clements put in a coin, called the Pentagon switchboard, and identified himself. He asked to be put through to the home of one of the most senior military officers in the country. Then he said: 'I've got Ross Perot from Texas with me. He's a friend of mine and a good friend to the military, and I want you to help him.' He handed the phone to Perot and walked away.

Half an hour later Perot was in an operations room in the Pentagon basement, surrounded by computer terminals, talking to half a dozen generals.

He had never met any of them before, but he felt he was among friends: they all knew of his campaign for the American prisoners-of-war in North Vietnam.

'I want to get two men out of Tehran,' Perot told them. 'Can you fly them out?'

'No,' said one of the generals. 'We're grounded in Tehran. Our air base, Doshen Toppeh, is in the hands of the revolutionaries. General Gast is in the bunker beneath MAAG headquarters, surrounded by a mob. And we have no communications because the phone lines have been cut.'

'Okay,' said Perot. He had half-expected that answer. 'I'm going to have to do it myself.'

'It's on the other side of the world, and there's a revolution going on,' said a general. 'It won't be easy.'

Perot smiled. 'I have Bull Simons over there.'

They broke up. 'Damn it, Perot!' said one of them. 'You aren't giving the Iranians an even chance!'

'Right,' Perot grinned. 'I may have to fly in myself. Now, can you give me a list of all the airfields between Tehran and the Turkish border?'

'Sure.'

'Could you find out whether any of those airfields are obstructed?'

'We can just look at the satellite photographs.'

'Now, what about radar? Is there a way to fly in there without appearing on the Iranians' radar screens?'

'Sure. We'll get you a radar map at five hundred feet.'

'Good.'

'Anything else?'

Hell, thought Perot, this is just like going into McDonald's! 'That'll do for now,' he said.

The generals started pushing buttons.

T. J. Marquez picked up the phone. It was Perot.

'I got your pilots,' T.J. told him. 'I called Larry Joseph, who used to be head of Continental Air Services in Vientiane, Laos – he's in Washington now. He found the guys – Dick Douglas and Julian Kanauch. They'll be in Washington tomorrow.'

'That's great,' said Perot. 'Now, I've been to the Pentagon and they can't fly the guys out – they're grounded in Tehran. But I have all kinds of maps and stuff so we can fly in ourselves. Now this is what I need: a jet plane, capable of crossing the Atlantic, complete with a crew, and equipped with a single-sideband radio, like we used to have in Laos, so we can make phone calls from the plane.'

'I'll get right on it,' said T.J.

'I'm at the Madison Hotel.'

'Got it.'

T.J. started calling. He contacted two Texas charter companies: neither of them had a transatlantic jet. The second, Jet Fleet, gave him the name of Executive Aircraft out of Columbus, Ohio. They could not help, and they did not know of anyone who could.

T.J. thought of Europe. He called Carl Nilsson, an EDS executive who had been working on a proposal for Martinair. Nilsson called back and said Martinair would not fly into Iran, but had given him the name of a Swiss outfit who would. T.J. called Switzerland: that company had stopped flying into Iran as of today.

T.J. dialled the number of Harry McKillop, a Braniff vice-president who lived in Paris. McKillop was out.

T.J. called Perot and confessed failure.

Perot had an idea. He seemed to remember that Sol Rogers, the president of Texas State Optical Company down in Beaumont, had either a BAC 111 or a Boeing 727, he was not sure which. Nor did he have the phone number.

T.J. called information. The number was unlisted. He

called Margot. She had the number. He called Rogers. He had sold his plane.

Rogers knew of an outfit called Omni International, in Washington, which leased planes. He gave T.J. the home phone number of the president and vice-president.

T.J. called the president. He was out.

He called the vice-president. He was in.

'Do you have a transatlantic jet?' T.J. asked.

'Sure. We have two.'

T.J. breathed a sigh of relief.

'We have a 707 and a 727,' the man went on.

'Where?'

'The 707 is at Meachem Field in Forth Worth—',

'Why, that's right here!' said T.J. 'Now tell me, does it have a single-sideband radio?'

'Sure does.'

T.J. could hardly believe his luck.

'This plane is rather luxuriously fitted out,' the vice-president said. 'It was done for a Kuwaiti prince who backed out.'

T.J. was not interested in the decor. He asked about the price. The vice-president said the president would have to make the final decision. He was out for the evening but T.J. could call him first thing in the morning.

T.J. had the plane checked out by Jeff Heller, an EDS vice-president and former Vietnam pilot, and two of Heller's friends, one an American Airlines pilot and the other a flight engineer. Heller reported that the plane seemed to be in good shape, as far as they could tell without flying it. The decor was kind of over-ripe, he said with a smile.

At seven-thirty the following morning T.J. called the president of Omni and got him out of the shower. The president had talked to his vice-president and he was sure they could do business.

'Good,' said T.J. 'Now what about crew, ground facilities, insurance—'

'We don't *charter* planes,' said the president. 'We *lease* them.'

'What's the difference?'

329

'It's like the difference between taking a cab and renting a car. Our planes are for rent.'

'Look, we're in the computer business, we know nothing about airlines,' said T.J. 'Even though you don't normally do it, will you make a deal with us where you supply all the extras, crew and so on? We'll pay you for it.'

'It'll be complicated. The insurance alone . . .'

'But you'll do it?'

'Yes, we'll do it.'

It *was* complicated, T.J. learned during the course of the day. The unusual nature of the deal did not appeal to the insurance companies, who also hated to be hurried. It was hard to figure out which regulations EDS needed to comply with, since they were not an airline. Omni required a deposit of sixty thousand dollars in an offshore branch of a US bank. The problems were solved by EDS executive Gary Fernandes in Washington and EDS house lawyer Claude Chappelear in Dallas: the contract, which was executed at the end of the day, was a sales demonstration lease. Omni found a crew in California and sent them to Dallas to pick up the plane and fly it on to Washington.

By midnight on Monday the plane, the crew, the extra pilots and the remnants of the rescue team were all in Washington with Ross Perot.

T.J. had worked a miracle.

That was why it took so long.

3

The negotiating team – Keane Taylor, Bill Gayden, John Howell, Bob Young and Rich Gallagher, augmented now by Rashid, Cathy Gallagher, and the dog Buffy – spent the night of Sunday 11 February at the Hyatt. They got little sleep. Close by, the mob was attacking an armoury. It seemed part of the Army had now joined the revolution, for tanks were used in the attack. Towards morning they blew a hole in the wall and got in. From dawn on, a stream of orange cabs ferried weapons from the armoury downtown, to where the fighting was still heavy.

The team kept the line to Dallas open all night: John Howell lay on the couch in Gayden's sitting-room with the phone to his ear.

In the morning Rashid left early. He was not told where the others were going – no Iranians were to know the location of the hideout.

The others packed their suitcases and left them in their rooms, just in case they should get a chance to pick them up later. This was not part of Simons's instructions, and he would certainly have disapproved, for the packed bags showed that the EDS people were no longer living here – but by morning they all felt Simons was overdoing his security precautions. They gathered in Gayden's sitting-room a few minutes after the seven o'clock deadline. The Gallaghers had several bags, and did not really look as if they were going to the office.

In the foyer they met the hotel manager. 'Where are you going?' he asked incredulously.

'To the office,' Gayden told him.

'Don't you know there's a civil war going on out there? All night long we've been feeding the revolutionaries out of our kitchens. They asked if there were any Americans here – I told them there was nobody here. You must go back upstairs and stay out of sight.'

'Life must go on,' said Gayden, and they all walked out.

Joe Poché was waiting in a Range Rover, silently fuming because they were fifteen minutes late and he had instructions from Simons to be back at seven forty-five with or without them.

As they walked to the cars, Keane Taylor saw a hotel clerk drive in and park. He went over to speak to the man. 'How are the streets?'

'Roadblocks all over the place,' said the clerk. 'There's one right here, at the end of the hotel driveway. You shouldn't go out.'

'Thank you,' said Taylor.

331

They all got into the cars and followed Pochés Range Rover. The guards at the gate were preoccupied, trying to jam a banana clip into a machine pistol which did not take that kind of ammunition, and they paid no attention to the three cars.

The scene outside was scary. Many of the weapons from the armoury had found their way into the hands of teenage boys who had probably never handled firearms before, and the kids were running down the hill, yelling and waving their guns, and jumping into cars to tear off along the highway, shooting into the air.

Poché headed north on Shahanshahi, following a roundabout route to avoid roadblocks. At the intersection with Pahlavi there was the remains of a barricade – burned cars and tree trunks across the road – but the people manning the roadblock were celebrating, chanting and firing into the air, and the three cars drove straight through.

As they approached the hideout they entered a relatively quiet area. They turned into a narrow street then, half a block down, they drove through gates into a walled garden with an empty swimming pool. The Dvoranchik place was the bottom half of a duplex, with the landlady living upstairs. They all went in.

During Monday, Dadgar continued to search for Paul and Bill.

Bill Gaydon called Bucharest, where a skeleton staff of loyal Iranians continued to man the phones. Gayden learned that Dadgar's men had called twice, speaking to two different secretaries, and asked where they could find Mr Chiapparone and Mr Gaylord. The first secretary had said she did not know the names of any of the Americans, which was a brave lie – she had been working for EDS for four years and knew everyone. The second secretary had said: 'You will have to speak to Mr Lloyd Briggs, who is in charge of the office.'

'Where is he?'

'Out of the country.'

'Well, who is in charge of the office in his absence?'

'Mr Keane Taylor.'

'Let me speak to him.'

'He's not here right now.'

The girls, bless them, had given Dadgar's men the runaround.

Rich Gallagher was keeping in touch with his friends in the military (Cathy had a job as secretary to a Colonel). He called the Evin hotel, where most of the military were staying, and learned that 'revolutionaries' had gone to both the Evin and the Hyatt showing photographs of two Americans for whom they were looking.

Dadgar's tenacity was almost incredible.

Simons decided they could not stay at the Dvoranchik house more than forty-eight hours.

The escape plan had been devised for five men. Now there were ten men, a woman, and a dog.

They had only two Range Rovers. An ordinary car would never take those mountain roads, especially in snow. They needed another Range Rover. Coburn called Majid and asked him to try to get one.

The dog worried Simons. Rich Gallagher was planning to carry Buffy in a knapsack. If they had to walk or ride horseback through the mountains to cross the border, a single yap could get them all killed – and Buffy barked at everything. Simons said to Coburn and Taylor: 'I want you two to lose that fucking dog.'

'Okay,' Coburn said. 'Maybe I'll offer to walk it, then just let it go.'

'No,' said Simons. 'When I say lose it, I mean permanently.'

Cathy was the biggest problem. That evening she felt ill – 'Feminine problems.' Rich said. He was hoping that a day in bed would leave her feeling stronger; but Simons was not optimistic. He fumed at the Embassy. 'There are so many ways the State Department could get someone out of the country and protect them if they wanted to,' he said. 'Put them in a case, ship them out as cargo . . . if they were interested it would be a snap.'

Bill began to feel like the cause of all the trouble. 'I think it's insane for nine people to risk their lives for the sake of two,' he said. 'If Paul and I weren't here none of you would be in any danger – you could just wait here until flights out resume. Maybe Paul and I should throw ourselves on the mercy of the US Embassy.'

Simons said: 'And what if you two get out, then Dadgar decides to take other hostages?'

Anyway, Coburn thought, Simons won't let these two out of his sight now, not until they're back in the USA.

The bell at the street gate rang, and everybody froze.

'Move into the bedrooms, but quietly,' Simons said.

Coburn went to the window. The landlady still thought there were only two people living here, Coburn and Poché – she had never seen Simons – and neither she nor anyone else was supposed to know that there were now eleven people in the house.

As Coburn watched, she walked across the courtyard and opened the gate. She stood there for a few minutes, talking to someone Coburn could not see, then closed the gate and came back alone.

When he heard her door slam shut upstairs, he called 'False alarm.'

They all prepared for the journey by looting the Dvoranchik place for warm clothes. Paul thought: Toni Dvoranchik would die of embarrassment if she knew about all these men going through her drawers. They ended up with a peculiar assortment of ill-fitting hats, coats and sweaters.

After that they had nothing to do but wait: wait for Majid to find another Range Rover, wait for Cathy to get better, and wait for Perot to get the Turkish Rescue Team organized.

They watched some old football games on a Betamax video. Paul played gin with Gayden. The dog got on everybody's nerves, but Coburn decided not to slit its throat until the last minute, in case there was a change of plan and it could be saved. John Howell read *The Deep* by Peter Benchley: he had seen part of the movie on the flight over and had missed the ending because the plane landed before the movie finished, and he had never figured out who were the good guys and who were the bad guys. Simons said: 'Those who wish to drink can do so, but if we have to move fast we'll be much better without any alcohol in our systems,' but despite the warning both Gayden and Gallagher surreptitiously mixed Drambuie with their coffee. The bell rang once more, and they all went through the same routine, but again it was for the landlady.

They were all remarkably good-tempered, considering how many of them were crammed into the living-room and three bedrooms of the place. The only one to get irritable was – predictably – Keane Taylor. He and Paul cooked a big dinner for everyone, almost emptying the freezer, but by the time Taylor came in from the kitchen, the others had eaten every scrap and there was nothing for him. He cursed them all roundly for a bunch of greedy hogs, and they all laughed, the way they always did when Taylor got mad.

During the night he got mad again. He was sleeping on the floor next to Coburn, and Coburn snored. The noise was so awful that Taylor could not get to sleep. He could not even wake Coburn to tell him to stop snoring, and that made him even madder.

It was snowing in Washington that night. Ross Perot was tired and tense.

With Mitch Hart, he had spent most of the day in a last-ditch effort to persuade the Government to fly his people out of Tehran. He had seen Under Secretary David Newsom at the State Department, Thomas V. Beard at the White House, and Mark Ginsberg, a young Carter aide whose job was liaison between the White House and the State Department. They were doing their best to arrange to fly the remaining one thousand Americans out of Tehran, and they were not about to make special plans for Ross Perot.

Resigned to going to Turkey, Perot went to a sporting goods store and bought himself cold-weather clothes. The leased 707 arrived from Dallas, and Pat Sculley called from Dulles Airport to say that some mechanical problems had surfaced during the flight: the transponder and the inertial navigation system did not work properly, the number one engine was using oil at twice the normal rate, there was insufficient oxygen aboard for cabin use, there were no spare tyres, and the water tank valves were frozen solid.

While mechanics worked on the plane, Perot sat in the Madison Hotel with Mort Meyerson, a vice-president of EDS.

At EDS there was a special group of Perot associates, men such as T. J. Marquez and Merv Stauffer, to whom he turned for help with matters that were not part of the day-to-day business of computer software: schemes like the prisoners-of-war campaign, the Texas War on Drugs, and the rescue of Paul and Bill. Although Meyerson did not get involved in Perot's special projects, he was fully informed about the rescue plan and had given it his blessing: he knew Paul and Bill well, having worked alongside them in earlier years as a systems engineer. For business matters he was Perot's top man, and he would soon become President of EDS. (Perot would continue to be Chairman of the Board.)

Now Perot and Meyerson talked business, reviewing each of EDS's current projects and problems. Both knew, though neither said, that the reason for the conference was that Perot might never come back from Turkey.

In some ways the two men were as different as chalk and cheese. Meyerson's grandfather was a Russian Jew who had saved for two years to buy his rail ticket from New York to Texas. Meyerson's interests ranged from athletics to the arts: he played handball, was involved with the Dallas Symphony Orchestra and was himself a good pianist. Making fun of Perot and his 'eagles', Meyerson called his own close colleagues 'Meyerson's toads'. But in many ways he was like Perot, a creative and daring businessman whose bold ideas often scared more conventional executives in

EDS. Perot had given instructions that, if something were to happen to him during the rescue, all his stock would be voted by Meyerson. EDS would continue to be run by a leader, not a bureaucrat.

While Perot discussed business and worried about the plane and fumed against the State Department, his deepest concern was for his mother. Lulu May Perot was sinking fast, and Perot wanted to be with her. If she were to die while he was in Turkey he would never see her again, and that would break his heart.

Meyerson knew what was on his mind. He broke off the business talk to say: 'Ross, why don't I go?'

'What do you mean?'

'Why don't I go to Turkey instead of you? You've done your share – you went to Iran. There's nothing you can do that I can't do in Turkey. And you want to stay with your mother.'

Perot was touched. Mort didn't have to say that, he thought. 'If you're willing . . .' He was tempted. 'That's something I'd sure want to think about. Let me think about it.'

He was not sure he had the right to let Meyerson do this instead of him. 'Let's see what the others think.' He picked up the phone, called Dallas, and reached T. J. Marquez. 'Mort's offered to go to Turkey instead of me,' he told T.J. 'What's your reaction to that?'

'It's the worst idea in the world,' T.J. said. 'You've been close to this project from the start, and you couldn't possibly tell Mort everything he needs to know in a few hours. You know Simons, you know how his mind works – Mort doesn't. Plus, Simons doesn't know Mort – and you're aware of how Simons feels about trusting people he doesn't know. Well, he *won't* trust them, that's how he feels.'

'You're right,' Perot said. 'It's not for consideration.'

He hung up. 'Mort, I sure appreciate your offer, but I'm going to Turkey.'

'Whatever you say.'

A few minutes later Meyerson left, to return to Dallas in

the chartered Lear jet. Perot called EDS again and spoke to Merv Stauffer. 'Now I want you guys to work in shifts and get some sleep,' Perot said. 'I don't want to be talking to a bunch of zombies back there.'

'Yes, sir!'

Perot took his own advice and got some sleep.

The phone woke him at two a.m. It was Pat Sculley, calling from the airport: the plane's mechanical problems were fixed.

Perot got a cab to Dulles Airport. It was a hair-raising thirty-mile ride on icy roads.

The Turkish Rescue Team was now together: Perot; Pat Sculley and Jim Schwebach – the deadly duo; young Ron Davis; the crew of the 707; and the two extra pilots, Dick Douglas and Julian 'Scratch' Kanauch. But the plane was *not* mended. It needed a spare part which was not available in Washington. Gary Fernandes – the EDS manager who had worked on the leasing contract for the plane – had a friend who was in charge of ground support for one of the airlines at New York's LaGuardia Airport: he called the friend, and the friend got out of bed, found the part, and put it on a plane for Washington. Meanwhile Perot lay down on a bench in the terminal and slept for a couple more hours.

They boarded at six a.m. Perot looked around the interior of the aircraft in amazement. It had a bedroom with a king-size bed, three bars, a sophisticated hi-fi system, a television, and an office with a phone. There were plush carpets, suede upholstery and velvet walls. 'It looks like a Persian whorehouse,' said Perot, although he had never seen a Persian whorehouse.

The plane took off. Dick Douglas and Scratch Kanauch immediately curled up and went to sleep. Perot tried to follow their example: he had sixteen hours of nothing to do in front of him. As the plane headed out across the Atlantic Ocean, he wondered again whether he was doing the right thing.

He might, after all, have left Paul and Bill to take their chances in Tehran. Nobody would have blamed him: it was the Government's job to rescue them. Indeed, the Embassy might even now be able to get them out unharmed.

On the other hand, Dadgar might pick them up and throw them in jail for twenty years – and the Embassy, on past performance, might not protect them. And what would the revolutionaries do if *they* got hold of Paul and Bill? Lynch them?

No, Perot could not leave his men to take their chances – it was not his way. Paul and Bill were *his* responsibility – he did not need his mother to tell him that. The trouble was that he was now putting more men at risk. Instead of having two people hiding in Tehran, he would now have eleven employees on the run in the wilds of north-west Iran, and another four, plus two pilots, searching for them. If things went wrong – if someone got killed – the world would see this whole thing as a foolhardy adventure by a man who thought he was still living in the Wild West. He could imagine the newspaper headlines: MILLIONAIRE TEXAN'S IRAN RESCUE BID ENDS IN DEATH . . .

Suppose we lose Coburn, he thought; what would I tell his wife? Liz might find it hard to understand why I staked the lives of seventeen men to gain the freedom of two.

He had never broken the law in his life, and now he was involved in so many major illegal activities he could not count them.

He put all that out of his mind. The decision was made. If you go through life thinking about all the bad things that can happen, you soon talk yourself into doing nothing at all. Concentrate on the problems that can be solved. The chips are on the table and the wheel is in spin. The last game has begun.

4

On Tuesday the US Embassy announced that evacuation flights for all Americans in Tehran would leave during the coming weekend.

Simons got Coburn and Poché in one of the bedrooms of the Dvoranchik place and closed the door. 'This solves some of our problems,' he said. 'I want to split them up at this point in the game. Some can take the Embassy evacuation flight, leaving a manageable group for the overland trip.'

Coburn and Poché agreed.

'Obviously, Paul and Bill have to go overland,' Simons said. 'Two of us three have to go with them: one to escort them across the mountains and the other to cross the border legitimately and meet up with Boulware. We'll need an Iranian driver for each of the two Range Rovers. That leaves us two spare seats. Who takes them? Not Cathy – she'll be much better off on the Embassy flight.'

'Rich will want to go with her,' said Coburn.

'And that fucking dog,' Simons added.

Buffy's life is saved, Coburn thought. He was rather glad. Simons said: 'There's Keane Taylor, John Howell, Bob Young and Bill Gayden. Here's the problem: Dadgar might pick people up at the airport, and we'll end up back where we started – with EDS men in jail. Who is at most risk?'

'Gayden,' said Coburn. 'He's President of EDS World. As a hostage, he'd be better than Paul and Bill. In fact, when Dadgar arrested Bill Gay*lord*, we wondered whether it was a mistake, and he really wanted Bill Gay*den*, but got confused because of the similarity of the names.'

'Gayden comes out overland with Paul and Bill, then.'

'John Howell is not even employed by EDS. And he's a lawyer. He should be all right.'

'Howell goes out by air.'

'Bob Young is employed by EDS in Kuwait, not Iran. If Dadgar has a list of EDS names, Young won't be on it.'

'Young flies. Taylor drives. Now, one of us has to go on the evacuation flight with the Clean Team. Joe, that's you. You've kept a lower profile than Jay. He's been on the streets, at meetings at the Hyatt – whereas nobody knows you're here.'

'Okay,' said Poché.

'So the Clean Team is the Gallaghers, Bob Young and

340

John Howell, led by Joe. The Dirty Team is me, Jay, Keane Taylor, Bill Gayden, Paul, Bill, and two Iranian drivers. Let's go tell 'em.'

They went into the living room and got everyone sat down. As Simons talked, Coburn admired how he announced his decision in such a way that they all thought they were being asked for their opinions rather than being told what to do.

There was some discussion of who should be in which team – both John Howell and Bob Young would have preferred to be in the Dirty Team, feeling themselves vulnerable to arrest by Dadgar – but in the end they all reached the decision Simons had already made.

The Clean Team might as well move into the Embassy compound as soon as possible, Simons said. Gayden and Joe Poché went off to find Lou Goelz, the Consul General, and talk to him about it.

The Dirty Team would leave tomorrow morning.

Coburn had to organize the Iranian drivers. These were to have been Majid and his cousin the professor, but the professor was in Rezaiyeh and could not get to Tehran, so Coburn had to find a replacement.

He had already decided on Seyyed. Seyyed was a young Iranian systems engineer like Rashid and the Cycle Man, but from a much more wealthy family: relatives of his had been high in politics and the army under the Shah. Seyyed had been educated in England and spoke with a British accent. His great asset, from Coburn's point of view, was that he came from the north-west, so he knew the territory and he spoke Turkish.

Coburn called Seyyed and they met at Seyyed's house. Coburn told him lies. 'I need to gather intelligence on the roads between here and Khoy,' Coburn said. 'I'll need someone to drive me. Will you do it?'

'Sure,' said Seyyed.

'Meet me at ten forty-five tonight at Argentine Square.'

Seyyed agreed.

Simons had instructed Coburn to go through all this.

Coburn trusted Seyyed, but of course Simons did not; so Seyyed would not know where the team was staying until he got there, and he would not know about Paul and Bill until he saw them; and from that moment on he would not be out of Simons's sight.

When Coburn returned to the Dvoranchik place, Gayden and Poché were back from seeing Lou Goelz. They had told Goelz that a few EDS men were staying in Tehran to look for Paul and Bill, but the others wanted to leave on the first evacuation flight, and stay at the Embassy in the meantime. Goelz said that the Embassy was full, but they could stay at his house.

They all thought that was pretty damn good of Goelz. Most of them had got mad at him once or twice over the last two months, and had made it pretty clear that they blamed him and his colleagues for the arrest of Paul and Bill: it was big of him to open his house to them after all that. As everything came unglued in Iran, Goelz was becoming less of a bureaucrat and showing that his heart was in the right place.

The Clean Team and the Dirty Team shook hands and wished each other luck, not knowing who needed it most; then the Clean Team left for Goelz's house.

It was now evening. Coburn and Keane Taylor went to Majid's house to pick him up: he would spend the night at the Dvoranchik place like Seyyed. Coburn and Taylor also had to get a 55-gallon drum of fuel which Majid had been keeping for them.

When they got to the house Majid was out.

They waited, fretting. At last Majid came in. He greeted them, welcomed them to his home, called for tea, the whole shooting match. Eventually Coburn said: 'We're leaving tomorrow morning. We want you to come with us now.'

Majid asked Coburn to step into another room with him, then he said: 'I can't go with you.'

'Why not?'

'I have to kill Hoveyda.'

'What?' said Coburn incredulously. 'Who?'

'Amir Abbas Hoveyda, who used to be Prime Minister.'

'Why do you have to *kill* him?'

'It's a long story. The Shah had a land reform programme; and Hoveyda tried to take away my family's tribal lands, and we rebelled, and Hoveyda put me in jail . . . I have been waiting all these years for my revenge.'

'You have to kill him right away?' said Coburn, astonished.

'I have the weapons and the opportunity. In two days' time all may be different.'

Coburn was nonplussed. He did not know what to say. It was clear Majid could not be talked around.

Coburn and Taylor manhandled the fuel drum into the back of the Range Rover, then took their leave. Majid wished them luck.

Back at the Dvoranchik place, Coburn started trying to reach the Cycle Man, hoping he would replace Majid as driver. The Cycle Man was as elusive as Coburn himself. He could normally be reached at a certain phone number – some kind of revolutionary headquarters, Coburn suspected – just once a day. The regular time for him to drop by this place was now past – it was late evening – but Coburn tried anyway. The Cycle Man was not there. He tried a few more phone numbers without success.

At least they had Seyyed.

At ten-thirty Coburn went out to meet Seyyed. He walked through the darkened streets to Argentine Square, a mile from the Dvoranchik place, then picked his way across a construction site and into an empty building to wait.

At eleven o'clock Seyyed had not arrived.

Simons had told Coburn to wait fifteen minutes, no longer; but Coburn decided to give Seyyed a little more time.

He waited until eleven-thirty.

Seyyed was not coming.

Coburn wondered what had happened: given Seyyed's family connections, it was quite possible he had fallen victim to the revolutionaries.

For the Dirty Team this was a disaster. Now they had *no* Iranians to go with them. How the hell will we get through all those roadblocks? wondered Coburn. What a shitty break:

343

the professor drops out, Majid drops out, the Cycle Man can't be found, then Seyyed drops out. Shit.

He left the construction site and walked away. Suddenly he heard a car. He looked back, and saw a jeep full of armed revolutionaries swing around the Square. He ducked behind a convenient bush. They went by.

He went on, hurrying now, wondering whether the curfew was in force tonight. He was almost home when the jeep came roaring back towards him.

They saw me last time, he thought, and they've come back to pick me up.

It was very dark. They might not have spotted him yet. He turned and ran back. There was no cover on this street. The noise of the jeep became louder. At last Coburn saw some shrubbery and flung himself into it. He lay there listening to his heartbeat as the jeep came closer. Were they looking for him? Had they picked up Seyyed and tortured him, and made him confess that he had an appointment with a capitalist American pig at Argentine Square at ten forty-five . . .?

The jeep went by without stopping.

Coburn picked himself up.

He ran all the way to the Dvoranchik place.

He told Simons they now had no Iranian drivers.

Simons cursed. 'Is there another Iranian we can call?'

'Only one, Rashid.'

Simons did not want to use Rashid, Coburn knew, because Rashid had led the jailbreak, and if someone who remembered him from that should see him driving a carload of Americans there might be trouble. But Coburn could not think of anyone else.

'Okay,' said Simons. 'Call him.'

Coburn dialled Rashid's number.

He was at home.

'This is Jay Coburn. I need your help.'

'Sure.'

Coburn did not want to give the address of the hideout over the phone, in case the line was wiretapped. He recalled that Bill Dvoranchik had a slight squint. He said: 'You remember the guy with the funny eye?'

'With a funny eye? Oh, yeah—'

'Don't say his name. Remember where he used to live?'

'Sure—'

'Don't say it. That's where I am. I need you here.'

'Jay, I live miles from there and I don't know how I'm going to get across the city—'

'Just try,' Coburn said. He knew how resourceful Rashid was. Give him a task and he just hated to fail. 'You'll get here.'

'Okay.'

'Thanks.' Coburn hung up.

It was midnight.

Paul and Bill had each picked a passport from the ones Gayden had brought from the States, and Simons had made them learn the names, dates of birth, personal details, and all the visas and country stamps. The photograph in Paul's passport looked more or less like Paul, but Bill's was a problem. None of them was right, and he ended up with the passport of Larry Humphreys, a blond, rather Nordic type who really did not look like Bill.

The tension mounted as the six men discussed details of the journey they would begin within the next few hours. There was fighting in Tabriz, according to Rich Gallagher's military contacts; so they would stick to the plan of taking the low road, south of Lake Rezaiyeh, passing through Mahabad. The story they would tell, if questioned, would be as close to the truth as possible – always Simons's preference when lying. They would say they were businessmen who wanted to get home to their families, the airport was closed, and they were driving to Turkey.

In support of that story, they would carry no weapons. It was a difficult decision – they knew they might regret being unarmed and helpless in the middle of a revolution – but Simons and Coburn had found, on the reconnaissance trip, that the revolutionaries at the roadblocks always searched for weapons. Simons's instinct told him they would be better

345

off talking their way out of trouble than trying to shoot their way out.

They also decided to leave behind the 55-gallon fuel drums, on the grounds that they made the team look too professional, too organized, for businessmen quietly driving home.

They would, however, take a lot of money. Joe Poché and the Clean Team had gone off with fifty thousand dollars, but Simons's crew still had around a quarter of a million dollars, some of it in Iranian rials, deutschmarks, sterling and gold. They packed fifty thousand dollars into kitchen baggies, weighted the bags with shot, and put them in a gas can. They hid some in a Kleenex box and more in the battery hold of a flashlight. They shared the rest out for each to conceal about his person.

At one o'clock Rashid still had not arrived. Simons sent Coburn to stand at the street gate and watch for him.

Coburn stood in the darkness, shivering, hoping Rashid would show up. They would leave tomorrow with or without him, but without him they might not get far. The villagers in the countryside would probably detain Americans just on general principles. Rashid would be the ideal guide, despite Simons's worries: the kid had a silver tongue.

Coburn's thoughts turned to home. Liz was mad at him, that he knew. She had been giving Merv Stauffer a hard time, calling every day and asking where her husband was and what was he doing and when he was coming home.

Coburn knew he would have to make some decisions when he got home. He was not sure that he was going to spend the rest of his life with Liz; and after this episode, maybe she would begin to feel the same way. I suppose we were in love, once upon a time, he thought. Where did all that go?

He heard footsteps. A short, curly-haired figure was walking along the pavement toward him, shoulders hunched against the cold.

'Rashid!' hissed Coburn.

'Jay?'

'Boy, am I glad to see you!' Coburn took Rashid's arm.

'Let's go inside.'

They went into the living room. Rashid said hello to everyone, smiling and blinking: he blinked a lot, especially in moments of excitement, and he had a nervous cough. Simons sat him down and explained the plan to him. Rashid blinked faster.

When he understood what was being asked of him, he became a little self-important. 'I will help you on one condition,' he said, and coughed. 'I know this country and I know this culture. You are all important people in EDS, but this is not EDS. If I lead you to the border, you must agree always to do everything I say, without question.'

Coburn held his breath. *Nobody* talked like this to Simons.

But Simons grinned. 'Anything you say, Rashid.'

A few minutes later Coburn got Simons in a corner and said quietly: 'Colonel did you mean that about Rashid being in charge?'

'Sure,' said Simons. 'He's in charge as long as he's doing what I want.'

Coburn knew, better than Simons, how hard it was to control Rashid even when Rashid was *supposed* to be obeying orders. On the other hand, Simons was the most skilled leader of small groups Coburn had ever met. Then again, this was Rashid's country, and Simons did not speak Farsi . . . The last thing they needed on this trip was a power struggle between Simons and Rashid.

Coburn got on the phone to Dallas and spoke to Merv Stauffer. Paul had encoded a description of the Dirty Team's proposed route to the border, and Coburn now gave Stauffer the coded message.

Then they discussed how they would communicate en route. It would probably be impossible to call Dallas from countryside pay phones, so they decided they would pass messages through an EDS employee in Tehran, Gholam. Gholam was not to know he was being used this way. Coburn would call Gholam once a day. If all was well he would say: 'I have a message for Jim Nyfeler. We are okay.' Once the team reached Rezaiyeh he would add: 'We are at the staging area.' Stauffer, in his turn, would simply call Gholam and ask whether there were any messages. So long as all went well, Gholam would be kept in the dark. If things went wrong, the pretence would be abandoned: Coburn would level with Gholam, tell him what the trouble was and ask him to call Dallas.

Stauffer and Coburn had become so familiar with the code that they could hold a discussion, using mostly ordinary English mixed with a few letter-groups and key code words, and be sure that anyone listening in on a wiretap would be unable to figure out what they meant.

Merv explained that Perot had contingency plans to fly into north-west Iran from Turkey to pick up the Dirty Team if necessary. Perot wanted the Range Rovers to be clearly identifiable from the air, so he proposed that each of them should have a large 'X' on its roof, either painted or made of black electrician's tape. If a vehicle had to be abandoned – because it broke down, or ran out of gas, or for any other reason – the 'X' should be changed to an 'A'.

There was another message from Perot. He had talked with Admiral Moorer, who had said that things were going to get worse and the team should get out of there. Coburn told Simons this. Simons said: 'Tell Admiral Moorer that the only water here is in the kitchen sink – I look out the window and I see no ships.' Coburn laughed, and told Stauffer: 'We understand the message.'

It was almost five a.m. There was no more time to talk. Stauffer said: 'Take care of yourself, Jay.' He sounded choked up. 'Keep your head down, y'hear?'

'I sure will.'

'Good luck.'

'Bye, Merv.'

Coburn hung up.

As dawn broke, Rashid went out in one of the Range Rovers to reconnoitre the streets. He was to find a route out of the city avoiding roadblocks. If the fighting was heavy, the team would consider postponing their departure another twenty-four hours.

At the same time Coburn left in the second Range Rover to meet with Gholam. He gave Gholam cash to cover the next payday at Bucharest, and said nothing about using Gholam to pass messages to Dallas. The object of the exercise was a pretence of normality, so that it would be a few days before the remaining Iranian employees began to suspect that their American bosses had left town.

When he got back to the Dvoranchik place, the team discussed who should go in which car. Rashid should drive the lead car, obviously. His passengers would be Simons, Bill, and Keane Taylor. In the second car would be Coburn, Paul and Gayden.

Simons said: 'Coburn, you're not to let Paul out of your sight until you're in Dallas. Taylor, the same goes for you and Bill.'

Rashid came back and said the streets were remarkably quiet.

'All right,' said Simons. 'Let's get this show on the road.'

Keane Taylor and Bill went out to fill the gas tanks of the Range Rovers from the 55-gallon drum. The fuel had to be siphoned into the cars, and the only way to start the flow was to suck the fuel through: Taylor swallowed so much gasoline that he went back into the house and vomited, and for once nobody laughed at him.

Coburn had some pep pills which he had bought, on Simons's instructions, at a Tehran drugstore. He and Simons had had no sleep for twenty-four hours straight, and now they each took a pill to keep them awake.

Paul emptied the kitchen of every kind of food that would keep: crackers, cup cakes, canned puddings and cheese. It was not very nutritious but it would fill them.

Coburn whispered to Paul: 'Make sure *we* get the cassette tapes, so we can have some music in our car.'

Bill loaded the cars with blankets, flashlights and can openers.

They were ready.

They all went outside.

As they were getting into the cars, Rashid said: 'Paul, you

drive the second car, please. You are dark enough to pass for Iranian if you don't speak.'

Paul glanced at Simons. Simons gave a slight nod. Paul got behind the wheel.

They drove out of the courtyard and into the street.

Eleven

1

As the Dirty Team drove out of the Dvoranchik place, Ralph Boulware was at Istanbul Airport, waiting for Ross Perot.

Boulware had mixed feelings about Perot. Boulware had been a technician when he joined EDS. Now he was a manager. He had a fine big house in a white Dallas suburb, and an income few black Americans could ever hope for. He owed it all to EDS, and to Perot's policy of promoting talent. They didn't give you all this stuff for *nothing*, of course: they gave it for brains and hard work and good business judgement. But what they did give you for nothing was the chance to show your stuff.

On the other hand, Boulware suspected Perot wanted to own his men body and soul. That was why ex-military people got on well at EDS; they were comfortable with discipline and used to a twenty-four-hours-a-day job. Boulware was afraid that one day he might have to decide whether he was his own man or Perot's.

He admired Perot for going to Iran. For a man as rich and comfortable and protected as that to put his ass on the line the way he had . . . that took some balls. There was probably not one other Chairman of the Board of an American corporation who would *conceive* the rescue plan, let alone participate in it.

And then again, Boulware wondered – all his life he would wonder – whether he could ever really trust a white man.

Perot's leased 707 touched down at six a.m. Boulware went on board. He took in the lush decor at a glance and then forgot about it: he was in a hurry.

He sat down with Perot. 'I'm catching a plane at six-thirty so I got to make this fast,' he said. 'You can't buy a helicopter and you can't buy a light plane.'

'Why not?'

'It's against the law. You can charter a plane, but it won't take you just anywhere you want to go – you charter for a specified trip.'

'Who says?'

'The law. Also, chartering is so unusual that you'll have the government all over you asking questions and you might not want that. Now—'

'Just a minute, Ralph, not so fast,' said Perot. He had that I'm-the-boss look in his eye. 'What if we get a helicopter from another country and bring it in?'

'I have been here a month and I have looked into all this thoroughly, and you can't rent a helicopter and you can't rent a plane, and I have to leave you now to meet Simons at the border.'

Perot backed off. 'Okay. How are you going to get there?'

'Mr Fish got us a bus to go to the border. It's on its way already – I was going with it, then I had to stay behind to brief you. I'm going to fly to Adana – that's about half way – and catch up with the bus there. I got Ilsman with me, he's the secret service guy, and another guy to translate. What time do the fellows expect to reach the border?'

'Two o'clock tomorrow afternoon,' said Perot.

'It's going to be tight. I'll see you guys later.'

He ran back to the terminal building and just made his flight.

Ilsman, the fat secret service policeman, and the interpreter – Boulware did not know his name so he called him Charlie Brown – were on board. They took off at six-thirty.

They flew east to Ankara, where they waited several hours for their connection. At midday they reached Adana, near the Biblical city of Tarsus in south central Turkey.

The bus was not there.

They waited an hour.

Boulware decided the bus was not going to come.

352

With Ilsman and Charlie Brown, he went to the information desk and asked about flights from Adana to Van, a town about a hundred miles from the border crossing.

There were no flights to Van from *anywhere*.

'Ask where we can charter a plane,' Boulware told Charlie.

Charlie asked.

'There are no planes for charter here.'

'Can we buy a car?'

'Cars are very scarce in this part of the country.'

'Are there no car dealers in town?'

'If there are, they won't have any cars to sell.'

'Is there *any* way to get to Van from here?'

'No.'

It was like the joke about the tourist who asks a farmer for directions to London, and the farmer replies: 'If I was going to London I wouldn't start from here.'

They wandered out of the terminal and stood beside the dusty road. There was no sidewalk: this was *really* the sticks. Boulware was frustrated. So far he had had it easier than most of the rescue team – he had not even been to Tehran. Now that it was his turn to achieve something it looked like he would fail. Boulware hated to fail.

He saw a car approaching with some kind of markings in Turkish on its side. 'Hey,' he said, 'is that a cab?'

'Yes,' said Charlie.

'Hell, let's get a cab!'

Charlie hailed the cab and they got in. Boulware said: 'Tell him we want to go to Van.'

Charlie translated.

The driver pulled away.

After a few seconds the driver asked a question. Charlie translated: 'Van, where?'

'Tell him Van, Turkey.'

The driver stopped the car.

Charlie said: 'He says: "Do you know how far it is?"'

Boulware was not sure but he knew it was half across Turkey. 'Tell him yes.'

353

After another exchange Charlie said: 'He won't take us.'

'Does he know anyone who will?'

The driver shrugged elaborately as he replied. Charlie said: 'He's going to take us to the cab stand so we can ask around.'

'Good.'

They drove into the town. The cab stand was just another dusty piece of road with a few cars parked, none of them new. Ilsman started talking to the drivers. Boulware and Charlie found a little shop and bought a sack of hard-boiled eggs.

When they came out, Ilsman had found a driver and negotiated a price. The driver proudly pointed out his car. Boulware looked at it in dismay. It was a Chevrolet, around fifteen years old, and it looked as if it still had the original tyres.

'He says we'll need some food,' Charlie said.

'I got some eggs.'

'Maybe we'll need more.'

Boulware went back into the shop and bought three dozen oranges.

They got into the Chevrolet and drove to a filling station. The driver bought a spare tank of fuel and put it in the trunk. 'Where we're going, there are no gas stations,' Charlie explained.

Boulware was looking at a map. The journey was about five hundred miles through mountain country. 'Listen,' he said. 'There is no way this car is going to get us to the border by two o'clock tomorrow afternoon.'

'You don't understand,' Charlie said. 'This man is a *Turkish* driver.'

'Oh, boy,' said Boulware; and he sat back in the seat and closed his eyes.

They drove out of town and headed up into the mountains of central Turkey.

The road was dirt and gravel, with enormous potholes, and in places it was not much wider than the car. It snaked over the mountainsides, with a breathtaking sheer drop at one edge. There was no guard rail to stop an incautious driver shooting over the precipice into the abyss. But the scenery was spectacular, with stunning views across the sunlit valleys, and Boulware made up his mind to go back one day, with Mary and Stacy and Kecia, and do the trip again, at leisure.

Up ahead, a truck was approaching them. The cabbie braked to a halt. Two men in uniform got out of the truck. 'Army patrol,' said Charlie Brown.

The driver wound down his window. Ilsman talked to the soldiers. Boulware did not understand what was said, but it seemed to satisfy the patrol. The cabbie drove on.

An hour or so later they were stopped by another patrol, and the same thing happened.

At nightfall they spotted a roadside restaurant and pulled in. The place was primitive and filthy dirty. 'All they have is beans and rice,' said Charlie apologetically as they sat down.

Boulware smiled. 'I been eating beans and rice all my life.'

He studied the cab driver. The man was about sixty years old, and looked tired. 'I guess I'll drive for a while,' said Boulware.

Charlie translated, and the cabbie protested vehemently.

'He says you won't be able to drive that car,' Charlie said. 'It's an American car with a very peculiar gearshift.'

'Look, I *am* American,' Boulware said. 'Tell him that lots of Americans are black. And I know how to drive a 'sixty-four Chevy with a standard shift, for Pete's sake!'

The three Turks argued about it while they ate. Finally Charlie said: 'You can drive, so long as you promise to pay for the damage if you wreck the car.'

'I promise,' said Boulware, thinking: Big deal.

He paid the bill, and they walked out to the car. It was beginning to rain.

Boulware found it impossible to make any speed, but the big car was stable, and its powerful engine took the gradients without difficulty. They were stopped a third time by an army patrol. Boulware showed his American passport, and once again Ilsman made them happy somehow. This time,

355

Boulware noted, the soldiers were unshaven and wore somewhat ragged uniforms.

As they pulled away, Ilsman spoke, and Charlie said: 'Try not to stop for any more patrols.'

'Why not?'

'They might rob us.'

That's great, thought Boulware.

Near the town of Maras, a hundred miles from Adana and another four hundred from Van, the rain became heavy, making the mud-and-gravel road treacherous, and Boulware had to slow down even more.

Soon after Maras, the car died.

They all got out and lifted the hood. Boulware could see nothing wrong. The driver spoke, and Charlie translated: 'He can't understand it – he has just tuned the engine with his own hands.'

'Maybe he didn't tune it right,' said Boulware. 'Let's check a few things.'

The driver got some tools and a flashlight out of the trunk, and the four men stood around the engine in the rain, trying to find out what had gone wrong.

Eventually they discovered that the points were incorrectly set. Boulware guessed that either the rain, or the thinner mountain air, had made the fault critical. It took a while to adjust the points, but finally the engine fired. Cold and wet and tired, the four men got back into the old car and Boulware drove on.

The countryside grew more desolate as they travelled east – no towns, no houses, no livestock, nothing. The road became even worse: it reminded Boulware of a trail in a cowboy movie. Soon the rain turned to snow and the road became icy. Boulware kept glancing over the sheer drop at the side. If you go off this sucker, he said to himself, you ain't going to get hurt – you're going to *die*.

Near Bingol, half way to their destination, they climbed up out of the storm. The sky was clear and there was a bright moon, almost like daylight. Boulware could see the snow clouds and the flashing lightning in the valleys below. The mountainside was frozen white, and the road was like a bobsleigh run.

Boulware thought: man, I'm going to die up here, and nobody's even going to know it, because they don't know where I am.

Suddenly the steering wheel bucked in his hands and the car slowed: Boulware had a moment of panic, thinking he was losing control, then realized he had a flat tyre. He brought the car gently to a halt.

They all got out and the cab driver opened the trunk. He hauled out the extra fuel tank to get at the spare wheel. Boulware was freezing: the temperature had to be way below zero. The cabbie refused any help and insisted on changing the wheel himself. Boulware took off his gloves and offered them to the cabbie: the man shook his head. Pride, I guess, thought Boulware.

By the time the job was done it was four a.m. Boulware said: 'Ask him if he wants to take over the driving – I'm bushed.'

The driver agreed.

Boulware got into the back. The car pulled away. Boulware closed his eyes and tried to ignore the bumps and jerks. He wondered whether he would reach the border in time. Shit, he thought, nobody could say we didn't try.

A few seconds later he was asleep.

2

The Dirty Team blew out of Tehran like a breeze.

The city looked like a battlefield from which everyone had gone home. Statues had been pulled down, cars burned, and trees felled to make roadblocks; then the roadblocks had been cleared – the cars pushed to the kerbs, the statues smashed, the trees burned. Some of those trees had been hand-watered every day for fifty years.

But there was no fighting. They saw very few people and little traffic. Perhaps the revolution was over. Or perhaps the revolutionaries were having tea.

They drove past the airport and took the highway north, following the route Coburn and Simons had taken on their reconnaissance trip. Some of Simons's plans had come to nothing, but not this one. Still Coburn was apprehensive. What was ahead of them? Did armies rage and storm in towns and hamlets still? Or was the revolution done? Perhaps the villagers had returned to their sheep and their ploughs.

Soon the two Range Rovers were bowling along at seventy miles an hour at the foot of a mountain range. On their left was a flat plain; on their right, steep green hillsides topped by snowy mountain peaks against the blue sky. Coburn looked at the car in front and saw Taylor taking photographs through the tailgate window with his Instamatic. 'Look at Taylor,' he said.

'What does he think this is?' said Gayden. 'A package tour?'

Coburn began to feel optimistic. There had been no trouble so far: maybe the whole country was calming down. Anyway, why should the Iranians give them a hard time? What was wrong with foreigners leaving the country?

Paul and Bill had false passports and were being hunted by the authorities, that was what was wrong.

Thirty miles from Tehran, just outside the town of Karaj, they came to their first roadblock. It was manned, as they usually were, by machine-gun-toting men and boys in ragged clothes.

The lead car stopped, and Rashid jumped out even before Paul had brought the second car to a halt, making sure that he rather than the Americans would do the talking. He immediately began speaking loud and rapid Farsi, with many gestures. Paul wound down the window. From what they could understand, it seemed Rashid was not giving the agreed story: he was saying something about journalists.

After a while Rashid told them all to get out of the cars. 'They want to search us for weapons.'

Coburn, remembering how many times he had been

frisked on the reconnaissance trip, had concealed his little Gerber knife in the Range Rover.

The Iranians patted them down then perfunctorily searched the cars: they did not find Coburn's knife, nor did they come across the money.

A few minutes later Rashid said: 'We can go.'

A hundred yards down the road was a filling station. They pulled in: Simons wanted to keep the fuel tanks as full as possible.

While the cars were being fuelled Taylor produced a bottle of cognac, and they all took a swig, except Simons who disapproved and Rashid whose beliefs forbade him to take alcohol. Simons was mad at Rashid. Instead of saying the group were businessmen trying to go home, Rashid had said they were journalists going to cover the fighting in Tabriz. 'Stick to the goddam story,' Simons said.

'Sure,' said Rashid.

Coburn thought Rashid would probably continue to say the first thing that came into his head at the time: that was how he operated.

A small crowd gathered at the filling station, watching the foreigners. Coburn looked at the bystanders nervously. They were not exactly hostile, but there was something vaguely menacing about their quiet surveillance.

Rashid bought a can of oil.

What now?

He took the fuel can, which contained most of the money in weighted plastic bags, out of the back of the car, and poured oil into it to conceal the money. It was not a bad idea, Coburn thought, but I would have mentioned it to Simons before doing it.

He tried to read the expressions on the faces in the crowd. Were they idly curious? Resentful? Suspicious? Malevolent? He could not tell, but he wanted to get away.

Rashid paid the bill and the two cars pulled slowly out of the filling station.

They had a clear run for the next seventy miles. The road, the new Iranian State Highway, was in good condition. It ran through a valley, alongside a single-track railroad, with snow-capped mountains above. The sun was shining.

The second roadblock was outside Qazvin.

It was an unofficial one – the guards were not in uniform – but it was bigger and more organized than the last. There were two checkpoints, one after another, and a line of cars waiting.

The two Range Rovers joined the queue.

The car in front of them was searched methodically. A guard opened the trunk and took out what looked like a rolled-up sheet. He unrolled it and found a rifle. He shouted something and waved the rifle in the air.

Other guards came running. A crowd gathered. The driver of the car was questioned. One of the guards knocked him on the ground.

Rashid pulled the car out of the line.

Coburn told Paul to follow.

'What's he doing?' Gayden said.

Rashid inched through the crowd. The people made way as the Range Rover nudged them – they were interested in the man with the rifle. Paul kept the second Range Rover right on the tail of the first. They passed the first checkpoint.

'What the fuck is he doing?' asked Gayden.

'This is asking for trouble,' said Coburn.

They approached the second checkpoint. Without stopping, Rashid yelled at the guard through the window. The guard said something in reply. Rashid accelerated. Paul followed.

Coburn breathed a sigh of relief. That was just like Rashid: he did the unexpected, on impulse, without thinking through the consequences; and somehow he always got away with it. It just made life a little tense for the people with him.

Next time they stopped, Rashid explained that he had simply told the guard the two Range Rovers had been cleared at the first checkpoint.

At the next roadblock Rashid persuaded the guards to write a pass on his windscreen in magic marker, and they

360

were waved through another three roadblocks without being searched.

Keane Taylor was driving the lead car when, climbing a long, winding hill, they saw two heavy trucks, side by side and filling the whole width of the road, coming downhill fast toward them. Taylor swerved off the road and bumped to a halt in the ditch, and Paul followed. The trucks went by, still side by side, and everyone said what a lousy driver Taylor was.

At midday they took a break. They parked near a ski-lift and lunched on dry crackers and cup cakes. Although there was snow on the mountainsides, the sun was shining and they were not cold. Taylor got out his bottle of cognac, but it had leaked and was empty: Coburn suspected that Simons had surreptitiously loosened the cork. They drank water.

They passed through the small, neat town of Zanjan, where on the reconnaissance trip Coburn and Simons had talked to the chief of police.

Just beyond Zanjan the Iranian State Highway ended – rather abruptly. In the second car, Coburn saw Rashid's Range Rover suddenly disappear from view. Paul slammed on the brakes and they got out to look.

Where the tarmac ended, Rashid had gone down a steep slope for about eight feet and landed nose-down in mud. Off to the right, their route continued up an unpaved mountain road.

Rashid re-started the stalled engine and put the car into four-wheel drive and reverse gear. Slowly he inched back up the bank and on to the road.

The Range Rover was covered with mud. Rashid turned on the wipers and washed the windscreen. When the mud splashes were gone, so was the pass which had been written on with magic marker. Rashid could have re-written it, but nobody had a magic marker.

They drove west, heading for the southern tip of Lake Rezaiyeh. The Range Rovers were built for tough roads, and they could still do forty miles per hour. They were climbing all the time: the temperature dropped steadily, and the countryside was covered with snow, but the road was clear. Coburn wondered whether they might even make the border tonight, instead of tomorrow as planned.

Gayden, in the back seat, leaned forward and said: 'Nobody's going to believe it was this easy. We better make up some war stories to tell when we get home.'

He spoke too soon.

As daylight faded they approached Mahabad. Its outskirts were marked by a few scattered huts, made of wood and mud-brick, along the sides of a winding road. The two Range Rovers swept around a bend and pulled up sharply: the road was blocked by a parked truck and a large but apparently disciplined crowd. The men were wearing the traditional baggy trousers, black vest, red-and-white chequered headress and bandolier of Kurdish tribesmen.

Rashid jumped out of the lead car and went into his act.

Coburn studied the guns of the guards, and saw both Russian and American automatic weapons.

'Everyone out of the cars,' said Rashid.

By now it was routine. One by one they were searched. This time the search was a little more thorough, and they found Keane Taylor's little switchblade knife, but they let him keep it. They did not find Coburn's knife, nor the money.

Coburn waited for Rashid to say: 'We can go.' It was taking longer than usual. Rashid argued with the Kurds for a few minutes, then said: 'We have to go and see the head man of the town.'

They got back into the cars. A Kurd with a rifle joined them in each car and directed them into the little town.

They were ordered to stop outside a small whitewashed building. One of the guards went in, came out again a minute later, and got back into the car without explanation.

They stopped again outside what was clearly a hospital. Here they picked up a passenger, a young Iranian in a suit.

Coburn wondered what the hell was going on.

Finally they drove down an alley and parked outside what looked like a small private house.

They went inside. Rashid told them to take off their shoes.

Gayden had several thousand dollars in hundred-dollar bills in his shoes. As he took them off he frantically stuffed the money up into the toes of the shoes.

They were ushered into a large room furnished with nothing but a beautiful Persian carpet. Simons quietly told everyone where to sit. Leaving a space in the circle for the Iranians, he put Rashid on the right of the space. Next to Rashid was Taylor, then Coburn, then Simons himself opposite the space. On Simons's right Paul and Bill sat, back a little from the line of the circle, where they would be least conspicuous. Gayden, completing the circle, sat on Bill's right.

As Taylor sat down he saw that he had a big hole in the toe of his sock, and hundred-dollar bills were poking through the hole. He cursed under his breath and hastily pushed the money back towards his heel.

The young man in the suit followed them in. He seemed educated and spoke good English. 'You are about to meet a man who has just escaped after twenty-five years in jail,' he said.

Bill almost said: Well, how about that. I've just escaped from jail myself! – but he stopped himself just in time.

'You are to be put on trial, and this man will be your judge,' the young Iranian went on.

The words *on trial* hit Paul like a blow, and he thought: we've come all this way for nothing.

3

The Clean Team spent Wednesday at Lou Goelz's house in Tehran.

Early in the morning a call came through from Tom Walter in Dallas. The line was poor and the conversation confused, but Joe Poché was able to tell Walter that he and the Clean Team were safe, would move into the Embassy as soon as possible, and would leave the country whenever the

363

Embassy got the evacuation flights finally organized. Poché also reported that Cathy Callagher's condition had not improved, and she had been taken to hospital the previous evening.

John Howell called Abolhasan, who had another message from Dadgar. Dadgar was willing to negotiate a lower bail. If EDS located Paul and Bill the company should turn them in and post the lower bail. The Americans should realize that it would be hopeless for Paul and Bill to try to leave Iran by regular means and very dangerous for them to leave otherwise.

Howell took that to mean that Paul and Bill would not have been allowed to get out on an Embassy evacuation flight. He wondered again whether the Clean Team might be in more danger than the Dirty Team. Bob Young felt the same. While they were discussing it, they heard shooting. It seemed to be coming from the direction of the US Embassy.

The National Voice of Iran, a radio station broadcasting from Baku across the border in the Soviet Union, had for several days been issuing 'news' bulletins about clandestine American plans for a counter-revolution. On Wednesday the National Voice announced that the files of SAVAK, the Shah's hated secret police force, had been transferred to the US Embassy. The story was almost certainly invented, but it was highly plausible: the CIA had created SAVAK and was in close contact with it, and everyone knew that US embassies – like all embassies – were full of spies thinly disguised as diplomatic attachés. Anyway, some of the revolutionaries in Tehran believed the story, and – without consulting any of the Ayatollah's aides – decided to take action.

During the morning they entered the high buildings surrounding the Embassy compound and took up position with automatic weapons. They opened fire at ten-thirty.

Ambassador William Sullivan was in his outer office, taking a call at his secretary's desk. He was speaking to the

Ayatollah's deputy foreign minister. President Carter had decided to recognize the new, revolutionary government in Iran, and Sullivan was making arrangements to deliver an official Note.

When he put the phone down he turned around to see his press attaché, Barry Rosen, standing there with two American journalists. Sullivan was furious, for the White House had given specific instructions that the decision to recognize the new government was to be announced in Washington, not Tehran. Sullivan took Rosen into the inner office and chewed him out.

Rosen told him that the two journalists were there to make arrangements for the body of Joe Alex Morris, the *Los Angeles Times* correspondent who had been shot during the fighting at Doshen Toppeh. Sullivan, feeling foolish, told Rosen to ask the journalists not to reveal what they had learned in overhearing Sullivan on the phone.

Rosen went out. Sullivan's phone rang. He picked it up. There was a sudden tremendous crash of gunfire, and a hail of bullets shattered his windows.

Sullivan hit the floor.

He slithered across the room and into the next office, where he came nose to nose with his deputy, Charlie Naas, who had been holding a meeting about the evacuation flights. Sullivan had two phone numbers which he could use, in an emergency, to reach revolutionary leaders. He now told Naas to call one and the army attaché to call the other. Still lying on the floor, the two men pulled telephones off a desk and started dialling.

Sullivan took out his walkie-talkie and called for reports from the Marine units in the compound.

The machine-gun attack had been covering fire for a squad of about seventy-five revolutionaries who had come over the front wall of the Embassy compound and were now advancing on the ambassadorial residence. Fortunately most of the staff were with Sullivan in the chancery building.

Sullivan ordered the Marines to fall back, not to use their rifles, and to fire their sidearms only in self-defence.

Then he crawled out of the executive suite and into the corridor.

During the next hour, as the attackers took the residence and the cafeteria building, Sullivan got all the civilians in the chancery herded into the communications vault upstairs. When he heard the attackers breaking down the steel doors of the building, he ordered the Marines inside to join the civilians in the vault. There he made them pile their weapons in a corner, and ordered everyone to surrender as soon as possible.

Eventually Sullivan himself went into the vault, leaving the army attaché and an interpreter outside.

When the attackers reached the second floor, Sullivan opened the vault door and walked out with his hands over his head.

The others – about a hundred people – followed him.

They were herded into the waiting room of the executive suite and frisked. There was a confused dispute between two factions of Iranians, and Sullivan realized that the Ayatollah's people had sent a rescue force – presumably in response to the phone calls by Charlie Naas and the army attaché – and the rescuers had arrived on the second floor at the same time as the attackers.

Suddenly a shot came through the window.

All the Americans dropped to the floor. One of the Iranians seemed to think the shot had come from within the room, and he swung his AK-47 rifle wildly at the tangle of prisoners on the floor; then Barry Rosen, the press attaché, yelled in Farsi: 'It came from outside! It came from outside!' At that moment Sullivan found himself lying next to the two journalists who had been in his outer office. 'I hope you're getting all this down in your notebooks,' he said.

Eventually they were taken out into the courtyard, where Ibrahim Yazdi, the Ayatollah's new Deputy Prime Minister, apologized to Sullivan for the attack.

Yazdi also gave Sullivan a personal escort, a group of students who would henceforth be responsible for the safety of the US Ambassador. The leader of the group explained to

Sullivan that they were well qualified to guard him. They had studied him, and were familiar with his route, for until recently their assignemnt had been to assassinate him.

Late that afternoon Cathy Gallagher called from the hospital. She had been given some medication which solved her problem, at least temporarily, and she wanted to rejoin her husband and the others at Lou Goelz's house.

Joe Poché did not want any more of the Clean Team to leave the house, but he also did not want any Iranians to know where they were; so he called Gholam and asked him to pick up Cathy at the hospital and bring her to the corner of the street, where her husband would meet her.

She arrived at around seven-thirty. She was feeling better, but Gholam had told her a horrifying story. 'They shot up our hotel rooms yesterday,' she said.

Gholam had gone to the Hyatt to pay EDS's bill and pick up the suitcases they had left behind, Cathy explained. The rooms had been wrecked, there were bullet-holes everywhere, and the luggage had been slashed to ribbons.

'Just our rooms?' Howell asked.

'Yes.'

'Did he find out how it happened?'

When Gholam went to pay the bill, the hotel manager had said to him: 'Who the *hell* were those people – the CIA?' Apparently, on Monday morning, after all the EDS people left the hotel, the revolutionaries had taken it over. They had harassed all the Americans, demanding their passports, and had shown pictures of the two men whom they were seeking. The manager had not recognized the men in the photographs. Nor had anyone else.

Howell wondered what had so enraged the revolutionaries that they had smashed up the rooms. Perhaps Gayden's well-stocked bar offended their Muslim sensibilities. Also left behind in Gayden's suite were a tape recorder used for dictation, some suction microphones for taping phone conversations, and a child's walkie-talkie set. The revolutionaries might have thought this was CIA surveillance gear.

367

Throughout the day, vague and alarming reports of what was happening at the Embassy reached Howell and the Clean Team through Goelz's houseman, who was calling friends. But Goelz returned as the others were having dinner, and after a couple of stiff drinks he was none the worse for his experience. He had spent a good deal of time lying on his ample belly in a corridor. Next day he went back to his desk, and he came home that evening with good news: evacuation flights would start on Saturday, and the Clean Team would be on the first.

Howell thought: Dadgar may have other ideas about that.

4

In Istanbul Ross Perot had a dreadful feeling that the whole operation was slipping out of control.

He heard, via Dallas, that the US Embassy in Tehran had been overrun by revolutionaries. He also knew, because Tom Walter had talked to Joe Poché earlier, that the Clean Team had been planning to move into the Embassy compound as soon as possible. But, after the attack on the Embassy, almost all telephone lines to Tehran had been disconnected, and the White House was monopolizing the few lines left. So Perot did not know whether the Clean Team had been in the Embassy at the time of the attack, nor did he know what kind of danger they might be in even if they were still at Goelz's house.

The loss of phone contact also meant that Merv Stauffer could not call Gholam to find out whether the Dirty Team had sent 'a message for Jim Nyfeler' saying either that they were okay or that they were in trouble. The whole seventh floor crew in Dallas was at work pulling strings to get one of the few remaining lines so they could talk to Gholam. Tom Walter had got on to A.T.&T. and spoken to Ray Johnson, who handled the EDS phone account. It was a very big account – EDS's computers in different parts of the USA talked to one another along telephone lines – and Johnson

368

had been keen to help a major customer. He had asked whether EDS's call to Tehran was a matter of life and death. You bet it is, said Tom Walter. Johnson was trying to get them a line. At the same time, T. J. Marquez was sweet-talking an international operator, trying to persuade her to break the rules.

Perot had also lost touch with Boulware, who was supposed to meet the Dirty Team on the Turkish side of the border. Boulware had last been heard from in Adana, five hundred miles from where he was supposed to be. Perot presumed he was now on his way to the rendezvous, but there was no way of telling how far he had got or whether he would make it on time.

Perot had spent most of the day trying to get a light plane or a helicopter with which to fly into Iran. The Boeing 707 was no use for that, because Perot would need to fly low and search for the Range Rovers with 'X' or 'A' on their roofs, then land on tiny disused airfields or even on a road or in a meadow. But so far his efforts had only confirmed what Boulware had told him at six o'clock that morning: it was not going to happen.

In desperation Perot had called a friend in the Drug Enforcement Agency, and asked for the phone number of the Agency's man in Turkey, thinking that narcotics people would surely know how to get hold of light planes. The DEA man had come to the Sheraton, accompanied by another man who, Perot gathered, was with the CIA; but if they knew where to get a plane they weren't telling.

In Dallas, Merv Stauffer was calling all over Europe looking for a suitable aircraft which could be bought or rented immediately and flown in to Turkey: he, too, had failed so far.

Late in the afternoon Perot had said to Pat Sculley: 'I want to talk to the highest-ranking American in Istanbul.'

Sculley had gone off and raised a little hell at the American Consulate, and now, at ten-thirty p.m., a consul was sitting in Perot's suite at the Sheraton.

Perot was levelling with him. 'My men aren't criminals of

369

any kind,' he said. 'They're ordinary businessmen who have wives and children worrying themselves to death back home. The Iranians kept them in jail for six weeks without bringing any charges or finding any evidence against them. Now they're free and they're trying to get out of the country. If they're caught, you can imagine how much chance they'd have of justice: none at all. The way things are in Iran now, my men may not get as far as the border. I want to go in and get them, and that's where I need your help. I have to borrow, rent or buy a small aircraft. Now can you help me?'

'No,' said the consul. 'In this country it's against the law for private individuals to have aircraft. Because it's against the law, the planes aren't here even for someone who's prepared to break the law.'

'But *you* must have aircraft.'

'The State Department has no aircraft.'

Perot despaired. Was he to sit and do *nothing* to help the Dirty Team?

The consul said: 'Mr Perot, we're here to help American citizens, and I'm going to try to get you an aircraft. I'll pull whatever strings I can. But I'll tell you now that my chance of success is close to zero.'

'Well, I appreciate it.'

The consul got up to go.

Perot said: 'It's very important that my presence in Turkey is kept secret. Right now the Iranian authorities have no idea where my men are. If they should learn that I'm here, they will be able to figure out how my men are getting out, and that would be a catastrophe. So please be very discreet.'

'I understand.'

The consul left.

A few minutes later the phone rang. It was T. J. Marquez calling from Dallas.

'Perot, you're on the front page of the paper today.'

Perot's heart sank: the story was out.

T.J. said: 'The Governor just appointed you Chairman of the Drug Commission.'

Perot breathed again. 'Marquez, you *scared* me.'

T.J. laughed.

'You shouldn't do that to an old man,' Perot said. 'Boy, you really caught my attention there.'

'Wait a minute, Margot's on the other line,' said T.J. 'She just wants to wish you a happy Valentine's Day.'

Perot realized it was 14 February. He said: 'Tell her I'm completely safe, and being guarded at all times by two blondes.'

'Wait a minute, I'll tell her.' T.J. came back on the line a minute later, laughing. 'She says, isn't it interesting that you need *two* to replace her?'

Perot chuckled. He had walked into that one: he should have known better than to try to score points off Margot. 'Now, did you get through to Tehran?'

'Yes. The international operator got us a line, and we blew it on a wrong number. Then A.T.&T. got us a line and we reached Gholam.'

'And?'

'Nothing. He hasn't heard from them.'

Perot's temporary cheerfulness vanished. 'What did you ask him?'

'We just said: "Are there any messages?" and he said there weren't.'

'Damn.' Perot almost wished the Dirty Team had called to say they were in trouble, for then at least he would have known their location.

He said goodbye to T.J. and got ready for bed. He had lost the Clean Team, he had lost Boulware, and now he had lost the Dirty Team. He had failed to get hold of an aircraft in which to go looking for them. The whole operation was a mess – and there was not a thing he could do about it.

The suspense was killing him. He realized that never in his life had he experienced this much tension. He had seen men crumble under stress but he had never really been able to relate to their suffering because it had never happened to him. Stress did not upset him, normally – in fact he thrived on it. But this was different.

He broke his own rule, and allowed himself to think about

371

all the bad things that could happen. What was at stake here was his freedom, for if this rescue were to go wrong he would end up in jail. Already he had assembled a mercenary army, connived at the misuse of American passports, arranged the forgery of US military identity cards, and conspired to effect an illegal border crossing. He hoped he would go to jail in the US rather than in Turkey. The worst would be if the Turks sent him to Iran to be tried for his 'crimes' there.

He lay awake on his hotel bed, worrying about the Clean Team, about the Dirty Team, about Boulware, and about himself. There was nothing he could do but endure it. In the future he would be more sympathetic to the men *he* put under stress. If he had a future.

5

Coburn was tense, watching Simons.

They all sat in a circle on the Persian carpet, waiting for the 'judge'. Simons had told Coburn, before they left Tehran: 'Keep your eye on me.' So far Simons had been passive, rolling with the punches, letting Rashid do the talking, allowing the team to be arrested. But there might come a moment when he changed his tactics. If he decided to start a fight, he would let Coburn know a split-second before it happened.

The judge arrived.

Aged about fifty, he wore a dark blue jacket with a light tan sweater underneath, and an open-necked shirt. He had the air of a professional man, a doctor or a lawyer. He had a .45 stuck in his belt.

Rashid recognized him. His name was Habib Bolourian, and he was a leading communist.

Bolourian sat in the space Simons had intended for him.

He said something in Farsi, and the young man in the suit – who now took on the role of interpreter – asked for their passports.

This is it, Coburn thought; this is where we get into

372

trouble. He will look at Bill's passport and realize it belongs to someone else.

The passports were piled up on the carpet in front of Bolourian. He looked at the top one. The interpreter began to write down details. There was some confusion about surnames and given names: Iranians often got the two mixed up, for some reason. Rashid was handing the passports to Bolourian, and Gayden was leaning over and pointing out things; and it dawned on Coburn that between the two they were making the confusion worse. Rashid was giving Bolourian the same passport more than once, and Gayden, in leaning over to point out things in a passport, was covering up the photograph. Coburn admired their nerve. In the end the passports were handed back, and it seemed to Coburn that Bill's had never actually been opened.

Bolourian began to interrogate Rashid in Farsi. Rashid seemed to be telling the official cover story, about their being ordinary American businessmen trying to go home, with some embellishments about family members on the point of death in the States.

Eventually the interpreter said in English: 'Would you tell us exactly what you're doing here?'

Rashid said: 'Well, you see—' then a guard behind him slammed in the bolt on his machine-gun and stuck the barrel into the back of Rashid's neck. Rashid fell silent. Clearly the interpreter wanted to hear what the Americans had to say, to see whether their story matched Rashid's; the guard's action was a brutal reminder that they were in the power of violent revolutionaries.

Gayden, as the senior EDS exective there, replied to the interpreter. 'We all work for a data processing company called PARS Data Systems, or PDS,' he said. In fact PDS was the Iranian company jointly owned by EDS and Abolfath Mahvi. Gayden did not mention EDS because, as Simons had pointed out before they left Tehran, Dadgar might put out a blanket arrest order on anyone connected with EDS. 'We had a contract with Bank Omran,' Gayden went on, telling the truth but by no means the whole truth.

'We weren't getting paid, people were throwing rocks at our windows, we had no money, we missed our families, and we just wanted to go home. The airport was closed so we decided to drive.'

'That's right,' said the interpreter. 'The same thing happened to me – I wanted to fly to Europe but the airport was closed.'

We may have an ally here, Coburn thought.

Bolourian asked, and the interpreter translated: 'Did you have a contract with ISIRAN?'

Coburn was astonished. For someone who had spent twenty-five years in jail, Bolourian was remarkably well-informed. ISIRAN – Information Systems Iran – was a data processing company which had once been owned by Abolfath Mahvi and had subsequently been bought by the government. The company was widely believed to have close links with the secret police, SAVAK. Worse, EDS *did* have a contract with ISIRAN: in partnership, the two companies had created a document control system for the Iranian Navy back in 1977.

'We have absolutely nothing to do with ISIRAN,' Gayden lied.

'Can you give us some proof of who you work for?'

That was a problem. Before leaving Tehran they had all destroyed any papers connected with EDS, under Simon's instructions. Now they all searched their pockets for anything they might have overlooked.

Keane Taylor found his health insurance card, with 'Electronic Data Systems Corp.' printed across the bottom. He handed it to the interpreter, saying: 'Electronic Data Systems is the parent company of PDS.'

Bolourian got up and left the room.

The interpreter, the armed Kurds, and the EDS men waited in silence. Coburn thought: What now?

Could Bolourian possibly know that EDS had once had a contract with ISIRAN? If so, would he jump to the conclusion that the EDS men were connected with SAVAK? Or had his question about ISIRAN been a shot in the dark?

In that case had he believed their story about being ordinary businessmen trying to go home?

Opposite Coburn, on the far side of the circle, Bill was feeling strangely at peace. He had peaked out on fear during the questioning, and he was simply incapable of worrying any longer. We've tried our hardest to get out, he thought, and if they put us up against the wall right now and shoot us, so be it.

Bolourian walked back in loading a gun.

Coburn glanced at Simons: his eyes were riveted on the gun.

It was an old M1 carbine that looked like it dated from World War Two.

He can't shoot us all with that, Coburn thought.

Bolourian handed the gun to the interpreter and said something in Farsi.

Coburn gathered his muscles to spring. There would be a hell of a mess if they opened fire in this room—

The interpreter took the gun and said: 'And now you will be our guests, and drink tea.'

Bolourian wrote on a piece of paper and handed it to the interpreter. Coburn realized that Bolourian had simply issued the gun to the interpreter and given him a permit to carry it. 'Christ, I thought he was going to shoot us,' Coburn muttered.

Simon's face was expressionless.

Tea was served.

It was now dark outside. Rashid asked whether there was somewhere the Americans could spend the night. 'You will be our guests,' said the interpreter. 'I will personally look after you.' Coburn thought: For that, he needs a gun? The interpreter went on: 'In the morning, our mullah will write a note to the mullah of Rezaiyeh, asking him to let you pass.'

Coburn murmured to Simons: 'What do you think? Should we stay the night here, or go on?'

'I don't think we have a choice,' Simons said. 'When he said "guests" he was just being polite.'

They drank their tea, and the interpreter said: 'Now we

375

will go and have dinner.'

They got up and put on their shoes. Walking out to their cars, Coburn noticed that Gayden was limping. 'What's the matter with your feet?' he said.

'Not so loud,' Gayden hissed. 'I got all the money stuffed up in the toes of my shoes and my feet are killing me.'

Coburn laughed.

They got into the cars and drove off, still accompanied by Kurdish guards and the interpreter. Gayden surreptitiously eased off his shoes and rearranged the money. They pulled into a filling station. Gayden murmured: 'If they weren't going to let us go, they wouldn't take us to gas up . . . would they?'

Coburn shrugged.

They drove to the town restaurant. The EDS men sat down, and the guards sat at tables around them, forming a rough circle and cutting them off from the townspeople.

A TV set was on, and the Ayatollah was making a speech. Paul thought: Jesus, it had to be now, when we're in trouble, that this guy comes to power. Then the interpreter told him that Khomeini was saying Americans should not be molested, but should be allowed to leave Iran unharmed, and Paul felt better.

They were served chella kebab – lamb with rice. The guards ate heartily, their rifles on the tables beside their plates.

Keane Taylor ate a little rice then put down his spoon. He had a headache: he had been sharing the driving with Rashid, and he felt as if the sun had been in his eyes all day. He was also worried, for it occurred to him that Bolourian might call Tehran during the night to check out EDS. The guards kept telling him, with gestures, to eat, but he sat and nursed a coke.

Coburn was not hungry either. He had recalled that he was supposed to phone Gholam. It was late: they would be worried sick in Dallas. But what should he tell Gholam – that they were okay, or that they were in trouble?

There was some discussion about who should pay the bill

when the meal was over. The guards wanted to pay, Rashid said. The Americans were anxious not to offend by offering to pay when they were supposed to be guests, but also keen to ingratiate themselves with these people. In the end Keane Taylor paid for everyone.

As they were leaving, Coburn said to the interpreter: 'I'd sure like to call Tehran, to let our people know we're all right.'

'Okay,' said the young man.

They drove to the post office. Coburn and the interpreter went in. There was a crowd of people waiting to use the three or four phone booths. The interpreter spoke to someone behind the counter, then told Coburn: 'All the lines to Tehran are busy – it's very difficult to get through.'

'Could we come back later?'

'Okay.'

They drove out of the town in the dark. After a few minutes they stopped at a gate in a fence. The moonlight showed a distant outline of what might have been a dam.

There was a long delay while keys to the gate were found, then they drove in. They found themselves in a small park surrounding an ornate modern two-storey building made of white granite. 'This is one of the Shah's palaces,' the interpreter explained. 'He has used it only once, when he opened the power station. Tonight we will use it.'

They went inside. The place was cosily warm. The interpreter said indignantly: 'The heating has been on for three years just in case the Shah should decide to drop by.'

They all went upstairs and looked at their quarters. There was a luxurious Royal suite with an enormous fancy bathroom, then along the corridor were smaller rooms, each containing two single beds and a bathroom, presumably for the Shah's bodyguard. Under each bed was a pair of slippers.

The Americans moved into the guards' rooms and the revolutionary Kurds took over the Shah's suite. One of them decided to take a bath: the Americans could hear him splashing about, hooting and hollering. After a while he came out. He was the biggest and burliest of them, and he had put on one of the Shah's fancy bathrobes. He came mincing down the corridor while his colleagues fell about laughing. He went up to Gayden and said in heavily-accented English: 'Complete gentleman.' Gayden broke up.

Coburn said to Simons: 'What's the routine for tomorrow?'

'They want to escort us to Rezaiyeh and hand us over to the head man there,' said Simons. 'It'll help to have them with us if we meet any more roadblocks. But when we get to Rezaiyeh, we may be able to persuade them to take us to the professor's house instead of the head man.'

Coburn nodded. 'Okay.'

Rashid looked worried. 'These are bad people,' he whispered. 'Don't trust them. We've got to get out of here.'

Coburn was not sure he trusted the Kurds, but he was quite certain there would be trouble if the Americans tried to leave now.

He noticed that one of the guards had a G3 rifle. 'Hey, that's a real neat firearm,' he said.

The guard smiled and seemed to understand.

'I've never seen one before,' Coburn said. 'How do you load it?'

'Load . . . so,' said the guard, and showed him.

They sat down and the guard explained the rifle. He spoke enough English to make himself understood with the help of gestures.

After a while Coburn realized that *he* was now holding the rifle.

He started to relax.

The others wanted to take showers, but Gayden went first and used all the hot water. Paul took a cold shower: he had sure as hell got used to cold showers lately.

They learned a little about their interpreter. He was studying in Europe and had been home on holiday when the revolution caught him and prevented his going back: that was how come he knew the airport was closed.

At midnight Coburn asked him: 'Can we try to place that call again?'

'Okay.'

One of the guards escorted Coburn back into town. They went to the post office, which was still open. However, there were no lines to Tehran.

Coburn waited until two o'clock in the morning, then gave up.

When he returned to the palace beside the dam, everyone was fast asleep.

He went to bed. At least they were all still alive. That was enough to be thankful for. Nobody knew what was between them and the border. He would worry about that tomorrow.

Twelve

1

'Wake up, Coburn, let's move, let's go!'

Simons's gravelly voice penetrated Coburn's slumber and he opened his eyes, thinking: where am I?

In the Shah's palace at Mahabad.

Oh, shit.

He got up.

Simons was getting the Dirty Team ready to go, but there was no sign of their guards: apparently they were all still asleep. The Americans made plenty of noise, and eventually the Kurds emerged from the Royal suite.

Simons said to Rashid: 'Tell them we're in a hurry, our friends are waiting at the border for us.'

Rashid told them, then said: 'We have to wait.'

Simons did not like this. 'What for?'

'They all want to take showers.'

Keane Taylor said: 'I don't see the urgency – most of them haven't taken a shower in a year or two, you'd think they could wait another day.'

Simons contained his impatience for half an hour, then told Rashid to tell the guards again that the team had to hurry.

'We have to see the Shah's bathroom,' Rashid said.

'Goddamn it, we've seen it,' said Simons. 'What's the delay?'

Everyone trooped into the Royal suite and dutifully exclaimed at the shameful luxury of an unused palace; and still the guards would not move out.

Coburn wondered what was happening. Had they changed their minds about escorting the Americans to the next town?

Had Bolourian checked up on EDS during the night? Simons would not be kept here much longer . . .

Finally the young interpreter showed up, and it turned out the guards had been waiting for him. The plan was unchanged: a group of Kurds would go with the Americans on the next leg of their journey.

Simons said: 'We have friends in Rezaiyeh – we'd like to be taken to their house, rather than go see the head man of the town.'

'It's not safe,' said the interpreter. 'The fighting is heavy north of here – the city of Tabriz is still in the hands of the Shah's supporters. I must hand you over to people who can protect you.'

'All right, but can we leave now?'

'Sure.'

They left.

They drove into the town and were ordered to stop outside a house. The interpreter went in. They all waited. Somebody brought bread and cream cheese for breakfast. Coburn got out of his car and went to Simons's. 'What's happening now?'

'This is the mullah's house,' Rashid explained. 'He is writing a letter to the mullah of Rezaiyeh, about us.'

It was about an hour before the interpreter came out with the promised letter.

Next they drove to the police station, and there they saw their escort vehicle: a big white ambulance with a flashing red light on top, its windows knocked out, and some kind of identification scrawled on its side in Farsi with red magic marker, presumably saying 'Mahabad Revolutionary Committee' or something similar. It was full of gun-toting Kurds.

So much for travelling inconspicuously.

At last they got on the road, the ambulance leading the way.

Simons was anxious about Dadgar. Clearly no one in Mahabad had been alerted to look out for Paul and Bill, but Rezaiyeh was a much bigger town. Simons did not know

381

whether Dadgar's authority extended into the countryside: all he knew was that so far Dadgar had always surprised everyone by his dedication and his ability to persist through changes of government. Simons wished the team did not have to be taken before the Rezaiyeh authorities.

'We have good friends in Rezaiyeh,' he told the young interpreter. 'If you could take us to their house, we'd be very safe there.'

'Oh, no,' said the interpreter. 'If I disobey orders and you get hurt, there will be hell to pay.'

Simons gave up. It was clear they were as much prisoners as guests of the Kurds. The revolution in Mahabad was characterized by communist discipline rather than Islamic anarchy, and the only way to get rid of the escort would be by violence. Simons was not yet ready to start a fight.

Just outside the town, the ambulance pulled off the road and stopped at a little cafe.

'Why are we stopping?' Simons said.

'Breakfast,' said the interpreter.

'We don't need breakfast,' Simons said forcefully.

'But—'

'We don't need breakfast!'

The interpreter shrugged, and shouted something to the Kurds getting out of the ambulance. They got back in and the convoy drove on.

They reached the outskirts of Rezaiyeh late in the morning.

Their way was barred by the inevitable roadblock. This one was a serious, military-style affair of parked vehicles, sandbags and barbed wire. The convoy slowed, and an armed guard waved them off the road and into the forecourt of a filling station which had been turned into a command post. The approach road was well covered by machine guns in the filling station building.

The ambulance failed to stop soon enough and ran right into the barbed-wire fence.

The two Range Rovers pulled up in an orderly fashion.

The ambulance was immediately surrounded by guards,

and an argument started. Rashid and the interpreter went over to join in. The Rezaiyeh revolutionaries did not automatically assume that the Mahabad revolutionaries were on their side. The Rezaiyeh men were Azerbaijainis, not Kurds, and the argument took place in Turkish as well as Farsi.

The Kurds were being ordered to turn in their weapons, it seemed, and they were refusing angrily. The interpreter was showing the note from the Mahabad mullah. Nobody was taking much notice of Rashid, who was suddenly an outsider.

Eventually the interpreter and Rashid came back to the cars. 'We're going to take you to a hotel,' said the interpreter. 'Then I will go and see the mullah.'

The ambulance was all tangled up in the barbed-wire fence, and had to be extracted before they could go. Guards from the roadblock escorted them into the town.

It was a large town by the standards of the Iranian provinces. It had plenty of concrete and stone buildings and a few paved roads. The convoy pulled up in a main street. Distant shouting could be heard. Rashid and the interpreter went into a building – presumably a hotel – and the others waited.

Coburn felt optimistic. You didn't put prisoners into a hotel before shooting them. This was just administrative hassle.

The distant shouting grew louder, and a crowd appeared at the end of the street.

In the rear car, Coburn said: 'What the hell is this?'

The Kurds jumped out of their ambulance and surrounded the two Range Rovers, forming a wedge in front of the lead car. One of them pointed to Coburn's door and made a motion like turning a key. 'Lock the doors,' Coburn said to the others.

The crowd came closer. It was some kind of street parade, Coburn realized. At the head of the procession were a number of army officers in tattered uniforms. One of them was in tears. 'You know what I think?' said Coburn. 'The army just surrendered, and they're running the officers down Main Street.'

The vengeful crowd surged around the vehicles, jostling the Kurdish guards and looking through the windows with hostile glares. The Kurds stood their ground and tried to push the crowds away from the cars. It looked as though it would turn into a fight at any moment. 'This is getting ugly,' said Gayden. Coburn kept an eye on the car in front, wondering what Simons would do.

Coburn saw the snout of a gun aimed at the window on the driver's side. 'Paul, don't look now, but someone's pointing a gun at your head.'

'Jesus . . .'

Coburn could imagine what would happen next: the mob would start rocking the cars, then they would turn them over . . .

Then, suddenly, it ended. The defeated soldiers were the main attraction, and as they passed on the crowd followed. Coburn relaxed. Paul said: 'For a minute, there . . .'

Rashid and the interpreter came out of the hotel. Rashid said: 'They don't want to know about a bunch of Americans going into their hotel – they won't take the risk.' Coburn took that to mean that feelings were running so high in the town that the hotel could get burned by the mob for taking in foreigners. 'We have to go to revolutionary headquarters.'

They drove on. There was feverish activity in the streets: lines of pick-up trucks of all shapes and sizes were being loaded with supplies, presumably for the revolutionaries still fighting in Tabriz. The convoy stopped at what appeared to be a school. There was a huge, noisy crowd outside the courtyard, apparently waiting to get in. After an argument, the Kurds persuaded the sentry to admit the ambulance and the two Range Rovers. The crowd reacted angrily when the foreigners went in. Coburn breathed a sigh of relief as the courtyard gate closed behind him.

They got out of the cars. The courtyard was crammed with shot-up automobiles. A mullah was standing on a stack of rifle crates conducting a noisy and passionate ceremony with a crowd of men. Rashid said: 'He is swearing-in fresh troops to go to Tabriz and fight for the revolution.'

The guards led the Americans towards the school building on one side of the courtyard. A man came down the steps and started yelling at them angrily, pointing at the Kurds. 'They must not go into the building armed,' Rashid translated.

Coburn could tell the Kurds were getting jumpy: to their surprise they found themselves in hostile territory. They produced the note from the Mahabad mullah. There was more argument.

Eventually Rashid said: 'You all wait here. I'm going inside to talk to the leader of the revolutionary committee.' He went up the steps and disappeared.

Paul and Gayden lit cigarettes. Paul felt scared and dejected. These people were bound to call Tehran, he felt, and find out all about him. Getting sent back to jail might be the least of his worries now. He said to Gayden: 'I really appreciate what you've done for me, but it's a shame, I think we've had it.'

Coburn was more worried about the mob outside the gate. In here, at least someone was trying to maintain order. Out there was a wolf pack. What if they persuaded some goofy guard to open the gate? It would be a lynch mob. In Tehran a fellow – an Iranian – who had done something to anger a crowd had been literally pulled apart, his arms and legs torn off by people who were just crazed, hysterical.

The guards jerked their weapons, indicating that the Americans should move to one side of the courtyard and stand against the wall. They obeyed, feeling vulnerable. Coburn looked at the wall. It had bullet holes in it. Paul had seen them too, and his face was white. 'My God,' he said. 'I think we bought the farm.'

Rashid asked himself: what will be the psychology of the leader of the revolutionary committee?

He has a million things to do, Rashid thought. He has just taken control of this town, and he has never been in power before. He must deal with the officers of the defeated army, he must round up suspected SAVAK agents and interrogate them, he must get the town running normally, he must guard against a counter-revolution, and he must send troops to fight in Tabriz.

All he wants to do, Rashid concluded, is *cross things off his list*.

He has no time or sympathy for fleeing Americans. If he must make a decision, he will simply throw us in jail for the time being, and deal with us later, at his leisure. Therefore I must make sure that he does not decide.

Rashid was shown into a schoolroom. The leader was sitting on the floor. He was a tall, strong man with the thrill of victory in his face; but he looked exhausted, confused and restless.

Rashid's escort said in Farsi: 'This man comes from Mahabad with a letter from the mullah – he has six Americans with him.'

Rashid thought of a movie he had seen in which a man got into a guarded building by flashing his driving licence instead of a pass. If you had enough confidence you could undermine people's suspicions.

'No, I come from the Tehran Revolutionary Committee,' Rashid said. 'There are five or six thousand Americans in Tehran, and we have decided to send them home. The airport is closed, so we will bring them all out this way. Obviously we must make arrangements and set up procedures for handling all these people. That is why I am here. But you have many problems to deal with – perhaps I should discuss the details with your subordinates.'

'Yes,' said the leader, and waved them away.

'I'm the deputy leader,' said Rashid's escort as they left the room. They went into another room where five or six people were drinking tea. Rashid talked to the deputy leader, loud enough for the others to hear. 'These Americans just want to get home and see their families. We're happy to get rid of them, and we want to treat them right so they won't have anything against the new regime.'

'Why do you have Americans with you now?' the deputy asked.

386

'For a trial run. This way, you know, we find out what the problems are . . .'

'But you don't have to let them cross the border.'

'Oh, yes. They are good men who have never done any harm to our country, and they have wives and children at home – one of them has a little child dying in hospital. So the Revolutionary Committee in Tehran has instructed me to see them across the border . . .'

He kept talking. From time to time the deputy would interrupt him with a question. Who did the Americans work for? What did they have with them? How did Rashid know they were not SAVAK agents spying for the counter-revolutionaries in Tabriz? For every question Rashid had an answer, and a long one. While he was talking, he could be persuasive; whereas if he were silent the others would have time to think of objections. People came in and went out continually. The deputy left three or four times.

Eventually he came in and said: 'I have to clear this with Tehran.'

Rashid's heart sank. Of course nobody in Tehran would verify his story. But it would take forever to get a call through. 'Everything has been verified in Tehran, and there is no need to re-verify,' he said. 'But if you insist, I'll take these Americans to a hotel to wait.' He added: 'You had better send some guards with us.' The deputy would have sent the guards anyway: asking for them was a way of allaying suspicion.

'I don't know,' said the deputy.

'This is not a good place to keep them,' Rashid said. 'It could cause trouble. They might be harmed.' He held his breath. Here they were trapped. In a hotel, they would at least have the chance to make a break of the border . . .

'Okay,' said the deputy.

Rashid concealed his relief.

Paul was deeply grateful to see Rashid coming down the steps of the schoolhouse. It had been a long wait. Nobody had actually pointed guns at them, but they had got an awful lot of hostile looks.

'We can go to the hotel,' said Rashid.

The Kurds from Mahabad shook hands with them and left in their ambulance. A few moments later the Americans left in the two Range Rovers, followed by four or five armed guards in another car. They drove to the hotel. This time they all went in. There was an argument between the hotel keeper and the guards, but the guards won, and the Americans were assigned four rooms on the third floor at the back, and told to keep the curtains drawn and stay away from windows in case local snipers thought Americans inviting targets.

They gathered in one of the rooms. They could hear distant gunfire. Rashid organized lunch and ate with them: barbecued chicken, rice, bread and coke. Then he left for the school.

The guards wandered in and out of the room, carrying their rifles. One of them struck Coburn as being evil. He was young, short and muscular, with black hair and eyes like a snake. As the afternoon wore on he seemed to get bored.

One time he walked in and said: 'Carter no good.'

He looked around for a reaction.

'CIA no good,' he said. 'America no good.'

Nobody replied. He went out.

'That guy is trouble,' Simons said calmly. 'Don't anybody take the bait.'

The guard tried again a little later. 'I am very strong,' he said. 'Wrestling. Wrestle champion. I went to Russia.'

Nobody spoke.

He sat down and fiddled with his gun, as if he did not know how to load it. He appealed to Coburn. 'You know guns?'

Coburn shook his head.

The guard looked at the others. 'You know guns?'

The gun was an M1, a weapon they were all familiar with, but nobody said anything.

'You want to trade?' the guard said. 'This gun for a backpack?'

Coburn said: 'We don't have a backpack and we don't want a gun.'

The guard gave up and went into the corridor again.

Simons said: 'Where the hell is Rashid?'

2

The car hit a pothole, jolting Ralph Boulware awake. He felt tired and groggy after his short, restless sleep. He looked through the windows. It was early morning. He saw the shore of a vast lake, so big he could not see the far side.

'Where are we?' he said.

'That's Lake Van,' said Charlie Brown, the interpreter.

There were houses and villages and civilian cars: they had come out of the wild mountain country and returned to what passed for civilization in this part of the world. Boulware looked at a map. He figured they were about a hundred miles from the border.

'Hey, this is good!' he said.

He saw a filling station. They really were back in civilization. 'Let's get gas,' he said.

At the filling station they got bread and coffee. The coffee was almost as good as a shower: Boulware felt raring to go. He said to Charlie: 'Tell the old man I want to drive.'

The cabbie had been doing thirty or forty miles per hour, but Boulware pushed the ancient Chevrolet up to seventy. It looked like he had a real chance of getting to the border in time to meet Simons.

Bowling along the lakeside road, Boulware heard a muffled bang, followed by a tearing sound; then the car began to buck and bump, and there was a screech of metal on stone: he had blown a tyre.

He braked hard, cursing.

They all got out and looked at the wheel: Boulware, the elderly cabbie, Charlie Brown, and fat Ilsman. The tyre was completely shredded and the wheel deformed. And they had used the spare wheel during the night, after the last blowout.

Boulware looked more closely. The wheel nuts had been

389

stripped: even if they could get another spare, they would not be able to remove the damaged wheel.

Boulware looked around. There was a house a way up the hill. 'Let's go there,' Boulware said. 'We can phone.'

Charlie Brown shook his head. 'No phones around here.'

Boulware was not about to give up, after all he had gone through: he was too close. 'Okay,' he said to Charlie. 'Hitch a ride back to the last town and get us another cab.'

Charlie started walking. Two cars passed him without stopping, then a truck pulled up. It had hay and a bunch of children in the back. Charlie jumped in, and the truck drove out of sight.

Boulware, Ilsman and the cabbie stood looking at the lake, eating oranges.

An hour later a small European station wagon came tearing along the road and screeched to a halt. Charlie jumped out.

Boulware gave the driver from Adana five hundred dollars then got into the new taxi with Ilsman and Charlie and drove off, leaving the Chevrolet beside the lake, looking like a beached whale.

The new driver went like the wind, and by midday they were in Van, on the eastern shore of the lake. Van was a small town, with brick buildings in the centre and mud-hut suburbs. Ilsman directed the driver to the home of a cousin of Mr Fish.

They paid their driver and went in. Ilsman got into a long discussion with Mr Fish's cousin. Boulware sat in the living room, listening but not understanding, impatient to get moving. After an hour he said to Charlie: 'Listen, let's just get another cab, we don't need the cousin.'

'It's a very bad place between here and the border,' Charlie said. 'We're foreigners, we need protection.'

Boulware forced himself to be patient.

At last Ilsman shook hands with Mr Fish's cousin and Charlie said: 'His sons will take us to the border.'

There were two sons and two cars.

They drove up into the mountains. Boulware saw no sign of the dangerous bandits against whom he was being protected: just snow-covered fields, scrawny goats, and a few ragged people living in hovels.

They were stopped by the police in the village of Yuksekova, a few miles from the border, and ordered into the little whitewashed police station. Ilsman showed his credentials and they were quickly released. Boulware was impressed. Maybe Ilsman really was with the Turkish equivalent of the CIA.

They reached the border at four o'clock on Thursday afternoon, having been on the road for twenty-four hours.

The border station was in the middle of nowhere. The guard post consisted of two wooden buildings. There was also a post office. Boulware wondered who the hell used it. Truck drivers, perhaps. Two hundred yards away, on the Iranian side, was a bigger cluster of buildings.

There was no sign of the Dirty Team.

Boulware felt angry. He had broken his neck to get here more or less on time: where the hell was Simons?

A guard came out of one of the huts and approached him, saying: 'Are you looking for the Americans?'

Boulware was surprised. The whole thing was supposed to be top secret. It looked like security had gone all to hell. 'Yes,' he said. 'I'm looking for the Americans.'

'There's a phone call for you.'

Boulware was even more surprised. 'No kidding!' The timing was phenomenal. Who the hell knew he was here?

He followed the guard into the hut and picked up the phone. 'Yes?'

'This is the American Consulate,' said the voice. 'What's your name?'

'Uh, what is this about?' Boulware said warily.

'Look, would you just tell me what you're doing there?'

'I don't know who you are and I'm not going to tell you what I'm doing.'

'Okay, listen, I know who you are and I know what you're doing. If you have any problems, call me. Got a pencil?'

Boulware took down the number, thanked the man, and hung up, mystified. An hour ago I didn't know I was going to be here, he thought, so how could anyone else? Least of all the American Consulate. He thought again about Ilsman. Maybe Ilsman was in touch with his bosses, the Turkish MIT, who were in touch with the CIA, who were in touch with the Consulate. Ilsman could have asked somebody to make a call for him in Van, or even at the police station in Yuksekova.

He wondered whether it was good or bad that the Consulate knew what was happening. He recalled the 'help' Paul and Bill had got from the US Embassy in Tehran: with friends in the State Department a man had no need of enemies.

He pushed the Consulate to the back of his mind. The main problem now was, where was the Dirty Team?

He went back outside and looked across no-man's-land. He decided to stroll across and talk to the Iranians. He called to Ilsman and Charlie Brown to come with him.

As he approached the Iranian side he could see that the frontier guards were not in uniform. Presumably they were revolutionaries who had taken over when the government fell.

He said to Charlie: 'Ask them if they've heard anything about some American businessmen coming out in two jeeps.'

Charlie did not need to translate the reply: the Iranians shook their heads vigorously.

An inquisitive tribesman, with a ragged headband and an ancient rifle, came up on the Iranian side. There was an exchange of some length, then Charlie said: 'This man says he knows where the Americans are and he will take you to them if you pay.'

Boulware wanted to know how much, but Ilsman did not want him to accept the offer at any price. Ilsman spoke forcefully to Charlie, and Charlie translated. 'You're wearing a leather coat and leather gloves and a fine wristwatch.'

Boulware, who was into watches, was wearing one Mary had given him when they got married. 'So?'

'With clothes like that they think you're SAVAK. They

392

hate SAVAK over there.'

'I'll change my clothes. I have another coat in the car.'

'No,' Charlie said. 'You have to understand, they just want to get you over there and blow your head off.'

'All right,' Boulware said.

They walked back to the Turkish side. Since there was a post office so conveniently nearby, he decided to call Istanbul and check in with Ross Perot. He went into the post office. He had to sign his name. The call would take some time to place, the clerk told him.

Boulware went back outside. The Turkish border guards were now getting edgy, Charlie told him. Some of the Iranians had wandered back with them, and the guards did not like people milling around in no-man's-land: it was disorderly.

Boulware thought: Well, I'm doing no good here.

He said: 'Would these guys call us, if the team comes across while we're back in Yuksekova?'

Charlie asked them. The guards agreed. There was a hotel in the village, they said; they would call there.

Boulware, Ilsman, Charlie and the two sons of Mr Fish's cousin got into the two cars and drove back to Yuksekova.

There they checked in to the worst hotel in the whole world. It had dirt floors. The bathroom was a hole in the ground under the stairs. All the beds were in one room. Charlie Brown ordered food, and it came wrapped in newspaper.

Boulware was not sure he had made the right decision in leaving the border station. So many things could go wrong: the guards might not phone as they had promised. He decided to accept the offer of help from the American Consulate, and ask them to seek permission for him to stay at the border station. He called the number he had been given on the hotel's single ancient wind-up telephone. He got through, but the line was bad, and both parties had trouble making themselves understood. Eventually the man at the other end said something about calling back, and hung up.

Boulware stood by the fire, fretting. After a while he lost patience, and decided to return to the border without permission.

On the way they had a flat tyre.

They all stood in the road while the sons changed the wheel. Ilsman appeared nervous. Charlie explained: 'He says this is a very dangerous place, the people are all murderers and bandits.'

Boulware was sceptical. Ilsman had agreed to do all this for a flat fee of eight thousand dollars, and Boulware now suspected the fat man was getting ready to up his price. 'Ask him how many people were killed on this road last month,' Boulware told Charlie.

He watched Ilsman's face as he replied. Charlie translated: 'Thirty-nine.'

Ilsman looked serious. Boulware thought: shit, this guy's telling the goddam *truth*. He looked around. Mountains, snow . . . He shivered.

3

In Rezaiyeh, Rashid took one of the Range Rovers and drove from the hotel back to the school which had been turned into revolutionary headquarters.

He wondered whether the deputy leader had called Tehran. Coburn had been unable to get a line, the previous night: would the revolutionary leadership have the same problem? Rashid thought they probably would. Now, if the deputy could not get through, what would he want to do? He had only two options: hold the Americans, or let them go without checking. The man might feel foolish about letting them go without checking: he might not want Rashid to know that things were so loosely organized here. Rashid decided to act as if he assumed the call had been made and verification completed.

He went into the courtyard. The deputy leader was there, leaning against a Mercedes. Rashid started talking to him about the problem of bringing six thousand Americans through the town on the way to the border. How many people could be accommodated overnight in Rezaiyeh? What facilities were there at the Sero border station for processing them? He emphasized that the Ayatollah Khomeini had given instructions for Americans to be well treated as they left Iran, for the new government did not want to quarrel with the USA. He got on to the subject of documentation: perhaps the Rezaiyeh committee should issue passes to the Americans authorizing them to go through Sero. He, Rashid, would certainly need such a pass today, to take these six Americans through. He suggested the deputy and he should go into the school and draft a pass.

The deputy agreed.

They went into the library.

Rashid found paper and pen and gave them to the deputy.

'What should we write?' said Rashid. 'Probably we should say, the person who carries this letter can take six Americans through Sero. No, say Barzagan or Sero, in case Sero is closed.'

The deputy wrote.

'Maybe we should say, um, "It is expected that all guards will give their best co-operation and assistance, they are fully inspected and identified, and if necessary escort them."'

The deputy wrote it down.

Then he signed his name.

Rashid said: 'Maybe we should put, "Islamic Revolution Commandant Committee."'

The deputy did so.

Rashid looked at the document. It seemed somewhat inadequate, improvised. It needed something to make it look official. He found a rubber stamp and an inking pad, and stamped the letter. Then he read what the stamp said: 'Library of the School of Religion, Rezaiyeh. Founded 1344.'

Rashid put the document in his pocket.

'We should probably print six thousand of these, so they can just be signed,' he said.

The deputy nodded.

'We can talk some more about these arrangements tomorrow,' Rashid went on. 'I'd like to go to Sero now, to discuss the problem with the border officials there.'

'Okay.'

Rashid walked away.

Nothing was impossible.

He got into the Range Rover. It was a good idea to go to the border, he decided: he could find out what the problems might be before making the trip with the Americans.

On the outskirts of Rezaiyeh was a roadblock manned by teenage boys with rifles. They gave Rashid no trouble, but he worried about how they might react to six Americans: the kids were evidently itching to use their guns.

After that the road was clear. It was a dirt road, but smooth enough, and he made good speed. He picked up a hitch-hiker and asked him about crossing the border on horseback. No problem, said the hitch-hiker. It could be done, and as it happened, his brother had horses . . .

Rashid did the forty-mile journey in a little over an hour. He pulled up at the border station in his Range Rover. The guards were suspicious of him. He showed them the pass written by the deputy leader. The guards called Rezaiyeh and – they said – spoke to the deputy, who vouched for Rashid.

He stood looking across to Turkey. It was a pleasant sight. They had all been through a lot of anguish just to walk across there. For Paul and Bill it would mean freedom, home and family. For all the EDS men it would be the end of a nightmare. For Rashid it meant something else: America.

He understood the psychology of EDS executives. They had a strong sense of obligation. If you helped them, they liked to show their appreciation, to keep the books balanced. He knew he only had to ask, and they would take him with them to the land of his dreams.

The border station was under the control of the village of Sero, just half a mile away down a mountain track. Rashid decided he would go and see the village chief, to establish a friendly relationship and smooth the way for later.

He was about to turn away when two cars drove up on the Turkish side. A tall black man in a leather coat got out of the first car and came to the chain on the edge of no-man's-land.

Rashid's heart leaped. He knew that man! He started waving and yelled: 'Ralph! Ralph Boulware! Hey, Ralph!'

4

Thursday morning found Glenn Jackson – hunter, Baptist and Rocket Man – in the skies over Tehran in a chartered jet.

Jackson had stayed in Kuwait after reporting on the possibility of Paul and Bill coming out of Iran that way. On Sunday, the day Paul and Bill got out of jail, Simons had sent orders, via Merv Stauffer, that Jackson was to go to Amman, Jordan, and there try to charter a plane to fly into Iran.

Jackson had reached Amman on Monday and had gone to work straight away. He knew that Perot had flown into Tehran from Amman on a chartered jet of Arab Wings. He also knew that the president of Arab Wings, Akel Biltaji, had been helpful, allowing Perot to go in with NBC's television tapes as a cover. Now Jackson contacted Biltaji and asked for his help again.

He told Biltaji that EDS had two men in Iran who had to be brought out. He invented false names for Paul and Bill. Even though Tehran Airport was closed, Jackson wanted to fly in and try to land. Biltaji was willing to give it a try.

However, on Wednesday Stauffer – on Simons's instructions – changed Jackson's orders. Now his mission was to check on the Clean Team: the Dirty Team was no longer in Tehran, as far as Dallas knew.

On Thursday Jackson took off from Amman and headed east.

As they came down towards the bowl in the mountains where Tehran nestled, two aircraft took off from the city.

The planes came closer, and Jackson saw that they were

fighter jets of the Iranian Air Force.

He wondered what would happen next.

His pilot's radio came to life with a burst of static. As the fighters circled, the pilot talked. Jackson could not understand the conversation, but he was glad the Iranians were talking rather than shooting.

The discussion went on. The pilot seemed to be arguing. Eventually he turned to Jackson and said: 'We have to go back. They won't let us land.'

'What will they do if we land anyway?'

'Shoot us down.'

'Okay,' said Jackson. 'We'll try again this afternoon.'

On Thursday morning in Istanbul, an English-language newspaper was delivered to Perot's suite at the Sheraton.

He picked it up and eagerly read the front-page story about yesterday's takeover of the American Embassy in Tehran. None of the Clean Team was mentioned, he was relieved to see. The only injury had been suffered by a Marine Sergeant, Kenneth Krause. However, Krause was not getting the medical attention he needed, according to the newspaper.

Perot called John Carlen, the captain of the Boeing 707, and asked him to come to the suite. He showed Carlen the newspaper and said: 'How would you feel about flying in to Tehran tonight and picking up the wounded Marine?'

Carlen, a laid-back Californian with greying hair and a tan, was very cool. 'We can do that,' he said.

Perot was surprised that Carlen did not even hesitate. He would have to fly through the mountains at night with no air traffic control to help him, and land at a closed airport. 'Don't you want to talk to the rest of the crew?' Perot asked.

'No, they'll want to do it. The people who own the airplane will go bananas.'

'Don't tell them. I'll be responsible.'

'I'll need to know exactly where that Marine is going to be,' Carlen went on. 'The Embassy will have to get him to the airport. I know a lot of people at that airport – I can talk my way out again or just take off.'

Perot thought: And the Clean Team will be the stretcher bearers.

He called Dallas and reached Sally Walther, his secretary. He asked her to patch him through to General Wilson, Commandant of the Marine Corps. He and Wilson were friends.

Wilson came on the line.

'I'm in Turkey on business,' Perot told him. 'I've just read about Sergeant Krause. I have a plane here. If the Embassy can get Krause to the airport, we will fly in tonight and pick him up and see he gets proper medical care.'

'All right,' said Wilson. 'If he's dying I want you to pick him up. If not, I won't risk your crew. I'll get back to you.'

Perot got Sally back on the line. There was more bad news. A press officer in the State Department's Iran Task Force had talked to Robert Dudney, Washington correspondent for the *Dallas Times Herald*, and revealed that Paul and Bill were on their way out overland.

Perot cursed the State Department yet again. If Dudney published the story, and the news reached Tehran, Dadgar would surely intensify border security.

The seventh floor in Dallas blamed Perot for all this. He had levelled with the consul who had come to see him the night before, and they believed the leak started with the consul. They were now frantically trying to get the story killed, but the newspaper was making no promises.

General Wilson called back. Sergeant Krause was not dying: Perot's help was not required.

Perot forgot about Krause and concentrated on his own problems.

The consul called him. He had tried his best, but he could not help Perot buy or rent a small aircraft. It was possible to charter a plane to go from one airport to another within Turkey, but that was all.

Perot said nothing to him about the press leak.

He called in Dick Douglas and Julian 'Scratch' Kanauch, the two spare pilots he had brought specifically to fly small

399

aircraft into Iran, and told them he had failed to find any such aircraft.

'Don't worry,' said Douglas. 'We'll get an airplane.'

'How?'

'Don't ask.'

'No, I want to know how.'

'I've operated in Eastern Turkey. I know where there are planes. If you need 'em, we'll steal 'em.'

'Have you thought this through?' said Perot.

'You think it through,' Douglas said. 'If we get shot down over Iran, what difference does it make that we stole the plane? If we don't get shot down, we can put the planes back where we got them. Even if they have a few holes in them, we'll be out of the area before anybody knows. What else is there to think about?'

'That settles it,' said Perot. 'We're going.'

He sent John Carlen and Ron Davis to the airport to file a flight plan to Van, the nearest airport to the border.

Davis called from the airport to say that the 707 could not land at Van: it was a Turkish-language-only airport, so *no* foreign planes were allowed to land except US military planes carrying interpreters.

Perot called Mr Fish and asked him to arrange to fly the team to Van. Mr Fish called back a few minutes later to say it was all fixed. He would go with the team as guide. Perot was surprised: until now Mr Fish had been adamant that he would not go to Eastern Turkey. Perhaps he had become infected by the spirit of adventure.

However, Perot himself would have to stay behind. He was the hub of the wheel: he had to stay in telephone contact with the outside world, to receive reports from Boulware, from Dallas, from the Clean Team and from the Dirty Team. If the 707 had been able to land at Van, Perot could have gone, for the plane's single-sideband radio enabled him to make phone calls all over the world; but without that radio he would be out of touch in Eastern Turkey, and there would be no link between the fugitives in Iran and the people who were coming to meet them.

400

So he sent Pat Sculley, Jim Schwebach, Ron Davis, Mr Fish, and the pilots Dick Douglas and Julian Kanauch to Van; and he appointed Pat Sculley leader of the Turkish Rescue Team.

When they had gone he was dead in the water again. They were just another bunch of his men off doing dangerous things in dangerous places. He could only sit and wait for news.

He spent a lot of time thinking about John Carlen and the crew of the Boeing 707. He had only known them for a few days: they were ordinary Americans. Yet Carlen had been prepared to risk his life to fly into Tehran and pick up a wounded Marine. As Simons would say: This is what Americans are supposed to do for one another. It made Perot feel pretty good, despite everything.

The phone rang.

He answered. 'Ross Perot.'

'This is Ralph Boulware.'

'Hi, Ralph, where are you?'

'I'm at the border.'

'Good!'

'I've just seen Rashid.'

Perot's heart leaped. 'Great! What did he say?'

'They're safe.'

'Thank God!'

'They're in a hotel, thirty or forty miles from the border. Rashid is just scouting the territory in advance. He's gone back now. He says they'll probably cross tomorrow, but that's just his idea, and Simons might think otherwise. If they're that close I don't see Simons waiting until morning.'

'Right. Now, Pat Sculley and Mr Fish and the rest of the guys are on their way to you. They're flying to Van, then they'll rent a bus. Now where will they find you?'

'I'm based in a village called Yuksekova, closest place to the border, at a hotel. It's the only hotel in the district.'

'I'll tell Sculley.'

'Okay.'

401

Perot hung up. Oh, boy, he thought; at last things were beginning to go right!

Pat Sculley's orders from Perot were to go to the border, ensure that the Dirty Team got across safely, and bring them to Istanbul. If the Dirty Team failed to reach the border, he was to go into Iran and find them, preferably in a plane stolen by Dick Douglas, or failing that by road.

Sculley and the Turkish Rescue Team took a scheduled flight from Istanbul to Ankara, where the chartered jet was waiting for them. (The charter plane would take them to Van and bring them back: it would not go anywhere they pleased. The only way of making the pilot take them into Iran would have been to hijack the plane.)

The arrival of the jet seemed to be a big event in the town of Van. Getting off the plane, they were met by a contingent of policemen who looked ready to give them a hard time. But Mr Fish went into a huddle with the police chief and came out smiling.

'Now, listen,' said Mr Fish. 'We're going to check in to the best hotel in town, but I want you to know it's not the Sheraton, so please don't complain.'

They went off in two taxis.

The hotel had a high central hall with three floors of rooms reached via galleries, so that every room door could be seen from the hall. When the Americans walked in the hall was full of Turks, drinking beer and watching a soccer match on a black and white TV, yelling and cheering. As the Turks noticed the strangers, the room quietened down until there was complete silence.

They were assigned rooms. Each bedroom had two cots and a hole in the corner, screened by a shower curtain, for a toilet. There were plank floors and whitewashed walls without windows. The rooms were infested with cockroaches. On each floor was one bathroom.

Sculley and Mr Fish went to get a bus to take them all to the border. A Mercedes picked them up outside the hotel

402

and took them to what appeared to be an electrical appliance store with a few ancient TV sets in the window. The place was closed – it was evening by now – but Mr Fish banged on the iron grille protecting the windows, and someone came out.

They went into the back and sat at a table under a single light bulb. Sculley understood none of the conversation, but by the end of it Mr Fish had negotiated a bus and a driver. They returned to the hotel in the bus.

The rest of the team were gathered in Sculley's room. Nobody wanted to sit on these beds, let alone sleep in them. They all wanted to leave for the border immediately, but Mr Fish was hesitant. 'It's two o'clock in the morning,' he said. 'And the police are watching the hotel.'

'Does that matter?' said Sculley.

'It means more questions, more trouble.'

'Let's give it a try.'

They all trooped downstairs. The manager appeared, looking anxious, and started to question Mr Fish. Then, sure enough, two policemen came in from outside and joined in the discussion.

Mr Fish turned to Sculley and said: 'They don't want us to go.'

'Why not?'

'We look very suspicious, don't you realize that?'

'Look, is it against the law for us to go?'

'No, but—'

'Then we're going. Just tell them.'

There was more argument in Turkish, but finally the policemen and the hotel manager appeared to give in, and the team boarded the bus.

They left town. The temperature dropped rapidly as they drove up into the snow-covered hills. They all had warm coats, and blankets in their backpacks, and they needed them.

Mr Fish sat next to Sculley and said: 'This is where it gets serious. I can handle the police, because I have ties with

403

them; but I'm worried about the bandits and the soldiers – I have no connections there.'

'What d'you want to do?'

'I believe I can talk my way out of trouble so long as none of you have guns.'

Sculley considered. Only Davis was armed anyway; and Simons had always worried that weapons could get you into trouble more readily than they could get you out of it: the Walther PPKs had never left Dallas. 'Okay,' Sculley said.

Ron Davis threw his .38 out of the window into the snow.

A little later the headlights of the bus revealed a soldier in uniform standing in the middle of the road, waving. The bus driver kept right on going, as if he intended to run the man down, but Mr Fish yelled and the driver pulled up.

Looking out of the window, Sculley saw a platoon of soldiers armed with high-powered rifles on the mountainside, and thought: If we hadn't stopped, we'd have been mown down.

A sergeant and a corporal got on the bus. They checked all the passports. Mr Fish offered them cigarettes. They stood talking to him while they smoked, then they waved and got off.

A few miles farther on, the bus was stopped again, and they went through a similar routine.

The third time, the men who got on the bus had no uniforms. Mr Fish became very jumpy. 'Act casual,' he hissed at the Americans. 'Read books, just don't look at these guys.' He talked to the Turks for something like half an hour, and when the bus was finally allowed to proceed, two of them stayed on it. 'Protection,' Mr Fish said enigmatically, and he shrugged.

Sculley was nominally in charge, but there was little he could do other than follow Mr Fish's directions. He did not know the country, nor did he speak the language: most of the time he had no idea what was going on. It was hard to have control under those circumstances. The best he could do, he figured, was to keep Mr Fish pointed in the right direction and lean on him a little when he began to lose his nerve.

At four o'clock in the morning they reached Yuksekova, the nearest village to the border station. Here, according to Mr Fish's cousin in Van, they would find Ralph Boulware.

Sculley and Mr Fish went into the hotel. It was dark as a barn and smelled like the men's room at a football stadium. They yelled for a while, and a boy appeared with a candle. Mr Fish spoke to him in Turkish, then said: 'Boulware's not here. He left hours ago. They don't know where he went.'

Thirteen

1

At the hotel in Rezaiyeh, Jay Coburn had that sick, helpless feeling again, the feeling he had had in Mahabad, and then in the courtyard of the schoolhouse: he had no control over his own destiny, his fate was in the hands of others – in this case, the hands of Rashid.

Where the hell was Rashid?

Coburn asked the guards if he could use the phone. They took him down to the lobby. He dialled the home of Majid's cousin, the professor, in Rezaiyeh, but there was no answer.

Without much hope he dialled Gholam's number in Tehran. To his surprise he got through.

'I have a message for Jim Nyfeler,' he said. 'We are at the staging area.'

'But where are you?' said Gholam.

'In Tehran,' Coburn lied.

'I need to see you.'

Coburn had to continue the deception. 'Okay, I'll meet you tomorrow morning.'

'Where?'

'At Bucharest.'

'Okay.'

Coburn went back upstairs. Simons took him and Keane Taylor in to one of the rooms. 'If Rashid isn't back by nine o'clock, we're leaving,' Simons said.

Coburn immediately felt better.

Simons went on: 'The guards are getting bored, their vigilance is slipping. We'll either sneak past them or deal with them the other way.'

'We've only got one car,' said Coburn.

'And we're going to leave it here, to confuse them. We'll walk to the border. Hell, it's only thirty or forty miles. We can go across country: we'll avoid roadblocks by avoiding roads.'

Coburn nodded. This was what he wanted. They were taking the initiative again.

'Let's get the money together,' Simons said to Taylor. 'Ask the guards to take you down to the car. Bring the Kleenex box and the flashlight up here and take the money out of them.'

Taylor left.

'We might as well eat first,' Simons said. 'It's going to be a long walk.'

Taylor went into an empty room and spilled the money out of the Kleenex box and the flashlight on to the floor.

Suddenly the door was flung open.

Taylor's heart stopped.

He looked up and saw Gayden, grinning all over his face. 'Gotcha!' Gayden said.

Taylor was furious. 'You bastard, Gayden,' he said. 'You gave me a fucking heart attack.'

Gayden laughed like hell.

The guards took them downstairs to the dining room. The Americans sat at a big circular table, and the guards took another table across the room. Lamb and rice was served, and tea. It was a grim meal: they were all worried about what might have happened to Rashid, and how they would manage without him.

There was a TV set on, and Paul could not take his eyes off the screen. He expected at any minute to see his own face appear like a 'Wanted' poster.

Where the hell was Rashid?

They were only an hour from the border, yet they were trapped, under guard, and still in danger of being sent back to Tehran and jail.

Someone said: 'Hey, look who's here!'

407

Rashid walked in.

He came over to their table, wearing his self-important look. 'Gentlemen,' he said, 'this is your last meal.'

They all stared at him, horrified.

'In Iran, I mean,' he added hastily. 'We can leave.'

They all cheered.

'I got a letter from the revolutionary committee,' he went on. 'I went to the border to check it out. There are a couple of roadblocks on the way, but I have arranged everything. I know where we can get horses to cross the mountains – but I don't think we need them. There are no government people at the border station – the place is in the hands of the villagers. I saw the head man of the village, and it will be all right for us to cross. Also, Ralph Boulware is there. I talked to him.'

Simons stood up. 'Let's move,' he said. 'Fast.'

They left their meal half-eaten. Rashid talked to the guards, and showed them his letter from the deputy leader. Keane Taylor paid the hotel bill. Rashid had bought a stack of Khomeini posters, and he gave them to Bill to stick on the cars.

They were out of there in minutes.

Bill had done a good job with the posters. Everywhere you looked on the Range Rovers, the fierce, white-bearded face of the Ayatollah glared out at you.

They pulled away, Rashid driving the first car.

On the way out of town Rashid suddenly braked, leaned out of the window, and waved frantically at an approaching taxi.

Simons growled: 'Rashid, what the fuck are you doing?'

Without answering, Rashid jumped out of the car and ran over to the taxi.

'Jesus *Christ*,' said Simons.

Rashid talked to the cab driver for a minute, then the cab went on. Rashid explained: 'I asked him to show us a way out of town by the back street. There is one roadblock I want to avoid because it is manned by kids with rifles and I don't know what they might do. The cabbie has a fare already, but he's coming back. We'll wait.'

'We won't wait very goddamn long,' Simons said.

The cab returned in ten minutes. They followed it through the dark, unpaved streets until they came to a main road. The cabbie turned right. Rashid followed, taking the corner fast. On the left, just a few yards away, was the roadblock he had wanted to avoid, with teenage boys firing rifles into the air. The cab and the two Range Rovers accelerated fast away from the corner, before the kids could realize that someone had sneaked past them.

Fifty yards down the road, Rashid pulled into a gas station.

Keane Taylor said to him: 'What the hell are you stopping for?'

'We've got to get gas.'

'We've got three-quarters of a tankful, plenty to jump the border on – let's get *out* of here.'

'It may be impossible to get gas in Turkey.'

Simons said: 'Rashid, let's *go*.'

Rashid jumped out of the car.

When the fuel tanks had been topped up, Rashid was still haggling with the taxi driver, offering him a hundred rials – a little more than a dollar – for guiding them out of town.

Taylor said: 'Rashid, just give him a handful of money and *let's go*.'

'He wants too much,' Rashid said.

'Oh, God,' said Taylor.

Rashid settled with the cabbie for two hundred rials and got back into the Range Rover, saying: 'He would have got suspicious if I didn't argue.'

They drove out of town. The road wound up into the mountains. The surface was good and they made rapid progress. After a while the road began to follow a ridge, with deep wooded gulleys on either side. 'There was a checkpoint around here somewhere this afternoon,' Rashid said. 'Maybe they went home.'

The headlights picked out two men standing beside the road, waving them down. There was no barrier. Rashid did not brake.

'I guess we better stop,' Simons said.

Rashid kept going right past the two men.

'I said stop!' Simons barked.

Rashid stopped.

Bill stared out through the windscreen and said: 'Would you look at that?'

A few yards ahead was a bridge over a ravine. On either side of the bridge, tribesmen were emerging from the ravine. They kept coming – thirty, forty, fifty – and they were armed to the teeth.

It looked very like an ambush. If the cars had tried to rush the checkpoint, they would have been shot full of holes.

'Thank God we stopped,' Bill said fervently.

Rashid jumped out of the car and started talking. The tribesmen put a chain across the bridge and surrounded the cars. It rapidly became clear that these were the most unfriendly people the team had yet encountered. They surrounded the cars, glaring in and hefting their rifles, while two or three of them started yelling at Rashid.

It was maddening, Bill thought, to have come so far, through so much danger and adversity, only to be stopped by a bunch of dumb farmers. Wouldn't they just like to take these two fine Range Rovers and all our money? he thought. And who would ever know?'

The tribesmen got meaner. They started pushing and shoving Rashid. In a minute they'll start shooting, Bill thought.

'Do nothing,' Simons said. 'Stay in the car, let Rashid handle it.'

Bill decided Rashid needed some help. He touched his pocket rosary and started praying. He said every prayer he knew. We're in God's hands now, he thought; it will take a miracle to get us out of this mess.

In the second car, Coburn sat frozen while a tribesman outside pointed a rifle directly at his head.

Gayden, sitting behind, was seized by a wild impulse, and whispered: 'Jay! Why don't you lock the door?'

410

Coburn felt hysterical laughter bubble up in his throat.

Rashid felt he was on the cliff-edge of death.

These tribesmen were bandits, and they would kill you for the coat on your back: they didn't care. The revolution was nothing to them. No matter who was in power, they recognized no government, obeyed no laws. They did not even speak Farsi, the language of Iran, but Turkish.

They pushed him around, yelling at him in Turkish. He yelled back in Farsi. He was getting nowhere. They're working themselves up to shoot us all, he thought.

He heard the sound of a car. A pair of headlights approached from the direction of Rezaiyeh. A Land Rover pulled up and three men got out. One of them was dressed in a long black overcoat. The tribesmen seemed to defer to him. He addressed Rashid. 'Let me see the passports, please.'

'Sure,' said Rashid. He led the man to the second Range Rover. Bill was in the first, and Rashid wanted the overcoat man to get bored with looking at passports before he got to Bill's. Rashid tapped on the car window, and Paul rolled it down. 'Passports.'

The man seemed to have dealt with passports before. He examined each one carefully, checking the photographs against the face of the owner. Then, in perfect English, he asked questions: 'Where were you born? Where do you live? What is your date of birth?' Fortunately, Simons had made Paul and Bill learn every piece of information contained in their false passports, so Paul was able to answer the overcoat man's questions without hesitation.

Reluctantly, Rashid led the man to the first Range Rover. Bill and Keane Taylor had changed seats, so that Bill was on the far side, away from the light. The man went through the same routine. He looked at Bill's passport last. Then he said: 'The picture is not of this man.'

'Yes, it is,' Rashid said frantically. 'He's been very sick. He's lost weight, his skin has changed colour – don't you understand that he's dying? He has to get back to America as

411

quickly as possible so he can have the right medical attention, and you are delaying him – do you want him to die because the Iranian people had no pity for a sick man? Is this how you uphold the honour of our country? Is—'

'They're Americans,' the man said. 'Follow me.'

He turned and went into the little brick hut beside the bridge.

Rashid followed him in. 'You have no right to stop us,' he said. 'I have been instructed by the Islamic Revolution Commandant Committee in Rezaiyeh to escort these people to the border, and to delay us is a counter-revolutionary crime against the Iranian people.' He flourished the letter written by the deputy leader and stamped with the library stamp.

The man looked at it. 'Still, that one American does not look like the picture in his passport.'

'I told you, he has been sick!' Rashid yelled. 'They have been cleared to the border by the revolutionary committee! Now get these bandits out of my way!'

'We have our own revolutionary committee,' the man said. 'You will all have to come to our headquarters.'

Rashid had no choice but to agree.

Jay Coburn watched Rashid come out of the hut with the man in the long black overcoat. Rashid looked really shaken.

'We're going to their village to be checked out,' Rashid said. 'We have to go in their cars.'

It was looking bad, Coburn thought. All the other times they had been arrested, they had been allowed to stay in the Range Rovers, which made them feel a little less like prisoners. Getting out of the cars was like losing touch with base.

Also, Rashid had never looked so frightened.

They all got into the tribesmen's vehicles, a pick-up truck and a battered little station wagon. They were driven along a dirt track through the mountains. The Range Rovers followed driven by tribesmen. The track twisted away into darkness. Well, shit, this is it, Coburn thought; nobody will

412

ever hear from us again.

After three or four miles they came to the village. There was one brick building with a courtyard: the rest were mud-brick huts with thatched roofs. But in the courtyard were six or seven fine jeeps. Coburn said: 'Jesus, these people live by stealing cars.' Two Range Rovers would make a nice addition to their collection, he thought.

The two vehicles containing the Americans were parked in the courtyard; then the Range Rovers; then two more jeeps, blocking the exit and precluding a quick getaway.

They all got out.

The man in the overcoat said: 'You need not be afraid. We just need to talk with you a while, then you can go on.' He went into the brick building.

'He's lying!' Rashid hissed.

They were herded into the building and told to take off their shoes. The tribesmen were fascinated by Keane Taylor's cowboy boots: one of them picked up the boots and inspected them, then passed them around for everyone to see.

The Americans were led into a big, bare room, with a Persian rug on the floor and bundles of rolled-up bedding pushed against the walls. It was dimly lit by some kind of lantern. They sat in a circle, surrounded by tribesmen with rifles.

On trial again, just like Mahabad, Coburn thought.

He kept an eye on Simons.

In came the biggest, ugliest mullah they had ever seen; and the interrogation began again.

Rashid did the talking, in a mixture of Farsi, Turkish and English. He produced the letter from the library again, and gave the name of the deputy leader. Someone went off to check with the committee in Rezaiyeh. Coburn wondered how they would do that: the oil lamp indicated there was no electricity here, so how could they have phones? All the passports were examined again. People kept coming in and going out.

What if they have got a phone? wondered Coburn. And what if the committee in Rezaiyeh has heard from Dadgar?

413

We might be better off if they *do* check us out, he thought; at least that way somebody knows we're here. At the moment we could be killed, our bodies would disappear without trace in the snow, and nobody would every know we had been here.

A tribesman came in, handed the library letter to Rashid and spoke to the mullah.

'It's okay,' Rashid said. 'We've been cleared.'

Suddenly the whole atmosphere changed.

The ugly mullah turned into the Jolly Green Giant and shook hands with everyone. 'He welcomes you to his village,' Rashid translated. Tea was brought. Rashid said: 'We are invited to be the guests of the village for the night.'

Simons said: 'Tell him definitely no. Our friends are waiting for us at the border.'

A small boy of about ten years appeared. In an effort to cement the new friendship, Keane Taylor took out a photograph of his son, Michael, aged eleven, and showed it to the tribesmen. They got very excited, and Rashid said: 'They want to have their picture taken.'

Gayden said: 'Keane, get out your camera.'

'I'm out of film,' said Taylor.

'Keane, get out your fucking camera.'

Taylor took out his camera. In fact he had three shots left, but he had no flash, and would have needed a camera far more sophisticated than his Instamatic for taking pictures by the light of the lantern. But the tribesmen lined up, waving their rifles in the air, and Taylor had no option but to snap them.

It was incredible. Five minutes earlier those people had seemed ready to murder the Americans: now they were horsing around, hooting and hollering and having a good time.

They could probably change again just as quickly.

Taylor's sense of humour took over and he started hamming it up, making like a press photographer, telling the tribesmen to smile or move closer together so he could get them all in, 'taking' dozens of shots.

414

More tea was brought. Coburn groaned inwardly. He had drunk so much tea in the last few days that he felt awash with it. He surreptitiously poured his out, making an ugly brown stain on the gorgeous rug.

Simons said to Rashid: 'Tell them we have to go.'

There was a short exchange, then Rashid said: 'We must drink tea once more.'

'No,' said Simons decisively, and he stood up. 'Let's move.' Smiling calmly, nodding and bowing to the tribesmen, Simons started giving very decisive commands in a voice which belied his courteous demeanour: 'On your feet, everybody. Get your shoes on. Come on, let's get out of here, let's *go*.'

They all got up. Every man in the tribe wanted to shake hands with every one of the visitors. Simons kept herding them towards the door. They found their shoes and put them on, still bowing and shaking hands. At last they got outside and climbed into the Range Rovers. There was a wait, while the villagers manouevred the two jeeps blocking the exit. At last they moved off, following the same two jeeps, along the mountain track.

They were still alive, still free, still moving.

The tribesmen took them to the bridge then said goodbye.

Rashid said: 'But aren't you going to escort us to the border?'

'No,' one of them replied. 'Our territory ends at the bridge. The other side belongs to Sero.'

The man in the long black overcoat shook hands with everyone in both Range Rovers. 'Don't forget to send us the pictures,' he said to Taylor.

'You bet,' said Taylor with a straight face.

The chain across the bridge was down. The two Range Rovers drove to the far side and accelerated up the road.

'I hope we don't have the same trouble at the next village,' said Rashid. 'I saw the head man this afternoon and arranged everything with him.'

The Range Rovers built up speed.

'Slow down,' said Simons.

'No, we must hurry.'

They were a mile or so from the border.

Simons said: 'Slow the goddam jeep down, I don't want to get killed at this point in the game.'

They were driving past what looked like a filling station. There was a little hut with a light on inside. Taylor yelled: 'Stop! Stop!'

Simons said: 'Rashid—'

In the following car, Paul honked and flashed his headlights.

Out of the corner of his eye Rashid saw two men running out from the filling station, locking-and-loading their rifles as they ran.

He stood on the brake.

The car screeched to a halt. Paul had already stopped, right by the gas station. Rashid backed up and jumped out.

The two men pointed their rifles at him.

Here we go again, he thought.

He went into his routine, but they weren't interested. One of them got into each car. Rashid climbed back into the driving seat.

'Drive on,' he was told.

A minute late they were at the foot of the hill leading to the border. They could see the lights of the frontier station up above. Rashid's captor said: 'Turn right.'

'No,' said Rashid. 'We've been cleared to the border and—'

The man raised his rifle and thumbed the safety.

Rashid stopped the car. 'Listen, I came to your village this afternoon and got permission to pass—'

'Go down there.'

They were less than half a mile from Turkey and freedom. There were seven of the Dirty Team against two guards. It was tempting . . .

A jeep came tearing down the hill from the border station and skidded to a stop in front of the Range Rover. An excited young man jumped out, carrying a pistol, and ran over to Rashid's window.

Rashid wound down the window and said: 'I'm under orders from the Islamic Revolution Commandant Committee—'

The excited young man pointed his pistol at Rashid's head. 'Go down the track!' he screamed.

Rashid gave in.

They drove along the track. It was even narrower than the last. The village was less than a mile away. When they arrived Rashid jumped out of the car, saying: 'Stay here – I'll deal with this.'

Several men came out of the huts to see what was going on. They looked even more like bandits than the inhabitants of the last village. Rashid said loudly: 'Where is the head man?'

'Not here,' someone replied.

'Then fetch him. I spoke to him this afternoon – I am a friend of his – I have permission from him to cross the border with these Americans.'

'Why are you with Americans?' someone asked.

'I am under orders from the Islamic Revolution Commandant Committee—'

Suddenly, out of nowhere, appeared the head man of the village, to whom Rashid had spoken in the afternoon. He came up and kissed Rashid on both cheeks.

In the second Range Rover, Gayden said: 'Hey, it's looking good!'

'Thank God for that,' said Coburn. 'I couldn't drink any more tea to save my life.'

The man who had kissed Rashid came over. He was wearing a heavy Afghan coat. He leaned through the car window and shook hands with everyone.

Rashid and the two guards got back into the cars.

A few minutes later they were climbing the hill to the frontier station.

Paul, driving the second car, suddenly thought about Dadgar again. Four hours ago, in Rezaiyeh, it had seemed sensible to abandon the idea of crossing the border on horseback, avoiding the road and the station. Now he was not so sure. Dadgar might have sent pictures of Paul and Bill to every airport, seaport, and border crossing. Even if there were no government people here, the photographs might be stuck up on a wall somewhere. The Iranians seemed to be glad of any excuse to detain Americans and question them. All along, EDS had underestimated Dadgar . . .

The frontier station was brightly lit by high neon lamps. The two cars drove slowly along, past the buildings, and stopped where a chain across the road marked the limit of Iranian territory.

Rashid got out.

He spoke to the guards at the station, then came back and said: 'They don't have a key to unloose the chain.'

They all got out.

Simons said to Rashid: 'Go over to the Turkish side and see if Boulware's there.'

Rashid disappeared.

Simons lifted the chain. It would not go high enough to let a Range Rover pass underneath.

Somebody found a few planks and leaned them on the chain, to see whether the cars could be driven over the chain on the planks. Simons shook his head: it was not going to work.

He turned to Coburn. 'Is there a hacksaw in the tool kit?'

Coburn went back to the car.

Paul and Gayden lit cigarettes. Gayden said: 'You need to decide what you want to do with that passport.'

'What do you mean?'

'Under American law there's a ten-thousand-dollar fine and a jail term for using a false passport. I'll pay the fine but you'll have to serve the jail term.'

Paul considered. So far he had broken no laws. He had shown his false passport, but only to bandits and revolutionaries who had no real right to demand passports anyway. It would be kind of nice to stay on the right side of the law.

'That's right,' said Simons. 'Once we're out of this goddam country we break no laws. I don't want to have to get you out of a Turkish jail.'

Paul gave the passport to Gayden. Bill did the same. Gayden gave the passports to Taylor, who put them down the sides of his cowboy boots.

Coburn came back with a hacksaw. Simons took it from him and started sawing the chain.

The Iranian guards rushed over and started yelling at him. Simons stopped.

Rashid came back from the Turkish side, trailing a couple of guards and an officer. He spoke to the Iranians, then told Simons: 'You can't cut the chain. They say we must wait until morning. Also the Turks don't want us to cross tonight.'

Simons muttered to Paul: 'You may be about to get sick.'

'What do you mean?'

'If I tell you so, just get sick, okay.'

Paul saw what Simons was thinking: the Turkish guards wanted to sleep, not spend the night with a crowd of Americans, but if one of the Americans was in urgent need of hospital treatment they could hardly turn him away.

The Turks went back over to their own side.

'What do we do now?' Coburn said.

'Wait,' said Simons.

All but two of the Iranian guards went into their guardhouse: it was bitterly cold.

'Make like we're prepared to wait all night,' said Simons.

The other two guards drifted off.

'Gayden, Taylor,' Simons said. 'Go in there and offer the guards money to take care of our cars.'

'Take care of them?' Taylor said incredulously. 'They'll just steal them.'

'That's right,' said Simons. 'They'll be able to steal them if they let us go.'

Taylor and Gayden went into the guardhouse.

'This is it,' said Simons. 'Coburn, get Paul and Bill and just walk across there.'

'Let's go, you guys,' said Coburn.

Paul and Bill stepped over the chain and started walking.

Coburn stayed close behind them. 'Just keep walking, regardless of anything else that might happen,' Coburn said. 'If you hear yelling, or gunfire, you run, but under no circumstances do we stop or go back.'

Simons came up behind them. 'Walk faster,' he said. 'I don't want you two getting shot out here in the bloody middle of nowhere.'

They could hear some kind of argument beginning back on the Iranian side.

Coburn said: 'Y'all don't turn round, just go.'

Back on the Iranian side, Taylor was holding out a fistful of money to two guards who were glancing first at the four men walking across the border and then at the two Range Rovers, worth at least twenty thousand dollars each . . .

Rashid was saying: 'We don't know when we'll be able to come back for these cars – it could be a long time—'

One of the guards said: 'You were all to stay here until the morning—'

'The cars are really very valuable, and they must be looked after—'

The guards looked from the cars, to the people walking across to Turkey, and back to the cars again, and they hesitated too long.

Paul and Bill reached the Turkish side and walked into the guard hut.

Bill looked at his wristwatch. It was 11.45 p.m. on Thursday, 15 February, the day after Valentine's Day. On 15 February 1960 he had slipped an engagement ring on Emily's finger. The same day six years later Jackie had been born – today was her thirteenth birthday. Bill thought: here's your present, Jackie – you still have a father.

Coburn followed them into the hut.

Paul put his arm around Coburn and said: 'Jay, you just hit a home run.'

Back on the Iranian side, the guards saw that half the Americans were already in Turkey, and they decided to quit while they were ahead and take the money and the cars.

Rashid, Gayden and Taylor walked up to the chain.

At the chain Gayden stopped. 'Go ahead,' he said. 'I want to be the last guy out of here.'

And he was.

2

At the hotel in Yuksekova, they sat around a smokey pot-bellied stove: Ralph Boulware, Ilsman the fat secret agent, Charlie Brown the interpreter, and the two sons of Mr Fish's cousin. They were waiting for a call from the border station. Dinner was served: some kind of meat, maybe lamb, wrapped in newspapers.

Ilsman said he had seen someone taking photographs of Rashid and Boulware at the border. With Charlie Brown translating, Ilsman said: 'If you ever have a problem about those photographs, I can solve it.'

Boulware wondered what he meant.

Charlie said: 'He believes you are an honest man, and what you are doing is noble.'

It was kind of a sinister offer, Boulware felt; like a Mafioso telling you that you are his friend.

By midnight there was still no word either from the Dirty Team or from Pat Sculley and Mr Fish, who were supposed to be on their way here with a bus. Boulware decided to go to bed. He always drank water at bedtime. There was a pitcher of water on a table. Hell, he thought, I haven't died yet. He took a drink, and found himself swallowing something solid. Oh, God, he thought; what was that? He made himself forget about it.

He was just getting to bed when a boy called him to the phone.

It was Rashid.

'Hey, Ralph?'

'Yes.'

'We're at the border!'

'I'll be right there.'

421

He rounded up the others and paid the hotel bill. With the sons of Mr Fish's cousin driving, they headed down the road where – as Ilsman kept saying – thirty-nine people had been killed by bandits last month. On the way they had yet another flat tyre. The sons had to change the wheel in the dark, because the batteries in their flashlight had gone dead. Boulware did not know whether to be frightened, standing there in the road waiting. Ilsman could still be a liar, a confidence trickster. On the other hand, his credentials had protected them all. If the Turkish secret service was like Turkish hotels, hell, Ilsman could be their answer to James Bond.

The wheel was changed and the cars moved off again.

They drove through the night. It's going to be all right Boulware thought. Paul and Bill are at the border, Sculley and Mr Fish are on their way here with a bus, Perot is in Istanbul with a plane. We're going to make it.

He reached the border. Lights were on in the guard huts. He jumped out of the car and ran inside.

A great cheer went up.

There they all were: Paul and Bill, Coburn, Simons, Taylor, Gayden and Rashid.

Boulware shook hands warmly with Paul and Bill.

They all started picking up their coats and bags. 'Hey, hey, wait a minute,' Boulware said. 'Mr Fish is on the way with a bus.' He took from his pocket a bottle of Chivas Regal he had been saving for this moment. 'But we can all have a drink!'

They all had a celebratory drink, except Rashid who did not take alcohol. Simons got Boulware in a corner. 'All right, what's happening?'

'I talked to Ross this afternoon,' Boulware told him. 'Mr Fish is on his way here, with Sculley, Schwebach and Davis. They're in a bus. Now, we could all leave right now – the twelve of us could get into the two cars, just about – but I think we should wait for the bus. For one thing, we'll all be together, so nobody can get lost any more. For another, the road out of here is supposed to be Blood Alley, you know;

bandits and like that. I don't know whether that's been exaggerated, but they keep saying it, and I'm beginning to believe it. If it's a dangerous road, we'll be safer all together. And, number three, if we go to Yuksekova and wait for Mr Fish there, we can't do anything but check into the worst hotel in the world, and attract questions and hassle from a new set of officials.'

'Okay,' Simons said reluctantly. 'We'll wait a while.'

He looked *tired*, Boulware thought; an old man who just wanted to rest. Coburn looked the same: drained, exhausted, almost broken. Boulware wondered just what they had been through to get here.

Boulware himself felt terrific, even though he had had little sleep for forty-eight hours. He thought of his endless discussions with Mr Fish about how to get to the border; of the screw-up in Adana when the bus failed to come; of the taxi ride through a blizzard in the mountains . . . And here he was, after all.

The little guardhouse was bitterly cold, and the wood-burning stove did nothing but fill the room with smoke. Everyone was tired, and the whisky made them drowsy. One by one they began to fall asleep on the wooden benches and the floor.

Simons did not sleep. Rashid watched him, pacing up and down like a caged tiger, chain-smoking his plastic-tipped cigars. As dawn broke he started looking out of the window, across no-man's-land to Iran.

'There's a hundred people with rifles across there,' he said to Rashid and Boulware. 'What do you think they would do if they should happen to find out exactly who it was who slipped across the border last night?'

Boulware, too, was beginning to wonder whether he had been right to propose waiting for Mr Fish.

Rashid looked out of the window. Seeing the Range Rovers on the other side, he remembered something. 'The fuel can,' he said. 'I left the can with the money. We might need the money.'

Simons just looked at him.

423

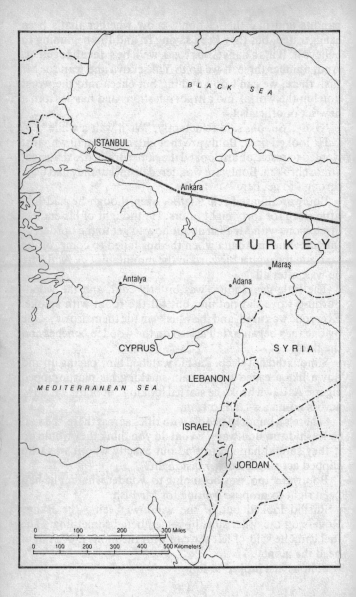

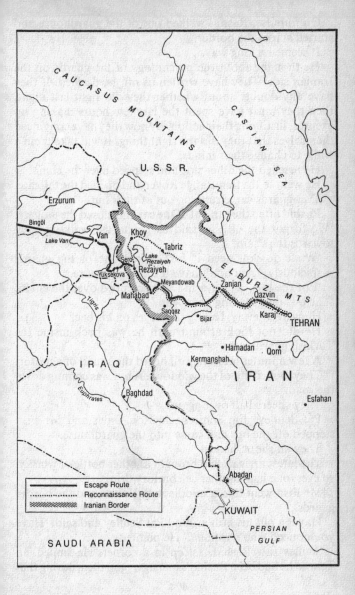

On impulse, Rashid walked out of the guardhouse and started across the border.

It seemed a long way.

He thought about the psychology of the guards on the Iranian side. They have written us off, he decided. If they have any doubts about whether they did right last night, then they must have spent the last few hours making up excuses, justifying their action. By now they have convinced themselves that they did the right thing. It will take them a while to change their minds.

He reached the other side and stepped over the chain.

He went to the first Range Rover and opened the tailgate.

Two guards came running out of their hut.

Rashid lifted the can out of the car and closed the tailgate. 'We forgot the oil,' he said as he started walking back towards the chain.

'What do you need it for?' asked one of the guards suspiciously. 'You don't have the cars any more.'

'For the bus,' said Rashid as he stepped over the chain. 'The bus that's taking us to Van.'

He walked away, feeling their eyes on his back.

He did not look around until he was back inside the Turkish guardhouse.

A few minutes later they all heard the sound of a motor.

They looked out of the windows. A bus was coming down the road.

They cheered all over again.

Pat Sculley, Jim Schwebach, Ron Davis and Mr Fish stepped off the bus and came into the guardhouse.

They all shook hands.

The latest arrivals had brought another bottle of whisky, so everyone had another celebratory drink.

Mr Fish went into a huddle with Ilsman and the border guards.

Gayden put his arm around Pat Sculley and said: 'Have you noticed who's with us?' He pointed.

Sculley saw Rashid, asleep in a corner. He smiled. In Tehran he had been Rashid's manager, and then, during that first meeting with Simons in the EDS boardroom – was it only six weeks ago? – he had strongly argued that Rashid should be in on the rescue. Now it seemed Simons had come round to the same point of view.

Mr Fish said: 'Pat Sculley and I have to go to Yuksekova and speak with the chief of police there. The rest of you wait here for us, please.'

'Now hold it,' Simons said. 'We waited for Boulware, then we waited for you. *Now* what are we waiting for?'

Mr Fish said: 'If we don't get clearance in advance, there will be trouble, because Paul and Bill have no passports.'

Simons turned to Boulware. 'Your guy Ilsman is supposed to have dealt with that problem,' he said angrily.

'I thought he did!' said Boulware. 'I thought he bribed them.'

'So what's happening?'

Mr Fish said: 'It's better this way.'

Simons growled: 'Make it goddam fast.'

Sculley and Mr Fish went off.

The others started a poker game. They all had thousands of dollars hidden in their shoes, and they were a little crazy. One hand Paul got a full house, with three aces in the hole, and the pot went over a thousand dollars. Keane Taylor kept raising him. Taylor had a pair of kings showing, and Paul guessed he had another king in the hole, making a full house with kings. Paul was right. He won $1,400.

A new shift of border guards arrived, including an officer who was mad as hell to find his guardhouse littered with cigarette butts, hundred-dollar bills, and poker-playing Americans, two of whom had entered the country without passports.

The morning wore on, and they all began to feel bad – too much whisky and not enough sleep. As the sun climbed in the sky, poker did not seem fun any more. Simons got jittery. Gayden started giving Boulware a hard time. Boulware wondered where Sculley and Mr Fish had got to.

Boulware was now sure he had made a mistake. They should all have left for Yuksekova as soon as he had arrived.

425

He had made another mistake in letting Mr Fish take charge. Somehow he had lost the initiative.

At ten a.m., having been away four hours, Sculley and Mr Fish came back.

Mr Fish told the officer that they had permission to leave.

The officer said something sharp, and – as if accidentally – let his jacket fall open to reveal his pistol.

The other guards backed away from the Americans.

Mr Fish said: 'He says we leave when *he* gives permission.'

'Enough,' said Simons. He got to his feet and said something in Turkish. All the Turks looked at him in surprise: they had not realized he spoke their language.

Simons took the officer into the next room.

They came out a few minutes later. 'We can go,' said Simons.

They all went outside.

Coburn said: 'Did you bribe him, Colonel – or frighten him to death?'

Simons gave the ghost of a smile and said nothing.

Pat Sculley said: 'Want to come to Dallas, Rashid?'

For the last couple of days, Rashid reflected, they had been talking as if he would go all the way with them; but this was the first time anyone had asked him directly whether he wanted to. Now he had to make the most important decision of his life.

Want to come to Dallas, Rashid? It was a dream come true. He thought of what he was leaving behind. He had no children, no wife, not even a girlfriend – he had never been in love. But he thought of his parents, his sister and his brothers. They might need him: life was sure to be rough in Tehran for some time. Yet what help could he give them? He would be employed for a few more days, or weeks, shipping the Americans' possessions back to the States, taking care of the dogs and cats – then nothing. EDS was finished in Iran. Probably computers were finished, too, for many years. Unemployed, he would be a burden to his family, just another mouth to feed in hard times.

But in America—

In America he could contine his education. He could put his talents to work, become a success in business – especially with the help of people like Pat Sculley and Jay Coburn.

Want to come to Dallas, Rashid?

'Yes,' he said to Sculley. 'I want to go to Dallas.'

'What are you waiting for? Get on the bus!'

They all got on the bus.

Paul settled into his seat with relief. The bus pulled away, and Iran disappeared into the distance: he would probably never see the country again. There were strangers on the bus: some scruffy Turks in improvised uniforms, and two Americans who – someone mumbled – were pilots. Paul was too exhausted to inquire further. One of the Turkish guards from the border station had joined the party: presumably he was just hitching a ride.

They stopped in Yuksekova. Mr Fish told Paul and Bill: 'We have to talk to the chief of police. He has been here twenty-five years and this is the most important thing that has ever happened. But don't worry. It's all routine.'

Paul, Bill and Mr Fish got off the bus and went into the little police station. Somehow Paul was not worried. He was out of Iran, and although Turkey was not exactly a western country, at least, he felt, it was not in the throes of a revolution. Or perhaps he was just too tired to be frightened.

He and Bill were interrogated for two hours, then released.

Six more people joined the bus at Yuksekova: a woman and a child who seemed to belong to the border guard, and four very dirty men – 'Bodyguards,' said Mr Fish – who sat behind a curtain at the back of the bus.

They drove off, heading for Van where a charter plane was waiting. Paul looked out at the scenery. It was prettier than Switzerland, he thought, but incredibly poor. Huge boulders littered the road. In the fields, ragged people were treading down the snow so that their goats could get at the frozen grass beneath. There were caves with wood fences across their mouths, and it seemed that was where the people lived. They passed the ruins of a stone fortress which might have dated back to the time of the Crusades.

427

The bus driver seemed to think he was in a race. He drove aggressively on the winding road, apparently confident that nothing could possibly be coming the other way. A group of soldiers waved him down and he drove right past them. Mr Fish yelled at him to stop, but he yelled back and kept going.

A few miles farther on the army was waiting for them in force, probably having heard that the bus had run the last checkpoint. The soldiers stood in the road with their rifles raised, and the driver was forced to stop.

A sergeant jumped on the bus and dragged the driver off with a pistol at his head.

Now we're in trouble, Paul thought.

The scene was almost funny. The driver was not a bit cowed: he was yelling at the soldiers as loudly and as angrily as they were yelling at him.

Mr Fish, Ilsman, and some of the mystery passengers got off the bus and started talking, and eventually they squared the military. The driver was literally thrown back on the bus, but even that did not quench his spirit, and as he drove away he was still yelling out of the window and shaking his fist at the soldiers.

They reached Van late in the afternoon.

They went to the town hall, where they were handed over to the local police. The scruffy bodyguards disappeared like melting snow. The police filled in forms, then escorted them to the airstrip.

As they were boarding the plane, Ilsman was stopped by a policeman: he had a .45 pistol strapped under his arm, and it seemed that even in Turkey passengers were not allowed to take firearms on board aircraft. However, Ilsman flashed his credentials yet again and the problem went away.

Rashid was also stopped. He was carrying the fuel can with the money in it, and of course inflammable liquids were not allowed on aircraft. He told the police the can contained suntan oil for the Americans' wives, and they believed him.

They all boarded the plane. Simons and Coburn, coming down from the effects of the stay-awake pills, both stretched

428

out and were asleep within seconds.

As the plane taxied and took off, Paul felt as elated as if it were his first plane trip. He recalled how, in jail in Tehran, he had longed to do that most ordinary thing, get on a plane and fly away. Soaring up into the clouds now gave him a feeling he had not experienced for a long time: the feeling of freedom.

3

According to the peculiar rules of Turkish air travel, the charter plane could not go where a scheduled flight was available, so they could not fly directly to Istanbul where Perot was waiting, but had to change planes in Ankara.

While they were waiting for their connection, they solved a couple of problems.

Simons, Sculley, Paul and Bill got into a taxi and asked for the American Embassy.

It was a long drive through the city. The air was brownish and had a strong smell. 'The air's bad here,' said Bill.

'High-sulphur coal,' said Simons, who had lived in Turkey in the fifties. 'They've never heard of pollution controls.'

The cab pulled up at the US Embassy. Bill looked out of the window and his heart leaped: there stood a young, handsome Marine guard in an immaculate uniform.

This was the USA.

They paid off the cab.

As they went in, Simons said to the Marine: 'Is there a motor pool here, soldier?'

'Yes, sir,' said the Marine, and gave him directions.

Paul and Bill went into the passport office. In their pockets they had passport-sized photographs of themselves which Boulware had brought from the States. They went up to the desk, and Paul said: 'We've lost our passports. We left Tehran in kind of a hurry.'

'Oh, yes,' said the clerk, as if he had been expecting them.

They had to fill in forms. One of the officials took them into a private office and told them he wanted some advice. The US Consulate in Tabriz, Iran, was under attack by revolutionaries, and the staff there might have to escape as Paul and Bill had. They told him the route they had taken and what problems they had encountered.

A few minutes later they walked out of there, each holding a sixty-day US passport. Paul looked at his and said: 'Did you ever see anything so beautiful in your whole damn life?'

Simons emptied the oil from the can and shook out the money in the weighted plastic bags. There was a hell of a mess: some of the bags had broken and there was oil all over the banknotes. Sculley started cleaning the oil off and piling the money up in ten-thousand-dollar stacks: there was $65,000 plus about the same again in Iranian rials.

While he was doing this a Marine walked in. Seeing two dishevelled, unshaven men kneeling on the floor counting out a small fortune in hundred-dollar bills, he did a double-take.

Sculley said to Simons: 'Do you think I ought to tell him, *Colonel*?'

Simons growled: 'Your buddy at the gate knows about this, soldier.'

The Marine saluted and went out.

It was eleven p.m. when they were called to board their flight to Istanbul.

They went through the final security check one by one. Sculley was just ahead of Simons. Looking back, he saw that the guard had asked to see inside the envelope Simons was carrying.

The envelope contained all the money from the fuel can.

Sculley said: 'Oh, shit.'

The soldier looked in the envelope and saw the sixty-five thousand dollars and four million rials; and all hell broke loose.

Several soldiers drew their guns, one of them called out, and officers came running.

Sculley saw Taylor, who had fifty thousand dollars in a little black bag, pushing his way through the crowd around Simons, saying: 'Excuse me, excuse me please, excuse me . . .'

Ahead of Sculley, Paul had already been cleared through the checkpoint. Sculley thrust his thirty thousand dollars into Paul's hands then turned and went back through the checkpoint.

The soldiers were taking Simons away to be interrogated. Sculley followed with Mr Fish, Ilsman, Boulware and Jim Schwebach. Simons was led into a little room. One of the officers turned, saw five people following, and said in English: 'Who are you?'

'We're all together,' Sculley said.

They sat down and Mr Fish talked to the officers. After a while he said: 'They want to see the papers which prove you brought this money into the country.'

'What papers?'

'You have to declare all the foreign currency you bring in.'

'Hell, nobody asked us!'

Boulware said: 'Mr Fish, explain to these clowns that we entered Turkey at a tiny little border station where the guards probably don't know enough to read forms and they didn't ask us to fill in any forms but we're happy to do it now.'

Mr Fish argued some more with the officers. Eventually Simons was allowed to leave, with the money; but the soldiers took down his name, passport number, and description, and the moment they landed in Istanbul Simons was arrested.

At three a.m. on Saturday 17 February 1979, Paul and Bill walked into Ross Perot's suite at the Istanbul Sheraton.

It was the greatest moment in Perot's life.

Emotion welled up as he embraced them both. Here they were, alive and well, after all this time, all those weeks of waiting, the impossible decisions and the awful risks. He looked at their beaming faces. The nightmare was over.

The rest of the team crowded in after them. Ron Davis was clowning, as usual. He had borrowed Perot's cold-weather clothes, and Perot had pretended to be anxious to get them back: now Davis stripped off his hat, coat and gloves, and threw them on the floor dramatically, saying: 'Here you are, Perot, here's your damned stuff!'

Then Sculley walked in and said: 'Simons got arrested at the airport.'

Perot's jubilation evaporated. 'Why?' he exclaimed in dismay.

'He was carrying a lot of money in a paper envelope and they just happened to search him.'

Perot said angrily: 'Darn it, Pat, *why* was he carrying money?'

'It was the money from the fuel can. See—'

Perot interrupted: 'After all Simons has done, why in the world did you let him take a completely unnecessary risk? Now see here. I'm taking off at noon, and if Simons isn't out of jail by then, *you* are going to stay in frigging Istanbul until he is!'

Sculley and Boulware sat down with Mr Fish. Boulware said: 'We need to get Colonel Simons out of jail.'

'Well,' said Mr Fish, 'it will take around ten days—'

'Bull shit,' said Boulware. 'Perot will not buy that. I want him out of jail *now*.'

'It's five o'clock in the morning!' Mr Fish protested.

'How much?' said Boulware.

'I don't know. Too many people know about this, in Ankara as well as Istanbul.'

432

'How about five thousand dollars?'

'For that, they would sell their mothers.'

'Fine,' said Boulware. 'Let's get it on.'

Mr Fish made a phone call, then said: 'My lawyer will meet us at the jail near the airport.'

Boulware and Mr Fish got into Mr Fish's battered old car, leaving Sculley to pay the hotel bill.

They drove to the jail and met the lawyer. The lawyer got into Mr Fish's car and said: 'I have a judge on the way. I've already talked to the police. Where's the money?'

Boulware said: 'The prisoner has it.'

'What do you mean?'

Boulware said: 'You go in there and bring the prisoner out, and *he* will give you the five thousand dollars.'

It was crazy, but the lawyer did it. He went into the jail and came out a few minutes later with Simons. They got into the car.

'We're not going to pay these clowns,' said Simons. 'I'll wait it out. They'll just talk themselves to death and let me go in a few days.'

Boulware said: 'Bull, please don't fight the programme. Give me the envelope.'

Simons handed over the envelope. Boulware took out five thousand dollars and gave it to the lawyer, saying: 'Here's the money. Make it happen.'

The lawyer made it happen.

Half an hour later, Boulware, Simons and Mr Fish were driven to the airport in a police car. A policeman took their passports and walked them through passport control and customs. When they came out on the tarmac, the police car was there to take them to the Boeing 707 waiting on the runway.

They boarded the plane. Simons looked around at the velvet curtains, the plush upholstery, the TV sets and the bars, and said: 'What the fuck is this?'

The crew were on board, waiting. A stewardess came up to Boulware and said: 'Would you like a drink?'

Boulware smiled.

The phone rang in Perot's hotel suite, and Paul happened to answer it.

A voice said: 'Hello?'

Paul said 'Hello?'

The voice said: 'Who is this?'

Paul, suspicious, said: 'Who is *this*?'

'Hey, Paul?'

Paul recognized the voice of Merv Stauffer. 'Hello, Merv!'

'Paul, I got somebody here wants to talk to you.'

There was a pause, then a woman's voice said: 'Paul?'

It was Ruthie!'

'Hello, Ruthie!'

'Oh, Paul!'

'Hi! What are you doing?'

'What do you mean, what am I doing?' Ruthie said tearfully. 'I'm waiting for you!'

The phone rang. Before Emily got to it, someone picked up the extension in the children's room.

A moment later she heard a little girl scream: 'It's Dad! It's Dad!'

She rushed into the room.

All the children were jumping up and down and fighting over the phone.

Emily restrained herself for a couple of minutes, then took the phone away from them.

'Bill?'

'Hello, Emily.'

'Gee you sound good. I didn't expect you to sound . . . Oh, Bill you sound so good.'

In Dallas, Merv began to take down a message from Perot in code.

Take . . . the . . .

He was now so familiar that he could transcribe the code as he went along.

434

. . . code . . . and . . .

He was puzzled, because for the last three days Perot had been giving him a hard time about the code. Perot did not have the patience to use it, and Stauffer had had to insist, saying: 'Ross, this is the way Simons wants it.' Now that the danger was past, why had Perot suddenly started to use the code?

. . . stick . . . it . . . where . . .

Stauffer guessed what was coming, and burst out laughing.

Ron Davis called room service and ordered bacon and eggs for everyone.

While they were eating, Dallas called again. It was Stauffer. He asked for Perot.

'Ross, we just got the *Dallas Times Herald*.'

Was this to be another joke?

Stauffer went on: 'The headline on the front page says: Perot men reportedly on way out. Overland exit route from Iran indicated.'

Perot felt his blood start to boil. 'I thought we were getting that story killed!'

'Boy, Ross, we tried! The people who own or manage the paper just don't seem to be able to control the editor.'

Tom Luce came on the line, mad as hell. 'Ross, those bastards are willing to get the rescue team killed and destroy EDS and see you jailed just to be the first to print the story. We've explained the consequences to them and it just doesn't matter. Boy, when this is over we should sue them, no matter how long it takes or how much it costs—'

'Maybe,' said Perot. 'Be careful about picking a fight with people who buy ink by the barrel and paper by the ton. Now, what are the chances of this news reaching Tehran?'

'We don't know. There are plenty of Iranians in Texas, and most of them will hear about this. It's still very hard to get a phone line to Tehran, but we've managed it a couple of times, so they could too.'

'And if they do . . .'

'Then, of course, Dadgar finds out that Paul and Bill have slipped through his grasp—'

'And he could decide to take alternative hostages,' Perot said coldly. He was disgusted with the State Department for leaking the story, furious with the *Dallas Times Herald* for printing it, and maddened that there was nothing he could do about it. 'And the Clean Team is still in Tehran,' he said.

The nightmare was not over yet.

Fourteen

1

At midday on Friday 16 February Lou Goelz called Joe
Poché and told him to bring the EDS people to the US
Embassy that afternoon at five o'clock. Ticketing and
baggage check-in would be done at the Embassy overnight,
and they could leave on a Pan Am evacuation flight on
Saturday morning.

John Howell was nervous. He knew, from Abolhasan,
that Dadgar was still active. He did not know what had
happened to the Dirty Team. If Dadgar were to find out that
Paul and Bill had gone, or if he were simply to give up on
them and take a couple more hostages, the Clean Team
would be arrested. And where better to make the arrests
than at the airport, where everyone had to identify himself
by showing his passport?

He wondered whether it was wise for them to take the first
available flight: there would be a series of flights, according
to Goelz. Maybe they should wait, and see what happened to
the first batch of evacuees, whether there was any kind of
search for EDS personnel. At least then they would know in
advance what the procedures were.

But so would the Iranians. The advantage of taking the
first flight was that everything would probably be confused,
and the confusion might help Howell and the Clean Team
slip out unnoticed.

In the end he decided the first flight was best, but he
remained uneasy. Bob Young felt the same way. Although
Young no longer worked for EDS in Iran – he was based in
Kuwait – he had been here when the Ministry contract was
first negotiated, he had met Dadgar face to face, and his

name might be on some list in Dadgar's files.

Joe Poché also favoured the first flight, although he did not say much about it – he did not say much at all: Howell found him uncommunicative.

Rich and Cathy Gallagher were not sure they wanted to leave Iran. They told Poché quite firmly that, regardless of what Colonel Simons had said, Poché was not 'in charge' of them, and they had the right to make their own decision. Poché agreed, but pointed out that if they decided to take their chances here with the Iranians, they should not rely on Perot sending another rescue team in for them if they got thrown in jail. In the end the Gallaghers also decided to go on the first flight.

That afternoon they all went through their documents and destroyed everything that referred to Paul and Bill.

Poché gave each of them two thousand dollars, put five hundred dollars in his own pocket, and hid the rest of the money in his shoes, ten thousand dollars in each. He was wearing shoes borrowed from Gayden, a size too large, to accommodate the money. He also had in his pocket a million rials, which he planned to give to Lou Goelz for Abolhasan, who would use the money to pay the remaining Iranian EDS employees their last wages.

A few minutes before five, they were saying goodbye to Goelz's houseman when the phone rang.

Poché took the call. It was Tom Walter. He said: 'We have the people. Do you understand? We have *the people*.'

'I understand,' Poché said.

They all got into the car, Cathy carrying her poodle, Buffy. Poché drove. He did not tell the others about his cryptic message from Tom Walter.

They parked in a side street near the Embassy, and left the car: it would stay there until somebody decided to steal it.

There was no relief of tension for Howell as he walked into the Embassy compound. There were at least a thousand Americans milling about, but there were also scores of armed revolutionary guards. The Embassy was supposed to be American soil, inviolate; but clearly the Iranian revolutionaries did not take any notice of such diplomatic niceties.

The Clean Team were herded into a queue.

They spent most of the night waiting in line.

They queued to fill in forms, they queued to hand in their passports, and they queued for baggage checks. All the bags were put in a huge hall, then the evacuees had to find their own bags and put the claim checks on. Then they queued to open their bags so the revolutionaries could search them. Every single piece was opened.

Howell learned that there would be two planes, both Pan Am 747s. One would go to Frankfurt, the other to Athens. The evacuees were organized by company, but the EDS people were included with Embassy personnel who were leaving. They would be on the Frankfurt flight.

At seven o'clock on Saturday morning they were boarded on buses to go to the airport.

It was a hell of a ride.

Two or three armed revolutionaries got on each bus. As they drove out of the Embassy gates, they saw a crowd of reporters and television crews: the Iranians had decided that the flight of the humiliated Americans would be a world television event.

The bus bumped along the road to the airport. Close to Poché was a guard about fifteen years old. He stood in the aisle, swaying with the motion of the bus, his finger on the trigger of his rifle. Poché noticed that the safety catch was off.

If he stumbled . . .

The streets were full of people and traffic. Everyone seemed to know that these buses contained Americans, and their hatred was palpable. They yelled and shook their fists. A truck pulled alongside, and the driver leaned out of his window and spat on the bus.

The convoy was stopped several times. Different areas of the city seemed to be under the control of different revolutionary groups, and each group had to demonstrate its authority by stopping the buses and then giving them permission to proceed.

It took two hours to drive the six miles to the airport.

The scene there was chaotic. There were more television

cameras and reporters, plus hundreds of armed men running around, some wearing scraps of uniform, some directing traffic, all of them in charge, all having a different opinion on where the buses should go.

The Americans finally got inside the terminal at nine-thirty.

Embassy personnel started distributing the passports they had collected during the night. Five were missing: those of Howell, Poché, Young and the Gallaghers.

After Paul and Bill had given their passports to the Embassy for safekeeping back in November, the Embassy had refused to return them without informing the police. Would they be so treacherous as to pull the same trick now?

Suddenly Poché came pushing through the crowd with five passports in his hand. 'I found them on a shelf behind a counter,' he said. 'I guess they got put there by accident.'

Bob Young saw two Americans holding photographs and scanning the crowd. To his horror, they started to approach the EDS people. They walked up to Rich and Cathy Gallagher.

Surely Dadgar would not take *Cathy* hostage?

The people smiled and said they had some of the Gallagher's luggage.

Young relaxed.

Friends of the Gallaghers had salvaged some of the bags from the Hyatt, and had asked these two Americans to bring them to the airport and try to give them to the Gallaghers. The people had agreed, but they did not know the Gallaghers – hence the photographs.

It had been a false alarm, but if anything it increased their anxiety.

Joe Poché decided to see what he could find out. He went off and located a Pan Am ticket agent. 'I work for EDS,' Poché told the agent. 'Are the Iranians looking for anyone?'

'Yes, they're looking pretty hard for two people,' said the agent.

'Anybody else?'

'No. And the stop list is several weeks old.'

'Thanks.'

Poché went back and told the others.

The evacuees were starting to go from the check-in concourse through to the departure lounge.

Poché said: 'I suggest we split up. That way we won't look like a group, and if one or two of you get into trouble the others may still get through. I'll be last, so if anyone has to stay behind, I'll stay too.'

Bob Young looked at his suitcase and saw that it bore a luggage tag saying: 'William D. Gaylord.'

He suffered a moment of panic. If the Iranians saw that, they would think he was Bill and arrest him.

He knew how it had happened. His own suitcases had been destroyed at the Hyatt by the revolutionaries who had shot up the rooms. However, one or two cases had been left more or less undamaged, and Young had borrowed one. This was it.

He tore the luggage tag off and stuffed it into his pocket, intending to get rid of it at the first opportunity.

They all went through the 'Passenger's Only' gate.

Next they had to pay the airport tax. This amused Poché: the revolutionaries must have decided that airport tax was the one good thing the Shah introduced, he thought.

The next queue was for passport control.

Howell reached the desk at noon.

The guard checked his exit documentation thoroughly, and stamped it. Next he looked at the picture in his passport, then looked hard at Howell's face. Finally he checked the name in the passport against a list he had on his desk.

Howell held his breath.

The guard handed him his passport and waved him through.

Joe Poché went through passport control last. The guard looked extra hard at him, comparing the face with the photograph, for Poché now had a red beard. But eventually he, too, was allowed through.

The Clean Team were in a jovial mood in the departure lounge: it was all over, Howell thought, now that they had come through passport control.

At two in the afternoon they began to pass through the gates. At this point there was normally a security check. This time, as well as searching for weapons, the guards were confiscating maps, photographs of Tehran, and large sums of money. None of the Clean Team lost their money, however; the guards did not look in Poché's shoes.

Outside the gates, some of the baggage was lined up on the tarmac. Passengers had to check whether any of theirs was there, and if so to open it for searching before it was loaded on to the plane. None of the Clean Team's bags had been picked out for this special treatment.

They boarded buses and were driven across the runway to where two 747s were waiting. Once again the television cameras were there.

At the foot of the ladder there was yet another passport check. Howell joined the queue of five hundred people waiting to board the Frankfurt plane. He was less worried than he had been: nobody was looking for him, it seemed.

He got on the plane and found a seat. There were several armed revolutionaries on board, both in the passenger cabin and on the flight deck. The scene became confused as people who were supposed to go to Athens realized they were on the Frankfurt plane, and vice versa. All the seats filled up, then the crew seats, and still there were people without seats.

The captain turned on the public-address system and asked for everyone's attention. The plane became quieter. 'Would passengers Paul John and William Deming please identify themselves,' he said.

Howell went cold.

John was the middle name of Paul Chiapparone.

Deming was the middle name of Bill Gaylord.

They were *still* searching for Paul and Bill.

Clearly it was not merely a question of names on a list at the airport. Dadgar was firmly in control here, and his people were relentlessly determined to find Paul and Bill.

Ten minutes later the captain came on the loudspeakers again. 'Ladies and gentlemen, we still have not located Paul John or William Deming. We have been informed that we cannot take off until these two people have been located. If anyone knows their whereabouts, will you *please* let us know.'

Will I hell, thought Howell.

Bob Young suddenly remembered the luggage tag in his pocket marked 'William D. Gaylord'. He went to the bathroom and threw it into the toilet.

The revolutionaries came down the aisle again, asking for passports. They checked each one carefully, comparing the photograph with the face of the owner.

John Howell took out a paperback book he had brought from the Dvoranchik place and tried to read it, in an effort to look unconcerned. It was *Dubai*, Robin Moore's thriller about intrigue in the Middle East. He could not concentrate on a paperback thriller: he was living a real one. Soon, he thought, Dadgar must realize that Paul and Bill are not on this plane.

And what will he do then?

He's so *determined*.

Clever, too. What a perfect way to do a passport check – on the plane, when all the passengers are in their seats and no one can hide!

But what will he do next?

He'll come aboard this damn plane himself, and walk down the aisle, looking at everyone. He won't know Rich, or Cathy, or Joe Poché, but he'll know Bob Young.

And he'll know me best of all.

In Dallas, T. J. Marquez got a call from Mark Ginsberg, the White House aide who had been trying to help with the problem of Paul and Bill. Ginsberg was in Washington, monitoring the situation in Tehran. He said: 'Five of your people are on a plane standing on the runway at Tehran Airport.'

'Good!' said T.J.

'It's not good. The Iranians are searching for Chiapparone and Gaylord, and they won't let the plane take off until they find the guys.'

'Oh, *hell*.'

'There's no air traffic control over Iran, so the plane has to take off before nightfall. We aren't sure what's going to happen, but there's not much time left. Your people may be taken off the plane.'

'You can't let them do that!'

'I'll keep you in touch.'

T.J. hung up. After all that Paul and Bill and the Dirty Team had been through, would EDS now end up with more of its people in a Tehran jail? It did not bear thinking about.

The time was six-thirty a.m. in Dallas, four p.m. in Tehran.

They had two hours of daylight left.

T.J. picked up the phone. 'Get me Perot.'

'Ladies and gentlemen,' said the pilot, 'Paul John and William Deming have not been located. The man in charge on the ground will now do another passport check.'

The passengers groaned.

Howell wondered who was the man in charge on the ground.

Dadgar?

It might be one of Dadgar's staff. Some of them knew Howell, some did not.

He peered along the aisle.

Someone came aboard. Howell stared. It was a man in a Pan Am uniform.

Howell relaxed.

The man went slowly down the plane, checking each of five hundred passports, doing a face-to-picture identification then examining the photographs and seals to see whether they had been tampered with.

'Ladies and gentlemen, captain speaking again. They have decided to check the baggage as it is loaded. If you hear your claim check number called would you please identify yourself.'

Cathy had all the claim checks in her handbag. As the first numbers were called, Howell saw her sorting through the checks. He tried to attract her attention, to signal her not to identify herself: it might be a trick.

More numbers were called, but nobody got up. Howell guessed everyone had decided they would rather lose their luggage than risk getting off this plane.

'Ladies and gentlemen, please identify yourselves when these numbers are called. You will not have to get off the plane, just hand over your keys so the bags can be opened for searching.'

Howell was not reassured. He watched Cathy, still trying to catch her eye. More numbers were called, but she did not get up.

'Ladies and gentlemen, some good news. We have checked with Pan Am's European headquarters and have been given permission to take off with an overload of passengers.'

There was a ragged cheer.

Howell looked over at Joe Poché. Poché had his passport on his chest and he was sitting back with his eyes closed, apparently asleep. Joe must have ice in his veins, Howell thought.

There was sure to be a lot of pressure on Dadgar as the sun went down. It had to be obvious that Paul and Bill were not on the plane. If a thousand people were deplaned and escorted back to the Embassy, the revolutionary authorities would have to go through the whole rigmarole again tomorrow – and somebody up there was bound to say 'No way!' to that.

Howell knew that he and the rest of the Clean Team were certainly guilty of crimes now. They had connived at the escape of Paul and Bill, and whether the Iranians called that conspiracy, or being an accessory after the fact, or some other name, it had to be against the law. He went over in his mind the story they had all agreed to tell if they were arrested. They had left the Hyatt on Monday morning, they would say, and had gone to Keane Taylor's house. (Howell had wanted to tell the truth, and say the Dvoranchik place, but the others had pointed out that this might bring down trouble on the head of Dvoranchik's landlady, whereas Taylor's landlord did not live on the premises.) They had spent Monday and Tuesday at Taylor's then had gone to

Lou Goelz's house on Tuesday afternoon. From then on they would tell the truth.

The story would not protect the Clean Team: Howell knew all too well that Dadgar did not care whether his hostages were guilty or innocent.

At six o'clock the captain said: 'Ladies and gentlemen, we have permission to take off.'

The doors were slammed and the plane was moving within seconds. The passengers without seats were told by stewardesses to sit on the floor. As they taxied, Howell thought: Surely we wouldn't stop now, even if we were ordered to . . .

The 747 gathered speed along the runway and took off.

They were still in Iranian airspace. The Iranians could send up fighter jets . . .

A little later the captain said: 'Ladies and gentlemen, we have now departed Iranian airspace.'

The passengers gave a weary cheer.

We made it, Howell thought.

He picked up his paperback thriller.

Joe Poché left his seat and went to find the chief steward.

'Is there any way the pilot could get a message through to the States?' he asked.

'I don't know,' the steward said. 'Write your message, and I'll ask him.'

Poché returned to his seat and got out a paper and a pen. He wrote: *To Merv Stauffer, 7171 Forest Lane, Dallas, Texas.*

He thought for a minute about what his message should be. He recalled EDS's recruiting motto: 'Eagles don't flock – you have to find them one at a time.' He wrote:

The eagles have flown their nest.

2

Ross Perot wanted to meet up with the Clean Team before returning to the States: he was keen to get everyone together, so that he could see and touch them all and be absolutely sure they were safe and well. However, on Friday in Istanbul

446

he could not confirm the destination of the evacuation flight which would bring the Clean Team out of Tehran. John Carlen, the laid-back pilot of the leased Boeing 707, had the answer to that problem. 'Those evacuation planes must fly up over Istanbul,' he said. 'We'll just sit on the runway until they pass overhead, then call them on radio and ask them.' In the end that was not necessary: Stauffer called on Saturday morning and told Perot the Clean Team would be on the Frankfurt plane.

Perot and the others checked out of the Sheraton at midday and went to the airport to join Boulware and Simons on the plane. They took off late in the afternoon.

When they were in the air Perot called Dallas: with the plane's single-sideband radio it was as easy as calling from New York. He reached Merv Stauffer.

'What's happening with the Clean Team?' Perot asked.

'I got a message,' said Stauffer. 'It came from the European headquarters of Pan Am. It just says: "The eagles have flown their nest".'

Perot smiled. All safe.

Perot left the flight deck and returned to the passenger cabin. His heroes looked washed out. At Istanbul Airport, he had sent Taylor into the duty-free shop to buy cigarettes, snacks and liquor, and Taylor had spent over a thousand dollars. They all had a drink to celebrate the escape of the Clean Team, but nobody was in the mood, and ten minutes later they were all sitting around on the plush upholstery with their glasses still full. Someone started a poker game, but it petered out.

The crew of the 707 included two pretty stewardesses. Perot got them to put their arms around Taylor, then took a photograph. He threatened to show the photo to Taylor's wife, Mary, if Taylor ever gave him a hard time.

Most of them were too tired to sleep, but Gayden went back to the luxurious bedroom and lay down on the king-sized bed. Perot was a little miffed: he thought Simons, who was older and looked completely drained, should have had the bed.

But Simons was talking to one of the stewardesses, Anita Melton. She was a vivacious blonde Swedish girl in her twenties, with a zany sense of humour, a wild imagination, and a penchant for the outlandish. She was fun. Simons recognized a kindred soul, someone who did not care too much about what other people thought, an individual. He liked her. He realized that it was the first time since the death of Lucille that he had felt attracted to a woman.

He really had come back to life.

Ron Davis began to feel sleepy. The king-sized bed was big enough for two, he thought; so he went into the bedroom and lay down beside Gayden.

Gayden opened his eyes. 'Davis?' he said incredulously. 'What the hell are you doing in bed with me?'

'Don't sweat it,' said Davis. 'Now you can tell all your friends you slept with a nigger.' He closed his eyes.

As the plane approached Frankfurt, Simons recalled that he was still responsible for Paul and Bill, and his mind went back to work, extrapolating possibilities for enemy action. He asked Perot: 'Does Germany have an extradition treaty with Iran?'

'I don't know,' said Perot.

He got The Simons Look.

'I'll find out,' he added.

He called Dallas and asked for Tom Luce, the lawyer. 'Tom, does Germany have an extradition treaty with Iran?'

Luce said: 'I'm ninety-nine per cent sure they do not.'

Perot told Simons.

Simons said: 'I've seen men killed because they were ninety-nine per cent sure they were safe.'

Perot said to Luce: 'Let's get a hundred per cent sure. I'll call you again in a few minutes.'

They landed at Frankfurt and checked into a hotel within the airport complex. The German desk clerk seemed curious, and carefully noted all their passport numbers. This increased Simon's unease.

They gathered in Perot's room, and Perot called Dallas again. This time he spoke to T. J. Marquez.

448

T.J. said: 'I called an international lawyer in Washington, and he thinks there *is* an extradition treaty between Iran and Germany. Also he said the Germans are kind of legalistic about stuff like this, and if they got a request to pick up Paul and Bill, hell, they'd probably go right ahead and do it.'

Perot repeated all of that to Simons.

'Okay,' said Simons. 'We're not going to take any chances at this point in the game. There's a movie house with three screens down at the basement level in this airport. Paul and Bill can hide in them . . . where's Bill?'

'Gone to buy toothpaste,' someone said.

'Jay, go find him.'

Coburn went out.

Simons said: 'Paul goes in one theatre, with Jay. Bill goes in another, with Keane. Pat Sculley stands guard outside. He has a ticket so he can go in and check on the others.'

It was interesting, Perot thought, to see the switches turn and the wheels start rolling as Simons changed from an old man relaxing on a plane to a commando leader again.

Simons said: 'The entrance to the train station is down in the basement, near the movies. If there's any sign of trouble Sculley gets the four men out of the movies and they all take a subway downtown. They rent a car and drive to England. If nothing happens, we get them out of the movies when we're about to board a plane. All right, let's do it.'

Bill was down in the shopping precinct. He had changed some money and bought toothpaste, a toothbrush and a comb. He decided that a fresh new shirt would make him feel human again, so he went to change some more money. He was standing in line at the currency exchange booth when Coburn tapped him on the shoulder.

'Ross wants to see you in the hotel,' Coburn said.

'What for?'

'I can't talk about it now, you need to come on back.'

'You've got to be kidding!'

'Let's go.'

They went to Perot's room, and Perot explained to Bill what was happening. Bill could hardly believe it. He had thought for sure he was safe in modern, civilized Germany. Would he *ever* be safe? he wondered. Would Dadgar pursue him to the ends of the earth, never resting until Bill was returned to Iran or killed?

Coburn did not know whether there was any real chance of Paul and Bill getting into trouble here in Frankfurt, but he *did* know the value of Simons's elaborate precautions. Much of what Simons had planned, over the past seven weeks, had come to nothing: the attack on the first jail, the idea of snatching Paul and Bill from house arrest, the route out via Kuwait. But then some of the contingencies for which Simons planned *had* come to pass, often the most far-fetched ones: the Gasr Prison had been stormed and Rashid was there; the road to Sero, which Simons and Coburn had carefully reconnoitred, had in the end been their route out; even making Paul and Bill learn all the information on their false passports had turned out to be crucial when the man in the long black overcoat started asking questions. Coburn needed no convincing: whatever Simons said was okay with him.

They went down to the movie house. There were three films: two were porno movies and the third was *Jaws II*. Bill and Taylor got *Jaws II*. Paul and Coburn went in to see something about naked South Sea maidens.

Paul sat staring at the screen, bored and tired. The movie was in German, not that the dialogue appeared to count for much. What could be worse, he thought, than a bad X-rated movie? Suddenly he heard a loud snort. He looked at Coburn.

Coburn was fast asleep, snoring.

When John Howell and the rest of the Clean Team landed at Frankfurt, Simons had everything set up for a quick turnaround.

Ron Davis was at the arrival gate, waiting to pull the Clean Team out of the line and direct them to another gate where the Boeing 707 was parked. Ralph Boulware was watching from a distance: as soon as he saw the first member of the Clean Team arrive, he would go down to the movie theatre and tell Sculley to round up the guys inside. Jim Schwebach was in the roped-off press area, where reporters were waiting to see the American evacuees. He was sitting next to writer Pierre Salinger (who did not know how close he was to a *really* good story) and pretending to read a furniture advertisement in a German newspaper. Schwebach's job was to tail the Clean Team from one gate to the other, just to make sure no one was following them. If there was trouble, Schwebach and Davis would start a disturbance. It would not matter much if they were arrested by the Germans, for there was no reason for them to be extradited to Iran.

The plan went like clockwork. There was only one hitch: Rich and Cathy Gallagher did not want to go to Dallas. They had no friends or family there, they were not sure what their future would be, they did not know whether the dog Buffy would be allowed to enter the USA, and they did not want to get on another plane. They said goodbye and went off to make their own arrangements.

The rest of the Clean Team – John Howell, Bob Young and Joe Poché – followed Ron Davis and boarded the Boeing 707. Jim Schwebach tailed them. Ralph Boulware rounded up everyone else, and they all got on board for the flight home.

Merv Stauffer in Dallas had called Frankfurt airport and ordered food for the flight. He had asked for thirty superdeluxe meals each including fish, fowl and beef; six seafood trays with sauce, horseradish and lemon; six hors d'oeuvre trays; six sandwich trays with ham-and-cheese, roast beef, turkey and swiss cheese; six dip trays with raw vegetables and bluecheese-and-vinaigrette dip; three cheese trays with assorted breads and crackers; four deluxe pastry trays; four fresh fruit trays; four bottles of brandy; twenty Seven-Ups and twenty ginger ales; ten club sodas and ten tonics; ten quarts of orange juice; fifty cartons of milk; four gallons of freshly brewed coffee in Thermos bottles; one hundred sets of plastic cutlery consisting of knife, fork and spoon; six dozen paper plates in two sizes; six dozen plastic glasses; six dozen Styrofoam cups; two cartons each of Kent, Marlboro, Kool and Salem Light cigarettes; and two boxes of chocolates.

There had been a mix-up, and the airport caterers had delivered the order double.

Take-off was delayed. An ice storm had dropped out of nowhere, and the Boeing 707 was last in the queue for de-icing – commercial flights had priority. Bill began to worry. The airport was going to close at midnight, and they might have to get off the plane and return to the hotel. Bill did not want to spend the night in Germany. He wanted American soil beneath his feet.

John Howell, Joe Poché and Bob Young told the story of their flight from Tehran. Both Paul and Bill were chilled to hear how implacably determined Dadgar had been to prevent their leaving the country.

At last the plane was de-iced – but its No 1 engine would not start. Pilot John Carlen traced the problem to the start valve. Engineer Ken Lenz got off the plane and held the valve open manually while Carlen started the engine.

Perot brought Rashid to the flight deck. Rashid had never flown until yesterday, and he wanted to sit with the crew. Perot said to Carlen: 'Let's have a really spectacular take-off.'

'You got it,' said Carlen. He taxied to the runway then took off in a very steep climb.

In the passenger cabin, Gayden was laughing: he had just heard that, after six weeks in jail with all-male company, Paul had been forced to sit through an X-rated movie; and he thought it was funny as hell.

Perot popped a champagne cork and proposed a toast. 'Here's to the men who said what they were going to do, then went out and did it.'

Ralph Boulware sipped his champagne and felt a warm glow. That's right, he thought. We said what we were going to do, then we went out and did it. Right.

He had another reason to be happy. Next Monday was

Kecia's birthday: she would be seven. Every time he had called Mary she had said: 'Get home in time for Kecia's birthday.' It looked like he was going to make it.

Bill began to relax at last. Now there's nothing but a plane ride between me and America and Emily and the kids, he thought. Now I'm safe.

He had imagined himself safe before: when he reached the Hyatt in Tehran, when he crossed the border into Turkey, when he took off from Van, and when he landed at Frankfurt. He had been wrong each time.

And he was wrong now.

3

Paul had always been crazy about airplanes, and now he took the opportunity to sit on the flight deck of the Boeing 707.

As the plane flew across the north of England, he realized that pilot John Carlen, engineer Ken Lenz and first officer Joe Fosnot were having trouble. On autopilot the plane was drifting, first to the left and then to the right. The compass had failed, rendering the inertial navigation system erratic.

'What does all that mean?' Paul asked.

'It means we'll have to hand-fly this thing all the way across the Atlantic,' said Carlen. 'We can do it – it's kind of exhausting, that's all.'

A few minutes later the plane became very cold, then very hot. Its pressurization system was failing.

Carlen took the plane down low.

'We can't cross the Atlantic at this height,' he told Paul.

'Why not?'

'We don't have enough fuel – an aircraft uses much more fuel at low altitudes.'

'Why can't we fly high?'

'Can't breathe up there.'

'The plane has oxygen masks.'

'But not enough oxygen to cross the Atlantic. No plane carries that much oxygen.'

Carlen and his crew fiddled with the controls for a while, then Carlen sighed and said: 'Would you get Ross up here, Paul?'

Paul fetched Perot.

Carlen said: 'Mr Perot, I think we ought to take this thing and land it as soon as we can.' He explained again why they could not cross the Atlantic with a faulty pressure system.

Paul said: 'John, I'll be forever grateful to you if we don't have to land in Germany.'

'Don't worry,' said Carlen. 'We'll head for London, Heathrow.'

Perot went back to tell the others. Carlen called London Air Traffic Control on the radio. It was one in the morning, and he was told Heathrow was closed. This is an emergency, he replied. They gave him permission to land.

Paul could hardly believe it. An emergency landing, after all he had been through!

Ken Lenz began to dump fuel to reduce the plane below its maximum landing weight.

London told Carlen there was a fog over southern England, but at the moment visibility was up to half a mile at Heathrow.

When Ken Lenz shut off the fuel dump valves, a red light that should have gone out stayed on. 'A dump chute hasn't retracted,' said Lenz.

'I can't believe this,' said Paul. He lit a cigarette.

Carlen said: 'Paul, can I have cigarette?'

Paul stared at him. 'You told me you quit smoking ten years ago.'

'Just give me a cigarette, would you?'

Paul gave him a cigarette and said: 'Now I'm really scared.'

Paul went back into the passenger cabin. The stewardesses had everyone busy stowing trays, bottles and baggage, securing all loose objects, in preparation for landing.

Paul went into the bedroom. Simons was lying on the bed.

He had shaved in cold water and there were bits of stickum tape all over his face. He was fast asleep.

Paul left him. He said to Jay Coburn: 'Does Simons know what's going on?'

'Sure does,' Coburn replied. 'He said he doesn't know how to fly a plane and there's nothing he can do so he was going to take a nap.'

Paul shook his head in amazement. How cool could you get?

He returned to the flight deck. Carlen was as laid-back as ever, his voice calm, his hands steady; but that cigarette worried Paul.

A couple of minutes later the red light went out. The dump chute had retracted.

They approached Heathrow in dense cloud and began to lose height. Paul watched the altimeter. As it dropped through six hundred feet, then five hundred feet, there was still nothing outside but swirling grey fog.

At three hundred feet it was the same. Then, suddenly, they dropped out of the cloud and there was the runway, straight ahead, lit up like a Christmas tree. Paul breathed a sigh of relief.

They touched down, and the fire engines and ambulances came screaming across the tarmac towards the plane; but it was a perfect safe landing.

Rashid had been hearing about Ross Perot for years. Perot was the multi-millionaire, the founder of EDS, the business wizard, the man who sat in Dallas and moved men such as Coburn and Sculley around the world like pieces on a chessboard. It had been quite an experience for Rashid to meet Mr Perot and find he was just an ordinary-looking human being, rather short and surprisingly friendly. Rashid had walked into the hotel room in Istanbul, and this little guy with the big smile and the bent nose just stuck out his hand and said: 'Hi, I'm Ross Perot,' and Rashid had shaken hands and said: 'Hi, I'm Rashid Kazemi,' just as natural as could be.

Since that moment he had felt more than ever one of the EDS team. But at Heathrow Airport he was sharply reminded that he was not.

As soon as the plane taxied to a halt, a vanload of airport police, customs men and immigration officials boarded and started asking questions. They did not like what they saw: a bunch of dirty, scruffy, smelly, unshaven men, carrying a fortune in various currencies, aboard an incredibly luxurious airplane with a Grand Caymen Islands tail number. This, they said in their British way, was highly irregular, to say the least.

However, after an hour or so of questioning, they could find no evidence that the EDS men were drug smugglers, terrorists, or members of the PLO. And as holders of US passports, the Americans needed no visas or other documentation to enter Britain. They were all admitted – except for Rashid.

Perot confronted the immigration officer. 'There's no reason why you should know who I am, but my name is Ross Perot, and if you would just check me out, maybe with the US Customs, I believe you will conclude that you can trust me. I have too much to lose by trying to smuggle an illegal immigrant into Britain. Now I will assume personal responsibility for this young man. We will be out of England in twenty-four hours. In the morning we will check with your counterparts at Gatwick Airport, and we will then get on the Braniff flight to Dallas.'

'I'm afraid we can't do that, sir,' said the official. 'This gentleman will have to stay with us until we put him on the plane.'

'If he stays, I stay,' said Perot.

Rashid was flabbergasted. Ross Perot would spend the night at the airport, or perhaps in a prison cell, rather than leave Rashid behind! It was incredible. If Pat Sculley had made such an offer, or Jay Coburn, Rashid would have been grateful but not surprised. But this was Ross Perot!

The immigration officer sighed. 'Do you know anyone in Great Britain who might vouch for you, sir?'

Perot racked his brains. Who do I know in Britain? he thought. 'I don't think — no, wait a minute.' Of course! One of Britain's greatest heroes had stayed with the Perots in Dallas a couple of times. Perot and Margot had been guests at his home in England, a place called Broadlands. 'I know Earl Mountbatten of Burma,' he said.

'I'll just have a word with my supervisor,' said the officer, and he got off the plane.

He was away a long time.

Perot said to Sculley: 'As soon as we get out of here, your job is to get us all first-class seats on that Braniff flight to Dallas in the morning.'

'Yes, sir,' said Sculley.

The immigration officer came back. 'I can give you twenty-four hours,' he said to Rashid.

Rashid looked at Perot. Oh, boy, he thought; what a guy to work for!

They checked in to the Post House hotel near the airport, and Perot called Merv Stauffer in Dallas.

'Merv, we have one person here with an Iranian passport and no US visa – you know who I'm talking about.'

'Yes, sir.'

'He has saved American lives and I won't have him hassled when we get to the States.'

'Yes, sir.'

'You know who to call. Just fix it, will you?'

'Yes, sir.'

Sculley woke them all at six a.m. He had to drag Coburn out of bed. Coburn was still suffering the after-effects of Simons's stay-awake pills: ill-tempered and exhausted, he did not care whether he caught the plane or not.

Sculley had organized a bus to take them to Gatwick Airport, a good two-hour journey from Heathrow. As they went out, Keane Taylor, who was struggling with a plastic bin containing some of the dozens of bottles of liquor and cartons of cigarettes he had bought at Istanbul Airport, said:

'Hey, do any of you guys want to help me carry this stuff?'

Nobody said anything. They all got on the bus.

'Screw you, then,' said Taylor, and he gave the whole lot to the hotel doorman.

On the way to Gatwick, they heard over the bus radio that China had invaded North Vietnam. Someone said: 'That'll be our next assignment.'

'Sure,' said Simons. 'We could be dropped between the two armies. No matter which way we fired, we'd be right.'

At the airport, walking behind his men, Perot noticed other people backing away, giving them room, and he suddenly realized how terrible they all looked. Most of them had not had a good wash or a shave for days, and they were dressed in a weird assortment of ill-fitting and very dirty clothes. They probably smelled bad, too.

Perot asked for Braniff's passenger service officer. Braniff was a Dallas airline, and Perot had flown with them to London several times, so most of the staff knew him.

He asked the officer: 'Can I rent the whole of the lounge upstairs in the 747 for my party?'

The officer was staring at the men. Perot knew what he was thinking: Mr Perot's party usually consisted of a few quiet well-dressed businessmen, and now here he was with what looked like a crowd of garage mechanics who had been working on a particularly filthy engine.

The officer said: 'Uh, we can't rent you the lounge, because of international airline regulations, sir, but I believe if your companions go up into the lounge the rest of our passengers won't disturb you too much.'

Perot saw what he meant.

As Perot boarded, he said to a stewardess: 'I want these men to have anything they want on this plane.'

Perot passed on, and the stewardess turned to her colleague, wide-eyed. 'Who the hell is *he*?'

Her colleague told her.

The movie was *Saturday Night Fever*, but the projector would not work. Boulware was disappointed: he had seen the movie before and he had been looking forward to seeing it again. Instead he sat and chewed the fat with Paul.

Most of the others went up to the lounge. Once again Simons and Coburn stretched out and went to sleep.

Half way across the Atlantic, Keane Taylor, who for the last few weeks had been carrying around anything up to a quarter of a million dollars in cash and handing it out by the fistful, suddenly took it into his head to have an accounting.

He spread a blanket on the floor of the lounge and started collecting money. One by one, the other members of the team came up, fished wads of banknotes out of their pockets, their boots, their hats and their shirtsleeves, and threw the money on the floor.

One or two other first-class passengers had come up to the lounge, despite the unsavoury appearance of Mr Perot's party; but now, when this smelly, villainous-looking crew, with their beards and knit caps and dirty boots and go-to-hell coats, spread out several hundred thousand dollars on the floor and started *counting* it, the other passengers vanished.

A few minutes later a stewardess came up to the lounge and approached Perot. 'Some of the passengers are asking whether we should inform the police about your party,' she said. 'Would you come down and reassure them?'

'I'd be glad to.'

Perot went down to the first-class cabin and introduced himself to the passengers in the forward seats. Some of them had heard of him. He began to tell them what had happened to Paul and Bill.

As he talked, other passengers came up to listen. The cabin crew stopped work and stood nearby; then some of the crew from the economy cabin came along. Soon there was a whole crowd.

It began to dawn on Perot that this was a story the world would want to hear.

Upstairs, the team were playing one last trick on Keane Taylor.

While collecting the money Taylor had dropped three bundles of ten thousand dollars each, and Bill had slipped them into his own pocket.

The accounting came out wrong, of course. They all sat

around on the floor, Indian fashion, suppressing their laughter, while Taylor counted it all again.

'How can I be thirty thousand dollars out?' Taylor said angrily. 'Damn it, this is all I've got! Maybe I'm not thinking clearly. What the hell is the matter with me?'

At that point Bill came up from downstairs and said: 'What's the problem, Keane?'

'God, we're thirty thousand dollars short, and I don't know what I did with all the rest of the money.'

Bill took the three stacks out of his pocket and said: 'Is this what you're looking for?'

They all laughed uproariously.

'Give me that,' Taylor said angrily. 'Damn it, Gaylord, I wish I'd left you in jail!'

They laughed all the more.

4

The plane came down towards Dallas.

Ross Perot sat next to Rashid and told him the names of the places they were passing over. Rashid looked out of the window, at the flat brown land and the big wide roads that went straight for miles and miles. America.

Joe Poché had a good feeling. He had felt this way as captain of a rugby club in Minnesota, at the end of a long match when his side had won. The same feeling had come to him when he had returned from Vietnam. He had been part of a good team, he had survived, he had learned a lot, he had grown.

Now all he wanted to make him perfectly happy was some clean underwear.

Ron Davis was sitting next to Jay Coburn. 'Hey, Jay, what'll we do for a living, now?'

Coburn smiled. 'I don't know.'

It would be strange, Davis thought, to sit behind a desk again. He was not sure he liked the idea.

He suddenly remembered that Marva was now three months pregnant. It would be starting to show. He wondered how she would look, with a bulging tummy.

I know what I need, he thought. I need a coke. In the can. From a machine. In a gas station. And Kentucky Fried Chicken.

Pat Sculley was thinking: no more orange cabs.

Sculley was sitting next to Jim Schwebach: they were together again, the short but deadly duo, having fired not a single shot at anyone during the whole adventure. They had been talking about what EDS could learn from the rescue. The company had projects in other Middle Eastern countries and was pushing into the Far East: should there perhaps be a permanent rescue team, a group of troubleshooters trained and fit and armed and willing to do covert operations in faraway countries? No, they decided: this had been a unique situation. Sculley realized he did not want to spend any more time in primitive countries. In Tehran he had hated the morning trial of squeezing into an orange cab with two or three grumpy people, Persian music blaring from the car radio, and the inevitable quarrel with the driver over the fare. Wherever I work next, he thought, whatever I do, I'm going to ride to the office by myself, in my own car, a big fat American automobile with air-conditioning and soft music. And when I go to the bathroom, instead of squatting over a hole in the damn floor, there will be a clean white American toilet.

As the plane touched down Perot said to him: 'Pat, you'll be last out. I want you to make sure everyone gets through the formalities and deal with any problems.'

'Sure.'

The plane taxied to a halt. The door was opened, and a woman came aboard. 'Where is the man?' she said.

'Here,' said Perot, pointing to Rashid.

Rashid was first off the plane.

Perot thought: Merv Stauffer has all *that* taken care of.

The others disembarked and went through customs.

On the other side, the first person Coburn saw was stocky, bespectacled Merv Stauffer, grinning from ear to ear. Coburn put his arms around Stauffer and hugged him.

Stauffer reached into his pocket and pulled out Coburn's wedding ring.

Coburn was touched. He had left the ring with Stauffer for safekeeping. Since then, Stauffer had been the lynch-pin of the whole operation, sitting in Dallas with a phone to his ear making everything happen. Coburn had talked to him almost every day, relaying Simons's orders and demands, receiving information and advice: he knew better than anyone how important Stauffer had been, how they had all just relied on him to do whatever had to be done. Yet, with all that happening, Stauffer had remembered the wedding band.

Coburn slipped it on. He had done a lot of hard thinking about his marriage, during the empty hours in Tehran; but now all that went out of his mind, and he looked forward to seeing Liz.

Merv told him to walk out of the airport and get on a bus which was waiting outside. Coburn followed directions. On the bus he saw Margot Perot. He smiled and shook hands. Then, suddenly, the air was filled with screams of joy, and four wildly excited children threw themselves at him: Kim, Kristi, Scott and Kelly. Coburn laughed out loud and tried to hug them all at the same time.

Liz was standing behind the kids. Gently, Coburn disentangled himself. His eyes filled with tears. He put his arms around his wife, and he could not speak.

When Keane Taylor got on the bus, his wife did not recognize him. Her normally elegant husband was wearing a filthy orange ski jacket and a knitted cap. He had not shaved for a week and he had lost fifteen pounds. He stood in front of her for several seconds, until Liz Coburn said: 'Mary, aren't you going to say hello to Keane?' Then his children, Mike and Dawn, grabbed him.

Today was Taylor's birthday. He was forty-one. It was the happiest birthday of his life.

John Howell saw his wife, Angela, sitting at the front of the bus, behind the driver, with Michael, eleven months, on her lap. The baby was wearing blue jeans and a striped rugby

462

shirt. Howell picked him up and said: 'Hi, Michael, do you remember your Daddy?'

He sat next to Angie and put his arms around her. It was kind of awkward, on the bus seat and Howell was normally too shy for public displays of affection, but he kept right on hugging her because it felt so good.

Ralph Boulware was met by Mary and the girls, Stacy and Kecia. He picked Kecia up and said: 'Happy birthday!' Everything was as it should be, he thought as he embraced them. He had done what he was supposed to do, and the family was here, where they were supposed to be. He felt like he had proved something, if only to himself. All those years in the Air Force, tinkering with instrumentation or sitting in a plane watching bombs drop, he had never felt his courage was being tested. His relations had medals for ground fighting, but he had always had the uncomfortable feeling that he had an easy role, like the guy in the war movies who slops out the food at breakfast time before the real soldiers go off to fight. He had always wondered whether he had the right stuff. Now he thought about Turkey, and getting stuck in Adana, and driving through the blizzard in that damn sixty-four Chevy, and changing the wheel in Blood Alley with the sons of Mr Fish's cousin; and he thought about Perot's toast, to the men who said what they were going to do then went out and did it; and he knew the answer. Oh, yes. He had the right stuff.

Paul's daughters, Karen and Ann Marie, were wearing matching plaid skirts. Ann Marie, the littlest, got to him first, and he swept her up in his arms and squeezed her tight. Karen was too big to be picked up, but he hugged her just as hard. Behind them was Ruthie, his biggest little girl, all dressed in shades of honey and cream. He kissed her long and hard, then looked at her, smiling. He could not have stopped smiling if he had wanted to. He felt very mellow inside. It was the best feeling he had ever known.

Emily was looking at Bill as if she did not believe he was really there. 'Gosh,' she said lamely, 'it's good to see you again, sweetie.'

463

The bus went rather quiet as he kissed her. Rachel Schwebach began to cry.

Bill kissed the girls, Vicki, Jackie and Jenny, then he looked at his son. Chris was very grown-up in a blue suit he had been given for Christmas. Bill had seen that suit before. He remembered a photograph of Chris, standing in front of the Christmas tree in his new suit; that photograph had been above Bill's bunk, in a prison cell, long ago and far away . . .

Emily kept touching him to make sure he was really there. 'You look marvellous,' she said.

Bill knew he looked absolutely terrible. He said: 'I love you.'

Ross Perot got on the bus and said: 'Is everybody here?'

'Not my Dad!' said a plaintive small voice. It was Sean Sculley.

'Don't worry,' said Perot. 'He'll be right out. He's our straight man.'

Pat Sculley had been stopped by a customs agent and asked to open his suitcase. He was carrying all the money, and of course the agent had seen it. Several more agents were summoned, and Sculley was taken into an office to be interrogated.

The agents got out some forms. Sculley began to explain, but they did not want to listen, they only wanted to fill out the form.

'Is the money yours?'

'No, it belongs to EDS.'

'Did you have it when you left the States?'

'Most of it.'

'When and how did you leave the States?'

'A week ago on a private 707.'

'Where did you go?'

'To Istanbul, then to the Iranian border.'

Another man came into the office and said: 'Are you Mr Sculley?'

'Yes.'

'I'm terribly sorry you've been troubled like this. Mr Perot is waiting for you outside.' He turned to the agents. 'You can tear up those forms.'

Sculley smiled and left. He was not in the Middle East any more. This was Dallas, where Perot was Perot.

Sculley got on the bus, and saw Mary, Sean and Jennifer. He hugged and kissed them all, then said: 'What's happening?'

'There's a little reception for you,' said Mary.

The bus started to move, but it did not go far. It stopped again a few yards away at a different gate, and they were all ushered back into the airport and led to a door marked Concorde Room.

As they walked in, a thousand people rose to their feet, cheering and clapping.

Someone had put up a huge banner reading:

JOHN HOWELL
NO. I
DADDY

Jay Coburn was overwhelmed by the size of the crowd and their reaction. What a good idea the buses had been, to give the men a chance to greet their families in private before coming in here. Who had arranged that? Stauffer, of course.

As he walked through the room towards the front, people in the crowd reached over to shake his hand, saying: Good to see you! Welcome back! He smiled and shook hands – there was David Behne, there was Dick Morrison, the faces blurred and the words melted into one big warm hello.

When Paul and Bill walked in with their wives and children, the cheering rose to a roar.

Ross Perot, standing at the front, felt tears come to his eyes. He was more tired than he had ever been in his life, but immensely satisfied. He thought of all the luck and all the coincidences that had made the rescue possible: the fact that he knew Simons, that Simons had been willing to go, that EDS had hired Vietnam veterans, that *they* had been willing to go, that the seventh floor knew how to get things achieved

465

around the world because of their experience with the POW campaign, that T.J. had been able to rent a plane, that the mob had stormed the Gasr Prison . . .

And he thought of all the things that might have gone wrong. He recalled the proverb: success has a thousand fathers, but failure is an orphan. In a few minutes he would stand up and tell these people a little of what had happened and how Paul and Bill were brought home. But it would be hard to put into words the risks that had been taken, the awful cost if the thing had gone bad and ended in the criminal courts or worse. He remembered the day he left Tehran, and how he had superstitiously thought of his luck as sand running through an hourglass. Suddenly, he saw the hourglass again, and all the sand had run out. He grinned to himself, picked up the imaginary glass, and turned it upside down.

Simons bent down and spoke in Perot's ear. 'Remember you offered to pay me?'

Perot would never forget it. When Simons gave you that icy look, you froze. 'I sure do.'

'See this?' said Simons, inclining his head.

Paul was walking towards them, carrying Ann Marie in his arms, through the crowd of cheering friends. 'I see it,' said Perot.

Simons said: 'I just got paid.' He drew on his cigar.

At last the room quietened down, and Perot began to speak. He called Rashid over and put his arm around the young man's shoulders. 'I want you to meet a key member of the rescue team,' he said to the crowd. 'As Colonel Simons said, Rashid only weighs a hundred and forty pounds, but he has five hundred pounds of courage.'

They all laughed and clapped again. Rashid looked around. Many times, many times he had thought about going to America; but in his wildest dreams he had never imagined that his welcome would be like this!

Perot began to tell the story. Listening, Paul felt oddly humble. He was not a hero. The others were the heroes. He was privileged. He belonged with just about the finest bunch of people in the whole world.

Bill looked around the crowd and saw Ron Sperberg, a good friend and a colleague for years. Sperberg was wearing a great big cowboy hat. We're back in Texas, Bill thought. This is the heartland of the USA, the safest place in the world; they can't reach us here. This time, the nightmare is *really* over. We're back. We're safe.

We're home.

THE END

Epilogue

Jay and Liz Coburn were divorced. Kristi, the second daughter, the emotional one, chose to live with her father. Coburn was made Manager of Human Resources for EDS Federal. In September 1982 he and Ross Perot Junior became the first men to fly around the world in a helicopter. The aircraft they used is now in the National Air and Space Museum in Washington, DC. It is called *Spirit of Texas*.

Paul became Comptroller of EDS and Bill became Medicaid Marketing Director in the Health Care Division.

Joe Poché, Pat Sculley, Jim Schwebach, Ron Davis and Rashid all continued to work for EDS in various parts of the world. Davis's wife Marva gave birth to a boy, Benjamin, on 18 July 1979.

Keane Taylor was made Country Manager for EDS in the Netherlands, where he was joined by Glenn Jackson. Gayden continued to be head of EDS World and therefore Taylor's boss.

John Howell was made a full partner in Tom Luce's law firm, Hughes and Hill. Angela Howell had another baby, Sarah, on 19 June 1980.

Rich Gallagher left EDS on 1 July 1979. An easterner, he had never quite felt one of the boys at EDS. Lloyd Briggs and Paul Bucha, two more easterners, left around the same time.

Ralph Boulware also parted company with EDS.

Lulu May Perot, Ross Perot's mother, died on 3 April 1979.

Ross Perot Junior graduated from college and went to

work for his father in the autumn of 1981. A year later Nancy Perot did the same. Perot himself just went on making more and more money. His real estate appreciated, his oil company found wells, and EDS won more and bigger contracts. EDS shares, priced around $18 apiece when Paul and Bill were arrested, were worth six times that four years later.

Colonel Simons died on 21 May 1979, after a series of heart attacks. In the last few weeks of his life, his constant companion was Anita Melton, the zany stewardess from the Boeing 707. They had an odd, tragic relationship: they never became lovers in the physical sense, but they were in love. They lived together in the guest cottage at Perot's Dallas house. She taught him to cook, and he started her jogging, timing her with a stopwatch. They held hands a lot. After Simons died, his son Harry and Harry's wife Shawn had a baby boy. They named him Arthur Simons, Junior.

On 4 November 1979 the US Embassy in Tehran was once again overrun by militant Iranians. This time they took hostages. Fifty-two Americans were held prisoner for more than a year. A rescue mission mounted by President Carter came to an ignominious end in the deserts of Central Iran.

But then, Carter did not have the help of Bull Simons.

Appendix

IN THE UNITED STATES DISTRICT COURT FOR THE NORTHERN DISTRICT OF TEXAS, DALLAS DIVISION

ELECTRONIC DATA SYSTEMS CORP. IRAN
VS.
SOCIAL SECURITY ORGANIZATION OF THE GOVERNMENT OF IRAN, THE MINISTRY OF HEALTH AND WELFARE OF THE GOVERNMENT OF IRAN, THE GOVT. OF IRAN

NO. CA3–79–218–F

(Extracts from the Findings of Fact)
Neither EDSCI nor anyone on its behalf procured the contract unlawfully. No evidence showed bribery of any official or employee of Defendants in order to secure the contract, nor did the evidence suggest the existence of fraud or public corruption in the procurement of the contract . . .

The price of the contract was not exorbitant; rather the evidence showed that the price was reasonable and in accordance with amounts charged by EDS to others for similar services. The price did not compare unfavourably with amounts charged by others in the health care industry for similar services . . .

The failure by SSO and the Ministry to provide written notice of non-acceptance of unpaid invoices was inexcusable and therefore constituted a breach of the contract. The assignment of Dr Towliati to SSO as Deputy Managing Director did not effect such an excuse. I do not find evidence that Dr Towliati's services influenced the process of approval for invoices, nor do I find evidence that Dr Towliati functioned improperly in his review of performance under the contract. Rather, the evidence showed that the Ministry and SSO had full and continuous opportunity to monitor EDSCI's performance. Moreover, I do not find credible evidence of trickery or that EDSCI conspired with anyone to gain wrongful approval for payment of its invoices or to deny the Defendants fair opportunity for their evaluation of EDSCI's performance under the contract . . .

EDSCI did not materially breach its performance obligations under the contract; rather, EDSCI substantially performed in accordance with the description and timing of its duties for each applicable phase up until January 16, 1978, the date of termination of the contract . . .

Recovery under the contract is not barred by Defendant's claims, unsupported by the evidence, that EDSCI procured the contract by fraud, bribery or public corruption. Specifically, the evidence did not demonstrate that EDS' relation-ship with the Mahvi Group was illegal. EDSCI's execution of and performance under the contract violated no Iranian law . . .

Plantiff introduced a plethora of evidence showing the fact and result of its services: testimony from those who managed and implemented the data processing systems, photographic evidence illustrating aspects of the data preparations functions developed, as well as reports jointly prepared by EDSCI and the Ministry of benefits being realized from the contract. Credible evidence failed to directly rebut this showing . . .

(Extract from the Final Judgment)
IT IS ORDERED, ADJUDGED and DECREED that Plaintiff Electronic Data Systems Corporation Iran have and recover of Defendants The Government of Iran, The Social Security Organization of The Government of Iran and the Ministry of Health and Welfare of The Government of Iran, jointly and severally, the sum of fifteen million, one hundred and seventy-seven thousand, four hundred and four dollars

($15,177,404), plus two million, eight hundred twelve thousand, two hundred and fifty-one dollars ($2,812,251) as prejudgment interest, plus one million, seventy-nine thousand, eight hundred and seventy-five dollars ($1,079,875) as attorneys' fees, plus interest on all such sums at the rate of nine per cent (9%) per annum from the date hereof, plus all costs of suit herein . . .

Acknowledgments

Many people helped me by talking to me for hours on end, by replying to my letters, and by reading and correcting drafts of the book. For their patience, frankness, and willing co-operation I thank especially the following:

Paul and Ruthie Chiapparone, Bill and Emily Gaylord; Jay and Liz Coburn, Joe Poché, Pat and Mary Sculley, Ralph and Mary Boulware, Jim Schwebach, Ron Davis, Glenn Jackson;

Bill Gayden, Keane Taylor, Rich and Cathy Gallagher, Paul Bucha, Lloyd Briggs, Bob Young, John Howell, 'Rashid', Toni Dvoranchik, Kathy Marketos;

T. J. Marquez, Tom Walter, Tom Luce;

Merv Stauffer, for whom nothing is too much trouble;

Margot Perot, Bette Perot;

John Carlen, Anita Melton;

Henry Kissinger, Zbigniew Brzezinski, Ramsey Clark, Bob Strauss, William Sullivan, Charles Naas, Lou Goelz, Henry Precht, John Stempel;

Dr Manuchehr Razmara;

Stanley Simons, Bruce Simons, Harry Simons;

Lt-Col Charles Krohn at the Pentagon;

Major Dick Meadows, Major-General Robert McKinnon;

Dr Walter Stewart, Dr Harold Kimmerling.

As usual, I was helped by two indefatigable researchers, Dan Starer in New York and Caren Meyer in London.

I was also helped by the remarkable switchboard staff at EDS headquarters in Dallas.

More than a hundred hours of taped interviews were transcribed, mainly by Sally Walther, Claire Woodward, Linda Huff, Cheryl Hibbitts, and Becky DeLuna.

Finally I thank Ross Perot, without whose astonishing energy and determination not only this book, but the adventure which is its subject, would not have been possible.

Bibliography

Beny, Roloff: *Persia, Bridge of Turquoise* London: Thames and Hudson, 1975

Carter, Jimmy: *Keeping Faith – Memoirs of a President* New York: Bantam, 1982

Forbis, William H: *Fall of the Peacock Throne* New York: Harper & Row, 1980

Ghirshman, R: *Iran* New York: Penguin, 1978

Graham, Robert: *Iran: The Illusion of Power* New York: St Martin's Press, 1980

Helms, Cynthia: *An Ambassador's Wife in Iran* New York: Dodd, Mead, 1981

Keddie, Nikki R. and Richard Tann: *Roots of Revolution* New Haven: Yale University Press, 1981

Ledeen, Michael and William Lewis: *Debacle: The American Failure in Iran* New York: Knopf, 1981

Maheu, René and Bruno Barbey: *Iran* Paris: Editions J.A., 1976

Pahlavi, Mohammed Reza: *Answer to History* New York: Stein & Day, 1980

Roosevelt, Kermit: *Countercoup: The Struggle for the Control of Iran* New York: McGraw-Hill, 1979

Schemmer, Benjamin F: *The Raid* New York: Harper & Row, 1976

Stempel, John D: *Inside the Iranian Revolution* Bloomington: Indiana University Press, 1981

Sullivan, William H: *Mission to Iran* New York: Norton, 1981

A SELECTED LIST OF NON-FICTION TITLES AVAILABLE FROM CORGI BOOKS

WHILE EVERY EFFORT IS MADE TO KEEP PRICES LOW, IT IS SOMETIMES NECESSARY TO INCREASE PRICES AT SHORT NOTICE. CORGI BOOKS RESERVE THE RIGHT TO SHOW NEW RETAIL PRICES ON COVERS WHICH MAY DIFFER FROM THOSE PREVIOUSLY ADVERTISED IN THE TEXT OR ELSEWHERE.

THE PRICES SHOWN BELOW WERE CORRECT AT THE TIME OF GOING TO PRESS (FEBRUARY '85).

All these books are available at your book shop or newsagent, or can be ordered direct from the publisher. Just tick the titles you want and fill in the form below.

CORGI BOOKS, Cash Sales Department, P.O. Box 11, Falmouth, Cornwall.

Please send cheque or postal order, no currency.

Please allow cost of book(s) plus the following for postage and packing:

U.K. Customers—Allow 55p for the first book, 22p for the second book and 14p for each additional book ordered, to a maximum charge of £1.75.

B.F.P.O. and Eire—Allow 55p for the first book, 22p for the second book plus 14p per copy for the next seven books, thereafter 8p per book.

Overseas Customers—Allow £1.00 for the first book and 25p per copy for each additional book.

NAME (Block Letters) . . . .

ADDRESS . . . .

. . . .